World Christianity and Public Religion Series, Volume 6
Series Editor: Raimundo C. Barreto

Praise for *World Christianity and Ecological Theologies*

World Christianity and Ecological Theologies represents a spread of essays on a subject of deep significance. Mostly from postcolonial settings in the Global South, these contributions reflect the ferment in current theological scholarship amidst the challenges faced by those most threatened by climate change. In assembling this fine collection, the editors have provided us with a rich resource for contemporary approaches to the theology of creation.

—David Fergusson, Regius Professor of Divinity, University of Cambridge

Only a polycentric yet dialogical approach can help us gain traction on the pressing ecological crises of our times, and thus, world Christianity has much to offer. Nuancing as well as concretizing conversations in religion and ecology from its interconfessional, interdisciplinary, and intercultural plethora, the series' culminating volume invites into ecological engagement and samples ecotheological concerns across diverse contexts and Christian traditions. This volume will be of interest for anyone seeking to be oriented and equipped in the face of our planetary crisis.

—Hanna Reichel, associate professor of reformed theology, Princeton Theological Seminary, and author of *After Method: Queer Grace, Conceptual Design, and the Possibility of Theology*

A successful contribution to pursue dialogue on ecotheology between North and South, East and West. A must-read for anyone interested in learning on key topics of ecological theology, addressed especially from the Global South and from Orthodox perspectives.

—Guillermo Kerber, coeditor of *Penser les relations écologiques en théologie à l'ère de l'anthropocène*

An excellent collection of essays that brings together diverse voices to a global dialogue on the intersection between religion and ecology. A global interdisciplinary dialogue that seeks to overcome the divide of power and

privilege by amplifying the voices and experiences of those often marginalized in this conversation with emphasis on the abundant wisdom these voices bring.
—Rev. Dr. Seforosa Carroll, academic dean and lecturer in cross-cultural ministry and theology, United Theological College, School of Theology, Charles Sturt University, Australia

The climate crisis has reached a tipping point, and it is clear that solutions will not come from the West, which has both caused and benefited from the exploitation of the earth's resources. Needed are the marginalized voices, especially from the Global South and Eastern Christianity, which have been largely ignored in the field of World Christianity, but also in the dialogue between religion and ecology. This volume marvelously fills that gap and offers hope for new ways of relating to the earth and to each other.
—Aristotle Papanikolaou, professor of theology, Archbishop Demetrios Chair in Orthodox Theology and Culture, and co-founding director of Orthodox Christian Studies Center, Fordham University

World Christianity and Ecological Theologies

World Christianity and Public Religion Series, Volume 6
Series Editor: Raimundo C. Barreto

WORLD CHRISTIANITY AND ECOLOGICAL THEOLOGIES

Raimundo C. Barreto
Graham McGeoch
Wanderley Pereira da Rosa

Editors

FORTRESS PRESS
MINNEAPOLIS

WORLD CHRISTIANITY AND ECOLOGICAL THEOLOGIES

Copyright © 2024 by Fortress Press, an imprint of 1517 Media. All rights reserved. Except for brief quotations in critical articles or reviews, no part of this book may be reproduced in any manner without prior written permission from the publisher. Email copyright@1517.media or write to Permissions, Fortress Press, PO Box 1209, Minneapolis, MN 55440-1209.

Library of Congress Cataloging-in-Publication Data

Names: Barreto, Raimundo, editor. | McGeoch, Graham, editor. | Rosa, Wanderley Pereira da, editor.
Title: World Christianity and ecological theologies / series editor, Raimundo C. Barreto ; Graham McGeoch, Wanderley Pereira da Rosa, editors.
Description: Minneapolis : Fortress Press, [2024] | Series: World Christianity and public religion series ; volume 6 | Includes bibliographical references and index.
Identifiers: LCCN 2024003137 (print) | LCCN 2024003138 (ebook) | ISBN 9798889831198 (paperback) | ISBN 9798889831204 (ebook)
Subjects: LCSH: Ecotheology. | Ecology--Religious aspects--Christianity. | Globalization--Religious aspects--Christianity.
Classification: LCC BT695.5 .W68 2024 (print) | LCC BT695.5 (ebook) | DDC 261.8/8--dc23/eng/20240512
LC record available at https://lccn.loc.gov/2024003137
LC ebook record available at https://lccn.loc.gov/2024003138

Cover image: A photograph showing sustainable farming and solar energy by Puneet Vikram Singh, Nature and Concept photographer, © 2023 Getty Images
Cover design: Alisha Lofgren

Print ISBN: 979-8-8898-3119-8
eBook ISBN: 979-8-8898-3120-4

CONTENTS

Acknowledgments ... ix

Contributors ... xi

The World Christianity and Public Religion Series
Raimundo C. Barreto, Series Editor ... xix

Introduction: World Christianity and Ecological Theologies
Raimundo C. Barreto, Graham McGeoch, and Wanderley Pereira da Rosa ... 1

Part 1: An Invitation to Dialogue on Christian Ecological Engagement

1. Ecology as the Capacity for Love
   Jürgen Moltmann ... 9

2. Interdependence, Christianity, and Environmental Crisis
   Ivone Gebara ... 21

Part 2: A Roadmap for the Conversation

3. The North/South Divide in Contemporary Christian Ecotheology: South Africa as a Case Study
   Ernst M. Conradie ... 45

4. Mother Earth, Mother Africa: African Ecofeminist Voices
   Sue Rakoczy ... 69

5. Seeking a Morally Viable Response to Climate Injustice: Informed by Voices from Its Underside
   Cynthia Moe-Lobeda ... 97

6. "For the Life of the World": Insights from the Eco-Praxis and Ecotheology of Eastern Orthodox Christianity
   Nikolaos Asproulis ... 129

Part 3: Sampling Ecotheological Concerns in Distinct Contexts and Christian Traditions

7. In Solidarity with Mother Earth: African Christianity and the Love of God in the Context of a Degraded Earth
   Ben-Willie Kwaku Golo — 155

8. Human Uniqueness, Divine Interrelationality, and the Hope of Ecofeminist Theology
   Rubén Rosario Rodríguez — 175

9. World Christianity and Ecology: Ecowomanism
   Melanie L. Harris — 197

10. Embracing Life and Cultivating Hope: The Ecological Dimension of Liberation Theology
    Luis Martínez Andrade — 211

11. Hearing the Words of Creatures: Contemplative Knowledge in the Orthodox Tradition
    Elizabeth Theokritoff — 229

Part 4: Earth-Keeping Approaches from the Global South

12. Native Religions and Hidden Moana Ecologies
    Jione Havea — 251

13. Two Million Trees Planted: The Green Reformation and Ghana's Church of Pentecost
    David Douglas Daniels III — 267

14. An Asian Eco-Spirituality
    Kwangsun Choi — 281

15. Christianity in Abya Yala: Motherland, Sustainability, and Ecocide
    Yenny Delgado-Qullaw — 297

Bibliography — 311

Index — 335

ACKNOWLEDGMENTS

This is the last volume of a six-volume series. Each volume began with a long gestation and conversations that took years and involved many participants. It all started with two initial conversations in 2016. The first one, between Raimundo Barreto and Wanderley Pereira da Rosa, was the starting point for the whole project. The original idea was to publish all volumes in English and Portuguese. A few months later, another crucial conversation occurred between Jesudas Athyal, then an acquisitions editor at Fortress Press, and Raimundo Barreto. Later on, Will Bergkamp, then Fortress Press's vice president of development, bought the idea, and Fortress Press decided to house this series, which had its first volume published in 2017. Wanderley Pereira da Rosa, president of Faculdade Unida de Vitoria in Brazil, and James Kay, then dean of academic affairs at Princeton Theological Seminary, joined this collaborative project to ensure this series would be translated and published in Portuguese. Without these individuals and others, this project would not have been birthed.

This volume in particular results from conversations started before our world was hit by the COVID-19 pandemic, and involved the collaboration of Elaine Nogueira-Godsey, who, for personal reasons, could not continue in the editorial team to see this work to publication. This volume's editors appreciate her ideas and initial suggestions, which helped us develop this volume. She also facilitated the translation of Jürgen Moltmann's chapter from German, done by Jeffrey Jaynes, Professor in the Warner Chair of Church History at the Methodist Theological School in Ohio, to whom we are equally grateful.

This volume is a collective enterprise that has demanded long hours of work from many people. Above all others, we are grateful to each contributor whose work fills the pages ahead. Some of them went through unexpected situations in their lives while working on their contributions. Still, as promised, all of them delivered the product of their meaningful scholarship, which we now share with the reader. We are grateful to Jesudas

Acknowledgments

Athyal at Fortress Press for his continuous support of this endeavor, and we would also like to recognize the contribution of Monika Ottermann as a translator from Portuguese to English, and Stephen R. Di Trolio Coakley, who also translated a chapter from Spanish into English and prepared the bibliography and index.

CONTRIBUTORS

Raimundo C. Barreto is associate professor of world Christianity at Princeton Theological Seminary. Prior to teaching at Princeton Seminary, he taught in his native Brazil and served as director of Freedom and Justice at the Baptist World Alliance. His most recent publications include *Protesting Poverty: Protestants, Social Ethics, and the Poor in Brazil* and the coedited volumes *Migration and Public Discourse in World Christianity*, *Decolonial Christianities: Latin American and Latinx Perspectives*, and *World Christianity, Urbanization, and Identity*. Barreto is the general editor of the series *World Christianity and Public Religion* and a coeditor of the *Journal of World Christianity*. He is also one of the conveners of the Princeton World Christianity Conference.

Wanderley Pereira da Rosa is the president of Faculdade Unida de Vitoria and a professor of the history of Christianity and of religion, democracy, and the public sphere. His main research interests are the social and political theology of the Reformation and the history of Protestantism. He is the coeditor of *Cristo e o processo Revolucionário Brasileiro* (Christ and the Brazilian Revolutionary Process), *Religião e sociedade (pós) secular* (Religion and (Post) Secular Society), and *World Christianity as Public Religion*. He is the author of *O dualismo na teologia Cristã* (Dualism in Christian Theology) and *Por uma fé encarnada: uma introdução à história do Protestantismo no Brasil* (For an Incarnate Faith: An Introduction to the History of Protestantism in Brazil).

Graham McGeoch is a minister of the Church of Scotland. He has worked in Africa, Europe, and Latin America. He has taught theology and religious studies at Faculdade Unida de Vitoria in Brazil; collaborated with UNIperiferias, a civil society university based in the favela Maré, Rio de Janeiro; and develops liberation and contextual theologies with the Council for World Mission. His most recent publication is *Russian Émigré Theology and Latin American Liberation Theology*.

Jürgen Moltmann is Professor Emeritus of Systematic Theology at the University of Tübingen in Germany and is one of the most widely read contemporary theologians. He has contributed many books to the field of theology, including *Theology of Hope*, *The Crucified God*, *The Church in the Power of the Spirit*, *The Trinity and the Kingdom of God*, *God in Creation*, and *The Spirit of Life*. His political theology has been deeply influenced by theologians in the Global South, and he was one of the first major theologians to turn his attention to ecology in the 1980s.

Ivone Gebara holds a PhD in philosophy from the Pontifical Roman Catholic University of São Paulo and a PhD in religious studies from the University of Louvain in Belgium. She is a Catholic nun who worked for many years in the northeastern part of Brazil, especially at the Instituto de Teologia in Recife. Gebara is a pioneering Latin American feminist liberation theologian and a renowned ecofeminist thinker who has taught and lectured at various universities and training institutes in Brazil and around the world. She currently lives in São Paulo, where she continues to advise many groups dedicated to popular education from a feminist and ecofeminist perspective. She has published a number of books and articles, including *Longing for Running Water: Ecofeminism and Liberation* and *Out of the Depths: Women's Experience of Evil and Salvation*.

Ernst M. Conradie is a senior professor in the Department of Religion and Theology at the University of the Western Cape in South Africa. Coming from the Reformed tradition, he works in the intersection between Christian ecotheology, systematic theology, and ecumenical theology. He is the author of *The Earth in God's Economy: Creation, Salvation and Consummation in Ecological Perspective*; *Redeeming Sin? Social Diagnostics amid Ecological Destruction*; and *Secular Discourse on Sin in the Anthropocene: What's Wrong with the*

World? He was the international convener of the Christian Faith and the Earth Project (2007–2014), the leading editor (with Sigurd Bergmann, Celia Deane-Drummond, and Denis Edwards) of *Christian Faith and the Earth: Current Paths and Emerging Horizons in Ecotheology*, and coeditor with Hilda Koster of *The T and T Clark Handbook on Christian Theology and Climate Change*.

Sue Rakoczy is an honorary professor in the School of Religion, Philosophy, and Classics at the University of KwaZulu-Natal (UKZN). In 2021 she completed thirty-two years of teaching and research at St. Joseph's Theological Institute, Cedara and the School of Religion at UKZN. She is a member of the Circle of Concerned African Women Theologians and has written widely in the areas of feminist theology, ecofeminism, and the intersection of spirituality.

Cynthia Moe-Lobeda has lectured in Africa, Asia, Australia, Europe, Latin America, and North America in theology, ethics, and matters of climate justice and climate racism, moral agency, globalization, economic justice, public church, ecofeminist theology, and faith-based resistance to systemic oppression. She is the author or coauthor of seven volumes, including the award-winning *Resisting Structural Evil: Love as Ecological-Economic Vocation* and over fifty articles and chapters. She serves as a professor of theological and social ethics at Pacific Lutheran Theological Seminary, Church Divinity School of the Pacific, and the Graduate Theological Union's Core Doctoral Faculty. She is the founding director of the Pacific Lutheran Theological Seminary (PLTS) Center for Climate Justice and Faith. She received her PhD in Christian ethics from Union Theological Seminary. She loves hiking in the forests and mountains and spending time with family and dear friends.

Nikolaos Asproulis is deputy director of the Volos Academy for Theological Studies-Research Center and lecturer at the Hellenic Open University in Greece. He is also chair of the first church-affiliated Energy Community in Volos, Greece and project manager of the Volos Academy's ecotheological projects. He has authored a number of articles on ecotheology from an Orthodox point of view. He is the coeditor of *Priests of Creation: John Zizioulas on Discerning an Ecological Ethos* and *The Orthodox Church Addresses Climate Crisis*.

Ben-Willie Kwaku Golo is a senior lecturer in world Christianity and religion and society in the Department for the Study of Religions at the University of Ghana. His research areas are African Pentecostalism, constructive African theologies, environmental theologies and ethics, religion, sustainability, and social change.

Rubén Rosario Rodríguez is the Clarence Louis and Helen Steber Professor of Theological Studies at Saint Louis University. His teaching and research interests include comparative religious ethics, theological anthropology, and liberation and political theologies. His most recent publications are *Christian Martyrdom and Political Violence* and *Dogmatics After Babel*. He is editor of the *T and T Clark Handbook of Political Theology*.

Melanie L. Harris is a professor of Black feminist thought and womanist theology jointly appointed with Wake Forest School of Divinity and the African American Studies Program at Wake Forest University. She is also the director of the Food, Health, and Ecological Well-Being Program. A graduate of the Harvard Leadership Program, she is a former American Council of Education Fellow and Founding Director of the Texas Christian University's African American and Africana Studies program. Her research and scholarship critically examine intersections between race, religion, gender, and environmental ethics. She is the author of many scholarly articles and books, including *Gifts of Virtue: Alice Walker and Womanist Ethics* and *Ecowomanism: Earth Honoring Faiths*, and she is the coeditor of *Faith, Feminism, and Scholarship: The Next Generation* as well as numerous journal articles and book chapters.

Luis Martínez Andrade received his PhD in sociology from École des Hautes études en Sciences Sociales in Paris. His previous books include *Religion without Redemption: Social Contradictions and Awakened Dreams in Latin America, Feminismos a la contra, Ecología y teología de la liberación: Crítica de la modernidad/colonialidad*

(Contrarian feminisms, ecology and liberation theology: Critique of modernity/coloniality), and *Textos sin disciplina: Claves para una teoría crítica anticolonial* (Texts without discipline: Keys to an anti-colonial critical theory). In 2009, he won the first international prize, Think against the Current, awarded by the Cuban Book Institute, the Ministry of Culture of Cuba, and the Social Sciences Edition. He currently holds the position of scientific collaborator at Université Catholique de Louvain, Belgium.

Elizabeth Theokritoff is an associate lecturer at the Institute for Orthodox Christian Studies and chair of the UK branch of Friends of the Institute for Orthodox Christian Studies (IOCS). She studied at Somerville and Wolfson Colleges, Oxford and earned a PhD in liturgical theology under the supervision of Metropolitan Kallistos (Ware) of Diokleia. From 1983 to 1990 she served as associate secretary and then general secretary of the Fellowship of St Alban and St Sergius. Since 1990, she has been an independent scholar and theological translator from Modern Greek. She taught liturgical theology for a semester at Holy Cross Orthodox School of Theology in Brookline, Massachusetts and has served several times as a visiting lecturer at IOCS. She has had a particular interest in theological ecology since 1988, when she served as visiting Orthodox tutor at the Ecumenical Institute in Bossey, Switzerland for the Graduate School on Justice, Peace, and the Integrity of Creation. Since then, she has given numerous conference presentations, lectures, and workshops on aspects of Orthodoxy and ecology. She is coeditor of the *Cambridge Companion to Orthodox Christian Theology* and author of *Living in God's Creation: Orthodox Perspectives on Ecology*. She lives in Cambridge.

Jione Havea is the parent of a multicultural daughter and celebrates girl power in "mala pilla" (her appointed caste), native pastor at the Methodist Church in Tonga, migrant to Naarm (renamed "Melbourne" by British colonizers) on the cluster of islands now known as Australia, and research fellow with Trinity Methodist Theological College in Aotearoa, New Zealand and the Centre for

Religion, Ethics and Society at Charles Sturt University, Australia. An activist in training, on the ground, and in meeting- and classrooms, Jione is easily irritated by bullies, suckers, and shitstems in and around scriptures.

David Douglas Daniels III is the Henry Winters Luce Professor of world Christianity at McCormick Theological Seminary, having joined the faculty in 1987 and become a professor of church history in 2003. He has been a member of the American Academy of Religion since 1989, the Society for the Study of Black Religion since 1993, and the Society for Pentecostal Studies since 1979. He is a member of the steering committee of the Evangelical Theology Group and Afro-American History Group of the American Academy of Religion. He is a member of the World Alliance of Reformed Churches and Pentecostal International Dialogue. He has served as commissioner for the Faith and Order Commission of the National Council of Churches of Christ in the USA. He is author of various articles on the history of Christianity and book reviews published on theological education in *Pneuma, Christianity Century, Encyclopedia of African American Religions*, and *A Sourcebook for the Community of Religions*. Daniels also served as an adviser to *Legacy of a Leader*, a 1991 video documentary on Charles Harrison Mason. He has been an ordained minister in the Church of God in Christ since 1980.

Kwangsun Choi is a pastor of the Presbyterian Church of Korea and a theologian who pursues ecotheology and eco-spirituality. He received his PhD from the University of St. Michael's College at the University of Toronto. He also holds a certificate of specialization in theology and ecology from the Elliott Allen Institute for Theology and Ecology (EAITE). His research interests lie in the area of Thomas Berry's cosmology and its implications to ecotheology and eco-spirituality, as well as in the field of religion and ecology.

Yenny Delgado-Qullaw is a PhD candidate at the Institut de sciences sociales des religions at Université de Lausanne. She is a Native American descendant and has a deep appreciation for her cultural roots and spiritualities. She is the founder and director of PUBLICA (www.publicatheology.org), a forum where theology, psychology, ethnicity, and politics meet in thoughtful and timely reflections, articles, and poems. She encourages active international theologians to distill thoughts into written works for sharing and discussion. She holds degrees from universities in Peru, Costa Rica, Spain, and the United States.

THE WORLD CHRISTIANITY AND PUBLIC RELIGION SERIES

During the latter half of the twentieth century, scholars began to pay closer attention to the polycentric and culturally diverse nature of Christianity worldwide. In particular, the rapid growth in the number of Christians living in the Global South caught the attention of Western scholars as a trend that would not be reversed in the near future.

A number of books have been written in an attempt to offer clues about how these drastic demographic changes are reshaping Christian identity and relations worldwide. Beyond the fascination with numbers, the rapid growth Global South Christianities and their respective diasporas have experienced in recent decades is giving birth to a new global Christian consciousness with profound cultural, social, and economic implications that demand further scholarly attention. World Christianity scholarship has demonstrated that Christianity can no longer be considered a Western religion. We have stepped into the threshold of a new era. New and creative theological insights have emerged, debunking a Eurocentric understanding of Christianity that has prevailed in the modern era. Contrary to some assumptions, conversion to Christianity in former Western colonies did not imply the Westernization of converts. On the contrary, Indigenous cultures and spiritualities that were expected to disappear or be absorbed into the colonial civilizational project remain alive and well. In fact, the end of the twentieth century saw a revitalization of Indigenous traditions and spirituality. Such resurfacing of Indigenous voices significantly contributed to renewed understandings of Christianity that are not at odds with traditional worldviews.

This series engages emerging voices from a variety of Christian expressions around the world, focusing not only on particular histories and practices but also on their theological articulations and impacts on the broader society. If in the modern and colonial world the study of Christianity was predominantly informed by Eurocentric perspectives and priorities, the study of world Christianity in the beginning of the twenty-first century is more representative of diverse contextual experiences, their interaction through the formation of multidirectional transnational networks, and the relationship between Christianity and other religions. Globalization and mass migration have contributed to deepened exchanges among peoples and cultures worldwide, creating a growing demand for making intercultural communication, intercultural theologies, and interfaith dialogue more central to the study of world Christianity. Likewise, questions about hybridity, liminality, border thinking, and cultural interweaving—particularly in the context of formerly colonized cultures—have also gained more attention.

While new tools have been added to the study of Christianity, particularly in response to the cultural turn in the social sciences, some long-existing problems nevertheless still linger and require attention. The scientific and technological progress of the past century has not mitigated persisting injustices and economic asymmetries. Socioeconomic injustice remains as fiercely prevalent as when the first theologies of liberation emerged in the 1960s. As Indian theologian Felix Wilfred reminds us, the demographic shift of world Christianity is not simply a shift "from the West to the South, but a shift of Christianity from the rich and middle classes to the poor." According to him, more than half of all Christians in the world live with less than 500 dollars of annual income.[1]

In a context marked by disparity and scarcity, standing in solidarity with the poor remains a priority. Yet a concern with economic justice is not enough. Christians living in contexts marked by widespread poverty and injustice in different parts of the world are asking challenging and complex questions about the reasons for such inequality. The inhumane treatment many migrants, refugees, asylum seekers, and stateless persons receive when crossing borders, for instance, helps increase awareness of the indivisibility of justice, demanding renewed moral commitments and

---

[1] Felix Wilfred, "Christianity between Decline and Resurgence," in *Christianity in Crisis?*, ed. Jon Sobrino and Felix Wilfred (London: SCM Press, 2005), 31.

creative responses to problems that are amounting to a global calamity. Unjust relations based on race, gender, and sexuality, along with land-related disputes and environmental concerns, are part of the public agenda Christians are called to engage in, both in the Global North and South. The growing awareness of the impact of the colonial hegemonic project on minoritized groups—especially the eclipsed non-European other—has produced new identity claims of previously silenced voices who are now more vocal about the epistemic injustice they have experienced. At the same time, their regained visibility is often used to justify the growing fear of difference and a relentless sense of insecurity that are at the heart of multiple forms of nationalist and xenophobic ideologies. Such ideologies are quickly poisoning societies across the world, increasing the risk of violence against those who, perceived as different, are feared and discriminated against.

Considering all these things, public reasoning has become an increasingly important dimension of the study of world Christianity. After all, Christians worldwide are key actors in what scholars commonly refer to as the "public sphere." Their public living and thinking are important sources for the interrogation of the impact of religion on public life vis-à-vis themes such as citizenship, public witness, peace, justice, environmental relations, and contemporary migration.

This series, which stems from a partnership between Princeton Theological Seminary and Faculdade Unida de Vitoria in Brazil, aims to provide a unique space for sustained dialogue on all these matters. It blends a number of methods and approaches in the burgeoning field of world Christianity, placing them in conversation with other fields of study and disciplines, including public theology, postcolonial/decolonial theory, intercultural studies, migration studies, critical gender theory, critical race theory, queer theory, and globalization studies. The series intentionally gathers religious scholars and theologians representative of diverse Christian traditions and continents into conversation with one another. At its root are two schools related to the Reformed tradition, one located in South America and the other in North America; one that is young (having existed for less than three decades) and the other that has a tradition spanning over two hundred years.

The World Christianity and Public Religion Series

In the first half of the twentieth century, Princeton Seminary appointed John A. Mackay as president after his tenure of almost two decades as a missionary in Latin America. That cross-cultural experience deeply influenced him and impacted his ecumenical thinking. By turning ecumenics into a field of study for the church in the twentieth century, Mackay in many ways anticipated the rise of the field we know today as world Christianity.

> A new reality has come to birth. For the first time in the life of mankind the Community of Christ, the Christian Church, can be found, albeit in nuclear form, in the remotest frontiers of human habitation. This community has thereby become "ecumenical" in the primitive, geographical meaning of that term. History is thus confronted with a new fact.[2]

Faculdade Unida de Vitoria, in turn, has a history marked by a commitment to the retrieval of a particular memory. Such memory is linked to theologians such as Richard Shaull and Rubem Alves. Shaull was a pioneer in encouraging young Latin American Christians, such as Rubem Alves himself, Jovelino Ramos, João Dias de Araújo, Joaquim Beato, and Beatriz Melano, to take their own sociocultural background as their theological and social locus. In other words, he called them to do theology as Latin Americans. By doing that, he inadvertently contributed to the rise of Latin American liberation theology. Rubem Alves, who studied under Shaull both at the Presbyterian Seminary of Campinas and in Princeton, wrote the first book-length treatise on liberation theology while living in the United States.[3] He was one of the most creative thinkers of his days, having also contributed to other subfields such as theopoetics.

As an heir of these combined stories, this series is deeply rooted in a long tradition, which continues to be renewed to respond to the challenges

---

2   John Alexander Mackay, *Ecumenics: The Science of the Church Universal* (Englewood Cliffs, NJ: Prentice Hall, 1964), vii.
3   Rubem Alves, "Towards a Theology of Liberation: An Exploration of the Encounter between the Languages of Humanistic Messianism and Messianic Humanism" (PhD diss., Princeton Theological Seminary, 1968).

and circumstances of a new era. It fosters a dialogue that places priority on voices from the Global South and also invites participants from the Global North to engage with their peers from the South.

Furthermore, the series is published in English and Portuguese. Its bilingual nature garners an inclusionary approach. The work of authors who write in Portuguese (some also in Spanish), and which otherwise would not be available to a broader English readership, are through this series brought to the attention of anglophone scholars, seminarians, and religious leaders. Similarly, the work of authors who, despite being known in the English-speaking world, remain largely unknown in Latin America are through this series made available to Latin American scholars who can read Portuguese. Above all, this series shows that it is possible to advance transnational and transcultural scholarly dialogues without placing priority on one particular language as a lingua franca.

The series has six volumes. The first one, published in Brazil in 2016 and in the United States in 2017, approaches world Christianity as a form of public religion, identifying areas for possible intercultural engagement. Each of the remaining five volumes focuses on specific topics deemed important for a public agenda for world Christianity scholarship in the twenty-first century. Volume two, published in English in 2019, examines migration as an important concern in world Christianity's public discourses. Volume three discusses current approaches to urbanization and identity in world Christianity. Volume four focuses on the public impact of interfaith relations. Volume five presents perspectives on race, ethnicity, gender, and sexuality in world Christianity as part of a broader reflection on the evasion of justice. Finally, volume six brings attention to pressing environmental concerns in world Christianity scholarship, engaging with Global South and Global North ecotheological responses to the imminent planetary crisis.

Finally, in the hope that this series becomes a platform for intercultural and intergenerational dialogue, the editors of all volumes have sought to increase the interaction between seasoned and emerging scholars from all parts of the world, creating a broad table, which may contribute to and enlarge international, intercultural, and interdisciplinary conversations.

Raimundo C. Barreto

INTRODUCTION

WORLD CHRISTIANITY AND ECOLOGICAL THEOLOGIES

This book, *World Christianity and Ecological Theologies*, brings attention to the intersection of religion and ecology as it is being developed in the Global South, and how this impacts scholarship emerging in conversation with the field of world Christianity, highlighting in particular examples of ecological theologies that have emerged in Africa, Asia, Latin America and the Caribbean, and more recently the Pacific. Despite its intentional focus on the Global South, the volume is attentive to interdisciplinary, interconfessional, and intercultural transversals, thus taking into account conversations taking place in the Global North and inviting them into a dialogue. This explains the decision the editors have made to invite two globally known theologians, Jürgen Moltmann (who adds a German/European voice to the conversation) and Brazilian ecofeminist Ivone Gebara, to start the conversation. They are joined by a select group of scholars from different disciplines and regions of the world that offers a number of approaches and perspectives meant to enlighten a path, which is still in the nascent stages of cultivating consistent dialogue and engagement involving world Christianity scholars and a plethora of contemporary scholars working on religion and ecology, in particular ecotheologians. As such, this book continues on the course started in the previous volumes of the series: Reversing the hegemonic flows of the spread of Christianity and Christian thought and theologies from North to South and West to East, thus recognizing, and reaffirming the polycentric nature of Christianity.

Within the study of religion, the fields of "religion and ecology" and "world Christianity" developed into subdisciplines of their own. Through the global pandemic, the connection between environmental rapacity, religion, and political interests has once again called scholarly attention to the important conversation on public religion and global environmental issues.

On the one hand, more scholars of religion engaging with ecological issues are using the language and concepts developed by scholars from the Global South. For example, they are using terms such as "coloniality" and "decoloniality" to frame their critical analysis. This became particularly evident in the Virtual Meeting of the American Academy of Religion in 2020 and even more so in the 2021 call for papers by its various units.

Despite these trends, Western scholars often fail to engage with the scholarship of those in the Global South or, indeed, in Eastern Christianity, neglecting to intersect religion and ecology as dialogue partners or knowledge producers. This book tries to address this failing by engaging epistemologies from the South, the decolonial turn, and Orthodox theology.

By way of contrast to hegemonic and colonial approaches, contemporary scholars in the field of world Christianity, engaging in transdisciplinary scholarship, have challenged the imperialistic aspects of religion's categorization as represented by the Western academic study of religion, including in world Christianity itself. Scholars have provided alternative theoretical and methodological approaches to the study of religion by engaging with religious experiences and scholarship globally.

We, however, acknowledge a deficit among scholars of world Christianity in addressing environmental concerns and the limited language to frame those concerns in the field. In light of this, volume six of the series *World Christianity and Public Religion* aims to bring the fields of study that became known as "religion and ecology" and "world Christianity" into a sustained conversation, with the goal of expanding the theoretical horizons of both areas of scholarship.

This volume builds upon the understanding that Christianity in the Global South emerges from a social matrix conditioned (culturally and linguistically) by preexisting religions. It reiterates that all Christian theologies are contextual, as they are shaped by specific historical and cultural circumstances. This volume also intentionally draws attention to Orthodox theological approaches to environmental concerns. This is in recognition of the fact that Orthodox studies have been often overlooked in world Christianity scholarship and emphasizes that world Christianity has important theological contributions from outside the Western epistemology that warrant closer examination. Such an approach enhances world Christianity frameworks and challenges lazy categorizations.

This volume aims at showcasing the ways in which the intersection of religion and ecology is approached by scholars in religious studies and theology in the Global South and in Eastern Christianity, and by those in conversation with them in the Global North. It points to what can be generated if these bodies of scholarship are engaged as dialogue partners to investigate new patterns of religious environmentalism.

The book is divided into four sections. The first part, comprising two essays from two pioneering scholars, is an invitation for ecological engagement and dialogue. German political theologian Jürgen Moltmann and Latin American ecofeminist liberation theologian Ivone Gebara have both made distinctive global contributions to the development of ecological theologies. Their essays reflect on the trajectories and roles of ecological theologies. The gradual process of restructuring and refining their respective theologies led Moltmann and Gebara to explore multiple contexts, including the contributions of political and militant debates and gender and race studies to theological approaches to ecology and North–South, East–West cross-cultural relationships. This volume builds on this dialogical dynamic present in Moltmann's and Gebara's theological trajectories and invites scholars in religious studies and theology from different continents, contexts, and disciplines to give continuation to this North–South/South–North/South–South/East–West dialogue through engaging topics within environmental ethics, political ecology, and ecofeminism.

Part two introduces a roadmap for the conversation. Ernst Conradie provides a succinct and masterful overview of recent trends in South African theological approaches to ecological theologies. Sue Rakoczy looks at the insights of contributions of the Circle of Concerned African Women Theologians. In particular, she presents the ecowomanist/ecofeminist influences of African women on theology (biblical studies, hermeneutics, and systematics), and looks for how African women speak to their sisters (and siblings, in general) around the world. Cynthia Moe-Lobeda, in a passionate text of scholarly activism, addresses the challenge of the volume by exploring methodological sources to guide the response of people in the Global North that include knowledge producers of the Global South and the crises of climate change and climate injustice, perceived through a lens that acknowledges causal links between the wealth and privilege of some people and the poverty and devastation of others. The section concludes with Nikolaos Asproulis's brief overview of certain initiatives of the ecumenical patriarchate of Constantinople, describing patterns of theologizing from an Orthodox ecological point of view. He notes that in the midst of this critical situation and in contrast to its own history, Eastern Orthodoxy has gradually developed a robust ecotheological narrative and practice, which places the urgency of environmental protection at the center of its agenda.

Part three explores distinct contexts (Africa, Asia, Latin America, and diaspora communities in the Global North) and Christian Traditions (Pentecostal, Protestant, and Orthodox). Sampling ecotheological concerns, the section begins with a contribution from Ben-Willie Kwaku Golo. He argues that the Indigenous African cosmology, which offers similarities to the biblical narrative, can contribute to developing an enriched African Christian theological virtue and praxis of loving God through loving the earth (God's creation), standing in solidarity with Mother Earth. Rubén Rosario Rodríguez enters more directly into a dialogue with the essays of Moltmann and Gebara. Using references from progressive theologians and contemporary scientists, Rosario Rodríguez argues for a theological turn from anthropocentrism to theocentrism. Melanie L. Harris presents ecowomanism as a method and praxis. Her contribution calls for decolonization, spirituality, and reparations, drawing particular attention to womanist theological activists and perspectives. Luis Martínez Andrade discusses the ecological dimension of Latin American liberation theology. Noting that this theological current is opposed to the individualistic and bourgeois ethos of capitalist civilization, he agrees with Moltmann's call for a green revolution rooted in an understanding of ecology as capacity to love. Finally, in a deeply theological contribution, Elizabeth Theokritoff challenges reductionist interpretations of Christianity that restrict it only to Roman Catholicism or Protestantism. Writing Orthodoxy back into the conversation, Theokritoff takes a deep dive into Eastern theological tradition and its three waves of creation theology: patristics, nineteenth-century Russian religious philosophy, and ecological theology as cosmological thinking.

Part four highlights earth-keeping approaches from the Global South. Jione Havea offers a Moana reading of two native Tongan sacred texts on creation and on fire, thus naming native religious ecological opinions and positions. It is the most decolonial contribution one will find in this volume. David Daniels looks at Moltmann's proposed green revolution through the perspective of a Ghanaian Pentecostal church's tree planting initiative. Drawing on the conservative commitment to Scripture and a conviction about the common good, Daniels argues that this Pentecostal church demonstrates a creation care and civic vision of the Church in a very holistic and concrete manner. Kwangsun Choi delves into the emergence of an Asian eco-spirituality rooted in a diverse religious and cultural context, which seeks to respond to the looming ecological disaster over the Earth community. He explores the profound cosmological and ecological worldview embedded in Asian cultures, drawing on examples from various Asian religions. Finally, emerging Indigenous scholar Yenny Delgado-Qullaw invites us to reframe our understanding of the land and its people by grounding her discussion on the land's name and location. Abya Yala presents Indigenous perspectives and spirituality of ecosystems and subsequent ecocide that can no longer be ignored by religious scholars engaging in ecotheological views.

The combination of voices, themes, interests, and theologies present in the chapters of this book, along with its interdisciplinary and intercontextual makeup, makes this volume an important and unique contribution for students, scholars, and religious leaders seeking to understand the intersection of religion and ecology as it is being developed in the Global South, and Orthodox Christianity. Underscoring the kinds of ecological theologies that have emerged in Africa, Asia, Latin America and the Caribbean, and the Pacific over the years, the volume invites the reader to be attentive to interdisciplinary, interconfessional, and intercultural transversals in the engagement of a theme of such relevance to the entire planet.

We hope that the readers will enjoy reading this book, a product of two years of hard work, commitment, and dedication by the editors and contributors.

PART 1

AN INVITATION TO DIALOGUE ON CHRISTIAN ECOLOGICAL ENGAGEMENT

CHAPTER 1

ECOLOGY AS THE CAPACITY FOR LOVE*

Jürgen Moltmann

From Dominion of the World to Cosmic Love (Love of the Cosmos)

We stand today not only at the end of the modern age but at the beginning of the ecological future of our world, if indeed our world should have a future and we want to survive. Since the Renaissance, the modern world has been regarded in an anthropocentric fashion. Humanity is at the "center of the world," proclaimed Pico della Mirandola in 1486.[1] "Science is power," declared Francis Bacon. Through science and technology, humanity becomes "lord and owner" of the world, prophesied René Descartes, and made the objective world predictable in order to dominate it. The notion of theological anthropology, *imago Dei–dominium terrae* [*imago Dei*–lordship of the world] justified—along with the "special position of humanity in the cosmos"—an entire age of scientific discoveries and European domination.[2]

Today we are aware of the nature of the world, and how this modern paradigm has reached its limit. Climate change has destroyed the balance of nature, and human consumption of the resources of the land has led to the extermination of its most vulnerable creatures. Long before the universal

---

* This chapter was translated from German into English by Jeffrey Jaynes.
1 Giovanni Pico della Mirandola, *Über die Würde des Menschen* (Zurich: Manesse, 1989 [1486]).
2 Max Scheler, *Die Stellung des Menschen im Kosmos* (Munich: Nymphenburger Verlagshandlung, 1947).

ecological crisis, Ernst Bloch concluded, "Our current technology exists in nature like an occupation force in enemy territory, with no knowledge of the terrain."[3]

There is a new paradigm, which binds human culture and the natural order together, no longer in an anthropocentric fashion but in a biocentric fashion. For that to happen, we need a new understanding of nature, a new view of humanity, and a new experience of God "in creation."[4] We need a "Green Reformation" in theology, in spirituality, and in our way of living. Ecological questions are no longer merely ethical questions; they call for an ecological shift to the entire theological enterprise. With his 2015 encyclical *Laudato Si': On Care for Our Common Home*, Pope Francis has given a decisive launching point. As a reformed theologian, I have chosen the expression "Green Reformation"[5] because every reformation in the church and in theology looks back to defining biblical texts from the Christian tradition in order to discover something new and grasp God's future. Biblical hermeneutics is the key to Christian theology. In this chapter, I will develop a doctrine of creation, which reads Genesis 1 no longer anthropocentrically but ecologically. Moreover, I look to replace the traditional readings of creation "from the beginning" with an eschatology reading "from the end," which designates the purpose of God's creative process through the life of the future world, as affirmed in the Nicene Creed. I will seek a theology of the earth, and a corporal and sensual spirituality, which sanctifies earthly life.

But is not the God of Abraham, Isaac, and Jacob revealed in human history and not in the power of nature? Is not Christianity itself, which exists thanks to the incarnation of God in Jesus Christ, anthropocentric from its very beginning? Ecology dedicates itself to research on the

---

3   Ernst Bloch, *Das Prinzip Hoffnung* (Frankfurt: Suhrkamp, 1959), 814.
4   Jürgen Moltmann, *Gott in der Schöpfung. Ökologische Schöpfungslehre* (Munich: Chr. Kaiser, 1985); "Ökologie," in *Theologische Realenzyklopädie* (TRE), ed. Gerhard Müller, vol. XXV, Berlin, 1995, 36–46; Anne-Marie Reijnen, "Is Green the Colour of Our Redemption?" in *Returning to Tillich. Theology and Legacy in Transition*, ed. Russell Re Manning and Samuel Andrew Shearn (Berlin: De Gruyter, 2018), 87–96.
5   Michael Biehl, Berndt Kappes, and Bärbel Wartenberg-Potter, eds., *Grüne Reformation* (Hamburg: Missionshilfe Verlag, 2017).

animal-environment connection; human ecology, therefore, focuses on research on the human-environment connection. It can also be anthropocentric.

Ecology calls for something else that changes the inner attitude of humanity. Some have called it "planetary solidarity."[6] It is a reversal that consists in passing from the gaze of humans on the earth to the gaze of the earth on the human race. The measurable world is only the external face of nature. We recognize its internal dimension in so far as we are able to love and thus to bind together affection with reverence. "We know insofar as we love," said Augustine. That holds not only for the knowledge of other people but also for the recognition of the animating spirit of nature. This knowledge is not the power of control but the wisdom of love. In a beautiful way, this cosmic love calls to mind words from the venerable Zosima in Dostoyevsky's *The Brothers Karamazov*:

> Love all God's creation, the whole and every grain of sand in it. Love every leaf, every ray of God's light. Love the animals, love the plants, love everything. If you love everything, you will perceive the divine mystery in things. Once you perceive it, you will begin to comprehend it better every day. And you will come at last to love the whole world with an all-embracing love.[7]

Or the words of the modern mystic and poet, Ernesto Cardenal, in his 1976 book *On Love*:

> All nature bears the initials of God and all creatures are God's love letters to us.... All of nature is burning with love, created through love in order to enkindle love in us.[8]

---

6 Grace Ji-Sun Kim and Hilda P. Koster, eds., *Planetary Solidarity: Global Women's Voice on Christian Doctrine and Climate Justice* (Minneapolis: Fortress Press, 2017).

7 Fyodor Dostoyevsky, *The Brothers Karamazov*, trans. Constance Garnett (Dar Es Salaam, Tanzania: Global Publishers, 2023), 447.

8 Ernesto Cardenal, *Amour, secret du monde*, Cerf, coll, "Terres de feu" 12, Paris, 1972, 16, cited in Jürgen Moltmann, "ou la capacité d'aimer," *Revue Lumen Vitae* vol. lxxiii, no. 4, 2018, 399–409, https://doi.org/10.2143/LV.00.0.0000000.

THE COMMUNITY OF CREATION

Before we humans cultivate the earth and protect it and assume responsibility for the world, the earth cares for us. It creates favorable living conditions for humanity and looks after it to the present. The earth is not entrusted to us; we are entrusted to the earth. The earth can live without human life and has done so for millions of years, but we cannot live without the earth. In the earth's biosphere we live off the intelligence of the plants, which are able to photosynthesize, something we cannot do. They produce the oxygen that we breathe to live.

The anthropocentric reading of the creation story in Genesis 1 is the traditional approach. According to this reading, humanity is the last of God's creatures, being therefore designated the crown of creation. Everything is created for the sake of humanity, because humanity alone is the image of God in creation. Therefore, humankind is also established as lord over the earth and all its inhabitants: "Subdue the earth and rule over the birds of the air and all the beasts of the ground" (Gen. 1:28). According to Psalm 8, God has even made humankind "lords over all the work of [God's] hands, and placed everything under their feet." As one can see in the depictions of Egyptian Pharaohs, the King "subdues" his enemies and they are "under his feet." According to Genesis 2, humankind should relate to the earth as gardeners, "cultivating and protecting" God's garden of Eden. This sounds more peaceful; nevertheless humankind is still the subject and earth its object.

These Genesis texts are approximately 2,500 years old, but it was not until the Renaissance that the concept of *imago Dei–dominium terrae* began to serve a cultural and political agenda of lordship of nature and European dominion of the world. As the almighty God is lord of the world, so must God's human likeness serve as lord of the earth. And humans are not only lords of the earth but masters of their own selves—they are their own invention, so asserted Pico della Mirandola. This *imago Dei* concept has become the theological signature of modern life in the Western world.

According to the ecological reading of the creation story in Genesis 1, humans are the last creature of God, and therefore the most dependent of all creatures. Human life depends on the existence of animals and plants, air and water, day and night, the sun, the moon, the stars, and light. There is only humanity because there are all these other creatures. They could exist without humans, but humans could not live without them. Thus, one cannot regard humankind as an almighty ruler of the earth or as a lone gardener in contrast to all other creatures. Humanity is first of all a creature in a grand community of God's creation. Only as part of this community of creation can humankind become aware of its position and destiny.

According to Genesis 2, before humankind is instilled with the divine breath and becomes a "living soul," it is "earth from the ground," and whenever humans cultivate the earth, they must know that they "are taken from the earth," and "to the earth they will return." The arrogance of power does not befit humanity, but rather a genuine "cosmic humility."[9] One can compare Psalm 8 with the great creation poem in Job 38–40: "Where were you, when I laid the foundation of the earth? Can you bind the chains of the Pleiades or loose the belt of Orion?" And Job answered: "See, I am of small account, what shall I say? I will place my hand on my mouth."

Did God, according to Genesis 1, create the world in six or in seven days? This is a question for a theological examination. I argued in a dialogue with the Catholic social ethicist, Alfons Auer, in Tübingen in 1985, that "the crown of creation is not the human being but the Sabbath, for with it [the Sabbath] God blessed not only humanity, but all of God's creatures," thus Genesis 2:2 says, "and so God brought to completion on the seventh day God's works, which God made." The Sabbath brings completion to creation "in the beginning" and points ahead to the messianic future of this initial creation.[10]

The German Animal Protection Act of 1986 sought a new concept for an animal.[11] An animal is not a legal subject, like a human being, but neither is an animal an object. An animal is a "fellow creature" according to German legal texts, which thereby affirms the community of creation

---

9   Richard Bauckham, *The Bible and Ecology: Rediscovering the Community of Creation* (London: Darton, Longman and Todd, 2010), 37.
10 Abraham J. Heschel, *The Sabbath: Its Meaning for Modern Man* (Boston: Shambhala, 2003).
11 Nicole Gerick, *Recht, Mensch und Tier, Nomos* (Baden-Baden, Germany: Verlag, 2005); Albert Lorz, *Tierschutzgesetz. Kommentar* (Munich: C.H. Beck, 1987).

between animals and humans, and introduces God as creator of this community of creation. Community is inherent in all creatures. Symbiosis is the secret of all living things. The love for life binds them together; it is the spirit of God in all things.

A Theology of the Earth

So, does the creator's command to "subdue the earth" contradict the reality of creation, "from the earth you are taken"? Jesus Sirach 40:1 calls the Earth "mother of us all." *Can one subdue one's own mother?* asks Leonardo Boff. Should one not love her as a child loves their mother?[12] But what is the earth?

According to the modern paradigm, the earth is a spiritless resource of material and kinetic goods—full of mineral resources—that must be put to use. But, according to contemporary geological sciences, the planet earth is a living organism because it generates life. I do not intend to go into James Lovelock's Gaia hypothesis here but simply put forward the biblical views of the earth.[13]

According to the creation account, the earth is a unique creative creature: "Let the earth bring grass and herbs . . ." (Gen. 1:11); "Let the earth bring forth living creatures after their kind" (Gen. 1:24). The earth does not reproduce itself, as other living things do; on the contrary, it brings forth other expressions of life. This cannot be said of any other part of creation, not even of human beings. The earth cries out for "the space for a manifold community of living things," as the Earth Charter of 2010 says, and is also the fruitful womb of all life. All living things owe their existence to the generative love of the earth.

The earth stands in covenant with God. Behind the Noahic covenant of Genesis 9, there stands a covenant of God with the earth, without any human mediation. The rainbow in the clouds shall "be a sign of the covenant between me and the earth" (Gen. 9:13). This divine covenant is the

---

12 For this idea in Boff, see Leonardo Boff, *Cry of the Earth, Cry of the Poor* (Maryknoll, NY: Orbis Books, 1997), 224.

13 James Lovelock, *Gaia: A New Look at Life on Earth* (Oxford: Oxford University Press, 2016).

mystery of the earth; God loves this earth before God loves humankind. The blood-soaked earth was a witness of the first fratricide among humans: "The voice of your brother's blood cries out to me from the earth," and Cain is cursed (Gen. 4:11).

The rights of the earth are revealed in the Sabbath law of Israel, "in the seventh year the land shall observe its sabbatical rest for the Lord" (Lev. 25:2). This is the religion of the earth.[14] Whoever despises it makes the land a wilderness and must abandon the land. In the book of Leviticus, there is an ecological meaning to the Babylonian exile of Israel. In the seventh year, the earth should remain free from all human use, breathe again, and regenerate its fruitfulness.

For the great prophets of Israel, the earth also holds the holy mystery of salvation: "Let the earth open up and bring salvation, let righteousness springs forth before me" (Isaiah 45:8). Here one is reminded of an Advent hymn, the stanza,

> O Savior, tear open the heavens,

Which is followed by the refrain,

> *O earth, sprout, O earth*
> *The mountain and the valley become entirely green.*
> *O earth, bring forth this little flower,*
> *O Savior, spring forth from the Earth.*
> (Evangelisches Gesangbuch 7, 3)

The advent of the cosmic Christ is awaited in the heavens and on earth. "Out of the earth God will come to meet us," wrote Christoph Blumhardt, who was deeply influenced by Karl Barth and Dietrich Bonhoeffer. "From the very depths begins the eternal rebirth of life."[15]

---

14   Jürgen Moltmann, "A Common Earth Religion: World Religions from an Ecological Perspective," *The Ecumenical Review*, 03/63 (2011): 16–25.

15   Christoph Blumhardt, *Ansprachen, Predigten, Reden, Briefe: 1865–1917*, vol. 2, ed. Johannes Harder (Neukirchener Verlag, 1978), 295.

In 1944, Bonhoeffer wrote to his fiancée Maria von Wedemeyer from prison,

> That requires faith, and may God grant it to us daily. I don't mean the faith that flees the world, but the faith that endures in the world and loves and remains true to that world in spite of all the hardships it brings us. Our marriage must be a "yes" to God's earth.[16]

The autobiography of my wife, Elisabeth Moltmann-Wendel, is entitled, *One Who Has No Concern for the Earth, Can Never Reach Heaven*.[17] From her I learned to touch the earth with all my senses.

An ecological spirituality is a spirituality of the senses and of the sanctification of earthly life. Human spirituality always develops where the spirit of God is expected and experienced. Whenever the spirit of God is "poured out into our hearts" (Rom. 5:5), it brings forth a piety of the heart. When the spirit of God is "poured out on all flesh" (Acts 2:17), it brings forth a spirituality of earthly life. For this spirituality of life, "God breathes through all of creation." God's spirit takes hold of us, then awakens an unfettered love for life, and all of our senses come alive. In the intensity of this quickened life, we feel the breath of God.

We should expand the double commandment of love to include the earth:

> *"You shall love the Lord your God*
> *with all your heart and with all your soul and with all your strength*
> *and with all your mind and your neighbor as yourself," (Deut. 6:*
> *5; Lev. 19:18; Luke 10:27)*
> *and the earth as yourself.*

---

16 Dietrich Bonhoeffer and Maria von Wedemeyer, *Love Letters from Cell 92: The Correspondence between Dietrich Bonhoeffer and Maria von Wedemeyer, 1943–45*, ed. Ruth Alice von Bismarck and Ulrich Kabitz (Nashville, TN: Abingdon Press, 1995), 64.

17 Elisabeth Moltmann-Wendel, *Wer die Erde nicht berührt, kann den Himmel nicht erreichen. Autobiographie* (Zurich: Benziger Verlag, 1997).

THE NEW CREATION

Christianity exists because there is a new creation. The new creation is the Christian notion of creation. The promise of a new creation goes back to the prophet Isaiah, "For I am to create new heavens and a new earth; the former things shall not be remembered or come to mind" (Isa. 65:17).

What is new in the new creation?

> "He [God] will swallow up death forever." (Isa. 25:8)

Has this happened already?

> "Do not remember the former things or consider the things of old. I am about to do a new thing; now it springs forth; do you not perceive it?" (Isa. 43:18–19)

In the broader sense of this hope of Israel, the witnesses of the New Testament glimpse the coming of Christ into this world and his resurrection for the new world of God.

The incarnation is not only the human incarnation of God but also the fleshly incarnation of the eternal Logos. "Flesh" here means "life," not only human life but the life of all living things. This is what Pope John Paul II wrote in his encyclical *Dominum et vivificantem* on May 18, 1986:

> The Incarnation of God the Son signifies the taking up into unity with God not only of human nature, but in this human nature, in a sense, of everything that is "flesh": the whole of humanity, the entire visible material world. The Incarnation, then, also has a cosmic significance, a cosmic dimension. (III: 50)

In the New Testament, there is a personal view of the resurrection of Christ: Christ is risen "from the dead," the "first of those who have fallen asleep" (1 Cor. 15:20). But there is also a cosmic view of the resurrection of Christ: In him God has conquered death itself and brought a new and eternal life into the world. Christ is the "leader of life" (Acts 3:15). Therefore, Paul says in 2 Corinthians 5:17:

So if anyone is in Christ, there is a new creation: everything old has passed away; look, new things have come into being!

With the resurrection of Christ, the new creation begins, that is the "life of the world to come," as the Nicene Creed states.[18]

THE COSMIC CHRIST: "AT HOME IN THE UNIVERSE"

The silence of the interstellar space and the coldness of the universe can drive humans to melancholy. "The eternal silence of these infinite spaces fills me with dread," confessed Pascal.[19] Were humans planned in the universe, or are we just a random product of the evolution of life on the small and insignificant planet Earth? If nature has a "strong anthropic principle," then we might feel "at home in the universe," as Stuart Kauffman asserts. Scientifically speaking, that remains controversial. If there is no "strong anthropic principle," then we end up with the sad conclusion of Steven Weinberg: "The more the universe seems comprehensible, the more it also seems pointless."[20] But how can we love life and affirm our existence if we indeed live in a senseless and purposeless world? Do the stars or genes tell us if humankind should be there or not?

According to the apostle Paul's teaching on reconciliation, through the submission of Christ to death and through his resurrection in the new creation, God first reconciled the cosmos before establishing among humans the "ministry of reconciliation."

"God was in Christ reconciling the world to Godself." (2 Cor. 5:19)

---

18   Jürgen Moltmann, "Der Gott der Auferstehung. Christi Auferstehung—Auferstehung des Fleisches—Auferstehung der Natur," in *"Sein Name ist Gerechtigkeit." Neue Beiträge zur christlichen Gotteslehre* (Gütersloh, Germany: Gütersloher Verlagshaus, 2008), 45–82.
19   Blaise Pascal, *Pensées*, trans. A.J. Krailsheimer, (New York: Penguin, 1995), 66.
20   Stuart Kauffman, *At Home in the Universe* (Oxford: Oxford University Press, 1995); Steven Weinberg, *Dreams of a Final Theory: The Search for the Fundamental Laws of Nature* (London: Hutchinson Radius, 1993), 204.

The blood of Christ on the cross, as the confessional expressions read, serves not only for the reconciliation of a godless humanity with God but for the reconciliation of a divinely alienated cosmos with God. There are found the "thrones, principalities, and powers" that manifestly shatter the foundations of the universe (Ps. 82:5). These "lordless powers," as Karl Barth called them, evidently constituted the cosmic problematic of early Christianity in an environment that feared, idolized, or demonized these powers. They responded with the message of the "reconciliation of all things,"

> [A]nd through Christ God was pleased to reconcile to Godself all things, whether on earth or in heaven, by making peace through his blood on the cross. (Col. 1:20)

We live in a world reconciled with God, which is why we can feel at home in the universe.

That is as relevant today as ever because life is threatened externally by earthquakes, tornadoes, and tsunamis, and internally by diseases such as cancer and dementia. However, it makes a difference whether people feel they are at the mercy of the unpredictable forces of nature or if the earth, the sky, and the seas deteriorate to waste dumps because of human irresponsibility: global warming, air pollution, the ocean plastic catastrophe. There is still the same Gospel of the cosmic peace in Christ. We live in a reconciled world. As he grew older, Karl Barth comforted himself by saying, "*Es wird regiert!*" (*It is ruled!*)

In the letter to the Ephesians, a second act of the reconciliation of the cosmos "through his blood" follows, referred to as the *anakephalaiōsasthai ta panta* (to bring together all things): "As a plan for the fullness of time, to unite all things in him [Christ], things in heaven, and things on earth" (Eph. 1:10). This new creation of all things begins with the elevation of Christ to lordship "far above all rule and authority and power and dominion" (Eph. 1:21). The ascended Christ receives all power in heaven as on earth in order to lead everything toward God's new world.

This is also called the "restoration of all things." Christ fills all the spaces of creation with his peace and all the eras of creation with his eternal life. Nothing is lost, nothing is forgotten, all that once existed will be restored, made right, and gathered together in the life of the world to come. This Christian hope of resurrection is the only hope that promises a future for the past.

I close with a short story. At the end of his temptation by Satan in the wilderness, Jesus was, "with the wild animals; and the angels ministered to him" (Mark 1:13). The wild animals were not with him like pets are with humans. Jesus was in the wilderness, in their environment. And Jesus did not "dominate" over the animals, as humans should do according to Genesis 1:28. He was with the wild animals as if he were among friends, "and the angels ministered to him." This is the reversal of the expected; Jesus was not with the angels while the animals served him; it was reversed. The wild animals may have experienced the aroma of peace that emanated from the Son of Man. There are also accounts of certain saints that affirm that they were with wild animals: Francis of Assisi and Sergius of Radonezh. They lived with the animals and healed them. These are signs of an ecology understood as the capacity for love.

CHAPTER 2

INTERDEPENDENCE, CHRISTIANITY, AND ENVIRONMENTAL CRISIS

Ivone Gebara

INTRODUCTION[1]

The three terms that constitute the title of this reflection must be understood in light of some of the challenges of the present times. The renewed interrelation that exists between them requires a new understanding and new interpretations of their contextual and provisional meanings. Each new generation in different places and situations apprehends and re-signifies them as part of its passage through earth's history. And each new approach to these relationships adds something to our previous understanding, reveals new insights, and also includes new limits inherent to all human understanding.

The first of the three words, "interdependence," represents the angle through which I propose an understanding of human beings in relation to themselves and to others, and their effects on Christianity and the environmental crisis. It will be a key word around which we can redesign our understanding of the human being in light of the turbulent moment in our world's history.

Initially, I will not define these words, as we all have a preconception of their meanings, which is sufficient to warrant some interrogation. And these meanings, which we once thought to be stable, may need to be

---

[1] This text was translated from Portuguese into English by Monika Ottermann.

questioned. I believe that a previous definition would excessively limit our thinking and make the perception of the pluralism of present approaches difficult.

In this text, the reflexive act is inspired by the contemporary world lived from the perspective of Latin America, more precisely from Brazil. Its content is marked by the observation of varied social and religious behaviors and by the multiple currents of thought that intertwine in it. I highlight in particular critical feminism in its different strands that have marked contemporary cultures. A vast array of literature written by important contemporary authors like Hannah Arendt, Monica Sjöö, Barbara Mor, Caroline Merchant, Catherine Keller, Alicia Puleo, Judith Ress, and Judith Butler form an important part of what I learned about the relationships between human societies and the environmental crisis.[2] The immediate purpose of this reflection is to understand more about the human world through the notion of interdependency and in a special way the world marked by contemporary Christianity in the face of the environmental and ethical crises that we are experiencing.

From this perspective, I situate myself within a plural and complex understanding of the origins and diversified expansion of Christianity. I find myself surrounded by doubts, contradictions, and ambiguities, above all in relation to the teachings of Christian institutions and the sacralization of their statements. Its current historical expressions and especially the crisis of its ethics and dogma reveal the extent to which they are being impacted by the current global crisis of ethical meanings with serious consequences that affect earth's ecosystems. This phenomenon challenges the alleged hegemony of Christianity in many parts of the world and invites it to leave its traditional location to transform itself and better respond to the great questions that mark the world today. Its answers cannot be separated from the current major questions of the world that equally touch all religious creeds.

My reflection is a small sketch of thought and imagination about us humans, about the world, about our possible beliefs and directions in view of a better coexistence with and respect for the life of the planet.

---

2   Some of these works are noted in the bibliography.

WHO ARE WE WHO TALK ABOUT INTERDEPENDENCE AND INTERPRET THE WORLD?

In order to reflect more directly on interdependence, I want to situate it especially in light of certain aspects of the general history of our perception of the world. In this perspective, it is worth remembering that it is we who speak about interdependence, who choose it and give it meaning because we see it as a vital law that interconnects all things. In it we include the world outside us and the world inside us in an evolutionary process of mutual engagement and continuous mutation. In this sense, interdependence is not only an external physical relation between different elements but a process of perceiving the world through varied attitudes, forms, and valuations that also emerge from our own selves. We are intrinsically implicated in our perceptions and discoveries. For this reason, interdependence refers not only to physical phenomena but also to our own subjectivity and, therefore, to the ethical relations that we establish in our world. We know well that our subjectivity can be theoretically affirmed in relation to the physical world but negated as constitutive of human relations. Consequently, it can also be denied as instantiating political and social relations that guarantee rights to the citizens of this planet.

In order to better understand its complexity, we are invited to think briefly about human beings' search for meaning throughout history as an initial hermeneutical point.

We know that in addition to the myths and wisdom of many Eastern and Western cultures, in Greek and Roman antiquity philosophers faced the challenge of defining the human being. It seemed clear how easy it was for human beings to define other beings and the things that surround them. However, it was difficult to explain themselves and justify their choices. The beings who try to understand the world in which they and others live are faced with greater enigmas when that gaze turns back on themselves. The ability to think and turn their gaze toward themselves astounds them. The complex diversity of their peers alarms and limits them. The emotions that emerge from that experience can generate life or death. The countless skills in everyday life and the new difficulties one has always to face do not cease to generate conflicts. The mobility of the thoughts that permeate them, and their many doubts and anxieties, confuse the search for clarity about oneself. Who orders human life? Who gives humans the directives for the search for truth? Who limits them? This seems to be an important and recurrent hallmark of thinking about ourselves at different times in our history. Where did it come from, or how did it originate?

I raise the hypothesis in an evolutionary line, that in reality such a condition or limit is due to our own ability to explain the things around us. We are authorities over them, having the power to distinguish them, to bring them together, shape them, transform them, and make them ours. However, the biggest problem lies with us. Who guarantees our word about ourselves? In order for us to be able to speak about ourselves with certain propriety, we had to appeal to religions and create gods to give us authority over ourselves. An anthropological process of parthenogenesis of meanings can be observed in several human groups. Thus, we can say that religions are the result of our own evolution and the increasing complexity of our social organization.

However, we observe that after some centuries, our divine creatures, sprouted from our entrails, gradually became detached realities from us. We came to believe that they exist as realities in themselves detached from the beings around us. And, being infinitely superior, they live in other spheres or dimensions called "spiritual."

From the spiritual realm they began to define us, and through language we started to assert ourselves as beings created by others, beings whose destiny was outlined and designated by other beings superior to us.

Undoubtedly, this creation took many forms and responded to various needs, but it was also the result of the experience of how much the phenomena of the outside world and our bodies seemed to be much larger than ourselves. This was a fact that gave rise to the experience that perhaps our origin, or even the life of our bodies, had interference from forces superior to our own. Another aspect, no less important, was the development of the ethical dimension in us, so that in view of the good we started to consider ourselves sinners and guilty before our divinities, which we made perfect. We became their servants, dependent on their will, and offered sacrifices to appease them. We also welcomed the forms of salvation that were imposed on us from dispossession or the sharing of goods all the way to martyrdom. We became judges of each other, dividing ourselves between good and evil and creating dualistic instances of earthly and heavenly judgment.

Over the years, despite many acquisitions, we started losing the sense of cohabitation and of collective intimacy and interdependence as we established hierarchies and supernatural powers over us. Thus, we started to think and believe as separate beings coming from the gods or from a single God, so much so that this mythical origin began to explain ourselves, our actions, and our destiny. Just as our existence depended on the gods or on God, so all beings on Earth came to depend on us as if we were their creators, their gods, or their representatives. We started to rank them, assess their value, and eliminate them according to our needs and stereotypes. Although everything was ultimately attributed to the gods or to God, we have come to understand ourselves as custodians of their works and designs and almost as dominators of everything that exists. We became the center of the world even though we affirmed our dependence on our gods. This is what is conventionally called "anthropocentrism."

Over time, our deities became powerful abstractions that allowed us to hide in or behind them and to believe that they were the ones who decided from within us, as an extraordinary force above us. However, our daily power over other animals, plants, rivers, seas, different matter, and over our relationships could be seen, managed, lived. We treated nature and lower beings as we thought our gods treated us. Our narcissistic passions for power emerged in a frightening way. There were conflicting visible and invisible powers. Furthermore, it was up to us to name the lower beings, and to name is to designate the type of life and the value of the life of things according to the utility that we attribute to them in the hierarchy that we ourselves established. However, once again, when it comes to humans in relation to themselves, a greater limit was experienced in relation to this same explanation. We who were able to name animals, plants, and things could not do the same in relation to ourselves—could not define and own ourselves. We needed the gods to define us and establish our rules of conduct. And we believed that our words of power were derived from them and we could not change anything about them. To this day, this belief survives in the phrase "in God we trust," which we affirm and inscribe in our political and economic decrees.

Even today, some still consider themselves to be custodians of God and do not hesitate to exploit people and dominate other beings to assert God's supposed will. There is a kind of experience of duplicity of wills unified in a single will—the divine—expressed and hierarchized in the actions of some humans. Reconstructing the process of birth of our gods through this initial parable seems to be a necessary path for understanding ourselves and the evolution of our theologies. In part, this path that I describe is inspired by the philosopher Hannah Arendt, who masterfully expressed the perplexity of human beings in relation to themselves and reminded us of the enormous limitation that affects us when we have to answer the question: Who are we?[3] Due to this issue, we sought and still seek superhuman or divine power to define the human, to give them guidance, to set limits to their understanding and action on earth. And this is because nothing that we were able to explain could fully explain us, since no element totally conditioned us, not even death. Therefore, we invent gods to justify our power and fears. We invent gods that divide us and oppose each other by determining our place in creation. We write texts and declare them the sacred word of God to order the world and our actions. We believe in the recorded tradition received without criticism. We read our own texts in a compliant and fundamentalist way. We enthrone men to interpret and represent the almighty God, the Father, the author, and inspirer of the sacred texts. We exclude women and ethnicities considered inferior from this official representation, believing in the ontological superiority of some beings over others. We kill and die for our gods! Aren't they just as mortal as we are?

There is much to think about the creation of our gods from the point of view of the phenomenology of religions. At the moment, the brief recollection presented seems to be sufficient for the next steps in view of the urgency of approaching religious phenomena from new perspectives. As we can see in many parts of the world, the metaphysical and hierarchical tendency is gaining ground again. This leads us to surrender collective responsibility to the will of the gods and their would-be political and

---

[3] Hannah Arendt, *The Human Condition* (Chicago: University of Chicago Press, 1958), 10–11.

religious representatives. It legitimizes the action of occult forces against the interest of the majority, relying on a metaphysics stripped of its traditional meaning and the contexts that saw it come into being.

Thus, the hierarchical religious tendency to legitimize life and human beings based on the will of hidden deities seems to be the order of the day. Authoritarian political regimes are implanted in different countries of the world, guaranteeing their power under the claim of being of divine inspiration. Others deify some of their old leaders by justifying behaviors of submitting the people to the figure of the great leader. They show themselves to be chosen by superior forces that the people cannot resist. They justify their social policies on the grounds of divine mandates considered fair and granted to some chosen ones as a privilege due to their fidelity to God.

Forsaken, divided into classes, abandoned to their own fate and ignoring their strength, most people submit themselves in the struggle to survive. It is a survival characterized by almost total dependence on what the owners of the world declare to be important to them. Without security, people are allowed to buy firearms to defend themselves; without drinking water, soft drinks are offered to them; without healthy nourishment, they eat affordable hamburgers as daily food. Most do not realize that through this food and drink, their pastures and fountains of pure water are stolen, and that another empire rules their lives. It is an empire full of lights and daily attractions that leads them to value what is offered to them by making them believe that their happiness and salvation are there. Once again, this parable makes us think of the cunning of the children of darkness who took possession of the light. They dress up in multicolored lights to attract and trap majorities to their will and close off their access to freedom.

The two parables characterize and to some extent introduce the concern that afflicts me: the invention and maintenance of our gods and the misuse of their power in the name of the fallacy of capitalist progress. I know well that through the gods, we also love and fight for justice among us. But today, we are being invited to go further. We are invited to review the discourse about our dependence and our interdependence in relation to our gods. What if we didn't have gods in heaven or on the Olympus? What would become of us? Who would we be? What if there were no powerful institutions that represented them and controlled us? How would we live? What if our gods were not as powerful and at the same time as powerfully invisible? How we would be?

To outline a reflection on these questions, I begin a path apparently different from interdependence. This has been recovered and affirmed by many groups, but not always in a way to enforce respect for the rights of all. For this reason, a reflexive alert is necessary.

The Chiaroscuro Path of Interdependence

Interdependence appears as a beautiful and uncontroversial word in mainstream media and several news outlets of the 'new age' movement. Undoubtedly, from the development of attention to interdependence and interrelationality, we begin to perceive ourselves as human beings included in the countless vital processes within and outside us. In this way, we affirm that we do not exist without the beings and all the things we name in our surroundings. We discover ourselves as individuals who only survive in dependence of all other bodies and of the immutable and changing laws of the universe. This brief initial explanation of what a current interpretation of interdependence looks like creates a bond between many people.

The problem arises when, conscious of interdependence, we hierarchize it through our political, social, and religious actions or use it as rhetoric to impress people and hide our selfish and predatory intentions. We have reduced interdependence to a pyramidal shape obedient to a single design. We do not make room for its creative freedom, its chance, its multiple designs, its shortcuts, and its exceptions. From the pyramid we go to the circle and again to the pyramid. With this, perhaps, we do not realize the risk of returning to the traditional hierarchical relational models in which others and the world in its diversity are felt and experienced as a threat to ourselves, especially when they present themselves differently from what we expect.

We highlight the different, the enemies, those who are outside the established order, outside the will of God. We create "others," always treating ourselves as more or less narcissistic centers. The other may be white people, black people, the poor, the LGBTQ community, women, foreigners, animals, insects, aggressors. The others are "hell," as Sartre said! The others are what I apparently am not or imagine I am not. The categorized others mark my difference in relation to them not simply as diverse others, as parts of the same rainbow that includes us all, or of the same planet that creates and sustains us. As Toni Morrison explains in her book *The Origin of Others*, when we say "race," we are referring to the natural world in its genetic diversity, and this world seems peaceful and acceptable.[4] But when we invent racism, we are in the realm of social relations in which we identify others not only by the different color of their skin but by the social place they occupy and our relations with that place. When we talk about racism, we are in the register of exclusion, in the breaking of relationships. The same is true in relation to sex and sexism, and also with the notion of interdependence. It can be transformed into new systems of social differentiation and exclusion insofar as it is only a theory, not an ethical experience respectful of differences. Such a reality is also present in religious traditions from which dependence on the gods or God was hierarchized and expressed through the most varied social power relations. Interdependence is transformed into dependence, dependence into submission, and submission into the absence of the rights of some, and so on.

To verify and affirm this means to introduce, once again, a level in which the human rationality present in interdependence appears submissive to a habitual rationality that we would analogously consider prior cultural, religious, or political rationality and which would condition the notion of interdependence. In other words, I want to underline that it is not enough to affirm interdependence as an evident and good idea, but it is necessary to understand it within the limits of human relational functioning and the knowledge of the everyday reality that surrounds us. For example, what scientists call knowledge representational model, which considers that knowledge is like a representation of the external reality in us. This model is strongly present in the patriarchal world and makes us believe that we do not interfere in the world by knowing it or that the world is different from us and can only become an object of knowledge. It is believed that there is an objectivity that comes to us from outside,

---

4   Toni Morrison, *The Origin of Others* (Cambridge, MA: Harvard University Press, 2017). See especially chapter 2, "Being or Becoming the Stranger."

a divine or natural truth such as, for example, that of the sacred texts, based on which it is believed that it is always possible to apprehend that truth within the limits of our subjectivity conditioned to a multiplicity of elements. However, this external reality exists as a reality almost independent of us. Our relationship to it does not change it, as if external things exist without change and interaction among themselves. So, for example, it would be enough to read the Bible to know what is the best way to lead us in history or what is the will of God. It would be enough to follow the teachings of the churches to learn how to discern the best path forward. It would be enough to follow the teachings of a guru to achieve inner peace.

Such a posture, to some extent magical, also reinforced the idea that the world "outside of us" is an object to be explored, that we are the kings and queens of nature. This mentality is very present today, especially in the production of monocultures, of the extractivism that takes the resources considered of interest and discard many others, causing disasters and ecological crimes. The same is true at the level of social and economic relations. Some people are considered subjects of rights while others are made completely disposable. Some are known and others unknown. Some welcomed and others rejected even as children. Despite these facts, we continue to speak of interdependence as a magically inclusive word, although one that creates social and cultural exclusions, in addition to many social and religious illusions.

For this reason, understanding a little more the meaning and consequences of a vital and interrelated conception of interdependence seems to be an important path also for theologies. They need to modify their epistemologies, their forms of expression, their language, their contents, and their policies to enter the new dynamics of the transformations that operate in us from our constitutive and always changing relationality.

Everything starts with a word of attention to life, a word that is also scientific, to affirm that our universe erupted through a great fire, an explosion from which everything, including our senses, our virtues and vices, our loves and our hates, came out all at the same time and in evolutive form, part of that scorching explosion expanding in a variety of directions. We have a common origin, derived from our evolving and expanding galaxy. Life in its diversity of forms since the birth of the universe, passing by the neighbor's baby and the calf of the farm or the flower on the field, has a common biological origin. It all starts with the cosmic fire, the fire of the passions, the fire of the attraction of the bodies, the fire that creates life, the fire of art, the fire that creates and devastates![5]

In addition to that, we cannot say much; only poetry of ecstasy and wonder as participants in this broader vastness, which also contains painful laments because this same vital energy can take various directions, of cruelties and destructions to which we can attest. This scientific sensibility and poetic consciousness is present in our times above all else due to the evolution that astrophysical science, biology, and some philosophies could glimpse from the outset. This beginning could be the beginning of interdependence in the very origin of life. This is enough for us to realize that we have in us this common force that moves in multiple directions and that without we cannot survive as living beings of different species.

Undoubtedly, this beginning, as we describe it, is not literally present in the tradition of monotheistic texts. As a result, we continue to live a theology of the superior divine distant from the human, although we affirmed its manifestation in the human. The divine, however, continues to be separated—the creator, the demiurge, the absolute, the savior with its own nature, different from that of the universe and with a primarily human and masculine social representation.

The question of how we know our world arises again and linked to it is the question of what we believe and how we believe concerning ourselves. Believing is not an affirmation of certainties, but changing and provisional propositions that help us to live the ordinary and provisional reality of life. Belief is also unbelief. When we believe in something, we disbelieve in other things so that belief is never a pure, perfect, absolutely safe action. However, when we speak of believing or faith, we think of absolute and immutable realities experienced by us, people who are so mutable and relative. Faith would touch a certain lack of rationality, a security in the insecurity of life, something immutable. We live in the shadows of absolutes; we hang on to them and are convinced that they are the ones that sustain and order our lives.

---

5   Brian Swimme and Berry Thomas, *The Universe Story: From the Primordial Flaring Forth to the Ecozoic Era—A Celebration of the Unfolding of the Cosmos* (San Francisco: HarperOne, 1992).

In fact, we have lived for millennia to affirm our gods as separate and superior to us. Now we will live perhaps millennia to discover our shared divinity in everything that exists; divinity as a vital force that connects us to each other simply so that life can continue to be in us and in everything. It is this constitutive fact of everything that, in Sallie McFague's words, allows us to speak of a "planetary agenda." Such a planetary agenda "involves everything and everyone. It involves everything because we now know that all things, all beings and processes on the planet, are interrelated, and that the well-being of each is connected with the well-being of the whole."[6]

In this sense, agendas limited only to the well-being of some human beings such as Christians, Buddhists, Black people, and Indian people are increasingly facing the larger needs of the planet and all living beings. This agenda does not eliminate differences and urgencies, but it understands and addresses them in other ways.

In the present times when, through communication technologies, our world has become just a village in which we can continuously communicate with one another, affirmations like "only mine" and "my group" no longer stand alone and hardly produce justice actions. A new understanding of the relationship between human beings and the planet as a whole is needed and is slowly beginning to emerge. Perhaps it is the mark of our collective responsibility and the awareness that we can no longer save ourselves and our group at the expense of the health of the planet in its vital diversity.

A shared planetary dimension must permeate all our actions, even the simplest of our daily tasks, and include all people in the responsibility for their lives and for the common life. It should also touch theologies as a means of explaining what we believe. For this to be the case, the most diverse educational processes must be woven by a broad and inclusive idea of interdependence and the common good in order to favor the necessary dialogue between different groups.

My question as a Christian philosopher and theologian is whether there exists a possibility of reactivating some traditional doctrines of

---

6   Sallie McFague, *The Body of God: An Ecological Theology* (Minneapolis: Fortress Press, 1993), 8.

Christianity in line with the real interdependence of bodies. I confess my initial doubt because of the long metaphysical patriarchal tradition that shaped our theology. However, believing in the mixture of all things, I integrate my doubts into positive possibilities. Believing and doubting have always been joint paths. And there are elements of great wealth in the biblical tradition and that of the Christian churches for the perspective we are proposing.

The Christian phenomenon that later became the official religion of the Roman Empire began with a rupture within Judaism, the proportions of which are difficult for us to assess. This rupture gave rise to a plural and varied Christian phenomenon according to the different communities and their leaders, having a fundamental ethical nucleus, that is the restoration of the lives of the needy reclaimed in different ways by the prophetic texts and the Gospels. However, from the fourth century onwards, this phenomenon was affirmed in a dogmatic fashion, something that persisted even with the contribution of religious movements like the Protestant Reformation in the sixteenth century. Its form and content continue to this day. It is affirmed and reaffirmed through the Nicene Creed repeatedly recited in our churches and appears as the letter of principles by which we adhere to Christianity. Such a creed seems to me quite questionable today and has consequences in the relationship between interdependence, Christianity, and the environmental crisis.

Is another creed necessary? I think so. A creed that is understandable for each time; a creed that can be renewed periodically and can be a common platform in light of our common survival. A creed that reveals our interdependence and reciprocity in our own bodies and through them with the planet and its ecosystems. In this sense, one could speak of the body of God as the body of everything that exists. Not a body above or distinct, but a mysterious sacred dimension present in everything. Not a perfect body that creates imperfect bodies, but a body in all past, present, and future bodies, a body that is not vitally separated from any other body in the Milky Way and beyond. An evolving living body that assumes varied forms, many of which are absolutely unpredictable. It will no longer be the divinity before which we bend our knees to ask for special graces, but instead it will be the divine in me and in others, the divine recognized in the diversity of lives and the awareness that we are only the fragile and limited thought of this larger body. The awareness that there is no higher being above the world that saves us, but that we are participants in the same creative energy base on which we are mutually saved or lost.

These intuitions seem impossible in the cognitive and political structures of today's Christian churches. Would this decree perhaps represent their historic end? Would it be a weapon that would blow up the temples and empty their coffers? Would it be a whirlwind that would erase the treaties between churches and states? Dionysius the Areopagite, the Neoplatonic and mystical philosopher from the first century, said that because of the shared origin of all things, all things are intimately united, and this fact justifies the usage of the word "universe" to designate the belonging of all things to a single reality, not in separate ways, but in an inseparable connection and unity, a kind of ontological friendship among everything that exists.[7] Thinking about ancient statements such as this, as well as new possibilities, could stimulate our collective creativity and invite us to assume the responsibility that belongs to us at this moment in the history of the planet and, in a special way, in the plural history of Christianity.

The Paradoxical Movements of Interdependence

Often, when we speak of interdependence, we are tempted to believe that it expresses only a positive relationship governed by safe laws inherent to its inner workings. Without realizing, we reduce it to the human universe and give it a moral qualification of goodness—of something good. We remove from it its contradictions, the terrifying unpredictability that constitutes its evolution, including the unpredictability of animal, plant, mineral, and climatic relationships and, above all, human animals. In reductionist ethical terms, we often affirm interdependence as a positive phenomenon and, in a sense, exempt from negativity. If we do so, we would be, from an anthropological standpoint, adopting a limited view of good and evil, reducing the broader and more complex understanding of interdependence to a simplistic human level. Interdependence would be just another one of the many words or set of magical expressions that we would be introducing into our socio-emotional vocabulary as if the new page of our common

---

7   Swimme and Thomas, *The Universe Story*, 266.

history depended on them. Without realizing it, we tend to reduce this concept to a positive horizon, as we did with other expressions that have become almost symbols of perfect realities. For example, "classless society," "social justice," "human rights," and "reign of God" are expressions that once had and continue to have an important historical-social function, but which cannot have closed, perfect, and absolute content for its many users. They cannot contain only postures considered beneficial for all people as if we could turn our utopias into finished topoi. We cannot end with the dynamics of hope and announce the happy end of times.

In the same way, the revealing interdependence of the interconnection between everything that exists contains contradictory, paradoxical, and unexpected aspects that escape us. In addition, even though we are aware of our vital interdependent reality, it is marked by, and is fundamentally based on, a negativity component, i.e., that which it is set in opposition to. This means that the positive force asserts itself in the negative and the negative in the positive, each "side" transforming the apparent opposite into its vital action potential. In its deepest aspect, interdependence could socially make us think of the master and slave dialectic in Hegel, in which the existence of the master makes the slave and vice versa. One is in the other and depends on the other. However, what we are affirming is much broader than human social relations; it is much broader than what the perceptions of our imagination can offer.

This complexity seems to be the fundamental point to be addressed from a theological point of view: the inseparable negativity and positivity contained in interdependence. What would that be in Christian theological terms? I believe that it is strongly present in different expressions of Christian theology, which perhaps need an adjustment on the basis of our contemporary knowledge and the challenges that life poses to us today.

One thing to note is that this perception has always been present in the tradition of the peoples of the Bible and in part of the long Christian tradition, even though the word "interdependence" cannot be found in the Bible. For example, the perception of the inexplicable origin of evil, translated by so many myths, reveals this mixture that characterizes us. Likewise, in the tradition of Jesus of Nazareth, one learns that although he spent his life doing good, he was condemned to death on the cross. Apparently, in human history evil triumphs while the good is defeated, even when we talk about the victory of good over evil. And we speak about it precisely because we need to be moved by the hope of attaining good. For this reason, other possible imaginary worlds are invented where evil would be eliminated, including death, which Saint Paul considered to be the final enemy. The transformation of the victory of good over evil becomes a religious and political myth, a utopian horizon to base our walk on, a compass that would always point to the path of peace and justice. That which is requested by emotions, urged by desire, and shaped by hope is transformed into a possible reality and, at the same time, a source of hope and alienation. It is a source of alienation because it produces excesses in relation to the possible and feeds the real negation of the interdependence that sustains life. However, by eliminating everything we call evil, we also eliminate that which we call good. The dialectic that mixes subjects and situations is necessary for the maintenance of life through the production of new forms of balance and mutation.

It is through this perspective that we could also re-situate and reinterpret interdependence. Some, perhaps naively, when affirming it, take the negativity out of it and build it as a positive and homogeneous idea without the presence of contradiction, unpredictability, and the impermanence of living beings, particularly humans. From this perspective, if we take away the certainty of the happy ending of utopias, of human history, of the reign of Heaven, where would we be able to fix the anchor of the good we need? This fundamental question leads us to a new interpretation of the journey of human history in line with the development of the valuation of that which is provisional, as if the definitive was merely the renewal of the many provisional situations. Thus, a less fatalistic view of human history presents itself, allowing us to live the present with more intensity.

I believe that despite the variety of needs and interpretations, the new awareness of interdependence could help us to realize how much the world is, in the first place, the world that surrounds us, of which we are builders and neighbors. However, it is a world that equally builds us. This world is a small world, of small and great passions, of love and hate, of pain and healing, all connected to the larger world. And the paths we take depend only in part on us, since countless factors determine the steps we take. As Humberto Mariotti writes in the preface to the book *The Tree of Knowledge*, "Not only the helmsmen steer the ships. The environment also pilots vessels, by means of the maritime currents, the winds, accidents on the way, storms and so on. In this way, pilots guide, but they are also guided."[8]

We do not know exactly if the vessel will arrive as we expect at the port of destination. Unpredictability involves us on many levels even though predictability is also present. And it is from it that we must act; it is that which constitutes human responsibility; and it is through it that we can choose our actions regarding other human beings and nature, especially in relation to ourselves. Predictability will tell us whether it is worthwhile to build a dam or tear a forest, decrease the size of fruits or add chemicals to make them look larger. It is predictability, characteristic of our rationality today, that will help us analyze our projects and choose the good we wish to do. But it is also marked by the unpredictable, the unexpected that touches the different dimensions of life.

All of this is to say that interdependence is much more complex than the way in which we conceive the world, hoping that everything will happen within its limits, however beautiful and romantic it may seem. We fertilize and are fertilized by each other and by the countless predictable and unpredictable natural forces that sustain our lives. And the fertilizer is not always the most adequate to the common needs. The fertilizer transforms its effects when it encounters other unexpected elements . . . causing surprises!

To introduce this dynamism into religious beliefs is to invite them to come out of the fixed schemes which they developed, imposing themselves as supernatural powers on poor human lives. It is to invite theologies to not value the tradition of the past at the expense of the questions of the present, and to not minimize the new questions of today, thinking that the past will answer them. This is the difficult challenge posed to theological thinking in this century.

Perhaps this work has to not only start but also grow outside official institutions, as they believe themselves to be the guardians of the form of the faith, forgetting the necessary change in content that is needed to assist life as it presents itself today. Blind obedience to the tradition maintained

---

8   Humberto Maturana and Francisco Varela, *A árvore do conhecimento. as bases biológicas do conhecimento humano* (São Paulo: Palas Athena, 1984), 11.

by the churches often hinders the processes of conscience and prevents subsequent changes, since they tend to get in the way of the established religious power. And in the battle between being faithful to the established power or obeying the appeals of the many, history has shown us that the established power is almost always victorious.

THE PATH OF SIMPLICITY AMID THE COMPLEXITY OF RELATIONS

There is a process of conversion to simplicity which seems to guide the new relations between humanism, Christianity, and the environmental crisis. By simplicity, I understand many things, but above all a movement to return to everyday life, to facts, to people's little anecdotes, listening to stories and learning to tell them, preparing and sharing food together. It is to reconnect with the real, the immediate reality, without necessarily analyzing it in the first place through established socio-analytical mediations, believing that there is an initial approach to bodies that can be expressed in different ways. We have to get close to the bodies, smell them, shiver with their presence. They may cause repugnancy, nausea, or empathy. They may cause fear or a desire for proximity. They are bodies in front of us, not ideas. From this multiformed simplicity we can get to know each other better and find immediate and intermediate paths to help and influence our lives. We can learn how to get to know people and our own personal reactions better. The ecological and ethical agenda thus becomes more palpable, closer, more collective, more personal, and more possible to be linked to the multiple initiatives of good will.

I also believe that the path of simplicity falls beyond theologies. It seems strange that a text that was meant to be theological presents doubts about the very reality of theology. Theology in my view should not speak of a perfect being, but of the search on the part of imperfect beings to sustain themselves in life. It should talk about meanings exchanged and sought for. It should speak about shared insecurities and security, disappointments, and new quests. It should talk about poetry and help in singing and crying in life.

I believe that by identifying itself as a university science, theological knowledge has distanced itself from the anxieties and needs of the people, especially the poorest. It began to express itself through erudite concepts that seem more like powerful magic words of the exclusive knowledge of learned elites. The supposed divine knowledge becomes hierarchical and is now administered to the people who do not understand it and do not need it. Those who welcome it only do it like those who welcome the constitution of a country—or those who welcome a boss—without, however, following and understanding its contents or ordinances. Bending one's knees and lowering one's head in the face of what is not understood is not an approximation to the Great Mystery, but perhaps only its manipulation. The Great Mystery silences its greatness in us, does not enslave us or eliminate our dignity. The Great Mystery is in us.

The theologian, the priest, and the pastor represent knowledge and power above ordinary life. They often reduce the mystery that surrounds us to an almost esoteric conceptual knowledge by fixing it on the knowledge and power of the absolute being, the almighty God the Father. To celebrate God, they need altars and special clothes, not to mention the long years of study, formation, and formatting, in order to diffuse the truths they found about their God. They hide from themselves in order to appear to the people who listen to them with authority, appreciation, and respect in the name of the invisible God. Many people today experience a significant distance from the representatives of God and the religious institutions that in God's name keep believers submissive and dependent on a higher magical power.

On the one hand, there are the theories of liberation, the criticisms of postcolonialism and postmodernism, made by those who have decreed the death of religions, and also those who do not see themselves in religious theories, who do not understand them anymore. The latter no longer trusts pastors who do not represent them and who do not help them find the fire they need in the provisory nature of their lives. And yet, there is the multitude of those who take refuge in the many magical services, believing that they will find in them the immediate solution to their problems. We are all lost like the uprooted, without firmament to support our feet and without water while exposed to the scorching sun.

For this reason, we need to liberate the creative fire like Prometheus, who stole the sacred fire from the gods and handed it to humanity, to whom the fire belonged. We need to release the fire like in the image of Pentecost because it is our life. But the owners of religions and their political allies always steal it again and set up the most varied traps so that it is not returned to humanity, women above all: the sacred fire of freedom, of the vital force, of joy, of collective responsibility, of the acceptance of our differences as an expression of life itself and of the initial cosmic explosion.

BRIEF CONCLUSION

After reflecting on the magnitude and limits of interdependence, there remains a strange sensation inhabiting the body, perhaps concentrating in the chest and throat, as a sort of dissatisfaction, of insecurity in the face of true reflections, which leaves even more open the need for something safe to cling to. We cannot make relationality or interdependence our immediate imaginary anchor. It is not possible to quickly eliminate the various models of relation to God and the multiple meanings of this word. Even though we can describe something of the reality of interdependence and can name it in the form of examples and murmurs, it remains materially enigmatic. We are repeatedly faced with a sensation of impotence circling any sense of potentiality, a feeling inherited and developed.

Perhaps if we could explain something about the Great Mystery that weaves, attracts, and saturates us with "interdependence," we could find in the religious traditions something that would lead us to realize that we are each and every one an image of each other, in need of each other. What we observe as being outside of us is in us, and we only survive together because we are together. We only survive because one plants the seed, another reaps, another prepares bread, another caresses, another opens doors, and another builds houses. We only survive if we believe that it is necessary to recycle the things that have turned into garbage outside and inside us. The garbage is not negligible, but it is a new humus that can give life to flowers and animals. We are the garbage in the process of transformation. Nothing is lost—everything is transformed!

In the current stage of humanity, as contradictory and diverse as ever, the sentiment of emptiness and insecurity continues to torment us. Our science and technology cannot eliminate the bitter taste of our finitude. As limited, contingent, and therefore imperfect beings, we would like to anchor ourselves in something that does not perish and be immortal. That is why I dare to say that we have to return to God, perhaps, no longer as the almighty Father, but as a consoling force of reciprocity, as a mystery that guides us or as a protection for our steps guaranteed by our neighbors, those who are our image and likeness. We have to return to God as a vital energy in everything and everyone, beyond moral judgments and the barriers we put on one another.

In the same vein, removing the exclusively patriarchal garments of God and putting on others according to the needs of different groups and people was and continues to be a path of the religious tradition of many women and men. This may be a way to be reclaimed in the simplicity of domestic relations. This means reclaiming God as an inexplicable force that is expressed through a name, a sound, a sigh, a constant babble in us, with us, with others, a God of different names, in different forms, with no single one made absolute. But, above all, the I God, the you God, the we God with us.

One must admit that one does not feel safe going out into the violent streets of large cities without hearing someone say, "go with God." Likewise, one cannot go looking for a job without some sort of confidence or inkling that one will find it. One cannot go to the hospital without the hope to be seen even if frustration can come later. The problem does not lie in the anthropological belief about the need for protection in a world where we feel unprotected. The problem lies in the use and abuse made by religious institutions that in their drive for power use the faithful as a maneuvering mass to favor their many personal benefits and powers. The problem lies in the alliances between public authorities that use our natural contingency to make it an object of human exploitation. The problem is to alienate ourselves from our condition of precarious beings and to introduce hopes proposed by the consumerist capitalist market, often fueled by religions. The problem is that preachers deceive us with false promises and commercialize our needs. They astutely play with our quest for truth and security by imposing submission to their ways of seeing the world, affirming it as divine will. The old prophets, on the other hand, rose against the false prophets and priests who led the people astray (Jer. 23). Today we must turn against them just like we turn against bad politicians and bad professionals.

There is no absolute outside of relative desires, and based on them each of us draws our gods and talks to them. That is why a monolithic discourse about God seems totalitarian. A single theory about the divine creator or a single form of praise are today increasingly unthinkable. This openness that is outlined is undoubtedly dangerous for the institutions of religion because it can lead to apparent disorder. However, religious polysemy, divine polysemy, polysemy of needs and sighs lead to the beauty of diversity, irreducible to a monolithic model, and maintains the beauty of life.

Couldn't the planetary agenda have a common horizon based on our very diverse concrete lives? Could it not be a kind of common public religion that would lead us to behavioral agreements aimed at the good of each person and the planet? That would mean believing in something much greater than the gods that religious enterprises present to us! Believing that life sustains us even if we don't know how, or that we need to hold hands with each other so as not to fall into the many narcissistic temptations that plague us! That is, holding hands to believe in the forces of life!

Holding hands to carry each other's burdens, to share bread, to lift the fallen, not to stone women or other marginalized groups, to comfort the afflicted, to respect forests, rivers, and seas. These are not simply ritualistic words that were part of old ethical codes; they are essential daily experiences. The great challenge is to inscribe them into our hearts so that they become performative values of new interdependent relationships. This is called ethical interdependence!

Despite these possible aspirations and hopes, we are still in the penumbra or in the dark . . . But it was precisely in the 'dark night' that Saint John of the Cross found some light inside himself. We must believe that light needs darkness and darkness is a precondition for capturing the strength and fragility of the light that will appear in our hearts. This is part of our creed! This is our interdependent life in the world today!

PART 2
A ROADMAP FOR THE CONVERSATION

CHAPTER 3

THE NORTH/SOUTH DIVIDE IN CONTEMPORARY CHRISTIAN ECOTHEOLOGY: SOUTH AFRICA AS A CASE STUDY

Ernst M. Conradie

This volume on *World Christianity and Ecology* attests to the global spread of Christian ecotheology. It is now found in the full spectrum of geographical and cultural contexts, confessional traditions, and theological schools, published in many languages, with multiple centers of excellence in ecotheology across the globe.[1]

However, such a global spread does not alter the way the production (using the word advisedly) of Christian ecotheology is still dominated by publishing houses in the Global North, by English as language of communication, and by the US and the UK in particular. The sheer volume of titles that could be classified as ecotheology is indicative of that.

Given the destructive impact of imperialism, colonialism, and neocolonialism; the role of extractive, industrialized capitalism; and the historical carbon emissions of countries of the Global North, such an interest in Christian ecotheology is to be welcomed and may be regarded as an appropriate form of self-critical contextual theology. As may be expected, one finds a wide spectrum of approaches in the Global North itself, from theologically orthodox to liberal, from ecomodernist to staunchly anti-capitalist approaches, from support for notions of human stewardship or priesthood to radical critiques of anthropocentrism, from those

---

1   For a survey, see my essay on "Ecotheology" for the online *St Andrews Encyclopaedia of Theology* (forthcoming).

who emphasize Christian particularity to those who emphasize multi-faith collaboration. Other lines of demarcation may be added, and these do not always overlap with each other.

The global spread of Christian ecotheology will tend to undermine such dominance by the Global North. This is strengthened by an emphasis on the local, the particular, a sense of place and embodiment. However, to speak of "*world* Christianity" is also to recognize the need to address *global* challenges such as climate change, ocean acidification, the loss of biodiversity, ozone depletion, nuclear threats, deforestation, and so forth. To do so together, i.e., ecumenically, requires coming to terms with global divides, especially the North/South divide, but also the East/West divide, and perhaps what some refer to as the "clash of civilizations."

Within Christian ecotheology, the North/South divide is well recognized, albeit it is addressed in different ways: by confronting it, covering it up, seeking to overcome it, or strategically radicalizing it.[2] In this

---

2   A few examples of edited volumes may illustrate the point: An early WCC volume edited by David Hallman, *Ecotheology: Voices from South and North* (Geneva: WCC, 1994) recognizes the need to listen to such voices. Another volume edited by Rosemary Ruether, *Women Healing Earth: Third World Women on Ecology, Feminism and Religion* (Maryknoll, NY: Orbis, 1997) focuses on the "third world" only and includes essays from religious traditions other than Christianity. *Christian Faith and the Earth: Current Paths and Emerging Horizons* in *Ecotheology* (London: T and T Clark, 2014), a volume that I coedited, recognizes the global spread of ecotheology but struggles to be fully representative. Another WCC volume entitled *Making Peace with the Earth: Action and Advocacy for Climate Justice* (Geneva: WCC, 2016), edited by Grace Ji-Sun Kim, recognizes the need to address climate change together. By contrast, *Planetary Solidarity: Global Women's Voices on Christian Doctrine and Climate Justice*, also edited by Grace Ji-Sun Kim with Hilda Koster (Minneapolis: Fortress, 2017) focuses on women's voices, seeking to overcome such divides through "planetary solidarity." *The T and T Clark Handbook on Christian Theology and Climate Change* (London: T and T Clark, 2020), which I edited with Hilda Koster, accentuates the divide by focusing on the culpability of Christianity in the Global North. Likewise, but following the opposite strategy, *Decolonizing Ecotheology: Indigenous and Subaltern Challenges* (Eugene, OR: Wipf and Stock, 2022), edited by Lily Mendoza and George

contribution I will focus on the South African context in order to understand the complexities of such North/South divides *within* one country. This is based on the observation that world Christianity has become polycentric and that there are now multiple but diverging centers of excellence in ecotheology (including South Africa), so that any North Atlantic hegemony is fractured, although the debate continues to be dominated by English-language literature. I will first offer some clarifications and demarcations, then sketch the current state of the debate in order to support the conclusion that such divides remain far from resolved and requires further ecumenical dialogue.

A FEW CLARIFICATIONS

For the purposes of this contribution, "ecotheology" is taken to refer to theological (*theos*) reflection (*logos*) on the planetary "household" (*oikos*). It recognizes the complex interplay between ecology (the underlying logic of the household), economy (household rules), and ecumenicity (inhabitation of the household) and therefore the relatedness of economic exploitation, ecological destruction, and a consumerist culture, together with various social divides based on domination in the name of difference. Ecotheology has to consider the biophysical environment (ecosystems, including human embodiment), not only the social, political, and economic dimensions of the environment.

Theological reflection is best understood in terms of *doing* theology—as distinct from studying, teaching or producing theology. "Doing theology" refers to the ways ordinary Christian people (individuals and communities) reflect on the content and meaning of their faith in and for their everyday lives. Such first order reflections are expressed in body language,

---

Zachariah, radicalizes the tension by focusing on Indigenous and subaltern voices, albeit in order to decolonize mainstream ecotheology. Finally, the massive recent *International Handbook on Creation Care and Eco-Diakonia* (Geneva: WCC, 2022), edited by Lesmore Gibson and others, despite its name, draws on contributions from the Global South only. Notably, these titles are all in English, given that this is often the preferred medium to make one's work widely accessible. It has to be stated that this skews the debate significantly.

mumbling to oneself, conversations with others, and stories that are told. In addition, one may mention the role of secondary reflections through sermons; Christian education; the work of the laity in multiple vocations and organizations, wherever environmental responsibility is exercised; letters to the press; and articles in popular ecclesial magazines. Tertiary teaching and academic research form in this sense only the proverbial tip of the iceberg, the ears of the hippopotamus, and is of lesser significance than the rest. Since academic research output is more readily accessible, it will have to suffice here.

Ecotheology covers all the traditional subdisciplines of Christian theology given work done on the interpretation of biblical texts, the history of Christianity, the Christian faith, a Christian ethos, and ecclesial praxis and mission. Given the focus on *theological* reflection, Christian ecotheology is distinct from the field of religion and ecology, where Christianity could be regarded as one religious tradition alongside others. For some scholars (crossing multiple disciplines), a clear distinction is not plausible, so that the focus here has to be on those who would accept "Christian ecotheology" as a description of (at least some of) their work.

It is important to add the adjective "Christian" to respect the differences between various theistic traditions, including Judaism, Christianity, and Islam, but also traditional African religions. In speaking of God and God's relationship with the planetary household, ecotheology remains a theological discipline. This is tricky because Biblical scholars employing an ecological hermeneutics will not always describe their work as "ecotheology." Speaking of God cannot be reduced in a modernist vein to words *about* God or to critical reflection on religious experience or *human* constructions of God, but allows for the possibility of speaking *to* God, to consider the word *of* God even where an apophatic reserve in speaking on God's behalf is advised and where a hermeneutics of suspicion is required regarding using the word of God to justify (male) authority.

The focus of this chapter is more specifically on *South African* contributions to ecotheology. What this means is not self-evident. South Africa as a nation-state has a human population of around sixty million. Despite resistance against apartheid race classification, it is, for statistical purposes, still racially divided, roughly between an 81 percent African, 9 percent Colored (mixed descent), 8 percent White, and 2 percent Indian population.[3] There are some three to four million migrants, mostly from Zimbabwe and elsewhere in Africa, and no fewer than eleven official languages. Christianity is the dominant religion (around 75–80 percent of people), alongside less than 2 percent Muslims and around 1 percent Hindus and observers of Indigenous African religions. Christians belong to a wide range of so-called mainline churches and numerous Pentecostal and Indigenous churches.

There are twenty-six public universities in South Africa and a host of private service providers, including many offering theological education but producing a very small proportion of research outputs. Some South African citizens have been working elsewhere in the world, while scholars from elsewhere have been working in South Africa. Students from other African countries obtain degrees from South African universities and live here for extended periods. This applies especially to southern African students who have produced a disproportionate number of postgraduate theses in ecotheology compared to their South African colleagues. Many contributions touch on ecological concerns but focus on urban ecology, human ecology, human embodiment, gender issues, food, and of course economic issues.

Many South African scholars publish research in book series or journals housed by publishers based in the UK and the US, often assuming readers based in the Global North, albeit that such readers also include persons originally from the Global South. Some edited volumes are initiated by scholars in the Global North but include contributions by South Africans; the inverse also applies. Some journals are administratively based in South Africa but are produced by conglomerates in the Global North. Indeed, a confusing and conflicting scene!

As I will argue below, these distinctions matter when one considers what constitutes South African ecotheology. The picture is especially skewed when one maintains a narrow focus on academic research

---

3   Such categories are still used for statistical purposes and then for the sake of affirmative action. The nomenclature is awkward to say the least: it compares a color (white), a category (colored), a continent (Africa), and a country (India) with each other.

contributions that use "ecotheology" as a key term and are authored by South African citizens based in South Africa at the time of writing, are published in journals or by publishers administratively based in South Africa, and are aimed primarily at South African readers.

Surveying South African Discourse on Ecotheology

Given such considerations, it is necessary to be quite blunt: South African contributions to ecotheology are, statistically, heavily dominated by white (as per the race classification under apartheid) scholars, most of whom are male and aging or deceased. At least at the surface level, this merely reflects a North/South divide instead of addressing it. Many qualifications and explanations may be offered, but this is the proverbial elephant in the room that has to be mentioned, or else there can be no further conversation.

To demonstrate this, I conducted literature searches in October 2022 through the Atla Religion Database, the most comprehensive database available in the field. I searched for "ecotheology" (1,579 entries) and "ecological theology" (335 entries) and extracted research articles by authors who are South African citizens. I also searched for entries that included "South Africa" and "conservation" (8 entries), "ecology" (60 entries), "environment" (34 entries), "environmental justice" (14 entries), "nature" (62 entries), "sustainability" (9 entries), "sustainable development" (44 entries), and "climate change" (11 entries). Using keys such as "creation care," "environmental stewardship," and "earth-keeping" did not yield any additional references. Excluding those that were clearly not relevant for Christian ecotheology, I identified 129 entries by sixty-seven authors and exported these into a single file.

It must be immediately added that this is a rather blunt instrument, as not all South African contributions to ecotheology will include "ecotheology" (or something akin to that) as one of the key terms. For example, contributions to African, Black, feminist, and liberation theology that touch on issues of environmental justice would not necessarily have "ecotheology" as a form of self-description. Many of the older contributions are not captured in the ATLA Religion Database. The corpus is much bigger so that no statistical conclusions can be derived from this survey.⁴ Nevertheless, this helped to identify those scholars who at least occasionally work in the field and who would regard "ecotheology" as a key term describing at least some of their work. One may search for each of these authors individually for further contributions and this will surely yield many more references. Other search engines (such as Google Scholar) may be more comprehensive but then also more difficult for users to select what is relevant.

The search engine also did not yield references to several significant South African publications resulting from ecumenical collaboration. These include a statement entitled "The Land is Crying for Justice" and produced by the Ecumenical Foundation of Southern Africa on the basis of a church leaders' consultation with a view to the World Summit on Sustainable Development, which was held in Johannesburg in 2002. "The Oikos Journey" was a 2006 paper produced by the Diakonia Council of Churches to argue that poverty and ecological destruction have to be addressed together in the household of God. There is also a 2009 discussion document published by the South African Council of Churches entitled "Climate Change—A Challenge to the Churches in South Africa" and a "Message from African Faith Leaders to the Seventeenth Conference of the Parties (COP17)," following a meeting at the United Nations Environmental Programme in Nairobi, June 7–8, 2011.⁵

Despite such obvious shortcomings of this bibliographic survey, allow me to nevertheless offer some general impressions.

First, the scholars who regularly contribute to the field of Christian ecotheology (arguably with more than one essay in the field) are indeed predominantly white and male. These include Anthony Balcomb, Johan

---

4   A bibliography from two decades ago already included eighty-six contributions by South African scholars. See Ernst M. Conradie and Andrew E. Warmback, "Theology and the Environment: A Select Bibliography of Contributions from Africa," *Bulletin for Contextual Theology in Africa* 8/2&3 (2002): 121–134.

5   This communiqué was compiled jointly by 130 faith leaders representing Muslim, Christian, Hindu, African traditional, Bahá'í, and Buddhist communities from thirty countries across Africa. It is included as an addendum in the report on the "We Have Faith Campaign": SAFCEI, "We Have Faith," http://safcei.org/wp-content/uploads/2015/06/We-have-faith.pdf.

Buitendag, Ernst Conradie, Marthinus Daneel, Geoff Davies, Steve de Gruchy, David Field, Peter Houston, Klaus Nürnberger, David Olivier, Attie van Niekerk, and Andrew Warmback. If only monographs were considered, the picture would be even more skewed.

Second, there are also some significant white female scholars working in ecotheology, such as Denise Ackermann, Kate Davies, Christina Landman, Nadia Marais, Rachel Mash, Susan Rakoczy,[6] and Annalet van Schalkwyk. It needs to be noted that elsewhere on the African continent there is a very lively interest in ecofeminist forms of spirituality,[7] typically employing notions of being embodied to explore the interplay between ecological destruction and violence against women, resisting the interlocking dualisms between body and soul, spirit and matter, heaven and earth, and nature and culture.

Third, one may mention contributions to biblical scholarship employing an ecological lens, e.g., work by Jannie du Preez, Jimmy Loader, Neels Redelinghuys, Izak Spangenberg, Peet van Dyk, Willie van Heerden, Danie van Zyl, Gerald West, and Günther Wittenberg (again all white males), although it must be said that Black women scholars such as Musa Dube from Botswana, Madipoane Masenya,[8] and Miranda Pillay have been at the forefront of the field, typically adopting a story-telling approach.

Fourth, practical theologians often address the theme of sustainable development, although the focus may be more on development than on sustainability. There are also some contributions that touch on issues of liturgy, preaching, congregational praxis, diakonia, and, especially in earlier contributions from the 1990s, Christian mission. These are again

---

6   See, for example, Susan Rakoczy, *In Her Name: Women Doing Theology* (Pietermaritzburg, South Africa: Cluster, 2004).

7   One may mention here a number of contributions by scholars from other African countries who studied or worked in South Africa, including Sophia Chirongoma, Fulata Moyo, Kuzipa Nalwamba, and Isabel Apowo Phiri.

8   See especially Madipoane Masenya, "All from the Same Source? Deconstructing a (Male) Anthropocentric Reading of Job (3) through an Eco-bosadi Lens," *Journal of Theology for Southern Africa* 137 (2010), 46–60; also Masenya, "Ecological Hermeneutics and Postcolonialism," in *The Oxford Handbook of the Bible and Ecology*, ed. Hilary Marlow and Mark Harris (Oxford: Oxford University Press, 2022), 49–62.

dominated by white males such as Johan Cilliers, Marthinus Daneel, Dons Kritzinger, Ignatius Swart, and Cas Vos.

Fifth, postgraduate theses are not always captured by the ATLA Religion Database, but strikingly these are often written by students coming from other African countries, including significant contributions by Robert Agyarko, Cyprian Alokwu, Sophia Chirongoma, Chammah Kaunda, Kivatsi Kavusa, Fulata Moyo, and Kuzipa Nalwamba (who each hold teaching positions outside South Africa). This picture is admittedly changing; there are now several recent postgraduate theses by South African citizens, but this is harder to search for with some precision.

Finally, contributions to Christian ecotheology by Black (including African, Colored, and Indian scholars) South African scholars remain few and far between. There will surely be more, but let me highlight six significant essays reflected in the search, which are written by Gabriel Setiloane, Puleng Lenkabula, Kelebogile Resane, Archbishop Thabo Makgoba, and Tinyiko Maluleke.[9]

APPROACHING AN ASSESSMENT

How, then must one interpret such an apparent racial divide in ecotheology in South Africa?[10] Can this be equated with a North/South divide? To be clear, the racial divide in contributing authors may be only a symptom of an underlying divide over the kind of issues that are selected for discussion,

---

9 See Gabriel Setiloane, "Towards a Biocentric Theology and Ethic—via Africa." *Journal of Black Theology* 9:1 (1995), 52–66; Puleng Lenkabula, "Economic Globalisation, Ecumenical Theologies and Ethics of Justice in the Twenty-first Century," *Missionalia* 38:1 (2010), 99–120; Kelebogile Resane, "The Theological Responses to the Socio-economic Activities that Undermine Water as a Resource," *HTS Theological Studies* 66 (2010), 1–7; Thabo Makgoba, "Hope and the Environment: A Perspective from the Majority World," *Anvil* 29:1 (2013), 55–70; "Water Is Life, Sanitation Is Dignity," *Anglican Theological Review* 100:1 (2018), 113–118; and Tinyiko Maluleke, "Black and African Theologies in Search of Comprehensive Environmental Justice," *Journal of Theology for Southern Africa* 167 (2020), 5–19.

10 In this section I am drawing partly on a recent article: Ernst Conradie, "Doing Ecotheology in the South African Context," *Journal of Systematic Theology* 1:5 (2022), 1–35.

vested economic interests, conflicting allegiances and agendas, interpretative frameworks and assumed cosmologies, philosophical assumptions, selected conversation partners, and sources consulted that would be reflected in a bibliography. It cannot be assumed that white scholars reflect a Eurocentric perspective; at the same time, Black scholars also draw from the North Atlantic and other Global North sources. A clear divide between colonial and decolonial perspectives also does not do justice to the available literature. Nevertheless, the racial divide may well prompt a hermeneutics of suspicion on all of the above and in particular over a persisting colonial matrix of power.

One option is to frame this merely in terms of diverging research interests among individual scholars. Accordingly, some would prioritize issues of poverty, unemployment and inequality, health (given the HIV/AIDS and COVID-19 pandemics), and gender-based violence over long-term ecological threats (e.g., climate change). Is there a divide on issues of whiteness, white supremacy, colonial conquest, land restitution, and coloniality? This does not appear to be the case. Most of the white scholars mentioned above have addressed the environmental impact of colonialism and issues of whiteness extensively, while most Black African scholars recognize ecological issues as a transversal for an adequate Black theology of liberation. There is more or less consensus, following the leads of Leonardo Boff and James Cone, that it is the same logic of domination that has led to ecological destruction and white supremacy.[11]

A related option is to understand the divide in terms of the so-called green and brown agendas. The focus of the green agenda is on nature conservation, attending to issues such as the loss of biodiversity, species extinction, soil erosion, waste management, and especially population growth. This is typically aligned with an (evangelical) emphasis on human stewardship. The nature conservation policies of the apartheid era provoked the suspicion that conservation boils down to the establishment of game reserves for a privileged few, often at the expense of the dislocation of local

---

11 See Leonardo Boff, *Cry of the Earth, Cry of the Poor* (Maryknoll, NY: Orbis, 1997); James Cone, "Whose Earth Is it Anyway?" in *Earth Habitat: Eco-injustices and the Church's Response*, ed. Dieter T. Hessel and Larry Rasmussen (Minneapolis: Fortress Press, 2001), 32–32.

people. Many Black residents of urban communities still view issues of nature conservation as a concern of the white middle class, the hobby of an affluent, leisured minority who would like to preserve the environment for purely aesthetic reasons and who seem more concerned about wildlife than the welfare of the unemployed.

In response, the focus of the brown agenda is on the link between environmental degradation and issues of social justice; for example, the plight of urban slum dwellers, factory workers, farm workers, and Indigenous groups removed from ancestral land for the sake of nature conservation areas. The primary concern is the day-to-day struggle of surviving in overcrowded, squalid, and unhealthy conditions. Indeed, finding employment may seem far more urgent than the long-term environmental impact of mining, manufacturing, business, farming, forestry, or fishing. However, the North American critique of environmental racism (around toxic waste dumping) applies in the South African context as well and is readily expanded to address the position of the poor in general.

One may argue that such a divide between the green and brown agendas is still found among white male scholars, but most South African scholars would agree that this divide is not fruitful. In fact, South African contributions to ecotheology have been at the forefront of attempts to bridge this divide. This can be framed in various ways; for example, in terms of an oikotheology (based on the etymology of the "whole household of God" as root metaphor),[12] an olive agenda,[13] ancestral notions of land,[14]

---

12   References may be easily multiplied here. See especially *The Oikos Journey* (2006).

13   See the essays collected in Steven M. de Gruchy, *Keeping Body and Soul Together: Reflections by Steve de Gruchy on Theology and Development* (Pietermaritzburg, South Africa: Cluster Publications, 2015).

14   Throughout the African continent there are many examples of theological reflections on a retrieval of Indigenous ecological wisdom where land plays a crucial role. See, for example, Kapya Kaoma, *God's Family, God's Earth: Christian Ecological Ethics of Ubuntu* (Zomba: Kachere Series, 2013) and Ebenezer Blasu, *African Theocology—Studies in African Religious Creation Care* (Eugene, OR: Wipf and Stock 2020). In the South African context, however, the focus is typically on land ownership, land rights, land redistribution, and land tenure. A major concern is that such Indigenous ecological wisdom hardly overcomes an urban-rural divide. Ancestral land on the periphery cannot be

feminist notions of embodiment, or by regarding ecology as a transversal so that there is an ecological dimension to any issue of social justice. Some may argue that the image of the household plays in the hands of domestication where women, children, and slaves were restricted to the private sphere, while others would respond that using this image in the public sphere precisely undermines such a public/private divide. This is celebrated in African women's contributions, where an important further distinction between a house (the physical structure), a home (*ikhaya*, "to feel at home in"), and a warm hearth is proposed.[15] This divide may have been present before 1994 but is no longer characteristic of the field as a whole.

Another option is to frame this as a divide between Christian ecotheology and discourse on religion and ecology. Both discourses have undeniable legitimacy, but one should not be subsumed under the other—for example, under the rubric of missiology or religious studies. The three Greek roots in the term "ecotheology" (*oikos*, *Theos*, and *Logos*) could be understood in a trinitarian way: there is an interplay between the inhabitation of the Spirit, the transcendence of God, and the mediating role of the *Logos*. From this perspective, the perichoresis between these terms should prevent the one from dominating the other. Yet, multiple distortions are possible in discourse on ecotheology. One danger is that *Logos* would come to dominate *Theos*. This is the modernist logic that underplays the brokenness of the cross; embodies hubris through knowledge, science, and technology; and tends to displace God as the focus of theology. Each of the classic theological subdisciplines is in danger of being reduced to, for example, literary studies, ancient culture, history, philosophy, ethics, sociology, psychology, or development studies. Spirituality, too, can easily be understood in anthropocentric terms as human experiences so that the focus remains on *anthropos* instead of *Theos*.

---

restored if threats are derived from the industrialized economic center. See in this regard the many contributions by Klaus Nürnberger on the structural divide between economic centers and economic peripheries, especially *Prosperity, Poverty and Pollution: Managing the Approaching Crisis* (Pietermaritzburg, South Africa: Cluster Publications, 1999); *Regaining Sanity for the Earth* (Pietermaritzburg, South Africa: Cluster Publications, 2011).

15 See Musimbi R. Kanyoro and Nyambura J. Njoroge, eds., *Groaning in Faith: African Women in the Household of God* (Nairobi: Acton Publishers, 1996).

These tensions are clearly played out in the South African context. Given the allegiance between Christianity and colonial powers, there is considerable resistance against any form of Christian dominance in South African society and a widespread call for religious tolerance and respect for religious diversity. The focus of interreligious dialogue is often on common environmental concerns, exemplified by the Southern African Faith Communities' Environment Institute (SAFCEI). There is a recognition that the *oikos* is a home shared with many others so that any ecclesiastic reduction of the household of God is simply arrogant.[16] Moreover, there is the recognition that environmental problems (e.g., climate change) can only be addressed through collaborative, multidisciplinary efforts.[17] However, given its historical allegiance with the industrialized West, Christianity is often regarded with suspicion as part of the problem. This yields a double temptation for Christian ecotheology to isolate itself from secular critics in order to retain Christian authenticity or to become subsumed under religious studies so that *Theos* is, in fact, replaced by *anthropos*. Where that happens, ecotheology arguably loses its critical and transformative power.

I would suggest that there is indeed a divide in the South African academy between ecotheology and religion and ecology, but this cannot be interpreted as a North/South divide and cannot be fully captured in terms of gender or race. On a personal note, I may add that most of my own work focuses on Christian particularity, but that this has precisely enabled (not inhibited) multi-faith and indeed multidisciplinary collaboration in addressing common challenges.[18]

One may argue that there is no real North/South divide in South African ecotheology except insofar as this reflects a racial divide in the

---

16 See Clive W. Ayre and Ernst M. Conradie, eds., *The Church in God's Household: Protestant Perspectives on Ecclesiology and Ecology* (Pietermaritzburg, South Africa: Cluster Publications, 2016).

17 See the volume edited by Ernst M. Conradie and Hilda P. Koster, eds., *T and T Clark Handbook on Christian Theology and Climate Change* (London: T and T Clark, 2019), with multiple contributions by scholars who studied or are based in South Africa.

18 For one example, see Larry Swatuk et al., eds., *Towards the Blue-Green City—Building Urban Water Resilience* (Pretoria: Water Research Commission, 2021).

South African academy a whole. Accordingly, there is a need to transform the academy to better reflect its location on the African continent and the South African demography. This has far-reaching implications for the vision and mission statements of universities, for resisting the corporatization of tertiary education, for decolonizing the curriculum, and for employment equity. There can be no doubt that the South African higher education sector has already gone through a significant transformation since 1994, partly on the basis of affirmative action policies, but also that there is some distance to travel before it can be claimed that the imbalances of the past have been eradicated.[19] A change in employment profile will translate into research outputs in the long run (and hence more publications in the field of ecotheology),[20] but this cannot be an instant process, as emerging young

---

19 See *Briefly Speaking* 21 (June 2022), Council on Higher Education. See https://www.che.ac.za/news-and-announcements/brieflyspeaking-no-21-dimensions-transformation-higher-education-south.

   According to the latest available report from South Africa's Council on Higher Education, entitled *Public Higher Education 2019* (published in 2021), the racial profile of academic staff members changed significantly from 2014 to 2019. Of the 50,491 academic staff members at public universities in 2014, 17,685 were classified as "African"; 2,819 as "Colored"; 4,402 as "Indian"; 24,652 as "white"; and 933 as "unknown." This changed to a total of 55,742 staff members in 2019 and corresponding figures of 24,922 for "African"; 3,476 for "Colored"; 4,394 for "Indian"; 22,077 for "white"; and 873 for "unknown." However, throughout this period, 64 percent of academic appointments were temporary. By 2019 the figures for permanent staff members by race were 8,223 for "African"; 1,447 for "Colored"; 1,619 for "Indian"; and 8,204 for "whites." If one then factors in the qualifications of permanent academic staff members, the overall picture again looks different, with 3,102 "African"; 597 "Colored"; 762 "Indian"; and 4,693 "white" permanent staff members holding a doctoral qualification (only 47 percent on average in 2019). The proportion of permanent staff members working in the fields of religion and theology could not be established, but it would be fewer than two hundred individuals. One may add retired academics, pastors with doctoral qualifications, postgraduate and postdoctoral students, and other research associates who also produce research outputs, probably doubling the numbers. This is a small pool, albeit one that produces a large volume of research.

20 The Department of Higher Education and Training's" Report on the Evaluation of the 2019 Universities' Research Output" (dated March 2021) shows

Black scholars need to reach academic maturity over decades in order to match the research output of senior colleagues (whether Black or white, male or female). It takes time to mature as a researcher.

In short, there is a plausible argument to be made that the employment profile at South African public universities has a significant impact on research output, but whether this suffices to explain the disproportionate contributions made by white male scholars to ecotheology in South Africa is debatable.[21]

One may also frame the underlying divide (albeit not really a North/South divide) in South African ecotheology in terms of the soteriological categories that are typically employed. Such categories coincide with long-standing confessional traditions and theological schools. I suggest that these can be clustered together under three rubrics, namely liberation (climate justice), reconciliation (land restoration), and reconstruction (sustainable development).

Some extend calls for political, economic, and psychological liberation (as in decolonial discourse) to the liberation of the whole earth. The target of such liberation remains the same; namely, liberation from enslavement, imperialism, colonialism, apartheid, and neoliberal globalized capitalism. Sin is thus understood in terms of domination. The environmental impact of such forces of domination and oppression is highlighted, while

---

that, for the year 2019, a total of 21,019 units of research outputs (in books, chapters in books, articles and conference proceedings) were produced by researchers and research associates at South African public universities. A disproportionate large number of these, 1,243 units, were in the category of philosophy, religious studies, and (especially) theology. The report also shows that "the contribution of BCIA authors has increased from approximately 15% in 2005 to more than 40% in 2019. Conversely the contribution of 'white' academics has declined from 85% in 2005 to less than 60% in 2019." In terms of seniority by age, 7,257 of the 19,901 permanent staff members in 2019 were older than fifty years of age. They produced a large portion of the research output, namely 41 percent in 2005, compared with 35 percent in 2019. See https://www.dhet.gov.za/Policy%20and%20Development%20Support/Research%20outputs%20report%202021_final.pdf.

21 This is recognized, for example, in Tinyiko Maluleke, "Black and African Theologies in Search of Comprehensive Environmental Justice," *Journal of Theology for Southern Africa* 167, 5–19.

the aim of such liberation is explained not only in terms of anthropocentric categories, such as freedom, self-governance, and self-sustenance, but also in terms of ecological well-being. In the same vein, others employ the softer category of healing or the harder category of exorcism to indicate the need to overcome the forces of destruction. In the South African context, the language employed by the *Kairos Document* comes to mind here. The environmental crisis, especially climate change, is thus portrayed as a new Kairos.[22]

Others extend the need for reconciliation between people to reconciliation with the earth as our God-given home. They root enmity between people in alienation—not only from the means of production or from nature (following the rise of industrialized capitalism) but ultimately in alienation from God. The Gospel is then understood as God's work of reconciliation in Jesus Christ and through the Spirit. Such reconciliation has to yield a sense of restorative justice. This has implications not only for the redistribution of land but also for the restoration of the (ancestral) land itself. Salvation is therefore best understood as reconciliation (or justification) and restoration (or sanctification). This may be extended toward the classic reformed notion of recreation (*recreatio* instead of *nova creatio*).[23] In the South African context, the language employed by the Belhar Confession and in the secular version of the Truth and Reconciliation Commission come to mind here.[24]

Some recognize that liberation and reconciliation are elusive and indeed ultimate categories. In this dispensation, liberation will always remain incomplete, while full justice is in a sense impossible. The impact

---

22 The SACC document *Climate Change—A Challenge to the Churches in South Africa* (2009) is representative of recognizing such a Kairos. An emphasis on liberation, healing, and indeed exorcism is found in the writings of Marthinus Daneel, culminating in his *African Earthkeepers Volume 2: Environmental Mission and Liberation in Christian Perspective* (Pretoria: Unisa, 1999). As yet few of the prominent South African exponents of liberation theology have explicitly extended notions of liberation to address ecological concerns.

23 For a discussion, see my *Saving the Earth? The Legacy of Reformed Views on "Re-creation"*, (Berlin: LIT Verlag, 2013).

24 See especially Desmond M. Tutu, *No Future without Forgiveness* (London: Rider, 1999).

of the past can perhaps be alleviated, but this is easier said than done. The horrors of history can never be undone as if they never happened. In the interim we need to live our lives in an imperfect world. To seek to eradicate evil completely may exacerbate evil, given the instruments employed to do so. We all need to eat, seek shelter, clothe ourselves, find or create employment, and address poverty. The discourse on Justice, Peace and Integrity of Creation recognizes the many faces of violence and the environmental side effects of a capitalist economy. In secular terms, this agenda is typically understood as one of "reconstruction and development." This was the African National Congress's election manifesto in 1994, but its core concerns also stimulated extensive theological discussions on environmental responsibilities. But the dominant discourse has been on theology and development. In the South African context, this was qualified as "sustainable development" following the World Summit on Sustainable Development held in Johannesburg in 2002 and according to the United Nations' Sustainable Development Goals of 2015.[25] This prompted further heated debate: Some welcome the emphasis on sustainability, while others reject the term as nothing more than the greening of capitalism, calling for a focus on sustainable livelihoods instead.[26]

In my own work, I have suggested that these three notions of salvation are aligned with the soteriological motifs described by Gustaf Aulén as the classic type (Christ's victory over evil, death, and destruction), the Latin type (atonement through satisfaction or penal substitution), and the modern type (moral influence, renewal, and reconstruction). I argued for

---

25 See the double issue of the *Bulletin for Contextual Theology* in partnership with the SACC on "Church, Environment and the World Summit on Sustainable Development", 8:2 & 8:3 (2002).

26 South African discourse on theology and (sustainable) development cannot be reviewed here. See: the special edition of *HTS Theological Studies* on "Engaging Development: Contributions to a Critical Theological and Religious Debate," ed. Ignatius Swart and Afe Adogame, *HTS Theological Studies* 72:4 (2016). This includes an essay of mine entitled "Why Can't the Term 'Development' Just be Dropped Altogether? Some Reflections on the Concept of Maturation as Alternative to Development Discourse," *HTS Theological Studies* 72:4 (2016), 1–11.

the legitimacy of all three types and their contemporary ecological equivalents.[27] Nevertheless, although such divides theoretically can be overcome, there are deeply ingrained theological differences at stake between various forms of liberation theology; Lutheran, reformed and evangelical theologies; and liberal theologies. Such differences are not readily overcome and may well capture the underlying divide in South African ecotheology. Such divergent soteriologies reflect a North/South divide insofar as the symbol of liberation is prioritized from a decolonial perspective. Nevertheless, an emphasis on reconciliation or on reconstruction and development is clearly also at home in the South African context.

A final way of framing the perceived North/South divide within South African ecotheology is in terms of conversation partners (or interlocutors). It has long been argued in theologies of liberation that it matters whether the cultured despisers of religion or the poor and the oppressed are assumed as the primary interlocutors for theological reflection. In postcolonial and decolonial discourse, there is a similar recognition of the danger that theological reflection can remain conditioned by conversation partners from the Global North. Instead, it is important "to drink from one's own wells" and not to define excellence with reference to the dominant publishing houses in the Global North. Admittedly, a selective use of conversation partners from the Global North is condoned—as is evident in references to Karl Marx, Jacques Derrida, and Alfred North Whitehead—prompting further decolonial and feminist critiques as well as an emphasis on the need for South–South dialogue across the Indian, Atlantic, and Pacific oceans.

My sense is that there is indeed a real divide here—and there is ample evidence for that in terms of the references and entries in the bibliography of the contributions of the authors cited above. As a result, even if scholars are saying more or less the same thing, it does not feel like that. This divide is not particular to Christian ecotheology (in South Africa) but is indeed applicable to it. It is a striking feature of South

---

27 See especially my "The Salvation of the Earth from Anthropogenic Destruction: In Search of Appropriate Soteriological Concepts in an Age of Ecological Destruction," *Worldviews: Global Religions, Culture, Ecology* 14:2–3 (2010), 111–140.

African theology in general that a very wide variety of conversation partners are adopted. This applies in terms of geographical contexts beyond South Africa; for example, other anglophone and francophone countries in Africa, Australia (significant for ecotheology), Germany, the Netherlands, the UK, the US, and Latin America (but not India, East Asia, or the Pacific). Understandably, there is also a divide in terms of confessional traditions that is then entangled with colonial and missionary history. In addition, there are divides in terms of widely diverging theological schools and multidisciplinary conversations (e.g., with other religious traditions, religious studies, philosophy, critical gender and race theory, the arts, literature, economics, political studies, and also the natural sciences [including climate science and ecology in the narrower sense]). A specific aspect is that of drawing on Indigenous ecological wisdom as derived from African traditional religion and culture (see especially Setiloane but also Daneel). The look and feel of contributions to ecotheology is very different depending on such conversation partners. The question, though, is whether such differences are aligned with ideological divides. That is of course possible, but one would also need to allow for authors coming to roughly similar conclusions but following different conversations that would be relevant to their implied readers. The interlocutors from whom one draws insights and the implied readers (who are addressed) are not necessarily the same!

Reading Moltmann and Gebara through South African Lenses

The reception of Ivone Gebara's and Jürgen Moltmann's oeuvres in the bibliographies of South African contributions to ecotheology would be an interesting postgraduate study. Both these scholars are from continents other than Africa, one from the Global South, the other from the Global North. There are issues of confessional tradition (Roman Catholic and Reformed), gender and language (German and Portuguese), and theological positions (which are harder to capture). The sizes of their oeuvres differ, but English translations of their work are widely available. Both scholars' bodies of work are widely read, and they recognize that they are addressing a global readership even if their contributions can be situated contextually.

There is some obvious congeniality in the positions adopted by Gebara and Moltmann in the two essays included in this volume (see chapters 1 and 2). There is a common concern over contemporary threats to life, a common critique of modernity and of patriarchy, a shared affirmation of an evolutionary worldview with an emphasis on symbiosis (living together in community, in love, and in interdependence based on an "ontological friendship among everything that exists"), and an appreciation for the significance of everyday life. The differences between their positions may be only in emphasis but are nevertheless striking. Let me mention the following:

- Gebara's polemic is especially with papal hierarchy, while Moltmann's polemic is arguably with the modernist assumptions of other German Protestant scholars. Gebara's dominant conversation partners are contemporary feminist theorists and some mystics, while Moltmann cites Western and other classics.

- Gebara finds the Nicene Creed "quite questionable," while the apophatic is for Moltmann embedded in an affirmation of that creed. For Gebara, beliefs are "changing and provisional propositions that help us to live the ordinary and provisional reality of life." She advises us not to "value the tradition of the past at the expense of the questions of the present, and not to minimize the new questions of today, thinking that the past will answer them." She thus warns against "blind obedience to the tradition."

- Moltmann recovers the ecological significance of the Christian faith with a tone of firm confidence, while Gebara frames her contribution as the ambiguous role of *religion* in society, questions Christian hegemony, and feels herself surrounded by "doubts, contradictions, and ambiguities."

- Moltmann (in confessing complicity) roots ecological destruction primarily in anthropocentrism (and hence subjugation), while Gebara (siding with victims) roots such destruction in domination in the name of hierarchical differences between species, class and race, and gender and sexual orientation, all in the name of service to God or the gods. Both scholars note the impact of alienation from other creatures and from the earth community itself.

- Moltmann expects a radically new creation on the basis of a cosmic resurrection, the life of the world to come, while Gebara's hope is rooted in recycling, in the new humus that can give life to flowers and animals because "nothing is lost, everything is transformed!"

- While Moltmann's position may be described as panentheistic, and he would agree with Gebara that the "Great Mystery is in us," Gebara subscribes to panentheism but at times still expresses views that come close to a form of pantheism. She offers a critique of totalitarian God-talk, insisting that the gods are "just as mortal as we are" and speaking of God as "a vital energy in everything and everyone." She speaks also of "our shared divinity in everything that exists," seeing "the body of God as the body of everything that exists" and noting "a mysterious sacred dimension present in everything."

- Gebara is suspicious of declaring texts to be the sacred word of God in order to order the world around us in a hegemonic way, while Moltmann freely quotes Scripture with affirmation.

- Gebara underplays soteriological metaphors, even speaking of the victory of good over evil as "a religious and political myth," relying instead on the "awareness that there is no higher being above the world that saves us, but that we are participants in the same creative energy base on which we are mutually saved or lost," while Moltmann uses terms such as "reconciliation," "restoration," and "the recapitulation of all things."

- While Moltmann speaks from the academy to a wider public, Gebara retains a healthy skepticism over the academic study of theology from within her religious community.

How, then, do South African scholars read Moltmann and Gebara? A few brief comments may suffice: Both authors are indeed widely recognized in South African contributions to ecotheology. Not surprisingly, Moltmann's work is especially cited by Reformed theologians such as Johan Buitendag, David Field, and myself (albeit also critically),[28] and also by Klaus Nürnberger as a Lutheran theologian. Equally, it is not surprising that Susan Rakoczy frequently cites Ivone Gebara as a fellow Catholic feminist scholar. Nevertheless, there are ample cross references, so that it is hard to say that there is a clear North/South divide here beyond the long-standing confessional divides.

A Tentative Conclusion

Can one then speak of a North/South divide in South African ecotheology that runs along racial lines and reflects either a Eurocentric or an Afrocentric orientation? From the above it should be clear that there are multiple divides, but that it is not so obvious that these are North/South divides; for example, if understood in terms of allegiances, vested interests, agendas, philosophical assumptions, or conversation partners. My impression is that this is more a matter of rhetoric. South African scholars are not really addressing each other but are playing for different national and international audiences. That is why, even when we are saying similar things, they does not always feel the same.

At the same time, given its location and history, South Africa has a distinctive role in bridging the various divides, including the North/South divide, at best through South–South dialogue. This is because of the multiple conversation partners that South African scholars typically adopt beyond the South African and wider African contexts—from Europe and North America traditionally, from Latin America and India on liberation theology, and also from Australia and the Pacific on ecotheology in particular. There may be less dialogue with East Asian scholars,[29] while language

---

28 See my critical engagement with Moltmann in *Saving the Earth?*, 277–320.
29 See, however, the volume edited by Ernst M. Conradie and Lai Pan-chiu, *Taking a Deep Breath for the Story to Begin . . .*, Eugene, OR: Wipf and Stock, 2021).

barriers with French-speaking Africa and with Spanish and Portuguese scholars may allow for English hegemony. In particular, ecotheology has an integrative function given its ability to link concerns over economic, gender, racial, and other forms of justice. What happens in the South African context therefore matters for global Christianity, even if the eyes of the world are no longer on South Africa as they used to be during the apartheid period. The presence of a racialized elephant in the room therefore has to be articulated and addressed.

CHAPTER 4

MOTHER EARTH, MOTHER AFRICA: AFRICAN ECOFEMINIST VOICES

Sue Rakoczy

Each day brings more dire news of climate change. Floods, hurricanes, and drought are all increasing. Although awareness of our climate emergency is growing, the will to end destructive practices such as the use of fossil fuels is often weak. Mother Earth is in the ICU ward and many beds are occupied by Africans. What can we do?

Mother Earth is home to Mother Africa, the cradle of humankind. The two are inseparable. This is clearly demonstrated in the writings of members of the Circle of Concerned African Women Theologians, whose members have published a number of books with titles that analyze the *Mother Earth, Mother Africa* unity.[1]

The Circle was founded in 1989 by Mercy Amba Oduyoye of Ghana. At that time African theology was developing as a contextual liberation theology, but the voices were all male.[2] In 1975, when the Ecumenical Association of Third World Theologians was founded in Accra, Ghana, only one

---

1 Among others, see *Mother Earth, Mother Africa and Biblical Studies: Interpretation in the Context of Climate Change*, ed. Sidney K. Berman et al. (Bamberg, Germany: University of Bamberg Press, 2021); *Mother Earth, Postcolonial and Liberation Theologies*, ed. Sophia Chirongoma and Esther Mombo (New York: Lexington Press, 2021) and *Mother Earth, Mother Africa and African Indigenous Religions*, ed. Nobuntu Penxa Matholeni, Georgina Kwanima Boateng, and Molly Manyonganise (Cape Town: SUN PReSS, 2020).
2 See Jonathan Gichaara, "Issues in African Theology," *Black Theology* 3 (1, 2005), 75–85.

woman was present as an observer. Thankfully things began to change, and Oduyoye became president in 2000.

Oduyoye's vision was of local Circles of women—ecumenical and interfaith—meeting to share their personal experience and theological reflections on diverse topics and to encourage and support one another to write and publish. The early efforts have born fruit since Circle authors have published hundreds of books and articles.

Circle women have addressed the stress that Mother Earth experiences in Mother Africa in many contexts: mission, theology, the Bible, and others. Their writings explore the tension between affirming the goodness of creation and the situation of African women living on a continent so severely impacted by climate change.

This chapter will begin with a discussion of the tension between women and the earth. The goodness of both has been and continues to be undermined by the power of patriarchy, which treats both as objects to be exploited and consumed. Theologically these tensions are discussed in the perspective of ecofeminism and ecowomanism. The first is a broad term referring to women in general; the second brings forth the voices of Black women throughout the world.

The second section of the chapter presents diverse ecofeminist and ecowomanist insights of African women on a broad variety of themes. These understandings of God, biblical hermeneutics, salvation, Christ, and other topics in reference to Mother Earth are linked to practical applications in land, agriculture, water issues, and other significant contexts.

The final section of the chapter addresses the importance of these Circle insights. Who is Mother Earth/Mother Africa? What are Circle women saying to their sisters (and brothers) around the world? In what ways does the Mother Earth/Mother Africa unity speak to all of humanity in our common challenge to ensure that Mother Earth is a healthy and strong mother?

Mother Earth/Mother Africa

To speak of Mother Earth is to name the home of all of humanity and of every living being. As mothers give birth to the next generation and nourish and care for their children physically and psychologically, so we humans find in Mother Earth all that we need: air, water, food, and companionship with other humans and with animals.

> The name 'Mother Earth' is associated with Greek mythology, where Gaia, the great goddess, is equated to 'Mother Earth' and 'Mother Nature.'... As 'Mother Nature,' Gaia personifies the entire ecosystem on Earth. The goddess was considered to have created the universe and was therefore worshiped as the universal Mother. According to Greek mythology, it is from the fertile womb of the goddess that all life begins, and therefore 'Mother Nature' or 'Mother Earth' nurtures, heals and supports all life in this planet.[3]

Mother Africa names the common and original home of all humanity. Hominid fossils from Southern and Eastern Africa date back about three million years.[4] Modern humans evolved in Africa about 250,000 years ago.[5] Mother Earth/Mother Africa is thus our common origin and ancestor.

THE GENESIS OF ECOFEMINISM

"Ecofeminism" entered the theological vocabulary in 1974. The word itself is derived from the French *ecofeminisme* and was first used by Francoise d'Eaubonne in her book *Le féminisme ou la mort*. Ecofeminism "brings together feminism and ecology into a matrix which exposes the domination of women by men and the domination of the natural world by human

---

3   Maitseo Bolaane and Gwen Lesetedi, "Women Shaping the Narrative within the Fire Churches Environment in Gabarone, Botswana," in *Mother Earth, Mother Africa and Mission*, ed. Seblewengel Daniel, Mmapula Diana Kebaneilwe and Angeline Savala (Stellenbosch: SUN PReSS 2021), 163.
4   Erin Wayman," How Africa Became the Cradle of Humankind", https://www.smithsonianmag.com/science-nature/how-africa-became-the-cradle-of-humankind-108875040/.
5   "Evolution of Modern Humans," https://www.yourgenome.org/stories/evolution-of-modern-humans/#:~:text=of%20much%20debate.-,Modern%20humans%20originated%20in%20Africa%20within%20the%20past%20200%.

beings."⁶ It evolved from radical feminism and includes analyses of race, class and culture.⁷

Karen Warren outlines four key foundations of ecofeminism:

- There are important connections between the oppression of women and the oppression of nature;

- Understanding the nature of these connections is necessary to any adequate understanding of the oppression of women and the oppression of nature;

- Feminist theory and praxis must include an ecological perspective;

- Solutions to ecological problems must include a feminist perspective.⁸

The goal of ecofeminism is a radical transformation of consciousness of how we as human beings view ourselves, our relationships with others, and our relationships with the earth itself.

Ecofeminism has a controversial history since some feminists accused its thinkers of essentialism because it links women and nature.

> Essentialism encapsulates the notion that certain characteristics or experiences are necessary to categorise an individual. Essentialism in ecofeminism goes beyond the shared oppression of the nature and woman by man to suggest that it is woman's affinity with nature, their shared role as mother and carer of the earth's population, that qualifies them more directly to speak on nature's behalf.⁹

---

6   Susan Rakoczy, *In Her Name: Women Doing Theology* (Pietermaritzburg, South Africa: Cluster Publications, 2004), 300.
7   See Mary Phillips and Nick Rumens, "Introducing Contemporary Ecofeminism," in *Contemporary Perspectives on Ecofeminism*, ed. Mary Phillips and Nick Rubens (London: Routledge 2015), 1–16.
8   Rakoczy, *In Her Name*, 302.
9   Sam Perrin, "Ecofeminism: The Essentialism Issue," https://ecologyforthemasses.com/2019/11/21/ecofeminism-the-essentialism-issue/.

Ecofeminist thought has developed a more nuanced understanding of women and nature in light of the initial critique of essentialism. To affirm the Earth as mother is not to claim that mothering is the sole purpose of women's existence.

Ecowomanism takes ecofeminism into the context of the experience of Black women, including African women. Melanie L. Harris describes ecowomanist approaches "as the reflective and contemplative study of the ecowisdom that is theorized, constructed and valued by women of African descent."[10] As a liberation theology, ecowomanism links theory and praxis—thought and transformative action.

Sinenhlanhla Chisale asserts that "black women use the ecowomanism theology to confront structural violence that is caused by white supremacy and colonialism that perpetuates societal and environmental oppression. . . . Their suffering is parallel to how the Earth suffers in the hands of those who undermine and pollute her."[11]

Ecowomanist theology also analyzes the "the connection of the theologies of the female body and the feminization of the Earth."[12] Ecowomanist theologians explain "that the exploitation of the Earth is because of her feminization that is linked to the control of slave women's bodies that were used as the property of white slave masters who used them for sexual gratification when they continuously raped her."[13] Chisale notes that "African women theologians use ecowomanism with reservations, because their struggle for environmental justice is intertwined with their roles as custodians of religion, ethnicity and culture in addition to class, gender and race."[14]

Naming the earth as Mother is thus a foundation of ecowomanist thought. Harris states that "A focus on gender in ecowomanist analysis

---

[10] Melanie L. Harris, *Ecowomanism: African American Women and Earth-Honoring Faiths* (Maryknoll, NY: Orbis, 2017), 14.

[11] Sinenhlanhla S. Chisale, "When Women and Earth Connect: African Ecofeminist or Ecowomanist Theology?', in *Mother Earth, Mother Africa and Theology*, ed. Sinenhlanhla S. Chisale and Rozelle Robson Bosch, (Cape Town: AOSIS), 12.

[12] Chisale, "When Women and Earth Connect," 12–13.

[13] Chisale, "When Women and Earth Connect," 13.

[14] Chisale, "When Women and Earth Connect," 13.

is paradoxical in that it simultaneously uncovers an innate solidarity between women and the earth."[15] Therefore "social justice is earth justice. Earth justice is social justice."[16] Ecowomanist theology is anchored in African cosmologies, and through womanist earth stories, African American agricultural knowledge, and African interconnectedness, a symbiotic connection is developed which is based in interconnectedness.[17]

In her analysis of Mark 5:24-43—the healing of the woman with a hemorrhage—Musa W. Dube uses the feminine to name Africa: "Mother Africa as a character thus personifies the story of Africa. Her role exposes the various gender oppressions and other forms of oppression encountered by African women in general."[18] The woman bled for a very long time; Dube asserts the same for Mother Africa, who is in dire need of healing. She states, "The subjugation of women and the Earth thus undergirds Christian/biblical understanding of salvation, for at the centre of its theological imagination is patriarchy and anthropocentricism."[19]

The dynamism of Mother Earth/Mother Africa opens up a new type of praxis in which to consider the state of our only home. To mistreat our biological mother is a universal scandal in all cultures. Yet we do this daily to the only home we shall ever have.

Part Two: The Praxis of Mother Earth/Mother Africa

The Mother Earth/Mother Africa volumes do not devote a great deal of attention to the theological meaning of this intrinsic connection. They present it as fact. The authors focus on praxis or transforming action for

---

15 Harris, *Ecowomanism*, 18.
16 Harris, *Ecowomanism*, 76.
17 See Harris, *Ecowomanism*, 76.
18 Musa W Dube, "Fifty Years of Bleeding: A Storytelling Reading of Mark 5:24-43," *The Ecumenical Review* 51(1, 1999), 11.
19 Musa W. Dube, "Mother Earth, Gender and Biblical Imagination," in *Mother Earth, Mother Africa and Biblical Studies: Interpretations in the Context of Climate Change*, ed. Sidney K. Berman et al. (Bamberg, Germany: University of Bamberg Press, 2021), 238.

radical change. The praxis is diverse, and this chapter will highlight only a few of the contexts in which the challenges Mother Earth/Mother Africa is experiencing are addressed.

However, some authors are explicit in their analysis of what this bond describes. Sylvia and Beatrice-Joy Owusu-Ansah write:

> The Christian tradition has used images that describe God as a caring and loving mother who protects and cares for her children, delivering them from oppressive systems and domination. God's care goes even beyond the care of a nursing mother. He or she vindicates the vulnerable and the weak from the strong and mighty. In other words, the degradation of the environment God created is part of God's saving agenda.[20]

Robson Bosch also articulates the Mother Earth language:

> Mother Earth is a metaphor that, in very intimate terms, describes the relationship between persons and the Earth—those persons come from the dust of the Earth and will return to dust. As such, speaking of Mother Earth not only means the created order but also the spiritual practices, prayers and beliefs of those persons who receive her as their mother.[21]

Bosch employs the theology of Julian of Norwich, a fourteenth century English mystic (1342–1416/23), to extend the concept of Mother. While she was dying, Julian experienced a series of visions of Christ in his Passion. She recovered and later became an anchoress, living a contemplative life in

---

20   Sylvia Owusu-Ansah and Beatrice-Joy Owusu-Ansah, "Women, Religion and Sustainable Development: Redeeming the Environment for Human Survival," in *Mother Earth, Mother Africa and Theology*, ed. Sinenhlanhla. S. Chisale and Rozelle Robson Bosch (Cape Town: AOSIS Publishing, 2021), 47.

21   Rozelle Robson Bosch, "Mother Earth in a Theological Perspective: A Sacramental Unveiling," in *Mother Earth, Mother Africa and Theology*, ed. Sinenhlanhla. S. Chisale and Rozelle Robson Bosch (Cape Town: AOSIS Publishing, 2021), 21.

a small cottage and reflecting on her visionary experiences with a distinct feminist perspective. She names Christ as our Mother.[22]

Bosch states, "The feminine grammar of Christ our mother proves to be a fruitful way of speaking of the relationship between God and the created order. This is because, as I have sought to show thus far, the Cross is the moment where God expresses God's continued creative activity in the restoration of the created order."[23] For Bosch, "Christ is our mother whose wound, or womb, perpetually incarnates God's encompassing vision for the created order,"[24] and the created order is sacred.

Using sacrament in an inclusive vision, Bosch concludes her reflections by asserting, "When Mother Earth comes to us as sacrament, one is necessitated to take seriously her health, her well-being and her flourishing."[25]

In the same volume, Kelebogile T. Resane discusses the Trinity in an earth-centered perspective. Her Trinitarian theology has practical implications: "The task of the church in Africa should go beyond the liberation of the oppressed. In her deliberations to liberate the oppressed, there must also be the liberation of Mother Earth from scandalous usurpation of responsibility because of greed and self-enrichment at the expense of Mother Nature."[26]

REFLECTIONS ON THE CLIMATE CRISIS

The current climate crisis—truly a climate emergency—is an important theme in these Circle books. In her chapter in *Mother Earth, Mother Africa:*

---

22 See Julian of Norwich, *Julian of Norwich: Showings*, trans. Edmund Colledge and James W. Walsh (New York: Paulist Press, 1978), ch. 58–63; Veronica Mary Rolf, *Julian's Gospel* (Maryknoll, NY: Orbis, 2014).
23 Bosch, "Mother Earth," 24.
24 Bosch, "Mother Earth," 27.
25 Bosch, "Mother Earth," 29.
26 Kelebogile T. Resane, "Earth-Centred Trinitarian Models: The Trinitarian Synergy and Symbiosis in the Creation Narrative," in *Mother Earth, Mother Africa and Theology*, ed. Sinenhlanhla. S. Chisale and Rozelle Robson Bosch (Cape Town: AOSIS Publishing, 2021), 42.

World Religions and Environmental Imagination, Megan Bedford-Strohm discusses the dynamic of grief and faith at this time.[27]

Using the work of Musa Dube, the Bedford-Strohm proposes that rather than seeing the Earth as a passive victim of climate change, humanity is invited to view "the Earth in the creation account as a co-creator with God, elevating Earth's status from that of an inanimate object that is simply the backdrop for the human drama to having a dignity of her own, to be respected."[28]

The climate crisis has three intertwined challenges. First, it is a gendered crisis.

In Africa, primarily women and girls are responsible for food production. Ecological degradation of an area means that they have to walk longer and longer distances for water and firewood. The water is often polluted and the firewood supply is dwindling.

Second, it is a justice crisis. Puleng Lenkabula of South Africa has stated that "the injustices in the economy and the ecology tended to make it impossible for Africans to breathe."[29] The Global South is already heavily impacted by the climate crisis, and it will worsen. The Global North is on alert since its time is coming soon, if it's not already here, with stronger hurricanes and rising waters.

Third, it is a religious challenge. Lynn White and others have called attention to the ways Christianity and Christians have not been friendly to Mother Earth. White wrote in the 1960s that "Christianity not only established a religion of man and nature but also insisted that man exploit nature for his proper ends."[30] Megan Bradford-Strohm asks Christians a very challenging question: Why has it taken so long for so many Christians

---

27   Megan Bedford-Strohm, "Your House is Left to You Desolate: On Christian Grief and Faith for Africa and Earth in Climate Crisis," in *Mother Earth, Mother Africa: World Religions and Environmental Imagination*, ed. Sophia Chirongoma and Wayua Kiilu (Stellenbosch, South Africa: SUN PReSS, 2022), 15-36.
28   Bradford-Strohm, "Your House," 31.
29   Bradford-Strohm, "Your House," 22.
30   Bedford-Strohm, "Your House," 24.

to engage in creation care, and why are some around the world "still turning a blind eye to the climate crisis?"[31]

The climate crisis has arrived in Zimbabwe, as in other African countries, with drought and lower food production, leading to widespread malnutrition, especially among children. However, before the colonial era beginning in the nineteenth century, the people were able to feed themselves and their children well using traditional knowledge and practices now termed "Indigenous Knowledge Systems (IKS)." Sophia Chirongoma and Silindiwe Zvingowanisei point out that for centuries the Shona people ate a healthy diet of locally produced foods. Now, however, "the Shona have lost or are losing the ability to address poverty, nutritional and environmental problems solely through their IKS because their environment has been altered by Western ideas and technology which were imposed through the introduction of colonial and postcolonial development projects."[32]

Chirongoma and Zvingowanisei describe the many dimensions of IKS that are useful in agriculture. These include weather forecasting, observations of trees, birds, animals and insects, wind patterns, and the sun and the moon. These practices can assure good harvests of cereals, grain, and grass crops; legumes; sugar crops; root crops; and tubers and nutrient rich vegetables such as pumpkin. The authors stress that the IKS the women know and practice should be part of Zimbabwe's climate change mitigation strategies and, by extension, "gender inclusive policies which acknowledge women's roles in mitigating climate change should be implemented in all African countries."[33]

The importance of IKS in Kenya is presented by Catherine Njagi, who focuses on the Mount Kenya Forest. Mount Kenya "is regarded as a holy mountain and as a realm of God by all the communities living adjacent to

---

31 Bedford-Strohm, "Your House," 25.
32 Sophia Chirongoma and Silindiwe Zvingowanisei, "Karanga Women's Utilisation of Indigenous Knowledge Systems on Climate Change Adaptation and Mitigation in Zimbabwe," in *Mother Earth, Mother Africa: World Religions and Environmental Imagination*, ed. Sophia Chirongoma and Wayua Kiilu (Stellenbosch, South Africa: SUN PReSS, 2022), 133.
33 Chirongoma and Zvingowanisei, "Karanga Women's Utilisation," 146.

it."³⁴ But the forest has been under threat because of illegal logging and other harmful practices, and this has led to less rainfall and the drying up of rivers, which severely impacts the people who depend on the forest.

The author's research with people living in the forest area revealed that the respondents agreed that various Indigenous methods could preserve the forest and its resources. These include "maintenance of sacred forests, sacred groves and sacred trees, reverence for totemic animals, limited entrance in the forests, special forest areas where no human activity is allowed and royal hunting preserves."³⁵

Njagi recommends that "there is need for revisiting some of the traditional religious belief systems and cultural practices that encourage the conservation of the forests and natural resources."³⁶ These belief systems emphasize having a harmonious relationship with the sacred forests, trees, groves, and special animals. The teachings of Christian missionaries and the policies of the colonial authorities significantly undermined these practices. They must now be restored.

Land Issues

Mother Earth is literal land, actual physical soil of diverse kinds. Some soils are naturally very fertile, while others need the help of various kinds of fertilizers so that food may grow. Some agricultural practices are not healthy for Mother Earth, and so the land degrades and is less fertile. Molly Manyonganise and Godfrey Museka analyze the Shona cultural context as they confront land degradation in Zimbabwe.

Traditional Shona land practices included taboos in reference to access to land and totems. These taboos prohibited access to certain mountains since chiefs were buried in caves there. "A totem is any natural or mythical animal, plant, bird or inset that serves as a symbol of a family

---

34   Catherine Njagi, "African Cosmological View: The Role of African Indigenous Knowledge Systems in the Preservation of Mount Kenya Forest," in *Mother Earth, Mother Africa: World Religions and Environmental Imagination*, ed. Sophia Chirongoma and Wayua Kiilu (Stellenbosch, South Africa: SUN PReSS, 2022), 116.
35   Njagi, "African Cosmological View," 121.
36   Njagi, "African Cosmological View," 123.

or clan whose members feel a close connection during their lives and these members do not eat, kill or trap such totemic, animals or fish."[37]

The Shona consider land to be sacred since a baby's umbilical cord is buried in the earth.

Shona people name themselves as *mwana wevhu* (a child of the soil). In raising children, mothers informally communicated their knowledge of the environment through songs and folktales.

Women were and are close to the land because they gather the firewood and fetch water, often carrying both long distances, for their families. Women and children tilled the land, and crop rotation and intercropping were used. Shona society is patriarchal, and men would usually decide what would be planted and where; however, the women did the work that fed the community.

Under colonial rule, practices were adopted that worked against the health of the land. Land was allocated to Black and white people in the 1930s and 1950s, but this resulted in African alienation of land, since some "holy places (were) situated on white farms."[38] Colonialists introduced their flora and fauna, which disrupted the natural ecological balance. They also "introduced a cash economy which prioritised male labour over female labour," and "the knowledge that women had in terms of environmental conservation was often not recognised."[39]

The Fast Track Land Reform Programme, which began in 2000, involved much violent seizure of white-owned farms. The owners with their families and their farm workers were driven from their homes. The land was then occupied by people who often did not respect it. Food production diminished, and hunger stalked the Shona people.

Women were neglected as men grabbed the land and were "practically silenced on what happens on the land, increasing environmental

---

37 Molly Mangonganise and Godfrey Museka, "The Sedated Sacred: A Socio-Religious Analysis of Zimbabwe's Land Reform Programme and Environmental Degradation," in *Mother Earth, Mother Africa and African Indigenous Religions*, ed. Nobuntu Penxa Matholeni, Georgina Mwanima Boateng and Molly Mangonganise (Stellenbosch, South Africa: SUN PReSS, 2020), 71.
38 Mangonganise and Museka, "The Sedated Sacred," 73.
39 Mangonganise and Museka, "The Sedated Sacred," 74.

degradation through government's failure to enable women to either own or co-own land."[40]

Mangonganise and Museka argue that "the environmental crisis that Zimbabwe faces requires the reawakening of the sacred," and this can be done by restoring "women's places in environmental conservation among the Shona people."[41] If this is not done, the authors predict, Zimbabwe's environmental degradation will continue with dire consequences for all.

Researcher Excellent Chireshe also analyses the relationship of land ownership and gender among the Shona people. She conducted interviews with fourteen women and contrasted land ownership rights between women in monogamous and polygamous marriages.

The communal structure of the Shona people means that "the land belongs to the community and is demarcated according to clans and families."[42] Historically communal land was owned by married males. "Thus, a woman in a man's life validated the man's manhood by making him qualify for land ownership."[43] The women work the land and produce the food but "they may not have decision-making powers on land use."[44]

While women do not own land, "they are the moral teachers when it comes to issues of land. They are custodians of knowledge for impartation to the youth."[45] Young people are taught that, while people may legally own land, "the real owners and guardians of the land are ancestral spirits and the Creator."[46]

When women marry they leave their family of origin and join their husband's family; if they owned land they would take it with them to

---

40   Mangonganise and Museka, "The Sedated Sacred," 78.
41   Mangonganise and Museka, "The Sedated Sacred," 78.
42   Excellent Chireshe, "Access to Land Ownership and Gender in the Light of African Indigenous Religion in Zimbabwe Amongst the Shona in Chiredzi District, Masvingo Province, Zimbabwe" in *Mother Earth, Mother Africa and African Indigenous Religions*, ed. Nobuntu Penxa Matholeni, Georgina Mwanima Boateng and Molly Mangonganise (Stellenbosch, South Africa: SUN PReSS, 2020), 157.
43   Chireshe, "Access to Land Ownership," 157.
44   Chireshe, "Access to Land Ownership," 157.
45   Chireshe, "Access to Land Ownership," 158.
46   Chireshe, "Access to Land Ownership," 159.

their new family. This cannot be allowed. Thus "women are denied land ownership rights because they do not extend the family line, and so do not contribute to the enlargement of the clans into which they are born."[47]

During the government of Zimbabwe's Fast Track Land Reform Programme, a 20 percent quota system was used for women, and thus the gender imbalance regarding land continued. The research conducted by Excellent Chireshe was based in the Chingwizi settlement area of Chiredzi District. Twenty persons—fourteen female and six male—were interviewed. The researcher discovered that "of the fourteen females, seven had independent land ownership, while seven who were in monogamous unions did not."[48] In contrast, the women in polygamous unions "had plots registered in their names because they were vetted as individuals who had left behind some dwellings."[49] Single women who now owned land "indicated that they had power to determine what to grow, how much, where and when. They felt empowered."[50]

Culture plays a large role in land ownership. Married women who were interviewed and did not own land "were [generally] satisfied about this on cultural grounds."[51] Most of the men did not have problems with women owning land but some did, defending the previous practice as their culture.

Although women owned land, it was not prime agricultural land. It was dry land that often suffered from drought, and so often the harvests were poor. Boreholes were few and irrigation facilities also weren't plentiful. Better land would have resulted in better harvests and healthier people, especially children.

FEMALE IMAGES FOR GOD: THE EJAGHAM OF CAMEROON

Female images for God can have a powerful impact on people's religious imagination, including how people view the land. An example is

---

47   Chireshe, "Access to Land Ownership," 159.
48   Chireshe, "Access to Land Ownership," 161.
49   Chireshe, "Access to Land Ownership," 163.
50   Chireshe, "Access to Land Ownership," 164.
51   Chireshe, "Access to Land Ownership," 164.

the Ejagham people of Southwest Cameroon, who have included female language for God in their tradition.

As Rev. Dr. Jennet Tabe, a lecturer of dogmatics at the Presbyterian Theological Seminary in Kumba, Cameroon, states:

> Before Christianity and colonisation arrived, Ndem was known as the Spirit (female Being) that protected the land through prophetic prediction of impending evil and ensured fertility and procreation. The name of God Almighty in the Kenyang language used by the Ejagham clan is called *Mandem* from two words: *Ma*, meaning Mother, and *Ndem*, meaning God. God is Mother God. But when the missionaries came, they insisted that this 'Ma' is a He and not a She. So they changed the gender of God, while the language still stipulates Him as Mother God.[52]

Among the Elagham is a group of women known as the Ngbokondems, who have "special knowledge of the spiritual universe who lived, thrived and sustained the living community from the pre-colonial era."[53] Oral tradition describes the first Ngbokondem as descending from the sky.

> The first Ngbokondem fell from the sky into a large Boma tree; she wore strange dancing attire and spoke to awed spectators in a queer language. She taught some women her secrets and was married in the area. Thereafter, parents started initiating their firstborn daughters and the association developed. Trees, forests, the sky, grass and the natural order became crucial for the Ngbokondem's survival since then.[54]

---

52 Jennet Tabe, "Gendered Bodies and the Forgotten Mothers of Nature: An African Woman's Rethinking of the Ngbokondems and Forest Preservation among the Ejagham of Cameroon," in *Mother Earth, Mother Africa and Mission*, ed. Seblewengel Daniel, Mmapula Diana Kebaneilwe, and Angeline Savala (Stellenbosch, South Africa: SUN PReSS, 2021), 123.
53 Tabe, "Gendered Bodies," 124.
54 Tabe, "Gendered Bodies," 124.

When Western missionaries arrived, they brought the Christian patriarchal ethos. They stigmatized Ngbokondems as witches and condemned their association and activities as demonic. However, they affirmed the rituals of the male associations, such as Ngbe, who had similar rituals to female Ngbokondems.

The Ngbokondems embodied "the very essence of the clan's survival as it ensured procreation and multiplication of society, where the Ndem priestess mediated between the community and the Ndem spirit to ensure fertility and procreation in the land."[55]

Unfortunately, male presence has led to the decline of the Ngbokondems. Tabe observes:

> Men succeeded in penetrating the most sacred realm of the Ndem association. Through introduction and initiation of Obales, firstborn sons were gradually introduced as initiates to become members of this female only association. Their role was to play the drums for the women to dance. The introduction of Obales placed men's presence at the heart of women's space and activities; some respondents think it was a ploy to regulate women.[56]

That this women's association is disappearing "while male cults such as Ngbe (Ekpe) and Njom that existed at the same pre-colonial period are still thriving today could be an indication of a patriarchal society that exalts the male."[57] It certainly appears so.

Domestic Ecology: Home Gardens

Home gardens are ubiquitous in Africa. Generally planned and worked by women, gardens' vegetables and fruits provide important nutrients for people's good health. Home gardens are discussed in the Circle books.

Linda Naicker describes and analyses the experience of women urban gardeners under the support of the Pietermaritzburg Agency for

---

55 Tabe, "Gendered Bodies," 134.
56 Tabe, "Gendered Bodies," 137.
57 Tabe, "Gendered Bodies," 137.

Community Social Action (PACSA). Founded in 1979 by white Christians to conscientize other white Christians on the structural evils of apartheid, PACSA evolved after 1994 to focus on engagement with poor communities. The people of these communities usually experience severe degrees of food insecurity sbecause they rely on the government's income grants as often their only income.

The food gardens "have become not just a measure to mitigate food insecurity but a space where women could unite in a common struggle against a myriad of social woes brought on by structural inequalities."[58] The women who organized and managed the community food gardens were between the ages of twenty-eight and sixty; "each of the ten community food gardeners belonged to a township or informal settlement in and around Pietermaritzburg. Deeply committed to their Christian faith, they represented various Christian denominations."[59]

As Naicker accompanied these urban gardeners, she became aware of how they embodied the principles of African Women's Theology (AWT). These women used urban community food gardens "as an important safe space to mobilize and draw on communal strength as they worked in solidarity to overcome poverty."[60] This solidarity gave them the energy and strength to unite in a common struggle. Naicker describes the strong sense of community that developed: "We sang as we worked, tilling the soil and invoking God's grace and aid in ensuring enough rain for the crops to grow and a bountiful harvest."[61]

Internalized Indigenous knowledge was evident in their gardens. "In tilling the soil, planting and harvesting, they rely on Indigenous knowledge handed down to them by their mothers and grandmothers. They know instinctively when to plant and when to harvest, when to water the soil and when to leave it up to the weather, which crops to plant in particular seasons, and the importance of crop rotation."[62] In addition to harvesting nutritious

---

58   Linda Naicker, "Sisters in Solidarity: Resistance and Agency through Urban Community Food Gardens," *African Journal of Gender and Religion*, 27, no. 2 (2021): 24.
59   Naicker, "Sisters in Solidarity," 27.
60   Naicker, "Sisters in Solidarity," 32.
61   Naicker, "Sisters in Solidarity," 32.
62   Naicker, "Sisters in Solidarity," 36.

food, "these women gardeners demonstrate how self-determination, self-reliance and agency in the face of overwhelming odds can contribute to community development and environmental sustainability."[63]

Esther Mombo also analyzed the effects of vegetable gardens on women's self-worth and dignity in her chapter "The Missionary Initiative of Vegetable Gardens: Benefits and Shortcomings from an Eco-centric Perspective." In Africa, it has traditionally been a woman's role to provide food and drink for the household, "a belief that has over time contributed to their repression, lack of land, and further degradation of land. This belief was adopted and replicated by the missionaries in their efforts to Christianize Africa through training women to keep vegetable gardens as a way of supplementing their family diet."[64]

African women have always borne the responsibility of providing food for the family. But patriarchal tradition has strongly limited their ability to own land. Christian missionaries who came to Africa brought Western patriarchy, which strengthened African patriarchy, including land ownership structures.

They also introduced the concept of a vegetable garden that supplemented the family diet. As Mombo states,

> The vegetable gardens had both positive and negative implications for the woman. A vegetable garden was important, because it meant that each woman had food available for her family. But at the same time, the vegetable garden was used by the church to reduce the social interactions among women except when it was for church meetings or doing church work. It was a symbol of hard work, discipline and the right moral behavior for the Christian women. For those women who did not have the discipline of creating and maintaining the vegetable gardens, they were perceived as lazy and busy bodies.[65]

---

63 Naicker, "Sisters in Solidarity," 39.
64 Esther Mombo, "The Missionary Initiative of Vegetable Gardens: Benefits and Shortcomings from an Eco-centric," in *Mother Earth, Mother Africa and Mission,* ed. Seblewengel Daniel, Mmapula Diana Kebaneilwe, and Angeline Savala (Stellenbosch, South Africa: SUN PReSS, 2021), 8.
65 Mombo, "The Missionary Initiative," 73–74.

African women may have hoped that the European missionaries would have a positive effect on their subjugated cultural position, but what they experienced was a strengthening of patriarchal norms. This was reinforced by the interpretation of Scripture. Christian women could not own land; nothing had changed.

Although vegetable gardens initially came in Western clothing, Mombo assesses them in a positive light.

> Vegetable gardening done and embraced by women is not an activity of reproach attracting demeaning associations, but a step toward the well-being and sustenance of the earth. Agro-ecological practices are normally inexpensive, simple and effective; there is a minimal dependence on external inputs. . . . For women, living in harmony with nature and choosing the agro-ecological path is ultimately a choice for autonomy. Women explicitly choose to follow a pathway with nature, not against it.[66]

WATER ISSUES

Water is literally life. We can fast from solid food for quite a long time, but three days is the accepted limit for not drinking water. Mother Africa supplies water in the form of rain and snow, rivers, lakes and streams. However, Africa is now a water-stressed continent suffering severe droughts. Circle writers address these water challenges.

Botswana is a land-locked country without rivers and thus totally dependent on rain as its source of water. However, at the present time the country is experiencing severe drought, although 2022 brought small periods of rain. Climate change is making the droughts longer and more severe. And as is the pattern in other parts of Africa, women who are responsible for providing the family household with water suffer severely.

In their chapter on water issues in Botswana, Tshenolo J. Madigele, Patricia K. Mogomotsi, and Goemeone E.J. Mogomotsi describe the effects of the water crisis in Botswana:

---

66 Mombo," The Missionary Initiative," 80.

> The crises are real for women and children every day. Moreover, women and children lose a lot of time gathering water and would not have much time for other things. If the water solution is put in place, people could practice sustainable agriculture. Children could focus on education when their parents may focus on taking care of family needs and expanding their economic activities. There is indeed so much gain if water is made accessible to all.[67]

These authors argue that the wisdom of the concept of *botho* in Tswana culture should be the foundation of ecological transformation in that country.

> This Tswana ethical value appreciates the interdependence and the interrelatedness of all earthly, creaturely and heavenly realms. No entity can survive on its own; therefore, human beings are implored to appreciate the worthiness of the other. Men, women and children depend on each other in as much as we depend on the world around us.[68]

The church, understood in an inclusive sense, has a very significant responsibility to help alleviate the multiple water crises in Botswana.

> It is recommended that the church should actively participate in developing water sources such as boreholes, underground water storages and dams. The church should also take part in negotiating usage and conservation of transboundary water resources such as the Okavango, Zambezi, etc. The church

---

67   Tshenolo J. Madigele, Patricia K. Mogomotsi and Goemeone E.J. Mogomotsi, "Water Deficiency, Poverty, Ecology and Botho Theology in Botswana," in *Mother Earth, Mother Africa and Theology*, ed. Sinenhlanhla S. Chisale and Rozelle Robson Bosch. (Cape Town: AOSIS Publishing 2021), 90.
68   Madigele, Mogomotsi, and Mogomotsi, "Water Deficiency," 93.

should also actively participate in water resource management and utilisation.[69]

Since women are primarily responsible for water management in the daily life of their families, they must be involved in the various levels of decision-making of water management. The principle of *Botho* is a strong foundation for women's inclusion, but can male patriarchy recognize that women must be at the decision-making table? The water needs of the people of Botswana must not continue to be held hostage to patriarchal norms.

Alease Brown researched the water crisis in Cape Town in 2017, which led to the concerns of a possible Day Zero, when water sources would run dry. Cape Town has many middle class and affluent families who saw Day Zero as a disaster they never thought would happen, but Brown points out that for poor Capetonians this is daily reality. And it is women who must find water when there is no water.

Brown describes their dilemma:

> It is women who bear the burden the most since it is women who mostly attend to retrieving water at the public spout, women who carry the water, women who use the water to do the cooking, cleaning, and washing. It is also women who are the most at risk when it comes to using the public toilet facilities.[70]

Brown argues that the reasons for this constant water deprivation are structural: "A substantial root of the problem of water access for the indigent in Cape Town, whether or not it is a time of drought, is the issue of racialized economic inequality."[71] Cape Town's unequal treatment of poor

---

69 Madigele, Mogomotsi, and Mogomotsi, "Water Deficiency," 95.
70 Alease Brown, "The Discourse of Drought: Ongoing Gendered Inequality of Water Access in Cape Town, and the Implications for Public Theology," in *Mother Earth, Postcolonial and Liberation Theologies*, ed. Sophia Chirongoma and Esther Mombo (New York: Lexington Books, 2021), 123.
71 Brown, "The Discourse of Drought," 126.

Black people in colonial systems of separation mean basic access to water is a source of continuing diminishment and dishonor for Black persons, and particularly for women.

FERTILITY ISSUES

Fertile land is a blessing. So too are fertile human beings who bring forth the next generation. Seblewengel Daniel analyses the intertwined fertility of Mother Earth and the land in the Ethiopian context. The Ethiopian culture denigrates women in its stories and proverbs, and she observes that "the numerous negative ones have greater impact on the mindset of little girls and women and hence affect their flourishing more than the positive ones."[72]

Childlessness in a marriage is almost always blamed on the woman since it is inconceivable that a man could be infertile. The birth of girl children is welcomed for the help they will give their mother, but boys are fiercely desired since they will carry the father's and thus the family's name.

Daniel observes that "ownership of land by women helps ensure the health of the family. Even though full control of land is difficult to attain, studies show that women who have children have a better access to land. . . . In fact, the more children they have, the better the access they can have. Sadly, women who are infertile are neglected or divorced sometimes without any hope to share the resources, even those that were acquired during their marriage."[73]

In addition to the social shame of not having children or not having male children (preferably many), Ethiopian women's faith and spirituality are questioned. Surely God is punishing this barren woman, people think. Women use various rituals to ward off the "evil eye" and God's displeasure. There are no similar rituals for men since all are presumed to be fertile.

---

72 Seblewengel Daniel, "Fertility of Women and Mother Earth: An Ethiopian Perspective," in *Mother Earth, Mother Africa and Theology*, ed. Sinenhlanhla S. Chisale and Rozelle Robson Bosch. (Cape Town: AOSIS Publishing, 2021), 130.

73 Daniel, "Fertility of Women," 133.

Daniel argues that it is imperative that women be involved in land issues since the health of the community is at stake. Infertile land and poor harvests lead to starvation. She comments that "studies show that when their right to own land is respected, women are more active and effective than men in soil conservation."[74] Since women do ecology on the ground every day—getting water and firewood, cooking, and tending the fields—they should be frontline advocates for ecological justice. But culture constrains them, and Mother Earth continues to lament.

RELIGION AND MOTHER EARTH

From its beginnings the Circle has always been ecumenical and interfaith. All voices and all perspectives are welcome. The challenges of Mother Earth in Mother Africa are described and analyzed from the perspectives of Christianity—mainline churches, Catholicism, and African Initiated Churches—and Islam. Christian and Muslim women face a variety of ecological challenges as they care for Mother Earth. Women's creativity and initiative demonstrate how religious commitment is a positive factor in caring for and sustaining our only home.

Maitseo Bolaane and Gwen Lesetedi examine the role of women in the Fire Churches in Gabarone, Botswana. This is an African Initiated Church, and generally in these churches women have marginal roles and seldom exercise leadership. However, the Fire Churches are an exception, and they credit the growth of these churches to the leadership opportunities they provide to women.

The women in the Fire Churches do not understand Mother Earth as a passive presence but through their leadership roles strive to use their gifts for the good of all. Mother Earth is the mother of us all and humanity must both honor her and ensure that she will always be a fruitful Mother for all on earth. Bolaane and Lesetedi stress that "understood through feminine perspective, 'Mother Nature' is viewed as always working to achieve and maintain harmony, wholeness and balance within the environment."[75]

---

74 Daniel, "Fertility of Women," 136.
75 Maitseo Bolaane and Gwen Lesetedi, "Women Shaping the Narrative within the Fire Churches Environment in Gabarone, Botswana," in *Mother Earth,*

Their analysis of Mother Earth does not include descriptions of specific earth-friendly practices by women in the Fire Churches, but the theological foundation is there.

In the Pentecostal context, Mmapula Diana Kebaneilwe and Scotch Kgomotso affirm that current Pentecostal teaching is moving from an otherworldly perspective to one that is also concerned about what happens to people on the Earth. But this is not sufficient since "contemporary Pentecostal movements, while emphasizing the welfare of people on Earth, tend to pay little or no attention to the welfare of the very Earth that sustains life."[76]

The Circle writings include reflections from the Catholic perspective. Nontando Hadebe found much to be commended in *Laudato Si'*, Pope Francis's 2015 encyclical on ecological justice. Among its strengths are, first, its insistence that ecology and social justice are inseparable and, second, its emphasis on everything being connected. Third is the call for "ecological conversion," a turn to the earth and all it contains so all may flourish.[77]

However, Hadebe critiques *Laudato Si'* because it pays no attention to the experience of women and the ecological challenges they face. She states that "it does not make any reference to the contributions of ecofeminism, raising questions on the claim made in the encyclical of engaging with everyone."[78]

Nelly Mwale analyzed the experiences of women in the Kasisi Agricultural Training Centre (KATC) in Zambia. The Jesuits, a Catholic male

---

Mother Africa and Mission, ed. Seblewengel Daniel, Mmapula Diana Kebaneilwe, and Angeline Savala (Stellenbosch, South Africa: SUN PReSS, 2021), 163.

76 Mmapula Diana Kebaneilwe and Kgomotso Scotch, "Re-Imagining Mission through Inculturation and Sustainable Environment," in *Mother Earth, Mother Africa and Mission*, ed. Seblewengel Daniel, Mmapula Diana Kebaneilwe, and Angeline Savala, (Stellenbosch, South Africa: SUN PReSS, 2021), 15.

77 Nontando Hadebe, "The Cry of the Earth Is the Cry of Women: Ecofeminisms in Critical Dialogue with *Laudato Si'*," in *Mother Earth, Mother Earth, Postcolonial and Liberation Theologies*, ed. Sophia Chirongoma and Esther Mombo, (New York: Lexington Books, 2021), 86–87.

78 Hadebe, "The Cry of the Earth," 84.

religious order, founded the mission station in 1905 and the agricultural training center in 1974. By the 1990s it shifted its focus to sustainable agriculture without the use of pesticides. The center was "modeled on the principles of the Catholic social teachings with a special emphasis on women's rights as part of social justice and ecology[.] KATC was largely renowned as a faith-based initiative in sustainable agriculture in Zambia."[79] Women are significantly involved in the work of the KATC. The training they have received in various aspects of agriculture has enabled them to exercise initiatives on behalf of Mother Earth.

The ethos of the center is Catholic social teaching exemplified in the theology of Vatican II, especially in the document *Gaudium et Spes: Pastoral Constitution on the Church in the Modern World*, which calls on Catholics to read the signs of the times and interpret them in the light of the Gospel and *Laudato Si'*.

Mwale comments that "the focus is on women not only because they constitute 64 percent of the rural population and approximately 80 percent of food producers in Zambia, but also because scholarship on religion, gender and environment has been devoid of the connectedness between women's contributions and the mission of the Church in the Zambian context from a Catholic perspective."[80]

The contributions of religious women to environmental education and action are also significant.[81] This is clearly evident in the work of the Comboni sisters in Zambia. Saint Daniel Comboni (1831–1881) founded congregations of men and women under the motto of "Save Africa with Africa." The Comboni Sisters arrived in Zambia in 1975. One of their most important ministry initiatives was the Mother Earth Centre and its work

---

79 Nelly Mwale, "Women and Sustainable Agriculture in the Context of the Kasisi Agricultural Training Centre: A Catholic Initiative in Zambia," in *Mother Earth, Mother Africa and Mission*, ed. Seblewengel Daniel, Mmapula Diana Kebaneilwe, and Angeline Savala. (Stellenbosch, South Africa: SUN PReSS, 2021), 143.

80 Mwale, "Women and Sustainable Agriculture," 144.

81 See Sarah McFarland Taylor, *Green Sisters: A Spiritual Ecology* (Cambridge, MA: Harvard University Press, 2007); Susan Rakoczy, "Green Sisters: An Inquiry into the Ecological Consciousness of Women Religious in South Africa," *Journal of Theology for Southern Africa* 151 (2015): 55–73.

with young farmers. Charcoal production was having a severely negative impact on the environment, and so the Sisters adopted a strategy of environmental sustainability through the adoption of moringa. This plant increased soil fertility and lessened charcoal production. They focused on ecological sustainability through a variety of initiatives such as "hosting a demonstration on organic farming and moringa production and a chicken-run for manure and as an income-generating activity."[82]

Muslim women also demonstrate commitment to ecological wholeness. The Varemba Muslim women in Zimbabwe experience the power of patriarchy since men own the land and women farm and work it to produce food for all.

For Varemba women the earth is feminine, and "it is common to hear them speaking of the motherland whenever they are referring to their homeland, particularly where one was born and raised."[83] The teachings of Islam mandate that the environment must be kept clean and that is the woman's responsibility. Women must fetch water and firewood, cultivate crops and gardens, take care of animals—and most importantly raise children.

Zvingowanisei stresses that women are part of creation and their roles are pivotal to the flourishing of all life. However, their patriarchal culture blocks their ownership of land. This must end. Land ownership will help women and all Varemba society to flourish.

MOTHER EARTH/MOTHER AFRICA IN CREATIVE TENSION

This overview and analysis of some of the Circle writings on ecological issues demonstrates that there are many layers of tension between Mother Earth and Mother Africa.

---

82 Nelly Mwale, "The Mother Earth Centre: A Narrative of the Comboni Missionary Sisters' Contributions to Environmental Sustainability" in *Mother Earth, Mother Africa: World Religions and Environmental Imagination*, ed. Sophia Chirongoma and Wayua Kiilu (Stellenbosch, South Africa: SUN PReSS, 2021), 104.

83 Silindiwe Zvingowanisei, "African Islam and Environmental Sustainability: A Case Study of the Varemba Muslim Women in Zimbabwe" in *Mother Earth, Mother Africa: World Religions and Environmental Imagination*, ed. Sophia Chirongoma and Wayua Kiilu (Stellenbosch, South Africa: SUN PReSS, 2021), 59.

Both experience the pervasive power of patriarchy; both are seen by men to be used and discarded. Both have little value in the patriarchal perspective except to provide for male needs—from water and food at the family table to exploitation of land and forests for male bank accounts.

The link between Mother Earth and Mother Africa has to be carefully delineated. Women give birth, and so they exemplify Mother Earth in a way that men do not. This is not a simple essentialism but fact. However, women are more than their reproductive ability; they have minds and emotions; they can analyze the situation of our only home and create new possibilities for abundance for all.

But this is very difficult, as patriarchy is stubborn and its thought patterns have been internalized by both men and women. Patriarchal structures limit African women in significant ways, including barring them from land ownership. However, African women are very strong, and the chant of South African women on August 9, 1956 as they marched to the seat of government to demand that the Pass Laws be revoked is also a chant for the twenty-first century: "You have struck a woman; you have struck a rock."

CHAPTER 5

SEEKING A MORALLY VIABLE RESPONSE TO CLIMATE INJUSTICE: INFORMED BY VOICES FROM ITS UNDERSIDE

Cynthia Moe-Lobeda

PART ONE: Moral Abomination and Moral Question

Our moment in time stuns. The next few years may be the most important in human history, from both a moral and a material perspective. Human decisions and actions will determine whether we arrest our suicidal rampage into climate disaster at its worst.

The moral abomination is layered, and the layers matter. First, the people most vulnerable to the ravages of climate change are—in general—not those most responsible for it.[1] Second, climate-privileged societies and sectors may respond to climate change with policies and practices that enable them to survive with some degree of well-being under the limited conditions imposed by the planet's warming while

---

[1] Maxine Burkett, "Climate Reparations," *Melbourne Journal of International Law* 10 [2009]: 2. Law professor Maxine Burkett articulates the legal and governance dimensions of this moral problem: Those who "suffer most acutely [from climate change] are also those who are least responsible for the crisis to date. That irony introduces a great ethical dilemma, one that our systems of law and governance are ill-equipped to accommodate. Indeed, attempts to right this imbalance between fault and consequence have resulted in a cacophony of political negotiation and legal action between and amongst various political scales that have yielded insufficient remedies."

relegating others—the most climate vulnerable—to death or devastation.[2] The third layer reveals that climate mitigation measures designed by privileged sectors may further endanger climate-vulnerable people. A team of Indian scholars points out that "poor and marginalized communities in the developing countries often suffer more from . . . climate mitigation schemes than from the impacts of actual physical changes in the climate."[3] Increasingly, Indigenous people and people of the Global South refer to this as "green and blue colonialism." Examples span the globe.[4] Fourth, the world's high-consuming and wealthier people have benefited greatly (in material terms) from the economic systems that have produced the climate crisis while also leaving impoverished people more vulnerable to it. These four layers of the moral travesty are intragenerational. The fifth is intergenerational. High-emitting sectors are limiting the life chances of future generations. The final layer is interspecific. Climate change and associated ecological devastation are extinguishing species and destroying habitats. These six dimensions of moral disgrace inherent in climate change also constitute dimensions of climate injustice.

---

2   *Third Assessment Report, Annex B: Glossary of Terms*, IPCC Working Group 2, 2001. "Climate vulnerable" refers to nations and sectors that are particularly vulnerable to the impacts of climate change-related disasters, including drought, fierce storms, rising sea levels, disease, and food shortages. As defined by the IPCC, "vulnerability" refers to "the degree to which a system is susceptible to, or unable to cope with, adverse effects of climate change." I use "climate privilege" to indicate nations and sectors most able to adapt to, prevent, or be less vulnerable to those disaste.

3   Soumya Dutta, Soumitra Ghosh, Shankar Gopalakrishnan, C. R. Bijoy, and Hadida Yasmin, *Climate Change and India* (New Delhi: Daanish Books, 2013), 12. This study notes that climate change has "two sets of impacts" on vulnerable sectors. One is the actual impact of climate change. The "second set of impacts originates from actions that our governments and corporate/industrial bodies undertake in the name of mitigating climate change. This includes large-scale agro-fuel and energy plantations in the name of green fuel . . . extremely risky genetically modified plants (in the name of both mitigation and adaptation to climate change), [and] more big dams for 'carbon-free' electricity."

4   For some examples, see later in this chapter under the seventh clue.

The first layer—the difference between who causes climate devastation and who suffers from it— needs more specificity. Increasingly, the term "carbon inequality" is used to signify this difference. Carbon inequality is calculated along three axes: inequality based on company emissions, national emissions, and individual emissions. The 2017 Carbon Majors Report shows that a hundred companies have been responsible for 71 percent of global industrial greenhouse gas emissions since 1988. The comparison between nations is reported by the Club of Rome: "Today's rich countries are responsible for nearly 80 percent of all human-related carbon emissions from 1850–2011." Yet these countries "account for only around 14 percent of today's global population."[5] The assessment "World Scientists' Warning of a Climate Emergency" vividly paints carbon inequality on the individual level: "The climate crisis is closely linked to excessive consumption of the wealthy lifestyle."[6] The scientists note in particular the high emissions produced by meat production, air travel, and other uses of fossil fuels. The World Inequality Report 2022 points to the

---

5   Club of Rome, "Just Transition," 5. While the national emissions of rising middle class (measured by GDP) in countries like China, India, and Brazil have risen to rival those of the US, when considered per capita, "the United States showed 8 times the per capital carbon emissions of India in production terms in 2015, and this difference increases to 12 times once final demand emissions are calculated."; In the words of the OECD itself: "G20 economies account for around 80% of global greenhouse gas emissions." https://web-archive.oecd.org/2021-10-27/614338-g20-economies-are-pricing-more-carbon-emissions-but-stronger-globally-more-coherent-policy-action-is-needed-to-meet-climate-goals-says-oecd.htm.

   The inequity is more complex when we combine the cross-country comparisons with comparisons of individual emissions. The difference in per capita carbon emissions across countries does not reveal the full extent of inequality in carbon emissions. According to data in the *World Inequality Report 2022*, "global carbon inequalities are now mainly due to inequalities *within* countries. . . . There are globally high emitters in low- and middle-income countries and globally low emitters in rich countries."

6   William J. Ripple et al., "World Scientists' Warning of a Climate Emergency," *BioScience* 70/1 (January 2020), 8–12. https://doi.org/10.1093/biosci/biz088. Note that in global terms, the "wealthy" includes middle strata North Americans.

even higher inequality related to the very rich: "The richest decile in North America are the most extravagant carbon emitters in the world with an average of . . . 73 times the per capital emission of the poorest half of the population of South and South East Asia. . . . Today, the richest 10 percent of people on the planet are responsible for nearly half of all carbon emissions."[7] The Oxfam report "Extreme Carbon Inequality," which compares the lifestyle consumption emissions of very rich people and poor people, indicates that the world's richest 1 percent were responsible for more than twice the greenhouse gas emissions of the poorest half of humankind. Yet, the poorest live overwhelmingly in locations most vulnerable to climate change.[8]

At this moment of dramatic urgency, unprecedented in human history, many voices of the Global South cry out in multiple modes of expression—art, music, poetry, protest, academic discourse of multiple disciplines, self-sacrifice—that the engines of global warming must cease their churning and reverse course. Thus far, the cries have been to little avail: the major forces of destruction go on and the window of time to improve matters creeps toward a close.

My purpose in this chapter is not to argue *whether* this situation is a moral crisis. Rather I presuppose that it is, and I ask a question related to this moral crisis. The development of that question is instructive. Initially

---

7 *World Inequality Report 2022*, produced by the Inequality Lab at the Paris School of Economics. Available at: https://wir2022.wid.world/. The "World Scientists' Warning of a Climate Emergency" confirms this: "The climate crisis is closely linked to excessive consumption of the wealthy lifestyle. The most affluent countries are mainly responsible for the historical GHG emissions and generally have the greatest per capita emissions."

8 Oxfam, "Extreme Carbon Inequality," Oxfam Media Briefing, 2 December, 2015, 1. The report goes on to show that "comparing the average lifestyle consumption footprints of richer and poorer citizens in a range of countries helps show that while some 'emerging economies' like China, India, Brazil and South Africa have high and rapidly rising emissions, the lifestyle consumption emissions of even their richest citizens remain way behind that of their counterparts in rich OECD countries, even though this is changing and will continue to do so without urgent climate action. The lifestyle emissions of the hundreds of millions of their poorest citizens, meanwhile, remain significantly lower than even the poorest people in the OECD countries."

I ask, At this moment in time, what is a morally viable response to the dual crises of climate change and climate injustice by scholars of the Global North working at the intersection of religion/theology and ecology? Yet, the focus of this volume leads me to formulate a different version of that question. The editors, in their invitation to contribute, wrote: "More scholars of religion engaging with ecological issues are using the language and concepts of scholars from the Global South, adopting such terms as 'coloniality/decoloniality' to frame their critical analysis. . . . Despite these trends, Western scholars often fail to engage with the scholarship of those in the Global South intersecting religion and ecology as sustained dialogue partners or knowledge producers." This volume "aims at showcasing what can be generated if these bodies of scholarship are engaged as dialogue partners."

This observation and purpose articulated by the editors render my question for this chapter: At this moment in time, what is a morally viable response to the dual crises of climate change and climate injustice by scholars of the Global North working at the intersection of religion/theology and ecology, *if that response is tutored and otherwise informed by voices of the Global South and indigenous voices, especially those who are situated at intersections of religion and ecology?*[9]

Having defined the question pursued in this chapter, we move in part two to consider the method shaping the inquiry, a danger inherent in this inquiry, and difficulties presented by it. Part three responds to the question.

PART TWO: METHOD, DANGER, AND DIFFICULTIES

The outcome of ethical inquiry is determined in significant part by the method employed. The method of ethical enquiry method has many approaches, and is a field of study in itself. For the purpose of this section, two of the most important approaches are related to sources and frames of analysis (or perception).

---

9 Let us acknowledge from the outset the ambiguity of the terms "Global South" and "Global North." They have varied connotations and problematics. Unraveling them is beyond the scope of this chapter.

Method: Sources

As determined by this chapter's question and this volume's purpose, my primary sources are scholars of the Global South working in the multifaceted intersection of religion and ecology. However—and this may be the most important methodological point—I reflect on what they have taught me not only through their formal scholarship but also through personal relationships and, to a lesser extent, through visual, literary, and musical arts. I define "scholarship" broadly to include knowledge produced not only through formal academic writing but also through lived experience and the articulation of it verbally and otherwise. Finally, I am including as scholars the knowledge producers who may not have access to channels of professional scholarship or who have chosen not to access those channels. These knowledge producers include both individuals and social movements led by subaltern and Indigenous people.

The decision to include social movements as sources has three roots. First is my experience with representatives of social movements whose truth about climate colonialism and appropriate responses to it have convinced me that knowledge from grassroots social movements is not only important but may be essential. Second are the writings of Maori theorist and activist Linda Tuhiwai Smith and African American theologian Willie James Jennings, who explicitly articulate that the violence of colonialism was and is not only material and cultural but epistemic. That epistemic violence included claiming that the collectively held knowledge and expertise of subjugated communities was not valid or valuable, and that truly valid knowing was the purview of individual experts.[10] I seek to resist that epistemic violence. Finally, I am influenced to value the knowledge of social movements by Indian scholar and activist, now in New Zealand, George Zachariah.[11]

---

10 Gayatri Spivak, "Can the Subaltern Speak?", in *Marxism and the Interpretation of Culture*, ed. Cary Nelson and Lawrence Grossberg (Basingstoke, England: Macmillan, 1988), 271–313. The term "epistemic violence" is used by Gayatri Spivak in "Can the Subaltern Speak?" to describe the silencing of marginalized groups.

11 George Zachariah, "Decolonizing Eco-Theology: Subaltern Social Movements as Theological Texts," *How Would We Know What God is Up To*, ed.

Method: Perspectival Frame

The outcome of the normative task in ethical inquiry (asking what ought we to do) depends on the frame of analysis and perception used in the descriptive task (asking what is actually going on). I am haunted by a frame that I cannot escape. It has been with me since age fourteen, and it directs my work. Naming that frame here is salient because it shapes my response to the question at hand, and also because it flows directly from my encounters at an early age with scholars and activists of the Global South (a primary source in this inquiry). While this perspectival lens has been a curse in the sense of creating anguish and confusion in me for decades, it also has been a blessing in conveying more authentic pictures of reality than I would have had without it.

The frame is this: The life-strangling poverty of many people is caused directly or indirectly by the economic systems (policies, practices, principles, and power arrangements) that generate the vast and obscene wealth of the world's richest and the material overconsumption and disproportionate ownership of land by many (including me) who are relatively wealthy in relationship to the world's people. Jesuit priest Jon Sobrino, speaking to a delegation of North Americans that I coled in El Salvador, put it with searing power: "In El Salvador, poverty means death, and people are not poor by chance. They are poor because the systems that bring your wealth make them poor." These systems constitute the political economy of advanced global capitalism. It goes by many names: neoliberal capitalism, economic globalization, corporate-and-finance-driven capitalism, predatory capitalism, and more.

This perspectival frame bears directly on this chapter's inquiry because neoliberal capitalism, together with its antecedents, is the engine driving both climate change and the climate injustice inherent in it. This economic system depends on and drives maximization of short-term profit, which demands maximization of economic growth (as defined by GDP), production, and consumption. This political economy and its direct antecedent, the colonial project begun some five hundred years ago, generated the materially consumptive lifestyle on which life in my society is

---

in Ernst Conradie and Cynthia Moe-Lobeda (Cape Town: AOSIS Publishing, 2022).

based, and it generated the disproportionate ownership of land and land-based resources by white and monied people. Some of us have benefited greatly (in material terms) from the political economy that is devastating or killing others through poverty and climate change. Alan Boesak nailed it: "While we are talking people are dying and somebody is responsible for that."[12]

Of course, the reality is more complex. At this point under neoliberal capitalism, many people who have benefited from this system are also being eaten alive by it. They are damaged or dying from the racism, lack of healthcare, unemployment, and environmental perils inherent in neoliberal capitalism.

These two methodological moves shape this essay. In addition, they comprise the first two clues that I offer in response to the question: (1) sources to guide the response of people in the Global North will include knowledge producers of the Global South, and (2) the crises of climate change and climate injustice will be perceived through a lens that acknowledges causal links between the wealth and privilege of some people and the poverty and devastation of others.

A Danger

I am wary of using the language of decolonization or anti-coloniality and wary of drawing from the body of theory related to it that is generated by Indigenous communities and people of the Global South. Any person from the colonizing side of history (such as me) should be wary. The danger, as I have learned from people speaking from the underside of the historic and ongoing rampage of colonialism, is multifold. One risk is using the discourse and receiving academic affirmation for so doing while not practicing or supporting the material moves that decoloniality prescribes. This failure reproduces ongoing colonialism by extracting theory and discourse and using it for self-enrichment.

I will address that danger shortly and will try not to fall into its trap. Still, I use decolonial and anti-colonial theory. Employing it is

---

12   Opening address at the first DARE Conference in 2017 in Bangkok, sponsored by the Council for World Missions.

a response to directives from colonized people to do so as a tool for acknowledging the history and ongoing realities of colonialism and for seeking reparatory justice, an end to colonialism, and a world less deformed by it.[13]

Two Difficulties

The difficulties attached to this chapter's question are intense. First, knowledge and wisdom are intimately linked to language and are expressed through language patterns. How is one to learn from the wisdom of a people if one does not know that people's language or the culture that it expresses? It seems to me that when historically colonized people attempt to express their wisdom in the colonizers' language in order to be heard by the colonizer society, vitally important meaning is lost.

A second and related difficulty is a daunting conundrum facing inquiry in most if not all academic disciplines.[14] It is this: the deadly trajectory on which humanity races—a trajectory toward almost unimaginable climate catastrophe imbued with racism and economic violence—is grounded in epistemologies that have been exposed as dangerous. The ways of knowing and resulting social systems that undergird Western consciousness and intellectual inquiry have shaped and been shaped by white supremacy, wealth supremacy, and an economic worldview that

---

13   For example, Sami theologian Tore Johnson, in his *Sami Nature-Centered Christianity in the European Arctic: Indigenous Theology beyond Hierarchical Worldmaking* (Lanham, MD: Lexington Books, 2022), unpacks the cosmological orientation of Indigenous Christianity in the North Sami people of Norway. His purpose includes the "decolonizing of Lutheran theology from the perspective of the indigenous experience in the European Arctic." That is, he is offering and asking for broader decolonizing not only by the colonized but by the colonizing culture. See also Pablo Mariman, Sergio Caniuqueo, Rodrigo Levil, and José Millalen, *¡. . .Escucha, winka. . .! Cuatro ensayos de Historia Nacional Mapuche y un epílogo sobre el future* (Santiago, Chile: LOM Ediciones, 2006).

14   This point and paragraph comes from my essay, "Method in Eco-theology: A Perspective from the Belly of the Beast," in *An Earthed Faith, Vol. 2: How Would We Know What God Is up To?*, ed. Cynthia Moe-Lobeda and Ernst Conradie (Capte Town: AOSIS Publishing, 2022).

prioritizes maximizing short-term wealth accumulation for a few and maximizing economic growth (as measured by GDP). Horrors upon horrors are rooted in the epistemologies and related ideological coding that structure worldviews and intellectual inquiry (including theological and religious inquiry) in the Western world. Genocide on the continents that became known as "the Americas" and the Atlantic slave trade are two of the most heinous. How, then, can minds and modes of inquiry shaped (largely unconsciously) by these lethal epistemological underpinnings—including the work of this essay—be exercised in ways that produce not death, destruction, and further colonization, but rather fullness of life for all and liberation from what thwarts it? In a sense this essay is itself an effort to grapple with that difficulty. Doing so is inherent throughout the essay and is explicit in the section entitled "Sixth clue: Practice "epistemological unmooring." Let dangers and difficulties provide wise guidance, but let them not dissuade us from pursuing a vital question!

PART THREE: A Response to the Question: Clues

"Clues" here refers to clues to a morally viable response to the crises of climate change and climate injustice by scholars of the Global North working at the intersection of religion and ecology, if that response is informed by voices from the Global South and Indigenous communities, and especially those who are situated at intersections of religion and ecology.

First clue: Re-see climate change as climate colonialism or climate debt

Many years ago, leaders in the National Council of Churches of India taught me to re-see climate change as climate colonialism. They declared that climate change is "caused by the colonization of the atmospheric commons. The subaltern communities are denied of their right to atmospheric commons and the powerful nations and the powerful within the developing nations continue to extract from the atmospheric common disproportionately. In that process they have emitted and continue to emit greenhouse gases beyond the capacity of the planet to withstand . . .

subaltern communities with almost zero footprint are forced to bear the brunt of the consequences."[15]

"Climate debt" is another term for this reality. I had been invited to India to work with Indian scholar-activists on eco-justice curricula for some forty seminaries. What I learned shaped the content of my subsequent teaching, writing, and speaking in the US and elsewhere. Why is the shift from climate change to climate colonialism or climate debt so consequential?[16] Response to climate change is frequently framed around the principle of sustainability. Climate change as a matter of sustainability calls for reducing carbon emission through technological advances, energy efficiency, and energy conservation, and replacing fossil fuels with renewable energy sources. The moves are crucial, to be applauded. If climate change were not connected, historically and contemporarily, to the power imbalances that have rendered climate debt, and if renewable energy development did not endanger climate vulnerable people, then this response—together with assistance to the victims of climate change—would be ethically adequate. It is, however, an inadequate and deceptive moral response for affluent societies and sectors if we: (1) are disproportionately responsible for climate change, (2) could choose sustainability measures that have adverse impact on climate vulnerable people and peoples, (3) are material beneficiaries of the fossil fuel economies that generated the climate crisis, and (4) have produced economic orders that impoverished or displaced vulnerable peoples, thus rendering them less able to survive disasters related to climate change.

A response organized around sustainability alone allows the world's high-consuming societies and people to address climate change in ways that do not take moral responsibility for these factors and for the

---

15   From the author's conversations with church leaders at the headquarters of the National Council of Churches in India located in Nagpur.

16   This paragraph and the following two are adapted from my chapter, "Climate Change as Race Debt, Class Debt, Climate Colonialism: Moral Conundrums, Vision, and Agency," in *Ecological Solidarities: Mobilizing Faith and Justice for an Entangled World*, ed. Krista Hughes, Dhawn Martin, and Elaine Padilla (University Park: Pennsylvania State University Press, 2019) 61–80.

disproportionate impact that climate change and efforts to mitigate it have on many communities of color, Indigenous communities, and economically impoverished people. In this case, the world's high-consuming and affluent minority could continue to

- respond to climate change in ways that reduce our carbon footprint and protect the more racially and economically privileged members of our society from the worst of the disastrous impact, at least for a time, but leave the other people to suffer the impacts;
- assume that all nations have *equal* obligations to reduce carbon emissions;
- implement mitigation efforts that harm vulnerable communities (e.g., see the examples of green and blue colonialism below); and
- fail to take on compensation for climate debt.

The probable consequences are sinister. And these are the very issues that people of the Global South emphasize in climate negotiations as unjust.

If, on the other hand, climate change is seen not only as a problem of ecological sustainability but also of climate colonialism or climate debt, damage done by one group to another, or human rights abused, then more is required in response. Debt owed by the enriched to the impoverished calls for compensation. Damage done or rights abused points to reparations. Climate colonialism evokes decolonial and anti-colonial directives. Foremost among these is reparations for "loss and damage." To this we turn presently.

Second clue: Listen ("Escucha Winka")

Scholars of the Global North are invited to listen to and learn from Afro-descended, Indigenous, and Global South voices, epistemologies, and cosmologies—to dare to open self to perceive differently. The essay collection "Escucha Winka," written collaboratively by a group of Mapuche scholar-activists, illustrates that. The set of four essays directs the *winka* (foreigner, invader, colonizer, or non-Indigenous person) to listen.[17] Above all, the collection is a "patient call for a listening practice."[18]

Listen for what?

Listen for: Worldviews, epistemes, and ways of perceiving life and reality that existed before the onslaught of colonialism and that were negated and subjugated by it, but that have survived in the lives and consciousness of Indigenous and Afro-descended peoples around the world.[19] Those worldviews, highly varied, contain wisdoms that humankind may need in order to escape from the hierarchical worldviews undergirding Western civilization that have justified and normalized extraction, exploitation, and domination as though they are necessary, natural, and even divinely mandated. Many subjugated worldviews and epistemologies escape, invert, or refuse the extractive view.[20] Our headlong dash into climate catastrophe reflects a profoundly diseased relationship to land (including oil, water, and soil) stemming from a worldview that perceives land primarily as a commodity and tool for private wealth creation.[21] Worldviews that see land and seas primarily as living kin, or as the bearer of sacred spirit, or as held by the community rather than the individual, invert that worldview.[22] This is not to idealize subaltern communities and

---

17 Luis Cárcamo Huechante, "Mapuche Historians Write and Talk Back: Background and Role of ¡. . .Escucha, winka. . .! Cuatro ensayos sobre Historia Nacional Mapuche y un epílogo sobre el futuro," *Decolonial Gesture* (11: 1) (2014), 4.

18 Macarena Gomez-Barris, *The Extractive Zone: Social Ecologies and Decolonial Perspectives* (Durham, NC: Duke University Press, 2017), 137.

19 Kristie Dotson, "Tracking Epistemic Violence, Tracking Practices of Silencing," *Hypatia* Vol. 26, No. 2 (Spring, 2011) 236–257. Kristie Dotson elaborates different ways in which marginalized communities are silenced. See

20 Gomez-Barris, *The Extractive Zone*, 133, 134.

21 Willie James Jennings documents that one of the colonizers' aims was to change Indigenous worldviews such that they would see land as private property to be commodified.

22 For an example of the second (land as bearer of sacred spirit), see: Marilú Rojas Salazar, "Decolonizing Theology: Panentheist Spiritualities and Proposals from the Ecofeminist Epistemologies of the South." *Journal of Feminist*

their knowledge. Rather it is a challenge to learn from them. To illustrate: a project initiated by the Pacific Theological University draws on Indigenous wisdoms of the Pacific islands for developing responses to the climate crisis. The project's initiator, Upolu Vaai, insists that these wisdoms—which have been ignored by Western climate science—are vitally important for humankind's effort to deal with climate change. In these Pacific islander worldviews (at least as I have understood them), the sea and land share kinship with the human creature.

Listen for: The realities of the historical and contemporary life of people and peoples on the underside of colonial history, global capitalism, and climate disaster. Listen in order to perceive the "untruths that have been so systematically constructed about" Indigenous and other subjugated peoples.[23] Listen in order to take seriously the often underreported ecological damage done to their lands and livelihoods (outsourced toxicity and waste dumps, corporate degradation of lands and waters, destruction by megadams, replacement of multi-cropping with export-oriented mono-cropping, etc.).[24] That is, recognize the zones of vulnerability, the sacrifice zones, that colonization and especially the recent decades of corporate-and-finance-driven global capitalism have left.[25]

Listen for: Proposals regarding lifeways that embody life-giving relationships between humans and the rest of the earth community. As

---

Studies in Religion 34, no. 2 (2018): 92–98. To illustrate the third (land held in common): "To us in Africa land was always recognized as belonging to the community. Each individual within our society had a right to use the land, because otherwise he could not earn his living and one cannot have the right to life without also having a right to some means of maintaining life. But the African's right to land was simply the right to use it; he had no other right to it, nor did it occur to him to try and claim one." Julius Kambarage Nyerere, "Ujamaa: The Basis of African Socialism," (April 1962), 5.

23   Tink Tinker, "Walking in the Shadow of Greatness: Vine Deloria Jr in Retrospect," *Wicazo Sa Review,* 21:2 (Autumn, 2006), 175.

24   See Rob Nixon, *The Slow Violence and the Environmentalism of the Poor* (Cambridge, MA: Harvard University Press, 2011), and the Indigenous Environmental Network's website.

25   "Colonial and Racialized Capitalism Always Create Sacrifice Zones." Mayra Rivera, Presidential Address to the American Academy of Religion, November 2022.

Macarena Gomez-Barris insists, in the extractive zones of South America, "there is already so much being done that what we require is a practice of listening to and then amplifying . . . analyses, responses, and proposals."[26] Proposals and projects for mitigating and adapting to climate change exist in plenitude.

Listen for: Christianities that have been developed by Indigenous and other subaltern voices and are based on their traditional epistemologies and on people's struggles to negotiate the interface of those epistemologies with the Christianity brought by colonizers. People of the Global North may encounter "other ways of being Christian" from theological voices in "what used to be the peripheries of Eurocentric modern Christianity."[27]

Third clue: Realize that the pain, trauma, and horror caused by colonialism, white supremacy, climate displacement, and devastation is unfathomable

This clue comes to me not from formal scholarship but from the pedagogy of friendships—in this case friendships with Indigenous and Afrodescended people who have had the courage and generosity to allow the depth of anguish to be glimpsed. Pain carried intergenerationally is real. The terror of one's child being hunted and shot for walking or driving while Black or Brown is beyond what I can imagine. Being forced from one's land by climate change may be exile from one's very life in ways that are incomprehensible to me, as a particular land is not my life. The ongoing microaggressions of well-intentioned white people are searing, traumatizing, terrifying, and exhausting for people of color and Indigenous people.

Recognizing that this pain is beyond what can be grasped by those not experiencing it is integral for a moral response to climate injustice. However, allowing oneself to glimpse the horror of these realities is not permission to be frozen by guilt or shame. Guilt and shame bear no liberative purpose unless they catalyze action and wisdom. The relationship between shame and guilt on the one hand and moral agency on the other

---

26 Gomez-Barris, *The Extractive Zone*, 134.
27 Raimundo C. Barreto, "A Response from a Latinx/Latin American Perspective," in *T and T Clark Handbook of Christian Theology and Climate Change*, ed. Hilda Koster and Ernst Conradie (London: T and T Clark, 2020) 177. See also: Johnson, *Sami Nature-Centered Christianity*.

is beyond the scope of this essay, but the warning here is to eschew the lure of inaction by shame.

Fourth clue: Acknowledge that ongoing neocolonialism is as real as is historical colonialism but takes different forms

The legal, political, economic, epistemological, and theological processes of colonialism that possessed by dispossessing are not only historical. They also are contemporary. "The enterprise of green energy is following colonial paths of extraction," noted Mayra Rivera in her address to the American Academy of Religion.[28] Those paths are manifest, for example, in the green and blue colonialism illustrated later in this chapter. Ongoing colonialism is manifest also in the continuing normativity of whiteness. Likewise, the assumption that economies must include extraction and exploitation remains tacitly accepted and often disguised as necessary, inevitable, or divinely mandated. Ngahuis Murphy, a Maori educator, explains: "[The] continuing colonial agenda . . . manifests itself in many ways. These include the denial of our right to autonomy as Indigenous peoples, the self-hatred that thrives in our communities as a consequence of ethnocidal policies that attempted to stamp out our philosophies and practices, and the relentless plundering of our elders—the land, the sea, the forests and rivers—under the banner of 'progress, 'civilization' and 'development.'"[29] Since colonialism is ongoing, its material beneficiaries are called to recognize it and subvert it.

Fifth clue: Assume that a life-giving future is possible and work toward it

If any people have reason to give up or to believe that a future for life in fullness is not possible, it seems to me that it would be Indigenous peoples, who have struggled against extinction and have seen so many

---

28   Mayra Rivera, "What Is the Role of the Study of Religion in Times of Catastrophe?" 2022 AAR Presidential Address, November 19, 2022.

29   Ngahuia Murphy, "Menstruation, Whakapapa and the Revival of Matrilineal Maori Ceremony," in *Decolonization in Aotearoa: Education, Research and Practice*, ed. Jessica Hutchings and Jenny Lee-Morgan (Wellington, New Zealand: NZCER Press, 2016), 182.

other Indigenous peoples and languages be killed, or it would be savagely oppressed people of the colonized world, who have suffered under brutal dictatorships and the threat of death by torture and disappearance. Yet, in all of my interactions with activists, theologians, and others in marginalized communities, I have never heard intimations of giving up the struggle because it is too late.

The implications are striking. Where a more equitable and life-giving future seems impossible, we are to cast ourselves with tenacious vigor and hope to render the impossible possible. Here is not the time to investigate the roots of that hope. Yet I will point to four possibilities that I have learned from listening. First, take seriously, celebrate, and build the alternatives that exist. Macarena Gomez-Barris, after a decade of engaged living with and studying Indigenous peoples in South America, concludes that their active "'dream of another world' is not merely a future oriented utopia but is already in motion, teeming with the alternatives we desire."[30]

Next, honor the ancestral past. Puzzled by the tenacious hope of Indigenous American communities, I have surmised (but am not certain) that hope for the future is rooted in the legacy of the ancestral heritage. "Before all else," declare leaders of the Indigenous NDN Collective, "we wish to acknowledge the work and the legacy of our ancestors and our elders. We carry their stories and their survivance with us every day, and know that their struggle and celebration, their commitment to their own humanity and the power of the life in the Earth, has given our future generations the audacity to dream."[31]

Third, I perceive, from the writings and anecdotes of friends and colleagues in the Pacific and Latin America, a firm belief in the power of life itself flowing within the earth, its waters, forests, and land. I sense an embodied conviction that this power is life-giving, life-sustaining, and life-saving, and that human agency is inseparable from it.

Finally, Ugandan theologian and activist Emmanuel Katongole dedicates an entire book to discovering how it was possible for people amid

---

30   Gomez-Barris, *The Extractive Zone*, 134.
31   Pennelys Droz and Julian Brave Noisecat, ed. "Position Paper: Mobilizing an Indigenous Green New Deal" (Rapid City, SD: NDN Collective), 2. https://ndncollective.org/app/uploads/2019/09/Position-paperR2.pdf.

seemingly unbearable personal and communal anguish and suffering to have hope and agency. He is considering the people of the Congo in the midst of twenty-five years of "wars and fighting that have left over 5.4 million dead, millions displaced from their homes, tens of thousands of women raped, and its sixty-seven million people among the worlds most impoverished." What enabled some people to productively transform their ruin, anguish, and loss? He concludes that "in the midst of suffering, hope takes the form of arguing and wrestling with God" as a "way of mourning, of protesting to, appealing to, and engaging God—and a way of acting in the midst of ruins. Lament sustains and carries forth Christian agency in the midst of suffering."[32] His findings call to mind the work of Emilie Townes in *Breaking the Fine Rain of Death*, which argues that, according to the Book of Joel, social healing after catastrophic social devastation comes in the wake of people's communal lament to God.[33]

Sixth clue: Practice "epistemological unmooring"[34]

While "decolonizing epistemologies and the theologies that underlie them is urgent and necessary in the Global South,"[35] I understand from various theorists and activists from Global South and Indigenous communities that it is also crucial within colonizing cultures. The authors of "Escucha Winka" issue "a loud request for epistemological unmooring, for the settler to think differently about our relations to social and ecological worlds."[36] Why, what does this mean, and how are we to go about it?

<u>Why?</u> Here we hearken back to the second difficulty identified earlier in this essay. The perilous trajectory into climate catastrophe laced with racism and economic violence has roots in dangerous epistemologies. They have shaped and been shaped by white supremacy, wealth supremacy, and

---

32   Emmanuel Katongole, *Born from Lament: The Theology and Politics of Hope in Africa* (Grand Rapids, IL: Eerdmans, 2017), 3, xiii, xvi.
33   Emile Townes, *Breaking the Fine Rain of Death* (Eugene, OR: Wipf and Stock, 2006).
34   Gomez-Barris, *The Extractive Zone*, 138.
35   Salazar, 93.
36   Gomez-Barris, *The Extractive Zone*, 138.

an economic worldview that prioritizes maximizing short-term wealth accumulation for a few. The consequence of the last five hundred years has been suffering of magnitudes unimaginable. We asked: "Can minds and modes of inquiry shaped (largely unconsciously) by these lethal underpinnings ... be done in ways that produce not death, destruction, and further colonization, but rather fullness of life for all and liberation from what thwarts it?" Without explicitly acknowledging and facing this challenge, it is unlikely. Hence, we face it here.

What does "decolonizing epistemologies and the theologies that underlie them" mean? In *After Whiteness*, Black theologian Willie James Jennings argues that theological education has been profoundly "distorted" by being "born in white hegemony."[37] What Jennings claims about theological education holds also for all disciplines in higher education. European-descended scholars of the Global North, then, will need to recognize and resist the distortion of our thinking and perceiving by whiteness and the colonial machine. That machine includes distortion by the presuppositions that people with wealth are worthier than people without wealth and that the purpose of economic life is to maximize profit, consumption, and growth. Epistemological unmooring includes asking: In what ways have white supremacy, wealth supremacy, and profit-maximizing economic life shaped the policies, practices, and presuppositions generating climate change and climate injustice?

How? This I am only beginning to unravel. The challenge stupefies. It is the challenge of recognizing the invisible air around us and acting on that recognition. Perhaps we begin in small pods of people (accountability pods) to note and list the manifestations of white supremacy that heretofore we have not noticed and to notice the manifestations of worth tied to wealth and of maximizing profit as normative. Then, after noticing, we choose to make them visible to more people and to counter them.

Another key to epistemological unmooring is the methodological point with which we began: hearing and heeding voices from the underside of colonization and climate injustice and learning from them.

---

37 Willie James Jennings, *After Whiteness: An Education in Belonging* (Grand Rapids, IL: Eerdmans, 2020) 5, 6.

Such reorientation assumes value in the cosmological orientations and ontological premises offered by Indigenous communities, including Indigenous Christianities. Tore Johnson, ed. argues that what distinguishes Indigenous methodology is its "centeredness on land and its commitment to promoting the self-determination of Indigenous peoples as distinct peoples." Tuvaluan theologian Maina Talia expands "lands" to "waters" and in particular the seas around the homeland islands of a people.³⁸ The message glares: For nonIndigenous people, epistemological unmooring—decolonizing epistemologies, theologies, social theories, and perspectives—includes or leads to: (1) protecting the lands and seas that give Indigenous people life, (2) protecting Indigenous people when they are threatened for protecting their lands and waters, and (3) protecting Indigenous people's rights to live on and with these lands, seas, and the communities of life that they offer. In my opinion, this shakes life as we know it to the core.

For Christians, epistemological unmooring entails acknowledging the roles of Christianity in the colonial process, the rise of capitalism and its neoliberal form, and subsequently the climate crises. This includes confessing that notions of God, sin, and salvation perpetuated by Christendom, theological anthropologies and cosmologies, and ecclesial power structures undergird colonization. Epistemological unmooring includes facing the reality of "Christianity's complicity in exterminating not only Indigenous people but also Indigenous notions of sacrality," and Indigenous spiritualities and ancestral knowledge.³⁹ It rests on people within Christian traditions to name this reality and dig into the many iron chains that bind Christianity to colonialism, white supremacy, and the climate crisis. This also invites those of us who are Christians of dominant cultures to recognize that *there are other ways of being Christian.*

In short, if scholars of the Global North are to help avert the worst kinds of climate catastrophe and help reorient life in ways that restore

---

38 Maina Talia, "The *Fakalofa* Lies before You," in *An Earthed Faith, Vol. 2: How Would We Know What God Is up To?*, ed. Cynthia Moe-Lobeda and Ernst Conradie (Cape Town: AOSIS Publishing, 2022).

39 Salazar, 92.

earth's life systems, we must unearth and actively undo our lives' epistemological moorings in white supremacy, wealth supremacy, and the normativity of profit-maximizing as way of life. While it has become mainstream in ecotheology to fault the epistemologies of Western modernity as a causal factor in the climate crisis, I name this clue here because I have heard it prevalent in voices of the Global South and of Indigenous communities.

I name this clue also because it is easy to ignore the real difficulties and dangers inherent in it. Consider to the difficulties and dangers named in this essay's first part; here we note another. Full acknowledgment of Christianity's complicity in exterminating Indigenous people, "notions of sacrality," Indigenous spiritualities, and ancestral knowledge is one thing.[40] But internalizing this knowledge is painful and enraging. Doing so has led many to leave the folds of Christian traditions, considering them irrevocably destructive. From my perspective, this is a justifiable decision. It also is highly lamentable. I believe that religions are as redeemable as humans, that is, infinitely so, and that religions are called on for moral and spiritual courage and wisdom to reshape human life on earth. This requires not deserting a religious tradition but staying critically and actively within it and gratefully seeking to draw on the wealth of life-giving wisdom within the tradition despite the ways it has betrayed the good that it was meant to serve.

Seventh clue: Engage in the struggle to stop extraction and exploitation, implement reparations (pay the debt), and protect the land and water protectors

These six clues raise the danger noted at the outset. It is the danger of making these moves and using this language but failing to take a necessary step that is inherent in a moral response to the climate crisis. That is the step of action—action of a particular kind. To claim the language and theory outlined above and not to act in accord with it is to perpetuate colonialism by extracting theory and discourse from subaltern communities. Drawing with integrity on and learning authentically from the wisdom

---

40   Salazar, 93.

of Indigenous and other subjugated peoples regarding a response to the climate crisis requires a commitment to join them in the movement to stop the extraction and exploitation, and also to begin paying the debt. This is heard from climate activists, scholars, theorists, theologians, and church leaders. That is, worldview change, epistemic humbling and diversifying, retracting and rethinking theologies, and ideologies that undergird colonialism and its attendant white supremacy, alone is—in the words of Tinyiko Maluleke—"farcical" unless these moves are accompanied by "dealing with the reality of the knowledge bearers' inherited and contemporary suffering at the hands of political, academic and commercial merchants of (white) superiority." This, she goes on to say, begins with "a reparation project."[41]

The largely Maori team that authored *Imagining Decolonization* says as much.[42] Reflecting on Paulo Freire's emphasis on praxis (reflection wed to action in the world in order to transform it),[43] the authors iterate that the intellectual and internal aspects of decolonizing consciousness lead to and interface with "action":

> The colonial machine and its blanketing mentalities is an exhausting, all-encompassing thing to break free of, and decolonization cannot be achieved without persistence and commitment. . . . [A]ction is imperative. Decolonizing actions range from simple, personal day-to-day changes, to society-wide collective endeavors.[44]

We thus arrive at a final clue for responding to the question of this essay. This last clue is to take action through striving to halt the exploitation and extraction, implement reparations and pay the debt, and protect the land and water defenders.

---

41 Tinyiko Maluleke, "A Response to Willis Jenkins," in *T and T Clark Handbook of Christian Theology and Climate Change*, ed. Hilda Koster and Ernst Conradie (London: T and T Clark, 2020), 83–89.
42 Bianca Elkington et al., *Imagining Decolonization* (Wellington, New Zealand: Bridget Williams Books: 2020), 55.
43 Paulo Freire, *Pedagogy of the Oppressed* (New York: Continuum, 1986).
44 Ocean Pipeka Mercier (Ngāti Porou), "What Is Decolonization?" in *Imagining Decolonization*, ed. Rebecca Kiddle et al. (Wellington, New Zealand: Bridget Williams Books), 62.

Protect the land and water defenders

An Indigenous colleague from Panama sat beside me at the World Council of Churches (WCC) General Assembly 2022 in Germany. A report had just been read outlining the commitments that the WCC was making to ecological and economic justice.[45] "What did you think of it?" I asked her, expecting a response similar to mine (that it was excellent). She looked at me and said, "It does not mention the Earth protectors who are persecuted or killed for defending the land against extractive industries." She was right. Michelle Bachelet, UN High Commissioner for Human Rights, has noted that women, farmers, and Indigenous peoples who fight against deforestation, extractives, or loss of cultural heritage or identity are the most exposed to abuse and reprisals.[46]

If these assassinations and harassment go on without being condemned by the larger public, they will continue. If, in contrast, global solidarity steps in, then protections are raised. It is less likely that protectors of the Amazon, for example, will be jailed, harassed, or killed if people the world over have made it clear that we stand against such reprisals. Within an hour of her comment to me, the Panamanian Indigenous woman, together with an eco-theologian from Latin America, had strategized to get this matter included in the WCC's statement. They succeeded.[47]

---

45   World Council of Churches (WCC), "The Living Planet: Seeking a Just and Sustainable Global Community," https://www.oikoumene.org/sites/default/files/2022-10/ADOPTED-PIC01.2rev-The-Living-Planet-Seeking-a-Just-and-Sustainable-Global-Community.pdf.

46   United Nations Human Rights Office of the High Commissioner, "Environmental Human Rights Defenders Must Be Heard and Protected," published March 2023, https://www.ohchr.org/en/stories/2022/03/environmental-human-rights-defenders-must-be-heard-and-protected.

47   The WCC statement now calls "all governments and authorities" to respect and fulfill human rights related to "a clean, healthy and sustainable environment, as described in the Escazú Agreement." That groundbreaking agreement includes the world's first binding provision on the human rights of land and water defenders, who "all too often subject to attacks and intimidation." The Regional Agreement on Access to Information, Public Participation and Justice in Environmental Matters in Latin America and the Caribbean signed in 2018 in Escazu, Costa Rica. https://www.cepal.org/en/escazuagreement.

Stop the extraction and exploitation including blue and green colonialism

Frontline communities of the Global South and Indigenous worlds underscore the harm that can come from renewable energy production and other efforts to reduce carbon emissions. They insist that the goal of net-zero emissions, while vitally important, is not morally viable without a specific restriction: paths to lowering emissions must disavow and discontinue mechanisms that damage or endanger climate vulnerable people and peoples.

Two forms of damage loom. One is justifying continued fossil fuel extraction by using the goal and language of net-zero emissions and carbon markets.[48] The Indigenous Environmental Network describes this ploy: "We reject net-zero emissions language (as well as carbon neutral and zero-carbon) because it . . . implies that the reduction of carbon and other greenhouse gases (GHG) emissions can be met through carbon market systems" such as carbon trading, which "allows polluters to buy and sell permits to pollute instead of cutting air pollution at source."[49] The Indigenous Environmental Network adds: "The carbon market does nothing to stop the fossil fuel industry from continuing its decimation of lands, communities, and climate. Worse, it gives the industry a false veneer of environmental and social responsibility while business as usual goes on."[50]

The other form of damage is the harm that renewable energy development may have on Indigenous and other frontline communities. Examples of this green and blue colonialism are endless. For communities of Northern Sami (the Indigenous of the European Arctic), for example, windmill farms are destroying reindeer herding lands that are necessary to people's economy and culture. In the Congo, horrific killing, rape, and

---

48 NDN Collective, "Position Paper: Mobilizing an Indigenous Green New Deal," Published September, 2019, https://ndncollective.org/app/uploads/2019/09/Position-paperR2.pdf.

49 Indigenous Environmental Network, "Talking Points on the Ocasio-Cortez—Markey Green New Deal (GND) Resolution," Published February 7, 2019, https://www.ienearth.org/green-new-deal/. See also "Indigenous Resistance against Carbon," Published August, 2021, https://www.ienearth.org/Indigenous-resistance-against-carbon.

50 Droz and Noisecat, "Mobilizing an Indigenous Green New Deal," 3.

other human rights abuses have accompanied mining for the cobalt used in electric car batteries. Pacific islanders' livelihoods are threatened by deep sea mining for minerals used in renewables.[51] For some Indigenous Native Americans, nuclear energy plants "carry deep toxic and damaging legacies within Indigenous communities and homelands."[52] In India and elsewhere, hydroelectric power dams have dislocated communities from their homelands of centuries.

These two problems do not mean stopping developing renewable energy sources. Rather they mean two things: first, renewable energy development must be guided by and accountable to a racial justice and an economic justice lens. Second, the world's high energy consumers, including Americans, may not continue to use the same high amounts of energy. We must accompany the move to renewables with significant reduction in use of energy so that renewables may be developed without exploitative impacts.[53]

Pay the debt and reparations

Angelica Navarro—Bolivian diplomate, climate negotiator, and ambassador to the World Trade Organization—brought to the world's attention, perhaps more than any other figure, the call by nations of the Global South to repay the climate debt owed to them by the wealthy world. She argued in 2009 at COP 15 that Bolivia is owed a debt because the lives of its people are endangered by climate change disproportionately caused by people of the industrialized and wealthy world. The appropriate response, she argued, is reparations by the industrialized world for the harm it has done.

---

51 See the excellent 80-page report produced by Blue Ocean Law and the Pacific Network on Globalization, "Resource Roulette: How Deep-Sea Mining and Inadequate Regulatory Frameworks Imperil the Pacific and Its Peoples," Published June, 2016, https://www.blueoceanlaw.com/blog/blue-ocean-law-releases-report-on-risks-and-pitfalls-of-deep-sea-mining-for-pacific-peoples-in-light-of-governments-inadequate-regulatory-frameworks.

52 Droz and Noisecat, 1.

53 Stan Cox, *The Green New Deal and Beyond* (San Francisco: City Lights Books, 2020).

People of the Global South have insisted since the first UN Climate Change Conference nearly thirty years ago that payment for climate-caused loss and damage is owed to the nations suffering it but not causing it.[54] With COP 27 (November 2022 in Egypt), loss and damage payments or financing was for the first time on the formal agenda and featured prominently in the talks. In light of this volume's purposes, it is notable that this was achieved through the insistence of leaders from the Global South. Saleemul Huq, director of the Bangladesh-based International Centre for Climate Change and Development, spoke for many in insisting that "loss and damage [funding] is by far the most important issue that needs to be discussed" at COP 27.[55]

Like Navarro and countless others, the Alliance of Small Island States (AOSIS), a group of thirty-nine small island and low-lying nations largely in the Caribbean and South Pacific, emphasizes that finance for loss and damage is not a favor but a payment of what is due to them. For this reason, many refer to loss and damage payments (or loss and damage finance) as "climate reparations," although the term "loss and damage" is more common in international climate negotiations. As early as 2009, the argument for and complexities of climate reparations were being voiced in the legal community.[56]

Climate reparations as some form of "payment of what is due to them because of what has been done to them" is complicated by the meaning of "what has been done to them." For many colonized peoples, this includes the forced removal from their land (for peoples for whom land was life, both spiritually and materially) and despoilment of their lands that left people sorely vulnerable to the ravages of climate change.[57]

---

54 The phrase "loss and damage" has varied connotations, but most refer to the loss of and damage to livelihoods, communities, lands, and lives caused directly or indirectly by climate change.

55 Sam Meredith, "A Showdown over Climate Reparations Is Brewing," Published November, 2022, https://www.cnbc.com/2022/11/04/cop27-climate-summit-loss-and-damage-funding-to-dominate-the-talks.html.

56 Burkett, "Climate Reparations," 2.

57 To illustrate: In writing about the devastating August 2022 floods in Pakistan that displaced fifty million people and killed more than 1,700, Amitav

This theme is key, and it is enormously controversial because it points to land repatriation/rematriation and to accountability. This is one reason why repatriation of land, land appropriation policies, land reform, land repossession and redistribution, and reparations for removal from lands are central for many Indigenous and colonized people discussing climate justice.[58] (Here again, I have experienced the value of the methodological move regarding sources noted in part one. Only by listening to people of the Global South and Indigenous people have I learned the centrality of land in discussions of climate justice.)

Rev. Dr. Gordon Cowan of Jamaica, for example, argued in an eloquent address that reparations for the devastating impact of colonialism on people, lands, economies, and cultures of the Caribbean must include both cancellation of the external debt and funding to recover from climate-related damage and rebuild their economies. The economic crises faced by Caribbean nations, he says, cannot "be divorced from the climate crisis. . . . The Caribbean's history has significantly contributed to a society in which indiscriminate exploitation of natural resources [by colonizing countries] has left nations more vulnerable to climate shocks. . . . Time has come for repair through reparatory justice."[59]

The complexity of calculating what is due is no reason to abandon climate reparations as a necessary step of climate justice. Many Indigenous and Global South players provide proposals for how such reparations are to be paid and warnings about untenable means. La Via Campesina, an

---

Ghosh points out that "one of the reasons why so many people were displaced in these floods is because, going back to colonial times, many nomads who moved with the rhythms of the river were forced to settle by river banks." Amitav Ghosh, "The Colonial Roots of Present Crises," *Green European Journal*, October 19, 2022, https://www.greeneuropeanjournal.eu/the-colonial-roots-of-present-crises.

58 See, for example, Sifiso Mpofu, "A Theology of the Land and Its Covenant Responsibility," in *People and Land: Decolonizing Theologies*, ed. Jione Havea (London: Rowman and Littlefield, 2020), 77–90; Garnett Roper, "Empire 2.0: Land Matters in Jamaica and the Caribbean," in Havea, ed. 101–112.

59 Gordon Cowan (paper presentation, the fifth meeting of the Global Ecumenical Panel for the NIFEA Initiative, Bali, October, 2022).

international network of small farmers, articulates a perspective of many Indigenous peoples in insisting that loss and damage payments not be done through mechanisms often promoted by wealthy nations, such as carbon markets and net-zero efforts. (Recall the similar warning above issued by the Indigenous Environmental Network.) La Via Campesina insists that these are "false solutions," arguing that:

> The legacy of carbon offsetting schemes so far has included environmental crimes, conflicts, corporate abuse, forced relocation, and threats to food sovereignty and cultural genocide, particularly for Indigenous Peoples, smallholder farmers, forest dwellers, young people, women and people of colour. Carbon offsetting schemes are responsible for atrocities inflicted upon vulnerable populations around the world, and we reject them as a form of climate colonialism. . . . We demand that rich countries stop shirking their responsibilities. . . . **We demand solutions that deliver emissions reductions at source** and lead us toward a more just and equitable world. We demand real, additional, public finance from rich countries so that developing countries can transition toward just energy systems, adapt to climate impacts, and be compensated for irreparable loss and damage as stipulated under article 6.6.[60]

La Via Campesina reflects other appeals from the Global South in promoting three forms of loss and damage payment:

- funding for climate mitigation that would enable impoverished nations to bypass dirty energy and move to renewables, thus reducing their national emissions;
- funding for adaptation;

---

60 La Via Campesina, "COP26: Adopt Peasant Agroecology to Achieve Climate Justice and Keep Carbon Markets out of the Paris Agreement," Published November, 5, 2021, https://viacampesina.org/en/cop26-adopt-peasant-agroecology-to-achieve-climate-justice-and-keep-carbon-markets-out-of-the-paris-agreement/. Bold in the original.

- cancellation of the odious debt owed by many impoverished countries to finance institutions and governments of wealthy nations.[61]

The situation in Pakistan after the floods that occurred in the fall of 2022 as described by the General Secretary of a network of twenty-six peasant organizations in Pakistan illustrates the case for climate reparations and two of the kinds of reparations noted above:

> As of Sept 2022, more than one-third of Pakistan is under water. Flash floods, generated by abnormal monsoon rains have so far claimed the lives of 1350 people. One million residential buildings are totally or partially damaged, leaving more than fifty million people displaced from their homes.... These impacts are undeniably a symptom of an accelerating climate.
>
> Despite producing less than one percent of global carbon emissions, Pakistan bears some of the worst consequences of the climate crisis globally. The nation has consistently ranked in the Global Climate Risk Index as among the top ten most vulnerable countries in the world over the past twenty years....
>
> The people of Pakistan are the latest victims of a global crisis to which they have contributed almost nothing— and which has instead been driven by the excess emissions of rich countries and corporate polluters. This fundamental injustice is at the root of increasing demands for climate reparations from Pakistan and the wider Global South.

---

61   Gordon Cowan in address to the World Council of Churches NIFEA team meeting in Bali, October, 2022: "It is time for the world to act towards the cancellation of debt of these struggling economies and the allocation of resources to them for development, recognizing the unique role that colonialism and enslavement played in stultifying economic progress in so many African and African descendant societies, leaving them more vulnerable to climate change damage."

One such demand is debt cancellation. Debt injustice and the climate crisis go hand-in-hand. As extreme weather events intensify, countries on the frontlines, such as Mozambique and island states in the Caribbean are facing increasing economic damages. After these events, low-income (and often already heavily indebted) governments face a shortfall in funding and have little choice but to take out further loans to rebuild livelihoods and communities.

If the West intends on supporting Pakistan through this crisis, it needs to implement a series of measures that tackle the scale of damage inflicted by the Global North upon the South since the Industrial Revolution. As a first step, this should include comprehensive debt cancellation, alongside greatly increased climate finance to support communities to adapt to the impacts of climate change.

In addition, many climate-vulnerable countries including Bangladesh, Ethiopia and Tuvalu are now also calling for compensation from rich countries for the disasters they are now facing. This is often termed as "loss and damage." ...

Why should Pakistan have to take out any loans at all to pay for the impacts of a crisis it has not caused? [62]

Taking action, then, is a final clue for responding to this essay's question.

In Closing

We began by identifying the moral abomination of climate injustice in its many layers. Then, in response to that reality, we posed a question to be pursued in this chapter. The question is: What is a morally viable response

---

62 Farooq Tariq, "After the Floods, Pakistan Needs Reparations, Not Charity," *Climate and Capitalism*, October, 10, 2022, https://climateandcapitalism.com/2022/10/10/after-the-floods-pakistan-needs-reparations-not-charity/. *Farooq Tariq is the general secretary of the Pakistan Kissan Rabita Committee, a network of twenty-six peasant organizations, and a coalition member of La Via Campesina.*

to the dual crises of climate change and climate injustice by scholars of the Global North working at the intersection of religion/theology and ecology, *if that response is tutored and otherwise informed by voices of the Global South and Indigenous voices, especially those who are situated at intersections of religion and ecology?*

After noting methodological basepoints, a danger that looms when people from colonizing cultures use language and theory of decolonization or anticolonization, and two difficulties that pervade this inquiry, we identified seven elements of a response to the question. These elements are clues to a morally viable response by scholars of the Global North to the abhorrent reality of climate injustice if our response is tutored by voices from the Global South and Indigenous voices.

The clues are unsettling. They entail deep listening and swimming upstream against fierce currents of deep-seated assumptions and practices. They entail opening to pain that I, for one, long to avoid. Most unsettling, these clues demand action. They affirm my growing conviction that we live and conduct our scholarship at an epic moment in time when it is no longer morally acceptable to theorize without practicing the knowledge gained. Too much is at stake.

Writing this essay has raised for me a sweet memory. It is the words of the path-breaking feminist ethicist Beverly Harrison, who insisted that, in doing courageous work to counter oppression and domination, we will find ourselves surrounded by a beautiful community of friends.

CHAPTER 6

"FOR THE LIFE OF THE WORLD": INSIGHTS FROM THE ECO-PRAXIS AND ECOTHEOLOGY OF EASTERN ORTHODOX CHRISTIANITY

Nikolaos Asproulis

INTRODUCTORY REMARKS

We live in an increasingly interconnected world facing an endless series of crises transcending national borders, one of them being the current climate crisis. In the midst of this critical condition and in contrast to its own history, the Orthodox Church has articulated a comprehensive ecotheological narrative and practice, which places the urgency of environmental protection at the center of its agenda. The numerous initiatives, pastoral messages, and acts of deep care for creation have been particularly effective in raising environmental awareness across the globe. This chapter provides a brief overview of certain initiatives (focusing on the ecumenical patriarchate of Constantinople) and describes patterns of theologizing from an ecological point of view.[1]

---

1   Purposely the chapter focuses on the role played by the Ecumenical Patriarchate for the following reasons: (1) it is the first throne of Eastern Orthodoxy, with a special historical and symbolic value; (2) the environmental concern has been at the center of its agenda for many decades now, even before it emerged as a critical problem for global community; and (3) its relative vision represents the most comprehensive account about environmental protection ever developed in the context of Eastern Orthodoxy. For a general account of the role played by other Orthodox primates in this regard, see:

CLIMATE CRISIS AS A GLOBAL CRISIS—SETTING THE CONTEMPORARY SCENE

Today climate crisis is considered the most urgent threat facing humanity. As a complex problem consisting of a variety of dimensions—such as climate change, meat production models, biodiversity loss, sea pollution from plastics, and even megafires—it puts at risk the entire environment, endangering the very survival of the human species and the natural world. It suffices here to mention the increasing risk of river and coastal flooding in northwestern Europe, the temperature rising much faster than the global average in the Arctic, and the expansion of habitats for southern disease vectors in the Mediterranean region.

Rooted in a selfish interpretation of the biblical account for the creation of world that dominated after the Enlightenment,[2] humanity has adopted a lifestyle that assumes a controlling role within the world. The work of major Enlightenment thinkers like Francis Bacon (1561–1626) and Immanuel Kant (1724–1804), and particularly René Descartes's (1596–1650) "cogito ergo sum," led to the gradual disassociation of humanity from the materiality of the world, determining a worldview that presents human beings, in Descartes's own words, as the "the lord(s) and possessor(s) of nature."[3] For centuries now, but especially at the dawn of (post)modernity, humanity has followed this path of a utilitarian exploitation and overconsumption of natural resources, indifferent to the preservation of the planet for future generations.

It was only in 1967 that Lynn White Jr. highlighted the historical responsibility of Christianity, bringing to the fore the spiritual and religious aspects of the ecological problem against the prevailing economic and political approaches. As White puts it,

---

Frederick W. Krueger, *Transfiguring the World: Orthodox Patriarchs and Bishops Articulate a Theology of Creation* (self-pub., 2022).

2   Gen., ch. 1–2; for instance: 2:15: "The Lord God took the man and put him in the Garden of Eden to work it and take care of it."

3   *Discours de la méthode*, part VI, accessed November 2, 2022, https://www.bartleby.com/34/1/6.html. Ivone Gabara, in her "Interdependence, Christianity, and Environmental Crisis," masterfully describes this same misunderstanding dominating human identity and its role within the world.

> The emergence in widespread practice of the Baconian creed that scientific knowledge means technological power over nature . . . marks the greatest event in human history since the invention of agriculture. . . . Man's relation to the soil was profoundly changed. Formerly man had been part of nature; now he was the exploiter of nature . . . What people do about their ecology depends on what they think about themselves in relation to things around them. Human ecology is deeply conditioned . . . by religion. . . . In Antiquity every tree, every spring, every stream, every hill had its own genius loci, its guardian spirit. . . . By destroying pagan animism, Christianity made it possible to exploit nature in a mood of indifference to the feelings of natural objects. . . . The roots of our trouble are so largely religious, the remedy must also be essentially religious.[4]

Along the same lines, Metropolitan of Pergamon John Zizioulas (1931–), the chief spokesperson of the ecumenical patriarchate's ecotheological vision, was among the first to turn our attention to White's detailed demonstration of the historical responsibility of Judeo-Christian theology for the environmental crisis.[5]

Climate crisis is not a condition that threatens a piece of land far away from one's own home. It puts at risk one's own villages and cities. Besides, today it has become unexceptional not only to hear about but also to experience exceptional weather, like long stretches of high temperatures, winter storms, forest fires, and floods. This was a situation unknown some decades ago, causing incalculable problems to the local environment, climate, and economy. It goes without saying, then, that the climate crisis is a consequence of globalization and modernity. It affects the whole planet and something should be done to reduce its consequences.

---

4   Lynn Townsend White Jr., "The Historical Roots of Our Ecologic Crisis," *Science* 155, no. 3767 (March 10, 1967): 1203–7. See also Jürgen Moltmann, "Ecology as the Capacity for Love."

5   Cf. John Chryssavgis and Nikolaos Asproulis, eds., *Priests of Creation: John Zizioulas on Discerning an Ecological Ethos* (London: T and T Clark, 2021), 61, 74, 96.

Recent Secular Initiatives

Against this background, how have people, governments, and Christians churches respond?

In recent years, certain important initiatives have been put into practice by the political leaders of the global community in an attempt to finally deal with the problem. Among the major initiatives, one should refer to the Paris Climate Agreement of 2015:

> Acknowledging that climate change is a common concern of humankind, Parties should, when taking action to address climate change, respect, promote and consider their respective obligations on human rights, the right to health, the rights of Indigenous peoples, local communities, migrants, children, persons with disabilities and people in vulnerable situations and the right to development, as well as gender equality, empowerment of women and intergenerational equity.

Among the ambitious decisions to be implemented in the following years were "holding the increase in the global average temperature to well below 2°C above pre-industrial levels and pursuing efforts to limit the temperature increase to 1.5°C above pre-industrial levels, recognizing that this would significantly reduce the risks and impacts of climate change."[6]

In a similar vein, the European Green Deal, which aims for climate neutrality in the European Union by 2050, did not come out of the blue. On the contrary, it seeks to transform our everyday lives to address the critical threat of climate change. In doing so, the European Green Deal suggests certain deeply transformative policies (e.g., modernizing the European economy, supplying clean and affordable energy, mobilizing industry for a clean economy, building in an energy and resource efficient way) for a sustainable future, taking into account, at least in principle, to not leave anyone behind (a just transition).[7]

---

6   UNFCC, "The Paris Agreement, November 5, 2022, https://unfccc.int/sites/default/files/english_paris_agreement.pdf
7   European Commission, "European Green Deal," November 7, 2022, https://ec.europa.eu/info/strategy/priorities-2019-2024/european-green-deal_en.

These are two of the major initiatives at a global scale recently undertaken by governments in their effort to reduce the climate catastrophe. Although quite ambitious in principle and not without strong reactions from various sides, they still point to the need to take radical action to save the planet...now!

Religious Initiatives: Orthodox Christianity Goes Greening

Not only governmental bodies and transnational organizations but also Christian churches have decided to align their efforts to address the climate crisis. In this regard, one should pay special attention to Pope Francis's encyclical *Laudato Si'*, which is the result of consultations with eco-experts, scientists, environmentalists, and theologians from all over the world. The encyclical calls for:

> A new dialogue about how we are shaping the future of our planet. We need a conversation which includes everyone, since the environmental challenge we are undergoing, and its human roots, concern and affect us all. The worldwide ecological movement has already made considerable progress, leading to the establishment of numerous organizations committed to raising awareness of these challenges. Regrettably, many efforts to seek concrete solutions to the environmental crisis have proved ineffective ... Obstructionist attitudes, even on the part of believers, can range from denial of the problem to indifference, nonchalant resignation or blind confidence in technical solutions. We require a new and universal solidarity.[8]

In this same direction, one can also refer to the joint statement by Pope Francis, Patriarch Bartholomew, and the Archbishop of Canterbury,

---

8 Pope Francis, *Laudato Si'*, November 2, 2022, https://www.vatican.va/content/francesco/en/encyclicals/documents/papa-francesco_20150524_enciclica-laudato-si.html. For an Orthodox reception of the Encyclical see Metropolitan John Zizioulas, "Pope Francis' Encyclical Laudato Si'," in, *Ecotheology, Climate Justice and Food Security*, ed. Dietrich Werner-Elizabeth Geglitza (Geneva: Globethics Publications, 2016), 179–186.

released in September 2021, which "call[s] on everyone, whatever their belief or worldview, to endeavor to listen to the cry of the earth and of people who are poor, examining their behavior and pledging meaningful sacrifices for the sake of the earth which God has given us."[9]

But what about Eastern Orthodoxy? It is true that Orthodoxy has often expressed a strong devotion to creation care, a concern deeply rooted in its life and spirituality. Although not transformed into a political program, care of creation has always found a central place in Eastern Orthodox theological vision and monastic life. It was only after the modern explosion of the climate crisis, however, that this vision started to take a more concrete form, being transformed into a specific strategy by the ecumenical patriarchate to increase awareness among the people on a global scale, while at the same time influencing policymakers to address the consequences of the climate crisis.

A. The Ecumenical Patriarchate of Constantinople

Although informal, the ecumenical patriarchate's prophetic environmental vision was initially expressed in clear theological terms in 1967, when the late Metropolitan of Pergamon John Zizioulas published an important article in Greek.[10] In this article, Zizioulas highlights the importance of White's critique of the Judeo-Christian tradition as part of the ecological crisis while stressing the relevance of the eucharistic ethos of the Orthodox Church as an alternative toward creation care.

This eucharistic vision of the world started to take specific shape in the context of the Pre-Conciliar Pan-Orthodox Conference in Chambésy

---

9 "Joint Statement, Pope Francis, Ecumenical Patriarch Bartholomew and Archbishop of Canterbury Urge Care for Future of the Planet," November 1, 2022, https://www.oikoumene.org/resources/documents/joint-statement-pope-francis-ecumenical-patriarch-bartholomew-and-archbishop-of-canterbury-urge-care-for-future-of-the-planet. For an Orthodox assessment of the statement see my "Un messaggio congiunto per la tutela del creato. Una riflessione ortodossa orientale," *Concilium* 58, no. 3 (2022): 151–155.

10 "Η ευχαριστιακή θεώρηση του κόσμου και ο σύγχρονος ανθρωπος" στο Χριστιανικόν Συμπόσιον επιμ. Κώστας Τσιροπουλος, Αθήνα [The Eucharistic vision of the world and modern man], in *Christianikon Symposium*, ed. Kostas Tsiropoulos (Athens, 1967), 183–190.

(Switzerland, October 28–November 6, 1986).[11] In that meeting, the representatives of the Orthodox Churches expressed their deep concern for the human abuse of the natural environment. At the same time, based on the traditional view of the value of creation and the dignity of humans created in the image and likeness of God, the meeting also highlighted the importance of respecting freedom and recognizing the harm caused to people but also to the whole creation by the deconstruction of the natural environment.

The Sixth Assembly of the World Council of Churches in Vancouver (1983) led to the organization of a number of inter-Orthodox meetings on the topic "Justice, Peace, and the Integrity of Creation."[12]

On September 23–25, 1988, at the Patmos conference organized by the ecumenical patriarchate with the support of the Hellenic Ministry of Cultural Affairs on the theme "Revelation and the Future of Humanity," it was decided that the ecumenical patriarchate should devote a particular day of the year to the protection of the natural environment. It is not an exaggeration to argue that this conference "proved to be a catalyst for the direction of many subsequent patriarchal initiatives on the environment."[13]

In 1989, the ecumenical patriarch Demetrios (1914–1991) released an encyclical letter to the entire Church declaring the first day of the new ecclesiastical calendar, known as the *indictus* (September 1), as a prayer day for the protection and preservation of the environment for all Orthodox Churches within the jurisdiction of the ecumenical patriarchate. This decision was followed by a composition of a special service with prayers for creation care in 1990 by the Mount Athos hymnographer Gerasimos Mikrayiannanites (1905–1991), upon the request of the ecumenical patriarchate.

---

11   For what follows on the Ecumenical Patriarchate, I mainly draw on: John Chryssavgis, *Creation as Sacrament. Reflections on Ecology and Spirituality* (London: T and T Clark, 2019); Ecumenical Patriarch Bartholomew, *In the World, Yet Not of the World. Social and Global Initiatives of Ecumenical Patriarch Bartholomew*, ed. John Chryssavgis, (New York: Fordham University Press, 2010).

12   Sofia, Bulgaria (1987); Patmos, Greece (1988); and Minsk, Belarus (1989).

13   Chryssavgis, *Creation as Sacrament*, 187.

A month after his 1991 election to the throne of Constantinople, the current ecumenical patriarch Bartholomew, the so-called Green Patriarch,[14] initiated and convened an ecological meeting on the island of Crete on the theme "Living in the Creation of the Lord." The meeting was attended and officially opened by Prince Philip, the Duke of Edinburgh and international chairman of the World Wildlife Foundation.

In addition, a series of special ecological seminars took place at the Theological School of Halki in Turkey on a wide range topics, including "Environment and Religious Education" (1994), "Environment and Ethics" (1995), "Environment and Communications" (1996), "Environment and Justice" (1997), and "Environment and Poverty" (1998). In addition to holding these seminars, H.A.H. Patriarch Bartholomew organized symposia all over the world to increase people's awareness of the climate crisis. The main objective of these symposia was to boldly communicate and disseminate the theological vision of the ecumenical patriarchate, establishing the first throne of Orthodoxy as a pioneer religious factor to this direction.

The first symposium on the topic "Revelation and the Environment" (1995) took place at the historic and sacred island of Patmos on the occasion of the celebration of the 1900th anniversary of the book of *Revelation*. During this historic meeting, the two hundred participants "identified the pollution of the world's waters as a threat to the survival of the planet and recommended the creation of a common language for scientific and theological thought,"[15] a move that meant to overcome the long rift between the two as a result of mutual misunderstandings.

The second symposium, on the theme "The Black Sea in Crisis," was held in 1997. This time, the symposium undertook a more focused work when members like H.A.H. Patriarch Bartholomew visited the countries of the region and assembled local religious leaders and environmental activists, as well as regional scientists and politicians, to jointly discuss and reflect on the relationship between faith and science. "During the second

---

14 The title has been bestowed on him for his long efforts against the environmental crisis, first formalized at the White House in 1997 by Al Gore, then vice president of the United States.

15 Chryssavgis, *Creation as Sacrament*, 191.

symposium, it became evident that no solution to the ecological collapse of the Black Sea could be determined without addressing the degradation of the rivers that flow into that sea."[16] The next symposium, on the "River of Life: Down the Danube to the Black Sea," took place in 1999, stressing the ecological impact of war, urban development, industrialization, and shipping and agriculture, especially in the context of the civil war in the former Republic of Yugoslavia. When interpreting the present war in Ukraine as a result of the Russian invasion of the country, it is easy to understand the relevance of these topics even today.

The fourth symposium, on "The Adriatic Sea: a Sea at Risk, a Unity of Purpose" (2002), opened in Durres, Albania, and concluded in Venice, Italy, where a serious effort took place to highlight the moral aspects of the discussion. The fifth symposium, titled "The Baltic Sea: A Common Heritage, A Shared Responsibility" (2003), focused on the responsibility of the nine countries surrounding the Baltic Sea in regards to the ongoing pollution. The sixth symposium on the general theme "The Amazon: Source of Life" was held in 2006 on the Amazon River, while the seventh symposium, entitled "The Arctic: Mirror of Life" (2007), intended to raise global awareness about the melting ice caps of Greenland and related consequences.

The next symposium, "Restoring Balance: The Great Mississippi River," was held in 2009 along the banks of the Mississippi River in New Orleans. The Mississippi River "has been acutely devastated by human domination in a chain of cities along its length, discharging domestic and industrial waste into the river for nearly two centuries."[17] In 2018, the ninth international symposium, entitled "Toward a Greener Attica: Preserving the Planet and Protecting Its People," was organized in Athens. The prime objective of the conference, which was attended by more than two hundred ecclesiastical and religious leaders, politicians, scientists, theologians, businessmen, activists, and journalists, was raising the international community's awareness of the environmental problems in the wider area of Attica, Greece.

---

16   Chryssavgis, *Creation as Sacrament*, 191.
17   Chryssavgis, *Creation as Sacrament*, 194.

The result of this important series of international, interfaith, and interdisciplinary on-ship environmental symposia was the launching of another series of meetings under the title "Halki Summit." In the words of the late ecumenical patriarch Bartholomew, "the Halki Summits are a vital step in this critical dialogue . . . to discuss ways of effecting positive and constructive change in the world." According to the official description, "the Halki Summit is a gathering of activists, scientists, journalists, business leaders, theologians, and academics engaging and working across intellectual boundaries to bring the global environmental discussion to a new and richer place. At the heart of that discussion is the belief that no effort can be successful without a fundamental change in values as manifested in ethics, spirituality, and religion."[18]

The first summit on "Global Responsibility and Environmental Sustainability: A Conversation on Environment, Ethics, and Innovation" took place in 2012, while the second, on "Theology, Ecology and the Word: A Conversation on the Environment, Literature and the Arts," occurred in 2015. "Theological Formation and Ecological Awareness: A Conversation on Education and the Environment" was organized in 2019. In 2020, due to COVID-19 sanitary measures, the summit turned virtual and focused on the general theme "COVID-19 and Climate Change: Living with and Learning from a Pandemic up to 2021." The last meeting took place from June 8 to 11, 2022, in Istanbul, on the topic "The Prophetic Ministry of Pope Francis and ecumenical patriarch Bartholomew."

The basic aim of all these initiatives was to highlight: (1) the urgency of the problem (since we do not have to tackle a future problem, but must react now to the worsening situation we are experiencing), (2) the moral dimension of the crisis (it is not enough simply to abstain from eating meat; a different spiritual attitude is required, which perceives everything as gift and not as individual property), (3) the need for a universal response to the challenge of the ecological crisis (the role of Christian churches and wider religious traditions is particularly critical), with the

---

18   See the official website of Halki Summit for the official statements and further information regarding the proceedings of the summits: https://www.halkisummit.com/.

cooperation of all the available powers (science, religions, technocrats, associations, individuals, etc.), so as to limit as much as possible the effects of the destruction of creation as a result of the arrogant behavior of humanity.

B. Holy and Great Synod of Crete (2016); "For the Life of the World" (2020)

After a long period of synodal aphasia, the Orthodox Church finally succeeded in convening a pan-orthodox synod in Crete upon the invitation and under the presidency of the ecumenical patriarch. Although only ten out of the fourteen Orthodox Churches gathered, the decisions of the synod were extremely important. In particular, the text entitled "The Mission of the Orthodox Church in Today's World" points to the role played by humanity in earth's destruction and humanity's responsibility to protect of the environment. As the text itself puts it: "The ecological crisis, which is connected to climate change and global warming, makes it incumbent upon the Church to do everything within her spiritual power to protect God's creation from the consequences of human greed.... Therefore, the Orthodox Church emphasizes the protection of God's creation through the cultivation of human responsibility for our God-given environment and the promotion of the virtues of frugality and self-restraint."[19]

The document titled "For the Life of the World: Toward a Social Ethos of the Orthodox Church," authored by a special commission of Orthodox scholars appointed by ecumenical patriarch Bartholomew, was partially prompted by the Holy and Great Council of the Orthodox Church held in 2016. It can definitely be as a *political manifesto* of Eastern Orthodoxy for the twenty-first century. In this document, a special section dedicated to the environment describes the role and responsibility of the Orthodox Church and the ontological interconnectedness

---

19 Holy Council, "The Mission of the Orthodox Church in Today's World," September 9, 2022, https://www.holycouncil.org/mission-orthodox-church-todays-world

of all creatures while criticizing the political and economic causes of the present disaster.[20] According to the text: "The Church calls, . . . upon the governments of the world to seek ways of advancing the environmental sciences, through education and state subventions for research, and to be willing to fund technologies that might serve to reverse the dire effects of carbon emissions, pollution, and all forms of environmental degradation."

C. Further Local Initiatives: *Archdiocese of America* and *Volos Academy for Theological Studies (Greece)* as Case Studies

"Greening Your Parish" Launched by Archdiocese of America[21]

Inspired by the work by ecumenical patriarch Bartholomew, the Department of Inter-Orthodox, Ecumenical and Interfaith Relations of the Archdiocese of America established a dedicated website that "provides resource material for fulfilling our vocation as stewards of creation and working toward greening our parishes." In this light the "'How-to' Green Your Parish" series of short videos is an initiative featuring ideas for implementing environment protection and sustainability on the parish level. The videos aim at offering a unique vision for creation care based on both the latest scientific information and the rich tradition of the Orthodox Church. In addition to this, the "Greening the Parish" webinar series explores various environmentally friendly practices, while implementing the theological vision of the salvation of the whole creation in the context of the local congregations. Another important initiative is the "Orthodox Creation Care Toolkit," which features practical methods and manuals for creation care useful on the local and parish levels. The toolkit includes diverse resources, including Sunday school lessons on the environment, ecclesiastical services devoted to the day for the protection of the environment, and list of books, articles, websites that give insights on how to green your parish.

---

20 "For the Life of the World: Towards a Social Ethos of the Orthodox Church," June 15, 2022, https://www.goarch.org/el/social-ethos.
21 See https://www.goarch.org/el/society/greening-the-parish.

Green Parish Initiative and Orthodox Faith-Based Energy Community: A Two-Step Project of the Volos Academy for Theological Studies

During the first phase of this project, the Volos Academy cooperated with World Wildlife Fund (WWF) Greece to achieve the core strategic objective of a theory of change.[22] This included encouraging and motivating Orthodox leaders from selected Balkan countries to be champions for coal phase-out and climate action. This initiative resulted in a major publication entitled *The Orthodox Church Address the Climate Change*,[23] as well as in a wider project consisting of activities carried out by the local parish the Annunciation of the Theotokos, like a series of public lectures for the general public on topical environmental issues, webinars, radio broadcasts, and blog posts.[24] In addition, a major international climate justice virtual conference was co-organized with WWF Greece in October 2021 under the general theme of the Orthodox Church's address of the climate crisis in consideration of UNFCC COP26. The conference revolved around possible good practices that take place in the various Orthodox Churches (with special emphasis on the Balkans) and relate to specific actions in parishes and monasteries, among other places, aimed at raising public awareness and addressing the consequences of climate crisis.[25]

The major objective of the second phase of the Volos initiative is the establishment of an energy community.[26] The energy community under

---

22 For a general overview of the activities and agenda of the Volos Academy for Theological Studies, see www.acadimia.org.
23 Theodota Nantsou and Nikolaos Asproulis, eds, *The Orthodox Church Address the Climate Change* (Volos: Volos Academy Publications, 2021).
24 Acidemia, "Prasini Enoria," https://www.acadimia.org/ylopoiimena-programmata/prasini-enoria.
25 Acadimia, "Prasini Enoria Vinteothiki," https://acadimia.org/ylopoiimena-programmata/prasini-enoria-vinteothiki. An official website include all the related material about the green initiatives taken on in Volos by the Volos Academy and the local diocese: http://churchgoesgreen.acadimia.org/.
26 Energy communities organize collective and citizen-driven energy actions that help pave the way for a clean energy transition while moving citizens to the fore. They contribute to increasing public acceptance of renewable energy projects and make it easier to attract private investments in the clean energy transition. At the same time, they have the potential to provide direct

consideration will be a legal entity primarily comprised of local Orthodox legal bodies (parishes of the local diocese in Volos, Greece: Metropolis of Demetrias) as well as potential individual consumers and small organizations representing the local society and economy. This development aims at producing, consuming, and sharing the needed energy between the members of the community. On a wider scale, this development is considered a unique (as an initiative of religious and faith-based bodies) pilot in the Greek context. In addition, based on the sociocultural impact of Orthodox religiosity on grassroots people for decisive change and transformation, the project seeks to carry forward a list of activities (webinar, workshop, and summer school). It encourages faith-based communities—that is parishes (priests and parishioners)—as well as ordinary people (believers or not) to become more engaged in issues of climate change, energy poverty, and green democracy. Church engagement on green issues is not only invaluable for the protection of the environment but is a journey for groups of people; not a list of moral commandments to blindly obey but a lifelong journey that needs to unfold gradually.

Despite the practical results of these initiatives, the majority of local churches, parishes, theologians, and faithful still remain, if not indifferent toward the destabilization of the climate and the catastrophe of the environment, at least without the necessary tools to conceptualize a proper ecotheological vision and relate the rich ecclesiastical tradition and doctrinal orthodoxy to our modern concerns and to the survival of the earth. If the Gospel cannot properly address the new existential challenges, then it is without meaning for the life of the world. On the contrary, if we believe that our faith has certain soteriological implications for the whole world, then an attempt is necessary to explore possible new paths of doing theology. In the remainder of this chapter, such a new way of theologizing will be outlined as a necessary step to seriously and successfully deal with climate crisis. Only if we regard the salvation of nature as an existential problem is it possible to find the proper solution. Otherwise, if we treat it in a managerial way, the result will be the overall destruction of life itself.

---

benefits to citizens by increasing energy efficiency, lowering their electricity bills, and creating local job opportunities. For more see: https://energy.ec.europa.eu/topics/markets-and-consumers/energy-communities_en.

Toward a New Way of Doing Theology: *Eco-Dogmatics*

It is well-known that dogmatics or dogmatic theology is the section of theology dealing with the arrangement and statement, as well as the interpretation, of the theoretical truths of faith concerning God *ad intra* (*theologia*) and God *ad extra* (*oikonomia*).[27] It is widely considered the core of Christian systematic theology on which all other theological disciplines are grounded.

But what about *eco-dogmatics*? This is not a new chapter of dogmatics or even a new discipline. On the contrary, by this neologism the need to use *ecology* as a *contextual* method of doing theology is expressed in view of the current climate crisis. It is not just about *creation theology*, that is an individual chapter of dogmatics that already exists in all traditional manuals, but the underlying background that substantiates every single chapter of theology (its prerequisites, method, and perspective).[28]

As a method, eco-dogmatics can make use of certain theoretical tools and assumptions of ecology, that is, the movement of materials and energy through living communities, the successional development of ecosystems, and the patterns of biodiversity and its effect on ecosystem processes. For instance, "ecosystem" itself as a concept can be useful in literal or metaphorical terms for Trinitarian theology or the eucharistic experience and practice since "an ecosystem is a geographic area where plants, animals, and other organisms, as well as weather and landscapes, work together to form a bubble of life."[29] Using all these tools that require a frank and open dialogue between (Orthodox) theology and science,[30] eco-dogmatics can

---

27 See the definition of dogmatics: Joseph Pohle, "Dogmatic Theology," in *The Catholic Encylopedia,* Vol. 14 (New York: Robert Appleton Company, 1912), https://www.newadvent.org/cathen/14580a.htm.

28 In chapter one, "Ecology as the Capacity for Love," Moltmann aims at developing a "creation teaching, which reads Genesis 1 no longer anthropocentrically but ecologically."

29 "Ecosystem," accessed November 5, 2022, https://education.nationalgeographic.org/resource/ecosystem

30 See, for example, Eftymios Nicolaidis, *Science and Eastern Orthodoxy: From the Greek Fathers to the Age of Globalization* (Baltimore: Johns Hopkins University Press, 2011); D. Buxhoeveden and Gayle Woloschak, eds., *Science and Eastern Orthodox Church* (Farnham, England: Ashgate Publishing, 2011); Al

approach in a new and constructive way certain aspects of doctrinal orthodoxy, such as the Trinitarian, Christological, anthropological, sacramental, ecclesiological, and eschatological doctrine, giving them an *incarnational* dimension badly needed today.

In this respect, the creation, *Ktisis*, the earth itself, and also matter, materiality, σάρξ (*sarx/flesh*), and animality, should no longer be regarded as external or secondary to theology. In contrast, it is the very ground through which *theologia* (λόγος περί Θεού) has become possible in the person of Christ in history. Otherwise, what we are doing is not theology but metaphysics, unrelated to creation and materiality, as an abstract reflection on first things.

Patterns of *Eco-dogmatics*

Eco-Christology: Christ as the Savior of the Whole World

So, what should we do? In more theological terms, "how did God want the world to survive?"[31] This question is not just a theoretical one but relates to both the Christian message and the current discussion about the survival of the earth. To this end, various answers have been proposed over time.

On the one hand, there is the notion of the *immortality of the soul*, an idea that dominated the ancient Greek world. However, if anything offers creation the possibility of existing in a natural way, it inevitably leads to an obligatory immortality. This is a view more or less shared today by romantics and even eco-activists who strongly oppose any human interference to provide green solutions to the climate crisis in favor of nature's own capacity to confirm its existence and survival. On the other hand, equally unacceptable is a relative solution based on *moral* or *juridical* foundations, supposing that a created being can improve itself by practicing or obeying divine, natural, or even human law. According to this view, creation can survive by putting into practice a certain political or cultural program. From a theological point of view, though, this is not the case. As Zizioulas clearly

---

Nesteruck, *Light from the East: Theology, Science and the Eastern Orthodox Tradition*, (Minneapolis: Fortress Press, 2003).

31 John Zizioulas, "Preserving God's Creation," in *The Eucharistic Communion and the World* (London: T and T Clark, 2011), 162.

states, "No, death is not conquered like that. The only thing conquered is preoccupation with the problem of death."[32]

Another way of thinking, or rather mode of life, is required here, which puts into question our given theological assumptions. Theology needs to appeal to the patristic concept of *hypostatic union*, which prioritizes personhood over the two natures of Christ without, however, bringing them into opposition. It was Maximus the Confessor (580–662), who, by working deeply in Christological lines, pointed out the need for a relationship between the created and the uncreated to overcome death. It is the human being who was meant to undertake this role. However, the fall foiled this divinely ordained task, necessitating a change of the divine plan. What was required now was for the Logos to become human.

The Chalcedonian Definition, particularly the clauses "without confusion" and "without division," describes the relationship between God and humanity in Christ.[33] The "without division" highlights the necessity of no separation between created and uncreated, since there must be also real communion at the ontological level to avoid the self-referentiality of the creation and of death. The former ("without confusion") guarantees freedom, personal otherness, and the dignity of the two realities; otherwise, the relationship would not be free, but mandatory. The two concepts are mediated in Christ, in whom communion and otherness coincide. Christ's resurrection offers the whole of creation salvation and a definitive victory over death. But still, is this perception of the close relation between created and uncreated in Christ sufficient to deal with the overturning of the catastrophic consequences of the climate crisis? It seems that another, more advanced step is required here, which construes Christology in a greener way. To this end, it needs to appeal to the concept of deep incarnation.

At the heart of the deep incarnation perspective is a fresh reception and interpretation of the historical roots of doctrinal orthodoxy. One by no means should understand deep incarnation as a development of Christian

---

32 John Zizioulas, *Communion and Otherness: Further Studies in Personhood and the Church* (London: T and T Clark, 2006), 258.

33 Bindley, *The Oecuminical Documents of the Faith*, https://earlychurchtexts.com/main/chalcedon/chalcedonian_definition.shtml.

doctrine. It has been mainly articulated as a response to the liberal Christology developed by Friedrich Schleiermacher (1768–1834), according to whom God is fully present only in Jesus's divine consciousness, while humanity (meaning body and flesh) is considered an instrument of sin and death, not of salvation. On the contrary, deep incarnation stresses the importance of both fleshliness (materiality) and human consciousness in Christ. Thus, it tries to combine the biology of growth, vulnerability, and decay (which characterizes created order) with religious awareness, creation in its entirety, and Jesus as a complete human being. In this respect, deep incarnation focuses not only on the person of Jesus and his personal history but takes into consideration the human, natural, and cultural environment of Jesus in its entirety—that is, his co-patriot Jews, his interlocutors (Samaritan people and others), and the fauna and flora of ancient Israel.

According to Niels Henrik Gregersen, a contemporary spokesperson of this theory, deep incarnation "was not only about evolutionary thinking but also about ecological thinking: how to rescue a flourishing and inhabitable planet from too linear, too anthropocentric ways of thinking." And he continues that it is about "divine assumption of the full ecospace of the material world of creation." Such a deep view of incarnation implies "an incarnation into the very tissue of biological existence, and system of nature." The focus here is "on the cross of Christ as a divine self-identification with the frailty and pain of biological creatures."[34]

Although protestant in its roots, deep incarnation bears sound patristic and medieval parallels, by which it gives to Christ the proper attention as the only mediator between created and uncreated, as the only person who assumed the fullness of cosmic materiality as the only condition for the entire planet to be ontologically saved. Without going into full details here, one can certainly refer to the well-known saying by Gregory Nazianzus: "What has not been assumed, has not been healed."[35]

---

34   Niels Henrik Gregersen, "Deep Incarnation: From Deep History to Post-axial Religion," *HTS Teologiese Studies/Theological Studies* 72/4 (2006): 9; Denis Edwards, *Deep Incarnation: God's Redemptive Suffering with Creatures* (Maryknoll, NY: Orbis, 2019).
35   Gregory Nazianzus, "Epistle 101," *PG* 37,181.

The meaning of the saying is clear: God became in Jesus not only fully human (not to say just man) but a complete created being, since he entered the created order to save the whole creation from corruption and death. In a similar vein, one can appeal to Maximus the Confessor's doctrine of the *Logos* and *logoi* of creation.[36] According to this doctrine, everything that exists bears within itself a logos, by which it enters into a constant dialogue with its source, the Logos of God. In this line, one can clearly argue that everything participates to some extent in the divine, without however the existing ontological break between created and uncreated to be naturally overcome. Panentheism (not pantheism) must also be understood in this same Christological direction of deep incarnation, where "God (i.e., Christ) is found in all things, yet at the same time is beyond and above all things."[37]

Creatio ex nihilo: The Inherent Value of Creation

The most basic question related to the biblical story of creation revolves around the proper understanding of the concept of *creation* itself. The fact that the world had a beginning in an absolute sense was, according to John Zizioulas, "utter nonsense and absurdity to all ancient Greek thinkers."[38] The idea of the radical beginning got, as a profound novelty, attention from the early period of Christianity and has been carefully unfolded by the early church fathers. For Athanasius of Alexandria, for instance, it was the idea of creation per se that required a beginning in an absolute sense, an argument underlining that between God and the world there is an ontological chasm. A Christian view of creation is founded on the acknowledgment of the radical beginning of created existence, as well as of the un-originated existence of the Creator. "Creation as 'ktisis' is a notion encountered for the first time . . . with Apostle Paul, and it clearly

---

36 Torstein Theodor Tollefsen, *The Christocentric Cosmology of St Maximus the Confessor* (Oxford: Oxford University Press 2008), 64–137.
37 Nikolaos Asproulis, "Metropolitan Kallistos Ware of Diokleia, between the Neo-patristic Synthesis and the Russian Religious Renaissance: An Example of the Reception of the Patristic Tradition," *International Journal for the Study of the Christian Church*, 19, no. 4, (2019): 212–229.
38 Chryssavgis and Asproulis, *Priests of Creation*, 109.

presupposes an absolutely ontological beginning."[39] With this, Zizioulas stresses the relevance of the term "creation" and further outlines the need to introduce a new concept, that of "ktisiology," to Christian vocabulary. By using the term "ktisis" rather than *demiourgia*," Zizioulas emphasizes the ontologically absolute character of the beginning of creation, which the church fathers ontologically interpreted as creation "from (absolute) nothing." As he further explains: "The idea that the world has an absolute beginning could only be expressed through the formula that the world was created 'out of nothing,' ex nihilo." Since the time of the early church (Athanasius and Nicaea I), an awareness gradually developed that between God and the world "there exists an absolute, 'abysmal' otherness."[40] If it is possible for something to arise from nothing, then it is also possible that a totally other being could exist vis-á-vis God's being. By emphasizing "creatio ex nihilo," one makes clear that the world is not eternal. If the world was eternal it would not need to be created, and if it was not created from nothing, then the world was created from something that has some other existence. This is clearly a reversal of the ancient view and leads to the conclusion that "existence is the fruit of freedom,"[41] since the self-referentiality of being, as perceived in ancient thought, is now abolished. The doctrine of creation out of nothing has clear ecological implications. Insofar as the world is considered a gift of God, then any dualism that undermines the dignity of the world's materiality is excluded. The fact that the world was created out of nothing and is not eternal means that there is also the possibility to return to nothing, and it cannot live eternally on its own right. On the other hand, if creation is a gift, then it by no means possesses any natural or other means to guarantee eternal survival. Today this is an uncontested reality, when the environmental crisis threatens the very sustainability and the future of the planet in its entirety. It is sufficient here to refer to global warming and the radical consequences of climate change for biodiversity and the survival of all creatures, including human beings, in order to realize that our world as such, meaning as created order, is, today as never before, under the yoke of death. *Creatio ex nihilo* grants to

---

39 Zizioulas, *Communion and Otherness*, 253.
40 Zizioulas, *The Eucharistic Communion*, 158.
41 Zizioulas, *Communion and Otherness*, 255.

the world a unique value, bringing to the fore its innate dignity. By doing so, the Christian view differs from other cosmological views like emanation, a concept developed in Far East spirituality, based on the conviction of a full equation between God and the world. While emanation provides the conceptual frame for a pantheistic reception of creation, the Christian innovation by the *creatio ex nihilo* doctrine emphasizes the fragility and uniqueness of the finite world understood as a living organism that requires constant dialogue with God to live eternally.

According to Daniel Munteanu, "Maximus the Confessor's theology of *creatio originalis* and of the new creation as transfigured universe, allows us to speak about the theological dignity of matter as the 'home of God,' as well as a field of dialogue between creator and human beings."[42]

Christian Anthropology: From *Imago Dei* to *Imago Mundi*

The time has come to focus on Christian anthropology and possible redefinitions from an ecological perspective. By redefining the image of God in a more inclusive way through the lens of "dinivanimality,"[43] theology can provide an all-embracing anthropology that would account for the particular place and reception of animals, as well as all creatures, and creation in toto not only in our discourse but also in our practice. If one defines the human from the standpoint of a personalist ontology,[44] then the human cannot be understood without a clear reference to a "You" and an "it." "Every part of creation matters,"[45] or every single creature of God matters. *Imago Dei* is incomplete unless the whole creation is recognized as being a constitutive part of it. Again, patristic tradition is quite illuminating here. In his effort to deal with the opponents of the hesychast tradition and the

---

42 Daniel Munteanu, "Cosmic Liturgy: The Theological Dignity of Creation as a Basis of an Orthodox Ecotheology," *International Journal of Public Theology* 4, no. 3 (2010): 332.

43 Stephen Moore, ed., *Divinanimality: Animal Theory, Creaturely Theology* (New York: Fordham University Press, 2014).

44 John Zizioulas, *Being as Communio: Studies in Personhood and the Church* (New York: St. Vladimir's Seminary Press, 1985).

45 See Kees Nieuwerth, Peter Pavlovic, and Adrian Shaw, eds., *Every Part of Creation Matters*, CEC Series No. 8 (Geneva: Globethics Publications, 2022).

role of the body in attaining the divine light, Gregory Palamas argues that "every kind of creature ... is also able to participate in the one who lies above everything, in order for the image of God to be completed."[46]

Such an inclusive understanding of *imago Dei* points, perhaps unconsciously, to the concept of *imago mundi*. Contemporary theologians have used this term to redefine human identity in light of the urgent climate crisis.[47] If the image of God in humanity cannot fully manifest without taking into account all the creatures, this clearly means that animals, as well as the whole creation, do share in the salvation of the whole creation, and that they do join heaven.[48] After all, this is the ultimate goal of the divine plan as it was finally realized through Christ's paschal mystery: the salvation (*theosis*) of the entire world, not only of humanity. Otherwise, the nonhuman creation would have been created in vain ("Man and beast thou savest, O Lord" [Ps. 36:6b]), and the Pauline premises that the whole earth will be saved, and Christ will "unite all things in Him, things in heaven and things on earth" (Eph. 1:9–10) would sound irrelevant.

In this vein, theological anthropology should ascribe priority to communion/relation as that dimension of the *imago* which points to the ontological affinity between all the existent nonhuman creatures.[49] In anthropology, it is the personalist and relational understanding of human beings that seeks to overcome the alleged fixed dichotomy between humanity and nature.

---

46   Gregory Palamas, "Against Akindynos," 7, 11, 36. 25–28.

47   As Moltmann puts it, "Before human beings are an *imago Dei*, they are an *imago mundi*, a microcosm in which all previous life forms are integrated," in his *Hope in These Troubled Times* (Geneva: WCC Publications, 2010), 19. See also A.C. Rabie-Boshoff, "Imago Mundi: Justice of Peace," *HTS Teologiese Studies/Theological Studies* 78 no. 2, (2022): 1–7.

48   Such a revisiting of the *imago Dei* should bear clear implications for all chapters of Christian doctrine, taking into account the cosmos itself (including of course humans) as a gift created by God out of nothing in order to share in his love and eternal salvation.

49   Quite interestingly, Ivone Gabara in chapter two ("Interdependence, Christianity, and Environmental Crisis") stresses this core and often forgotten dimension.

From Stewardship to the Priest of Creation?

According to the Greek patristic tradition, the human being functions as the bond or the bridge between God and creation. Against the prevailing understanding of the *imago Dei* as chiefly referring to the human mind (*ratio*), the Greek Fathers represent a different perception from the point of view of freedom. According to this understanding, freedom should be considered "the ability to affirm or deny the very existence of something . . . to either destroy creation or affirm its existence."[50] The current ecological crisis clearly highlights the relevance of such an understanding of human freedom. To be clear, contemporary currents of theology credit Darwinism (not always without reservations) and modern quantum physics for highlighting the innate interconnection, or rather ontological interdependence, between humanity, other creatures, and the whole earth. A human being is nothing but an animal, an "autexousious animal," though "with a difference of degree, but not of kind" to other creatures.[51] It is due to freedom that human beings possess the capacity to "transcend the limitations of nature to the point of denying nature itself or anything given."[52] It is exactly here that human's role as priest of creation emerges. In Eucharist, humanity undertakes this priestly role, acting on behalf of God himself by offering the creation in its entirety to God the Father so as to gain eternal life. This renders human beings an indispensable component for creation, in contrast with certain contemporary ecological views that deprive humanity of its role and responsibility in saving creation.

By Way of Conclusion

The climate crisis is not something to be dealt with in a managerial way. As the ultimate evil of our era, it should be clearly understood as an existential problem, or rather as an ecological sin, the fruit of human beings' disobedience to God's commandment to preserve and care for the planet. We live in

---

50 Zizioulas, "Creation Theology: An Orthodox Perspective," in *Priests of Creation*, ed. John Chryssavgis and Nikolaos Asproulis, 41.
51 Zizioulas, 42.
52 Zizioulas.

a critical time; radical action is required to change our egocentric lifestyle and consumerist culture that prevents us from finding real meaning in life. To this end we need a theology that will undertake the risk to closely work and cooperate with environmental sciences and ecology, and, by deeply diving in its own tradition and using an ecotheological hermeneutic, bring to the fore those elements necessary to address climate crisis. Both the long history of the church and the recent initiatives described above are nothing more than an attempt to cope with ecological evil and the disorder caused by creation, offering a new vision in the framework of cosmological *theosis* that remains the central goal of life in Christ.

PART 3

SAMPLING ECOTHEOLOGICAL CONCERNS IN DISTINCT CONTEXTS AND CHRISTIAN TRADITIONS

CHAPTER 7

IN SOLIDARITY WITH MOTHER EARTH: AFRICAN CHRISTIANITY AND THE LOVE OF GOD IN THE CONTEXT OF A DEGRADED EARTH

Ben-Willie Kwaku Golo

INTRODUCTION

Environmental degradation has become one of the most pressing challenges that humankind has to deal with in recent decades as it poses a significant threat to humanity. Negative environmental conditions place humankind in vulnerable and precarious situations. For instance, increased precipitation and extreme heat in different areas of sub-Saharan Africa will affect agriculture through increased plant growth but lower yields.[1] Already, the World Meteorological Organisation (WMO) reports that the rate of temperature in Africa has increased in recent decades, with severe climate-related hazards such as heatwaves, floods, tropical cyclones, and prolonged droughts affecting over 110 million people.[2] Climate change is a dire issue because its negative effects are far-reaching.

Admitting that Africa is most vulnerable to the impacts of climate change due to its low adaptive capacity and overdependence on natural resource-based livelihoods, André Pelser and Rujeko Chimukuche aver

---

[1] Thomas Ackerman, "A Scientist's Perspective," in *Loving the Least of These: Addressing a Changing Environment*, ed. Dorothy Boorse (Washington, DC: National Association of Evangelicals, 2011), 21.

[2] World Meteorological Organization, "Africa Suffers Disproportionately from Climate Change," 2023, https://public.wmo.int/en/media/press-release/africa-suffers-disproportionately-from-climate-change.

that two sources of livelihood, namely agriculture and fishing, are already under pressure from climate change. Projected trends in rainfall and temperature "are likely to exacerbate existing patterns of poverty, food insecurity, and forced migration in sub-Saharan Africa."[3] Similarly, noting that sub-Saharan Africa depends heavily on precipitation for water and food, thereby making the region's food systems highly sensitive to changes in precipitation,[4] many studies have projected how "current and future impacts of climate change on either water resources, land resources or food systems, and how these impacts further affect the lives of people who depend on them."[5] It has been further emphasized that discussions on climate change reveal "a fact that nature will suffer from the consequences, but we need to realize that humans who are the main perpetrators are equally the main victims of climate change. This is because our well-being depends on nature and its services."[6]

Thus, environmental problems do not create vulnerabilities only to human beings in Africa, but also to the entire creation of God, which believers have been admonished to take good care of (Gen. 2: 15). The church in Africa and its theology are confronted with a fundamental theological and ethical problem, which requires deep, convincing, and practical responses. This is crucial if the church is to give a good account of itself and show its readiness to respond to the times in which her followers and the society find themselves. In the following pages, I suggest the converging theological and ethical virtue of loving God as transformative in developing a contextualized Christian theology, ethic, and praxis aimed at a sustainable human-creation relationship and the well-being of the creation. Further, in the context of Africa, I submit that Indigenous ontologies and affirmations regarding the creation—Mother Earth—are quite

---

3   André J. Pelser and Rujeko Samanthia Chimukuche, "Climate Change, Rural Livelihoods, and Human Well-Being: Experiences from Kenya," *IntechOpen* (2022): 1, doi:http://dx.doi.org/10.5772/intechopen.104965.

4   Samuel Appiah Ofori, Samuel Jerry Cobbina, and Samuel Obiri, "Climate Change, Land, Water, and Food Security: Perspectives from Sub-Saharan Africa." *Front. Sustain. Food Syst.* 5, no. 680924 (2021): 2, doi: 10.3389/fsufs.2021.680924.

5   Ofori et al., "Climate Change and Food Security," 2.

6   Ofori et al, "Climate Change and Food Security." 2

similar to the biblical narrative and can be enriching to developing the Christian theological virtue and praxis of loving God through loving the earth (God's creation) and being in solidarity with Mother Earth.

In the following pages, I open the discussion with a theological ethical review of the theme of loving God in Christian theological ethics. This is followed by an exploration of what it means to love God in the context of a degraded earth, after which I examine African cosmology and idea of Mother Earth and its relationship with the biblical vision. The next section is devoted to discussing an African Christian perspective of solidarity with Mother Earth as loving God in the context of the degraded earth and environmental threats. The discussion ends with the conclusion that extending love to Mother Earth is also a way of expressing love to God and that the Indigenous African religious ecology provides a reservoir of sources relevant for enriching the scope and content of African Christian ecotheology.

GOD'S LOVE: A THEOLOGICAL ETHICAL PERSPECTIVE

According to Christian teaching, because Christian love flows from God as a measure of God's grace located within God's love itself, a foundation to understanding the love of God and neighbor is the understanding of the love of God, out of which we have been called and which we are required to extend to others. According to Carson, God is love intrinsically and constitutively to the extent that "he can no more abandon love than he can turn away from holiness."[7] The Bible speaks of this love of God in several distinguishable ways. Carson and Field have identified five of these as popular among Christians.[8]

First, the intra-Trinitarian love which is the perichoretic love that exists within the Trinity, especially between the Father and Son by which the Father was determined to show the Son everything he does

---

7   D.A Carson, "Love," in *New Dictionary of Biblical Theology*, ed. T. Desmond Alexander and Brian S. Rosner (Downers Grove: InterVarsity Press, 2000), 646.

8   Carson, "Love," 646–650; David H. Field, "Love," in *New Dictionary of Christian Ethics and Pastoral Theology*, ed. David J. Atkinson and David H. Field (Downers Grove, IL: InterVarsity Press, 1995), 9–10.

and to ensure that all honor the Son as they honor the Father; as well as the Son responding in love of the Father, which was displayed in the perfection of his obedience.[9] This Field sees as the true meaning of the love of God.[10] Second is God's providential love manifested in God's care and support of the products of God's own hand, which equally means products of God's love (as seen in Gen. 1:31 and Matt. 5:44–45).[11] The Bible paints this providential love as supporting, forgiving, and caring for God's people just as a farmer cares for the vineyard and a shepherd for their sheep.[12]

The third notable expression of the love of God is God's salvific and redemptive love, which moves toward human beings, even those who are rebellious and evil.[13] It is this love that moved God to send Jesus Christ to the created world to live among human beings for the salvation and deliverance of sinful and rebellious humanity. Identified also as practical, this salvific and redemptive love of God intervenes in human affairs, as in the case of Israel redeeming them from Egypt. Vulnerable minority groups, such as widows, orphans, and immigrants, benefited from this great support of love.[14] The fourth expression and exhibition of God's love is elective love, which saw God choose Israel for himself, not because they were his choice but "he loved them because he loved them: one cannot probe further back than that."[15]

The fifth expression is identified as God's conditional and covenantal love. This is the love that flows from God to human beings because they have kept the conditions of the covenant and have been obedient (see 1 John 4:10).[16] It is suggested that it is within the framework of the covenant that the most striking feature of God's love is displayed; this love can be described as "everlasting."[17]

---

9 Carson, "Love," 648; Field, "Love," 9.
10 Field, "Love," 9.
11 Carson, "Love," 648.
12 Field, "Love," 10.
13 Carson, "Love," 648.
14 Field, "Love," 10.
15 Carson, "Love," 648.
16 Carson, "Love," 648.
17 Field, "Love," 10.

Clearly, the Christian understanding of the love of God is that God's love springs from within God's self toward the world and pours out on sinners who, to some extent, may be regarded as enemies or rebellious of God. Hence, God's love is not dependent on the loveliness of the person or thing loved.[18] This love, as we have seen, is relational, providential, redemptive, elective, and covenantal; all of which suggests that the love of God is aimed at relationships that manifest toward others. Implied in God's love, therefore, is a concern for those in need of this love—the products of his hands. Similarly, the love of God does not manifest in vacuum—it manifests itself and operates toward an object. The highest point of display of this love is God's plan of redemption for humanity through his son, Jesus Christ, who himself symbolizes the love of God. Thus, it is noted by Field that 1 John 4:10–11 depicts the Christian love ethic as theocentric because the origin of genuine loving is located with God's gracious initiative. It is also Christocentric because the Son is the focal point of the Father's love.[19] As depicted practically in the death and resurrection of Christ, this love is active, self-sacrificial, and demands a reciprocal initiative response from its beneficiaries—Christians.[20]

Consequently, the Bible summons men and women again and again to live a life of love, and the self-giving of Jesus Christ spurs his brothers and sisters to live a life of love like his.[21] In the context of climate change and environmental degradation, this would mean living a life of sacrifice of the self for others—in this case, for the oppressed, poor victims of climate change. This is because love shown to God's people is love shown to God. In the Christian community, the New Testament view of God's love insists that love must be a distinguishing feature of church life as the archetype and kingpin of all relations, because to love the neighbor is both a sign of obedience to God and a genuine response to the love we receive from God.[22] This love, at times, will require that the person loving surrenders some personal rights and interests in solidarity of the one loved.

---

18 Carson, "Love," 649; Field, "Love," 12.
19 Field, "Love," 9.
20 Field, "Love," 9.
21 Field, "Love," 10.
22 Field, "Love," 11.

Therefore, in the teachings of Jesus, there is significant unity between loving God and loving the neighbor. This is clear in Jesus's commandment, "You must love the Lord your God with all your heart, all your soul, and all your mind" (Matt. 22:37-39).[23] This is the first and greatest and greatest commandment. A second is equally important: "Love your neighbor as yourself" (Mark 12:28-31). The answer provided by Jesus Christ is a bringing together of two crucial Old Testament passages, which are Deuteronomy 6:4-5 and Leviticus 19:18.[24] To Christian ethicists, the answer of Christ is profound and distinct: "Love shown to God's people is love shown to him . . . while the proof of genuine love for others is obedient love to their heavenly Father."[25] This is what some recognize as the cornerstone of Christian ethics and practice—the need to look beyond our immediate toward a dynamic and pragmatic vision of Christian affirmations. It's a life commitment.[26]

It has been debated how Christians practically express their claims of the love of God and the neighbor. This particularly concerns the Greek verb *agapao* and its derivatives that are rather obscure in pre-Christian literature.[27] However, in conformity to the New Testament and Christian ethical teachings, the most notable understanding of God's love is the Greek word *agape*, which is identified as the headline of all other virtues (Col. 3:14) and described as the nature of the Father.[28] According to Field, it is not surprising that the New Testament writers refused to use the various Greek words for love—*eros* (acquisitive love), *storge* (family love), *phillia/phileo* (friendly affection)—and instead chose *agape* as the Christian expression of love, a word that also reveals the characteristics of God's love.[29]

---

23 All quotations in this article are taken from the New Living Translation (NLT).
24 Field, "Love," 11; Carson, Love," 649.
25 Field, "Love," 11.
26 Glen S. Stassen and David P. Gushee 2003. *Kingdom Ethics: Following Jesus in Contemporary Context* (Downers Grove, IL: InterVaristy Press, 2003).
27 Field, "Love," 11; Carson, "Love," 646-647.
28 Field, "Love," 11.
29 Field, "Love," 12.

Glen Stassen and David Gushee identify four different strands of *agape*, with the kind that Jesus Christ taught being most important to Christians today.[30] The first strand, from the perspective of Anders Nygren, is *agape* as sacrificial love; the second strand, espoused by Daniel Day Williams, is *agape* as mutual love; the third is *agape* as equal regard; and the fourth is *agape* as liberating love, which Stassen and Gushee define as the kind of love taught and lived by Jesus Christ. Love here is not just a single principle but "a complex drama with different dramatic actions as the characters grow and interact."[31] This teaching was in response to the lawyer who came asking Jesus Christ how to attain eternal life and who his neighbor was—the story of the good Samaritan (Luke 10:25–37). Guided by the parable of the good Samaritan, proponents of delivering love identify four acts that should be considered as crucial in the practice of delivering love, especially in our world today, which is full of greed and individualism.[32] These acts, which correspond to the themes that run through the biblical books of Exodus, Leviticus, Hosea, Luke, and John, are: (1) love sees with compassion and enters into the situation of persons in bondage; (2) love does deeds of deliverance; it is action-oriented; (3) love (*agape*) invites people into community with freedom, justice, and responsibility for the future; and (4) love confronts those who exclude as it delivers from bondage and oppression.[33]

From an ethical perspective, therefore, while all the strands of *agape* are still relevant, what is notable in Jesus's teaching on the good Samaritan is a radicalized and enlarged definition of love (*agape*) in very comprehensive and practical ways that lend themselves to confronting and dealing with contemporary issues,[34] such as climate change and climate injustice. Consequently, the four acts taught by Jesus Christ become a preferred ethical framework for working toward a Christian ethic of love that solidarizes with Mother Earth in an era of degraded earth and environmental threats in Africa.

---

30   Stassen and Gushee, *Kingdom Ethics*, 327–344.
31   Stassen and Gushee, *Kingdom Ethics*, 333.
32   Stassen and Gushee, *Kingdom Ethics*, 334.
33   Stassen and Gushee, *Kingdom Ethics*, 334–338.
34   Stassen and Gushee, *Kingdom Ethics*, 340–341.

Loving God in the Context of a Degraded Earth

As loving God practically crystallizes in neighborly love, it is suggested: "For us to be faithful in loving God, we must love our neighbor."[35] This extends to taking care of the poor and oppressed, which is a resounding theme in both the Old and New Testaments, as emphasized in Deuteronomy 15:10–11.[36] Evidently, whatever the country in which the poor live, they are by and large the most vulnerable to the impacts of climate change and must remain the focus of concern and attention in the Christian love response to a degraded earth.[37] It is a call to neighborly love in response to a loving God and "the Christian thing to do."[38]

Therefore, Christians are invited into a loving relationship with God manifested in the reciprocal action of loving God through love and justice to fellow human neighbors, particularly the poor, vulnerable, and disenfranchised. Consequently, the church and its theology promote the well-being and flourishing lives of other humans—our neighbors—particularly those who have been rendered victims of negative environmental change. Within the context of a degraded earth, particularly climate change, and in light of the liberating love taught by Jesus Christ, the love required of Christians and the church identifies (with) poor victims of climate change with compassion, engaging in praxis that delivers them from the injustice and violence of negative environmental change and delivering them into a community that is dignifying and humane.

Practical and actionable engagements, as our expressions of love, would be required to deliver victims of climate change from further environmental harm, preventing the mortgaging of and working toward the well-being of future generations. In the context of a degraded earth, what

---

35 Ken Wilson, "A Biblical Basis for Christian Engagement: A Pastor's Perspective," in *Loving the Least of These: Addressing a Changing Environment*, ed. Dorothy Boorse (Washington, DC: National Association of Evangelicals, 2011), 11.
36 Wilson, "A Biblical Basis," 9.
37 David G. Hallman, "Climate Change and Poverty—Science, Theology and Ethics: A Discussion Paper for the National Religious Partnership on the Environment," (unpublished Paper, September, 2005), 5.
38 Leith Anderson, preface to *Loving the Least of These: Addressing a Changing Environment*, ed. Dorothy Boorse, 5.

is best required is solidarity with victims, which is the social expression of love and related to justice. It is important for Christians to understand that there is no tension between the two because there is an important dialectic between love and justice, for love presupposes and transcends justice in Christian ethics.[39] The love of God for justice, which is grounded in God's love for the victims of injustice, enjoins Christians to do justice and fight for the unjust treatment of others out of love.[40]

There is, however, another dimension to the discussion of neighborly love as loving God and what that means in the context of a degraded earth. Christian theology and teaching traditionally affirm that Christians only truly love God when they love their neighbors. However, one cannot claim neighborly love when they induce ecological imbalance and threaten the natural world, which is in a symbiotic relationship with humans. One sneezes and someone else catches a cold; such are the causes and effects of climate change in the human-nonhuman world relationship. Thus, it becomes clear, as Mercy Oduyoye avers, that the neighbor requiring Christian liberating love is not only the next door neighbor but also the earth, which is threatened with annihilation because when "air and water and vegetation are in danger, human life too is endangered. With the awareness of ecology, human vision of neighborliness has begun to expand to include all creation, seen and unseen. Loving our neighbor has come to mean recycling, reforestation and cleaning up the waters around us."[41] Consequently, the love of fellow human beings, whose lives and existences depend on the cosmic neighbor, the earth or creation, requires that we love the earth. This is because a genuine Christian love for others is largely measured by concerns for their living environment, whether they induce impoverishment and death or affirm human dignity and promote flourishing life. Protecting and safeguarding the dignity of the earth is as good as protecting and safeguarding the dignity of the human neighbor.

---

39 Cathriona Russell, "Burden-sharing in a Changing Climate: Which Principles and Practices Can Theologians Endorse?" *Studies in Christian Ethics* 24, no.1 (2011): 70.
40 Field, "Love," 13.
41 Oduyoye, *Beads and Strands: Reflections of an African Woman on Christianity in Africa* (Maryknoll, NY: Orbis, 2004), 46.

Furthermore, the creation remains a medium through which the Creator reveals (communicates) and interacts with humans (Rom. 1:20) and a place and context where the divine-human encounter takes place.[42] This neighbor has, for a long time, not been central in Christian theological thinking as a natural and ontological partner to human beings in God's plan of salvation and restoration through Jesus Christ. Hence, it is suggested that, while loving God will fundamentally mean spending time in worship and prayer, another way to express our love for God is active commitments to the things of God.[43] This includes, as already mentioned, fellow human beings and "caring about what happens to God's creation because God cares about it and because God gave us the job of caring for it. We worship God by caring for creation. We don't worship creation. God created the world for his glory, and because of this, it reveals his glory to us."[44] Thus, Christians are invited to love the creation of God, which is of the order of love,"[45] and our love of God enjoins us to love all that God loves. Christian solidarity can only be possible in an environment of a genuine Christian expression of the love of God toward the neighbor, broadly defined to include Mother Earth.

African Cosmology and the Biblical Vision

Strikingly reminiscent of the biblical story of creation from the earth (Gen. 2:7), many African Indigenous ideas of creation—cosmologies—indicate how humankind is physically a product from the earth and intrinsically of the earth.[46] These cosmologies, which are still widespread in African

---

42 Ben-Willie Kwaku Golo, "Redeemed from the Earth? Environmental Change and Salvation Theology in African Christianity," *Scriptura: International Journal of Bible, Religion and Theology in Southern Africa*, 111 (2012): 354.
43 Wilson, "A Biblical Basis," 9.
44 Wilson, "A Biblical Basis," 9.
45 Pope Francis, "Encyclical Letter Laudato Si' of the Holy Father Francis On the Care for Our Common Home" (2015): 56. Accessed at: https://www.vatican.va/content/dam/francesco/pdf/encyclicals/documents/papa-francesco_20150524_enciclica-laudato-si_en.pdf.
46 See John S. Mbiti, *African Religions and Philosophy* (London: Heinemann, 1969), 102.

societies, life, and thought, underscore that it is out of the earth that humans and nonhumans attain their forms of being. John Mbiti defines the ontological connection of human beings to plants, animals, and nonliving objects as kinship.[47] The earth, then, is our kindred.

Related to the ontological and intrinsic symbiotic relationship of humanity to the earth is an anthropomorphic understanding of the earth as a living female deity—a goddess—with diverse names in the African culture, largely translated as "Mother Earth." The idea of the earth as a mother and goddess (with feminine attributes and connotations) is not unpopular in African cosmology. The female attributes of the earth are conceptualized with the understanding that the earth is not just a thing but a living entity. This is similar to *Gaian* understandings of the earth in the science and ethics of ecology. For instance, in the Akan and the Ewes cultures of Ghana, the notion of the earth as a mother who has either hewn humankind with the help of God or from whom humans are hewn is popular. Among the Akans, this "Mother Earth" is known as *Asase Yaa*, a goddess born on a Thursday, and the Ewes refer to her as *Mianor Zordzie*, literally "our mother on whom we trek."

This deified view that Indigenous African cultures hold of the earth is due to their belief in its divine origin. The earth is understood as imbued by the divine creator with the capacity to generate, enhance, and support life or inversely to diminish, frustrate, and endanger—all in response to how humans treat it. Hence, from within African cosmology emerges the ontology that the earth is a unique and purposeful creation of God.[48] Thus, Indigenous people do not see the natural world just as any other object—it is an organism, a living organism capable of sustaining itself and those connected with it when properly maintained. Consequently, while seeing the earth as a goddess, Indigenous Africans affirm their love and care of the earth and natural world due to its embedded goodness as a divine creation and for the sustenance and benefit of human beings.[49]

---

47   Mbiti, *African Religions*, 102.
48   Ben-Willie Kwaku Golo, Hasskei Mohammed Majeed, and Nancy O. Myles, "Akan Religious Ontology and Environmental Sustainability in Ghana," *Worldviews*, 27 (2023): 101.
49   Golo, Majeed, and Myles, "Akan Ontology," 90, 98, 99.

Ontologically, African notions of communality underscore a symbiotic bondedness between human and nonhuman beings and communities, where nature is regarded as "an interconnected continuum of humans and all natural objects which exist in harmony."[50] This is because, as Bujo states, "no one can actually be free and articulate one's humanity if one does not live in harmony with nature."[51] The notion of the earth as a mother, therefore, implies that humans and the biophysical creation are offspring of Mother Earth. The clarity here is an affirmation of an ontological relationship between humans, the earth, and other created beings, which are more naturally considered to be of the earth than human beings. From this cosmology is derived the ontology of humans as naturally of the earth; and the vulnerability of human beings is regarded as the vulnerability of the earth and its nonhuman offspring, with the reverse also being true. This finds connection and analogs with the biblical vision of creaturely relationships. Within the biblical vision, reflected in instances such as God's covenant with Noah (Gen. 9: 9–10), which is significantly close to the Indigenous African worldview, humans live in covenanted and ontological connection with the creation, suggesting that creation is not only the neighborhood to humans but the neighbor.[52]

The biblical story of creation theologically grounds our ontological covenanted relationship with the earth. Just as Adam was hewn from the earth, thereby making him part of the creation (cosmos) and responsible to serve its ends rather than making him apart from it,[53] so is the whole of humanity was hewn from the earth, according to the Christian story. Here,

---

50 Polycarp A. Ikuenobe, "Traditional African Environmental Ethics and Colonial Legacy," *International Journal of Philosophy and Theology*, 2, no. 4 (2014): 1–21, 2.

51 Benezet Bujo, *The Ethical Dimension of Community: The African Model and the Dialogue between North and South* (Nairobi: Paulines Publications, 1998), 148.

52 Ben-Willie Kwaku Golo, "The Groaning Earth and the Greening of Neo-Pentecostalism in Twenty-first Century Ghana," *PentecoStudies: An Interdisciplinary Journal for Research on the Pentecostal and Charismatic Movements*, 13, no. 2 (2014): 207–8.

53 James Jones, "The Son of Man Came Eating and Drinking," in *Consumption, Christianity and Creation* (Paper presentation, Centre for Sustainable Consumption, Sheffield Hallam University, Sheffield, UK, July 5, 2002).

we see a similarity or convergence with the genesis of humanity linked to the natural world in Indigenous cosmology and ontology, suggesting the closeness and natural symbiosis between the cosmos and humans. Within this covenanted relationship with nature and other human beings, humans live, in the words of Santmire, as *homo cooperans* (humans as those who cooperate) and not as *homo faber* (humans as those who make).[54] This covenanted relationship with the natural world requires that humans are restrained in their exploitative and consumerist desires, for these conflict with God's plans for the creation and the desire of God for humans to cooperate with God and other beings within creation in maintaining the integrity of the creation (Gen. 2:15).

From this perspective, the Biblical vision of the story of the first humans in the garden God planted in Eden, and where the first human beings were placed (Gen. 2:8–3:24) in eco-communality with other creatures after been hewn from the earth, becomes paradigmatic. The ontological relationship between humans and the natural world became disrupted when humans fell out with God because of human beings' desire to "be like God" (Gen. 3.5b), which probably means to not die and to have creative knowledge of how to live eternally on the resources made available by God (Gen. 3:3–5). The consequence was human beings and the natural world becoming subject to decay and corruption—the reason for the groaning of creation (Rom. 8:22). The predilection of contemporary human beings toward runaway production and profligate consumption and materialism, which have largely brought humanity to this environmental tipping point, falls into the same category.

The love, care, and closeness that Indigenous Africans exhibit toward Mother Earth are, first, made in response to the love and goodness of God by returning love, worship, and commitment to him for the gift of creation; and second, they are an exhibit of their responsibility to themselves and the natural world, as they know well that their sustenance and continuous existence is dependent on their love and care for the earth. This knowledge, which correlates with the Christian story of creation, provides the African

---

54 Paul H. Santmire, "Healing the Protestant Mind: Beyond the Theology of Human Dominion," in *After Nature's Revolt: Eco-Justice and Theology*, ed. Dieter Hessel (Minneapolis: Fortress Press, 1992), 75.

Christian a rich repository of knowledge for an enriching theological ethic and praxis of loving God through loving the earth (God's creation), which is under degradation and decay, thereby exposing the nudity of Mother Earth. This becomes particularly important when one considers that it is crucial that the church considers salvaging the natural world from oppression and decay as an essential dimension of salvation and mission.[55]

The degradation of the natural world renders Mother Earth poor and vulnerable. The extension of love, which has hitherto been limited to fellow human beings, toward liberating the natural world from further degradation would be considered active commitments to solidarity with Mother Earth. As I have pointed out, there are similarities between the Christian faith and the Indigenous African religious ontology or religious ecology. Both cosmologies underscore how humans are ontologically of the earth and how loving the earth will literally mean responding to the love of God and being in solidarity of Mother Earth. Considering that the tapestry of Indigenous African religious ecology, like many Indigenous ecologies, offers rich sources of ecological knowledge, there must be no shying away from the fact that they can contribute to expand the scope of Christian ecological theologies locally and globally—and that the Christian faith can benefit tremendously from them. Particularly, this expansion of the scope of ecotheology will be the development of authentic constructive theologies on themes emerging from the exploration of these religious ecologies. In the next section, I constructively explore an African theological ethic of loving God in the context of a degraded earth and environmental threats.

AN AFRICAN CHRISTIAN PERSPECTIVE OF LOVING GOD IN THE CONTEXT OF A DEGRADED EARTH AND ENVIRONMENTAL THREATS

Practically, what will be required of the church in Africa to solidarize with Mother Earth is extending love to the beneficiaries of God's love, as does

---

55   Ben-Willie Kwaku Golo, "The Groaning Earth and the Greening of Neo-Pentecostalism in Twenty-first Century Ghana," *PentecoStudies: An Interdisciplinary Journal for Research on the Pentecostal and Charismatic Movements*, 13, No. 2 (2014).

God himself. Fundamentally, however, this requires the acknowledgment and affirmation of the church in Africa that, just as the love of God primarily manifests in its relationship with other humans, loving God is largely realizable within the fulfillment of relationships, both social and cosmological. This acknowledgment is necessary in affirming the identity of the African Christian, whose ontological roots suggests the human person is a "vital force in participation" and whose Christian faith sees creation "as a reality illuminated by the love which calls us together into universal communion."[56] If the church and Christians in Africa take loving God and their neighbors seriously, then they must come to terms with the affirmation that love for the creation—Mother Earth—is love for God and neighbors.

What would be required of the church and Christian theology in Africa is to further affirm and develop a Christian ethic of a love-driven human-earth relationship as the context within which loving God, and one's neighbors, is wholly attainable. In the papal encyclical *Laudato Si'*, which Weldon avers was not narrowly addressed to bishops or the Catholic faithful but was open to a wide readership both inside and outside of the Church,[57] Pope Francis calls humanity to its responsibility to act in love toward, what he terms as our "Sister, Mother Earth," rather than act in the irresponsible use and abuse of the goods she has been endowed by God and provides humanity.[58] Providing a remarkable insight relevant for a global Christian theological ethic and praxis of creation love and care, *Laudato Si'* has received a global acclaim as charting a theological and ethical course against the anthropocentrism and human greed of contemporary culture. In the case of the church in Africa, this may be approached in two related ways.

First, developing a theologically sound and convincing attitude of loving beyond the human other individually and communally becomes imperative—a theological ethic capable of sustaining commitments to

---

56 Gabriel M. Setiloane, *African Theology. An Introduction* (Johannesburg: Skotaville Publishers, 1986), 14; Francis, *Laudato Si'*, 56.

57 Stephen P. Weldon, "Laudato Si': On Care for Our Common Home," Inhabiting the Anthropocene, September 21, 2015, https://inhabitingtheanthropocene.com/2015/09/21/laudato-si-on-care-for-our-common-home/.

58 Pope Francis, *Laudato Si'*, 3.

human well-being and the well-being of the earth (creation). As indicated by Moltmann, humans need the natural world, as we live on its products, including the oxygen plants produce. Consequently, God blessed humans with their sustenance on creation (Gen. 1:29–30; 2:16). While there is no biblical evidence suggesting that the earth was created solely for the sake of humans, it would be theologically valid to define the earth as an exhibit of God's love. Particularly, reflections on the centrality of the earth to the sustenance of human life further reveals the love of God toward human beings, who were the last to be created (not necessarily as its crown), after the earth had been created, assessed, and approved as "very good" (Gen. 1:31). This should be humbling enough for human beings to love the natural world and take care of it—particularly when the Creator admonishes them to do so in Genesis 2:15. This should, particularly, be the case if we admit that humans live in a covenanted relationship with the earth and that Jesus Christ's teaching on love has "knocked down the fences which limited the concept of 'neighbour' to someone within the covenant community."[59]

So much ink has already been spilled correcting the human abuse of the biblical doctrine of humans as made in the image of God and the command to multiply and have dominion over the earth (Gen. 1:26–28), and it is unnecessary to recount this here. Consequently, it becomes worth underscoring that the degradation of the natural world largely reflects the failure of humans to love God, who created the earth. If Christians love God, they will love the earth God created out of love. Pope Francis wrote:

> The universe did not emerge as the result of arbitrary omnipotence, a show of force or a desire for self-assertion. Creation is of the order of love. God's love is the fundamental moving force in all created things. . . . Every creature is thus the object of the Father's tenderness, who gives it its place in the world. Even the fleeting life of the least of beings is the object of his love, and in its few seconds of existence, God enfolds it with his affection.[60]

---

59 Field, "Love," 11.
60 Francis, *Laudato Si'*, 56.

As noted earlier, it is important to underscore that God's love, which has been extended to humanity, shows up as an intense response to the object in need of love,[61] and the earth needs it. Thus, there is the need to return to the love of God if we would avert further environmental degradation. This return to loving God cannot be complete without loving what God has created out of love and an exhibit of his love. What can restore humanity to the love for God is seeking to respond to God's love through obedience to the covenant of love extended to humanity through Jesus Christ. This means living a life of love to which humans have been summoned by God and which Jesus Christ has instructed his followers to bear as the genuine mark of identity (John 13: 34-35). We love others just as God loves us, and when Christians love others it is in response to God's love, which has been extended to them through the grace of salvation in Jesus Christ (Col. 3:12-15; 1 Pet. 1:8; 1 John 4:11). God's gift of and grace of salvation to humankind through Jesus Christ, which is the highest point and symbol of God's practical manifestation of love, is aimed at restoring human brokenness and estrangement, manifesting in broken relationships with both God and the created order (cosmos), our first ontological neighbors (Gen. 3:1-19).

In the context of environmental degradation, this grace of deliverance through Jesus Christ must be understood against the consequences of human estrangement from God, initially through humankind's rejection of God's love—the gift of creation—and through the distortion of ontological relationships with the earth God created. This is depicted in the Biblical story of the fall of humankind from the garden God planted in Eden. Through humankind's desire for power—to be like God—they distorted their relationship with God and the creation. This was a fall from love and favor graciously extended by God. In our contemporary situation, this estrangement has become visible through human attempts to play God, facilitated by philosophies from the Enlightenment to modernity, which Moltmann also hinted at in this volume. This is because, courtesy of science and technology, which enhance the productive capabilities of meeting human desires, contemporary humans falsely repress the thought of the imminent—death—and vicissitudes of life through materialism.

---

61 Carson, "Love," 648.

This deifying of humanity further distanced modern and postmodern secular society from loving God and what God loves. This is because, courtesy of science and technology, which enhance the productive capabilities of meeting human desires, contemporary humans "seem to think that we can substitute an irreplaceable and irretrievable beauty with something which we have created ourselves."[62] This predilection to eternal human prowess further disables human beings' commitments to the things of God, which means unloving God. A consequence is the contemporary environmental degradation and environmental threats facing humankind today.

It would, therefore, be important for the church to emphasize and teach believers that loving God, which has been traditionally defined in Christian theology and ethics as manifesting in love for the neighbor, entails love and justice for Mother Earth, and that one cannot be divorced from the other. Christians cannot love one while unloving the other because, just as they are interrelated in the biblical vision and cosmology of the context, so is the Christian's expression of God-directed love. These are linked in the fulfillment and sustaining of God's love for the creation and work together to achieve the purposes of God for the realization of the kingdom of God; both in history, with regard to attaining sustainable communities and human flourishing here on earth, and eschatologically, in the future world of glory."[63] This requires an ethic of seeing and loving beyond the human self and others. Whenever human action undermines the well-being of the creation, the love for God means individuals and groups trade off their decision and choices, irrespective of how they desire them.

Second, affirming an African Christian ethic of love-driven and just earth-human relations would also mean the church in Africa must practically work toward sustaining the integrity and intrinsic worth of the natural world (creation). This goes hand in hand with affirming the

---

62   Francis, *Laudato Si'*, 26.
63   Golo Ben-Willie Kwaku, "In Search of a Sustainable Society in Africa: Christianity, Justice and Sustainable Peace in a Changing Climate," *Philosophia Reformata. An International Philosophical Journal of Christianity, Science and Society*, 83, no. 1, (2018): 82–3.

right of every human to a flourishing life and fair distribution of earth's resources. This is necessary to make certain that the vulnerabilities of human populations do not enforce the degradation of the natural world. This would mean the church must work to sustain the well-being of humans and the earth in response to the love of God and invitation to neighborly love. The aim would be to ensure balance between human well-being and the rhythms (well-being) of the natural world—to build a sustainable society. This would be the basis on which an ethic of maintaining human-ecological balance, which will seek human well-being, the welfare of others in community, and the sustainability of the natural world, would be grounded.

In practical terms, being in solidarity with Mother Earth and loving God will mean the church in Africa, as suggested by Hallman, should get involved in addressing the causes of environmental problems, particularly climate change, with a primary task being actively participating in processes toward reducing the causes.[64] Fundamentally, this necessitates the church in Africa's involvement in efforts toward making lifestyle changes and encouraging churches, church members, friends, and family to do the same: adopting modest and simple lifestyles and living in ways that do not burden ecosystems with waste and pollutants.[65] For instance, in the contemporary world of uncontrolled production and consumption, loving God would mean churches in Africa and Christian groups challenge unsustainable production and consumption, which continues to degrade and threaten God's creation. Through unsustainable production and consumption, human communities continue to subject the natural world (creation) to bondage and prevent it from experiencing the liberation and flourishing it groans for through Christ's liberation/the redemption of humanity (Rom. 8:22). Contemporary consumption, which drives unsustainable production, is therefore not only unloving but unjust. Furthermore, some practical demonstrations on the part of African churches of living God include: leading the way in energy efficiency, as models of good stewardship; switching to renewable energy sources such as wind

---

64 Hallman, "Climate Change and Poverty," 51.
65 Hallman, "Climate Change and Poverty," 51.

and solar, if they are available and affordable[66]; as well as involving local congregation and families in projects to reduce greenhouse gas emission.[67]

Conclusion

Christians cannot claim their love for God if they cannot reciprocate God's love and display this through love toward God's good earth. Consequently, a relationship of cooperation, in which Christians extend their love to the earth as a neighbor through care for it, would be loving God. Largely, this will involve actionable responses from the church and its theology in Africa to the love of God. Generally, the church in Africa must actively work toward sustainable ways of living, such as human levels of production and consumption, which have turned modern society and contemporary human beings into degraders and destroyers of mother earth. This must be prioritized while not abandoning liberating and transforming love to fellow human neighbors, particularly those who suffer from the effects of environmental degradation and climate change. These commitments of the African church and its theology to seeing the flourishing and sustainability of natural world will position them as standing in solidarity with Mother Earth.

Largely, the cosmology of the Indigenous African culture provides the Christian faith and its theology a reservoir of knowledge for contextualized Christian theologies and approaches to the earth, which are relevant for engaging the environmental predicament in sub-Saharan Africa, where Christianity still has a large following. However, this requires that the Christian community acknowledges the cosmologies of Indigenous cultures and their resourcefulness to create a rich and contextualized ecotheology in Africa, rather than disparaging these cultures as nature worshippers. This requires affirming the compatibilities of Indigenous cosmologies with the biblical vision and emphasizing why Christians must not undermine them but rather learn from them to enrich, particularly through collaboration, Christian ecotheologies and practices.

---

66 Christopher Shore, "A Development Worker's Perspective," in *Loving the Least of These*, 37.
67 Hallman, "Climate Change and Poverty," 51.

CHAPTER 8

HUMAN UNIQUENESS, DIVINE INTERRELATIONALITY, AND THE HOPE OF ECOFEMINIST THEOLOGY

Rubén Rosario Rodríguez

INTRODUCTION

For generations, scientists and ecologically minded theologians have been warning about the impending environmental collapse. As astrophysicist and planetary scientist Carl Sagan noted in an open letter to people of faith over thirty years ago, "Some of the short-term mitigations of these dangers such as greater energy efficiency, rapid banning of chlorofluorocarbons or modest reductions in nuclear arsenals are comparatively easy and at some level are already underway."[1] Yet despite such early warnings, society has not heeded the call to ecological justice, and now we are hearing panic from many of the voices that have been leading the charge for decades, like ecotheologian Catherine Keller:

> Time, our time, the time of human civilization, appears to be running out. The science of climate has been unhysterically, relentlessly, increasingly signaling: not that time will run out but that if we stay on the present course . . . we had a fighting chance of changing course within the narrow window of time

---

1 Carl Sagan, "An Open Letter to the Religious Community," presented at the Global Forum of Spiritual and Parliamentary Leaders Conference in Moscow, Russia, January 1990, http://earthrenewal.org/open_letter_to_the_religious_.htm.

that climate change allots. After the political shift, however, the window seemed to be slamming shut. Not on all of life, not on the earth, not necessarily even on our species. But on historic human civilization as it flows into its future. Yet it is precisely so-called civilization that had brought us to this moment of self-contradiction.[2]

Time is running out, the urgency is real, and we as a species need to come to terms with the facts concerning environmental degradation because, as Reformed theologian Jürgen Moltmann reminds us, "The earth can live without human life, and has done so for millions of years, but we cannot live without the earth."[3] There is growing consensus that a new paradigm is needed.

Throughout much of Western history, Christianity has lived with the assumption that humanity occupies a special place in the natural order as creatures made in the "image of God," a "little lower than God," with dominion over "the beasts of the field, the birds of the air, and the fish of the sea" (Gen. 1:26–28; Ps. 8:5–8 [NRSV]). With the publication of Charles Darwin's *On the Origin of Species* (1859), the theological narrative concerning human uniqueness was seriously undermined if not permanently discredited. Nevertheless, within scientific discourse there is an effort to reframe the conversation about human uniqueness given the severity of the ecological crisis now facing humanity. The complex evolutionary processes that led to sentient life-forms capable of self-awareness, of understanding and predicting complex events, and of reflective decision-making and goal-directed action mark humankind as *distinct* from other organic life on the planet. A defense of human uniqueness acknowledges and embraces the human capacity to transform nature on a broad scale to find positive solutions for adverse and destructive climate change through more meaningful dialogue and cooperation between religious beliefs and the natural sciences.

---

2   Catherine Keller, *Political Theology of the Earth: Our Planetary Emergency and the Struggle for a New Public* (New York: Columbia University Press, 2018), 1–2.

3   Jürgen Moltmann, "Ecology as the Capacity for Love," p. xx in this volume.

In *Light of the Stars: Alien Worlds and the Fate of the Earth* (2018), astrophysicist Adam Frank calls for a new narrative concerning humanity's place in the universe that affirms human uniqueness while embracing humanity's interdependence with the planet earth and its ecosystems. Frank's central insight, drawn from the relatively new field of astrobiology, resonates with the deep interrelationality sought by ecofeminism. Ivone Gebara has articulated a Trinitarian theology that rejects the human-centered and male-centered theologies of domination, offering in their place a sustaining matrix of immanent relationality. Within this feminist reconstruction of the doctrine of God, Gebara finds ample room for the insights and knowledge provided by the natural sciences, yet she is not satisfied with an abstract relationality. Given that divine transcendence is incarnated in human form, in Christ through whom God welcomes all of humanity into the divine interrelationality, God's preferential option for the poor becomes a *necessary* lens through which to see God in the world "outside us and the world inside us in an evolutionary process of mutual engagement and continuous mutation."[4]

A Theological Anthropology Beyond Contradiction

Catherine Keller describes the precipice on which Western civilization teeters as a "moment of self-contradiction."[5] Despite the popular perception that science and religion are always in conflict, scientists and theologians have long fostered an interdisciplinary space in which conceptual overlap leads to mutually beneficial conversation and practical cooperation on pressing concerns like climate change. Without denying humanity's place within the Darwinian tree of life, this essay advocates a revised conception of human uniqueness that does not reinforce outdated and dangerous theologies of domination but opens new vistas for human moral responsibility amid the impending ecological collapse. Notwithstanding our common descent, humanity is—for the moment at least—the only species capable of altering its natural habitat to such a degree that it

---

4 Ivone Gebara, "Interdependence, Christianity, and Environmental Crisis," p. xx in this volume.
5 Keller, *Political Theology of the Earth*, 2.

is affecting long-term evolutionary processes, as evidenced by the human impact on global climate change. The challenge facing both theologians and scientists is how to create the type of long-lasting change needed to reverse climate change, which will inevitably "encounter widespread inertia, denial and resistance," especially as humanity tries to wean itself "from fossil fuels to a nonpolluting energy economy."[6]

The world's religions have long recognized the gravity of this historic self-contradiction and unequivocally concede that human activity is negatively affecting biological processes and environmental systems, even to the point of destruction on a global scale. In 1989, prior to Carl Sagan's appeal to religious communities, Patriarch Dimitrios 1 of the Greek Orthodox Church issued a statement expressing concern for the environment: "The abuse by contemporary man of his privileged position in creation and of the Creator's order to him 'to have dominion over the earth' (Gen. 1, 28), has already led the world to the edge of apocalyptic self-destruction, either in the form of natural pollution which is dangerous for all living beings, or in the form of the extinction of many species of the animal and plant world, or in other forms."[7] Pope Francis, in his encyclical *Laudato Si'* (2015), makes one of the strongest ecclesial statements on ecological responsibility to date, acknowledging "the harm we have inflicted on her [Mother Earth] by our irresponsible use and abuse of the goods with which God has endowed her."[8] Similar statements have been made by all the major Christian communions,[9] as well as all the major religions of the

---

6 Sagan, "An Open Letter to the Religious Community."

7 Ecumenical Patriarch Dimitrios, Archbishop of Constantinople and New Rome, "Encyclical Letter on the Day of Protection of the Environment," September 1, 1989, https://www.orthtransfiguration.org/wpcontent/uploads/2016/05/Lecture_HAH-1989-Patr.-Dimitrios-on-Day-of-Prayer-for-Envir.pdf.

8 Pope Francis, *Encyclical Letter Laudato Si' of the Holy Father Francis on Care for Our Common Home*, 2015.

9 For example, see Presbyterian Church USA, "Affirmation of Creation," 222nd General Assembly, June 22, 2016, https://ncse.ngo/presbyterian-church-usa; Evangelical Environmental Network, "An Evangelical Declaration on the Care of Creation," 1994, https://creationcare.org/what-we-do/an-evangelical-declaration-on-the-care-of-creation.html; African Methodist Episcopal Church, "AME Church Climate Change Resolution," July 2016, http://www.

world, including Islam,[10] Judaism,[11] Buddhism,[12] and Hinduism.[13] Sadly, as Brazilian liberation theologian Ivone Gebara rightly discerns, when religion attempts to embrace biodiversity, especially within Christianity, it often encounters "great resistance on the part of the representatives of the dominant patriarchal theological traditions and is quickly repudiated as unorthodox, that is to say, not conforming with traditional theological thought."[14]

Ecofeminism represents the "radicalization that takes place as ecological consciousness is incorporated into feminist theology," which begins with the deconstruction and reconstruction of "the cosmological framework out of which the Christian worldview grew from its ancient

---

ame-church.com/wp-content/uploads/2016/07/AME-Climate-Change-Resolution.pdf; Episcopal Church, "A Pastoral Message on Climate Change," September 19, 2014, https://www.episcopalchurch.org/publicaffairs/a-pastoral-message-on-climate-change/.

10 See Islamic Foundation for Ecology and Environmental Studies, "Islamic Declaration on Global Climate Change," August 17, 2015, https://www.ifees.org.uk/about/islamicdeclaration/.

11 See Jewish Climate Initiative and The Interfaith Center for Sustainable Development, "Statement by Israel Orthodox Rabbis on The Climate Crisis," https://www.jewishecoseminars.com/statement-by-israel-orthodox-rabbis-on-the-climate-crisis/; The Shalom Center, "'Elijah's Covenant'—New Rabbinic Statement on the Climate Crisis," January 1, 2020, https://legacy4now.theshalomcenter.org/content/elijahs-covenant-boston-jewish-advocate-front-page-story.

12 See Yale, "The Time to Act is Now: A Buddhist Declaration on Climate Change," May 14, 2015 https://fore.yale.edu/files/buddhist_climate_change_statement_5-14-15.pdf; also see Global Buddhist Climate Change Collective, "Buddhist Climate Change Statement to World Leaders," October 29, 2015, https://plumvillage.org/articles/buddhist-climate-change-statement-to-world-leaders-2015.

13 See "Hindu Declaration on Climate Change," Parliament of the World's Religions, Melbourne, Australia, December 8, 2009, https://hinduclimatedeclaration2015.org/english.

14 Ivone Gebara, *Intuiciones ecofeministas: Ensayo para repensar el conocimiento y la religión*, trans. Graciela Pujol (Madrid: Editorial Tratto, 2000), 133 (all translations from the Spanish my own).

roots in the Hebrew and Greek worlds."[15] Rejecting the patriarchal dominion theology, feminist theologians like Rosemary Radford Ruether and Elisabeth Schüssler Fiorenza counter that the Genesis creation story lacks an "explicit mandate for the domination of some humans over others, as male over female, or master over slave," and that the doctrine of *imago Dei* can become the "basis for an egalitarian view of all humans as equal in God's image in later Christian movements that sought to dismantle slavery and sexism."[16] Feminist theology challenges patriarchal theologies by emphasizing the radically inclusive character of the earliest Christian communities while recognizing that "as Christianity was institutionalized in the patriarchal family and political order, it moved quickly to suppress these radical interpretations of redemption in Christ."[17] Ivone Gebara's vision of ecofeminism builds on this fundamental egalitarian assertion to critique the complicity of Christian patriarchal theologies "in the persistent domination of women and the unchecked exploitation of natural resources," arguing that not enough has been done to address the role of Christian colonialism in "the destruction of Indigenous divinities" through denying "other religious rapprochements" their due as "equally truthful" and ignoring the important role Indigenous and African religious narratives can play in fostering an "egalitarian and solidary dialogue."[18]

Ecofeminist theology seeks to overcome the dangerously anthropocentric and androcentric theologies of dominion, as well as the technocentric reductionism of Enlightenment rationality. In Moltmann's analysis, "The notion of theological anthropology, '*imago Dei—dominium terrae*' [*imago Dei*—lordship of the world] justified—along with 'the special position of humanity in the cosmos'—an entire age of scientific discoveries and European domination," have "destroyed the balance of nature" and led

---

15 Rosemary Radford Ruether, "Ecofeminism—The Challenge to Theology," *Deportate, esuli, profughe: Rivista telematica di studi sulla memoria femminile*, No. 20 (2012), 27.
16 Ruether, "Ecofeminism,"; Elisabeth Schüssler Fiorenza, *In Memory of Her: A Feminist Theological Reconstruction of Christian Origins*, revised and annotated (New York: Crossroad, 1994), 63.
17 Ruether, "Ecofeminism," 26; Schüssler Fiorenza, *In Memory of Her*, 105-53.
18 Gebara, *Intuiciones ecofeministas*, 28.

"to the extermination of its most vulnerable creatures."[19] Given the dominance of this two-faced god of consumption, ecofeminist theology begins with a critique of both theological and scientific false idols to identify that which we can no longer affirm as true if we are to forestall the ecological apocalypse: "the *via negativa*—devoted path of the ancient mystics—that is to say, what we can no longer say about God based on our personal and communitarian experience."[20] Accordingly, one of the divine attributes that ecofeminism rejects, based in part on knowledge derived from the ecological sciences, is the "image of the patriarchal God as dominating nature," with "nature in submission to God, which then God hands over to the man so that he can subdue nature under his proper dominion."[21] Mary Daly, in *Beyond God the Father* (1973), argued that "if God is male, then the male is God."[22] Gebara rejects dominion theology as idolatrous for the same reason, for any theology that contends that the male is "most fully image of God" inevitably leads to the development of "an anthropocentric and androcentric spirituality" wherein "Nature, other living beings, and the complex biological web in which we live," are "all placed in service to maleness."[23]

In her most recent work, Ivone Gebara draws inspiration from scientific and naturalist cosmologies to deconstruct the tyranny of old beliefs, especially the false idols of patriarchy and dominion theology: "Everything starts with a word of attention to life, a scientific word to affirm that our universe erupted through a great fire, an explosion from which everything including our senses, our virtues and vices, our loves and our hates came out, all being at the same time and evolutionarily part of that scorching explosion expanding in a variety of directions."[24] Drawing on the rich apophatic tradition within Christian theology that can be traced to the Platonism of Pseudo-Dionysius in the fifth or sixth century of the Common Era, that became institutionalized in the medieval synthesis of

---

19   Moltmann, "Ecology as the Capacity for Love," p. xx in this volume.
20   Gebara, *Intuiciones ecofeministas*, 134.
21   Gebara, *Intuiciones ecofeministas*, 135.
22   Mary Daly, *Beyond God the Father: Toward a Philosophy of Women's Liberation* (Boston: Beacon Press, 1993), 19.
23   Gebara, *Intuiciones ecofeministas*, 135.
24   Gebara, "Interdependence, Christianity, and Environmental Crisis," p. xx in this volume.

Thomas Aquinas, and that was radicalized in Paul Tillich's notion of the "God above God," Gebara pushes the critique of idolatry to its extreme, defining all theological constructs as human intellectual creations part of the mysterious, miraculous, and natural process that began with the creation of the material universe and led to the eventual evolution of intelligent life on Earth: "We cannot say much; only poetry of ecstasy and wonder as participants in this broader vastness.... This scientific sensibility and poetic consciousness is present in our times above all else due to the evolution that astrophysical science, biology and some philosophies could glimpse from the outset. This beginning could be the beginning of interdependence in the very origin of life."[25]

Many questions arise concerning what happens to divine revelation and divine agency once theological discourse moves in this direction, that is, fully embracing a materialistic explanation for religious belief. While these are fascinating and broad ranging questions, they cannot be adequately resolved within the parameters of the current investigation. Suffice it to say, Gebara's use of scientific cosmologies as a way of critiquing tyrannical theological traditions like patriarchy and dominion theology is part of the larger ecofeminist project to affirm "our shared divinity in everything that exists; divinity as a vital force that connects us to each other simply so that life continues to be in us and in everything."[26] In her earlier work, Gebara articulated a Trinitarian theology that rejected the human-centered and male-centered theologies of domination, attributing this androcentrism within Christian thought to the almost exclusive use of images of God as father and king with Christ as his son, offering in its place a "sustaining matrix of immanent relationality."[27] Gebara's reconstruction of Trinitarian doctrine refuses to visualize the Trinity as a "self-enclosed relation of two divine males with each other, mediated by the Spirit, but rather as the symbolic expression of the basic dynamic of

---

25 Gebara, "Interdependence, Christianity, and Environmental Crisis," p. xx in this volume.
26 Gebara, "Interdependence, Christianity, and Environmental Crisis," p. xx in this volume.
27 Ruether, "Ecofeminism," 30.

life itself as a process of vital interrelational creativity."[28] She conceives of the divine reality mediated by Christ as the incarnation of a life-affirming divine relationality. This divine relationality, unlike patriarchal visions of an aloof king on his throne who is sovereign over all of creation, offers a reconstruction of the Trinitarian God as transcendent yet everywhere immanent: "Transcendence is that feeling of always belonging to something greater—much greater—whose full breadth we barely know and are unable to express. . . . the human experience of transcendence is also the experience of beauty, the majesty of nature, and all its relationships and interdependencies."[29] This participation in the divine interrelationality grounds human existence in relationships of mutual interdependence, which in Gebara's opinion necessitates a new Christian creed, or more in keeping with the open-ended nature of rational and scientific inquiry, a "creed that is understandable for each time, a creed that can periodically be renewed and that can be a kind of common platform in light of our common survival. A creed that reveals our interdependence and reciprocity in our own bodies and through them with the planet and its ecosystems. In this sense, one could speak of the body of God as the body of everything that exists."[30]

Within this Trinitarian reconstruction of the doctrine of God, Gebara finds ample room for the insights and knowledge provided by the natural sciences: "All life from the evolution of the galaxies to the dynamics of the self manifests the presence of God as sustaining Wisdom of creation."[31] Yet, in describing the interrelationality demanded by such a concept of divinity, Gebara is not satisfied with abstract relationalities. Given that divine transcendence is incarnated in human form in the Christ, through whom God welcomes all of humanity into the divine interrelationality, God's preferential option for the poor becomes a *necessary* lens through which to see God in the world. For Gebara, the exploitation of

---

28 Ruether, "Ecofeminism," 30.
29 Gebara, *Intuiciones ecofeministas*, 136.
30 Gebara, "Interdependence, Christianity, and Environmental Crisis," p. xx in this volume.
31 Ruether, "Ecofeminism," 32.

the world's poor is indivisible from the exploitation of nature, as verified by the fact that "the dispossessed, like all marginalized groups and persons, reveal better than others the contradictory and destructive character of our actions. It is among the poor and in the ecosystems where they are found that today we see the most obvious signals of this destruction, the fruits of human action."[32] God's preferential option for the poor, as articulated by liberation theologians, "seeks to correct the destructive option for the rich at the expense of the well-being of the whole community of life. The ethic of preferential option for the poor calls us to feed and nurture the child of the poor dying from malnutrition and unclean water and rectify the conditions that are causing this untimely death, while the ethic of sustainability calls us to help the mother of this child limit her childbearing."[33] This preferential option leads to a life lived in solidarity with the victims of technocratic capitalism, which, as Catherine Keller contends, opposes a global common good: "Neoliberalism treats the multiple self-organizing ecologies of the earth—geological, biological, climatic—as externalities irrelevant to its own organization of the world. This world scheme with its extractions, exploitations, and extinctions ignores the fragilities of the world in which the most vulnerable but soon the all of us will be in peril."[34] But as Gebara makes clear, such solidarity must be nurtured and disseminated, which entails overturning and transcending the entrenched narratives of patriarchal dominion theology, finance-driven capitalism, and scientific materialism by articulating a different, more inclusive vision of the common good: "This option is a cultivated condition, a chosen lifestyle, a faith option insofar as it constitutes struggling on behalf of the most vulnerable, the victims of exclusionary systems whose numbers increase daily. This entails rejecting all sexist and racist ideologies originating from totalitarian regimes that seek to protect an elite group to the detriment of those considered impure, useless, marginalized."[35]

---

32   Gebara, *Intuiciones ecofeministas*, 142.
33   Ruether, "Ecofeminism," 33.
34   Keller, *Political Theology of the Earth*, 35.
35   Gebara, *Intuiciones ecofeministas*, 142.

CULTIVATING A SENSE OF WONDER AND INTERDEPENDENCE

Like Ivone Gebara, astrophysicist Adam Frank also affirms the need for a new narrative about humanity's interrelationship with the universe but approaches the topic from the relatively new field of astrobiology. Astrobiology is a multidisciplinary scientific field of study concerned with the origins, early evolution, distribution, and future of life in the universe. It primarily investigates the material conditions and contingent events necessary for life to arise in the universe and, to a lesser extent, considers the question of extraterrestrial life.[36] The central insight Frank draws from astrobiology resonates with the deep interrelationality sought by ecofeminism: "The evolution of the planet and its life cannot be separated. That is what our science has shown us. Earth and its life must be thought of as a whole that 'coevolves' together."[37] Science and religion are in agreement about the global environmental crisis, which Catherine Keller has described as our moment of self-contradiction:

> Two decades into the twenty-first century, we find ourselves facing the existential challenge of creating a sustainable version of human civilization. The scale of human activities is pushing hard on the tightly linked planetary systems that make up Earth's climate. As the planet begins to move off into a different climate state, our project of civilization will, at the very least, find itself under stress. At worst, Earth's changes may make our project impossible to maintain.[38]

Frank is not a naive idealist. Therefore, he is critical of environmentalists who think we can eliminate humanity's carbon footprint: "There is nothing wrong with such a goal, but the message often gets mangled in public debate from 'less impact' into 'no impact.' If we take the astrobiological view and start thinking like a planet, we see there's no such thing as 'no

---

36 See David C. Catling, *Astrobiology: A Very Short Introduction* (Oxford: Oxford University Press, 2013).
37 Adam Frank, *Light of the Stars: Alien Worlds and the Fate of the Earth* (New York: W. W. Norton, 2018), 13.
38 Adam Frank, *Light of the Stars*, 125.

impact.'"³⁹ Frank is not trying to undermine the best impulses of environmental activists but wants to make sure that whatever is proposed is built on a solid scientific foundation ensuring that all claims made adhere to the available data.

Adam Frank proposes a complex thought experiment—a multidisciplinary astrobiological exercise in civilization building—that will "require input from fields as diverse as atmospheric science, geology, energy science, and ecology. To create realistic models, we'll have to get the physics, chemistry, planetary science, and ecological interactions right in terms of what we build into the models."⁴⁰ His experiment identifies three distinct trajectories: (1) civilizations "die off," meaning that, as they use their energy resources, their populations grow beyond what the environment can sustain; (2) civilizations reach a "soft landing," meaning that, as the population grows and the planetary system changes due to increased energy consumption, the civilization makes the necessary changes by switching to a low-impact energy source to reach a sustainable ecological equilibrium; and (3) the "full-blown collapse," wherein a civilization grows so fast and impacts the planetary ecosystem so drastically that it leads to a massive extinction. Adam Frank grants that scientific models are not reality, but he contends that carefully constructed models are more than mere fictions. By relying on known natural laws applied on a planetary scale, astrobiologists are able to predict possible outcomes with reliable precision.

Given enough civilizational models accounting for a wide range of possible natural and artificial conditions, scientists can "ask what explicitly led some civilizations to achieve planetary sustainability and others to collapse. Like a doctor looking for a cure by studying the most pathological cases of a disease, we can see what common factors drove the civilizations that died to their fate. The models will have a lot to teach us that we can't see now with the tunnel vision of just our planet and just our own uncertain future."⁴¹ Frank's thought experiment shares a major conceptual overlap with ecofeminism: the realization that we cannot continue to treat human civilizations and technologies as distinct or removed from nature.

---

39 Adam Frank, *Light of the Stars*, 137.
40 Adam Frank, *Light of the Stars*, 141.
41 Adam Frank, *Light of the Stars*, 148.

The rise and fall of human civilizations are a natural part of the planet's evolutionary history, where every "civilization must be seen as a new form of biospheric activity arising within a planet's history of transformation and evolutionary innovation." As we direct our knowledge and resources to the question of ecological sustainability, our civilization must "enter into a long, cooperative relationship" with our planet or risk extinction.[42]

Reformed theologian Jürgen Moltmann, like Ivone Gebara and Adam Frank, values and emphasizes the interrelationality between humankind and the rest of creation in order to generate and nurture the necessary social change to reverse climate change: "Ecology calls for something else that changes the inner attitude of humanity. Some have named this 'planetary solidarity.'"[43] According to Moltmann, beyond dominion theology an equally important factor that has accelerated the exploitation and domination of the natural world is the anthropocentric worldview that arose during the Renaissance and came to dominate during the Enlightenment: a reductionist materialism that sees the world as objects to control, dominate, and exploit through the use of technology.

Controversial—yet widely influential—philosopher Martin Heidegger (1889-1976) attributes the dominance of technocratic capitalism in the West to a foundational metaphysical error: post-Enlightenment humanity views nature as the raw material for its technical activities, i.e., as the means to an end. With the rise of the scientific worldview, we have come to understand physics as an exact experimental science "dependent upon technical apparatus and upon progress in the building of apparatus."[44] Thus, the natural world becomes an object for our manipulation and exploitation:

> A tract of land is challenged in the hauling out of coal and ore. The earth now reveals itself as a coal mining district, the soil as a mineral deposit. The field that the peasant formerly cultivated and

---

42 Adam Frank, *Light of the Stars*, 156.
43 Moltmann, "Ecology as the Capacity for Love," p. xx in this volume.
44 Martin Heidegger, "The Question Concerning Technology," in *Martin Heidegger: Basic Writings*, ed. and trans. David Farrell Krell (New York: Harper and Row, 1977), 295-96.

set in order appears different from how it did when to set in order still meant to take care and maintain. . . . Agriculture is now the mechanized food industry. Air is now set upon to yield nitrogen, the earth to yield ore, ore to yield uranium, for example; uranium is set upon to yield atomic energy, which can be released either for destruction or for peaceful use.[45]

While the premodern world was characterized by a more interdependent relationship between humanity and the natural realm, the rise of science and technology accelerated the utilitarian relationship that views nature as the means of technological advancement. Heidegger warns that humanity's relationship to technology is inherently flawed: "Everywhere we remain unfree and chained to technology, whether we passionately affirm or deny it. But we are delivered over to it in the worst possible way when we regard it as something neutral; for this conception of it, to which today we particularly like to do homage, makes us utterly blind to the essence of technology."[46] In other words, despite a methodological commitment to neutrality, Heidegger warns that scientific knowledge is far from neutral, and its reliance on technology is grounded in an instrumental view of the world wherein all that exists—even other human beings—become objects for our use and abuse.

Echoing many of Heidegger's insights concerning the instrumental relationship to nature fostered by the scientific worldview, Moltmann counters this materialistic and exploitative relationship by rediscovering a sense of awe that locates humanity within the vast interconnected web of relationships constituted by the Creator at the creation:

> This basic trust in the wisdom of God which is presupposed and is spread out before us in the cosmos and in life can be understood as a pre-rational postulate of pure reason. Every scientific discovery discovers something of this wise rationality in the world. The structure of the world determined by Wisdom or the Logos hastens invitingly ahead of human knowledge—and yet at the same

---

45 Heidegger, "The Question," 296.
46 Heidegger, "The Question," 287–288.

time, in its divine sublimity, it is immeasurable and unfathomable. That is why human beings in their knowledge of the world become wise through the fear of God.[47]

Moltmann is aware that the "modern paradigm has reached its limit. Climate change has destroyed the balance of nature, and human consumption of the resources of the land has led to the extermination of its most vulnerable creatures."[48] Therefore, he argues the only way to overcome the *anthropocentrism* of modern science, with its inherently instrumental relationship to the material world, is through a critical retrieval of a *theocentric* perspective: "There is a new paradigm, that human culture and the natural order are bound together no longer in an anthropocentric fashion, but in a bio-centric fashion. And along with that, we need a new understanding of nature, and a new view of humanity, and a new experience of God 'in the creation.'"[49] A theocentric perspective, as Moltmann envisions it, begins with "the fear of God and the love of God, because with whatever we know it is wise to respect the dignity of the known object itself."[50]

Thus, rather than perpetuate the I-It relationship that modern science has cultivated, in which the natural world is an object to be controlled and manipulated, a theocentric perspective nurtures an I-Thou relationship between humanity and the creation, wherein the inherent dignity of the creation is honored and our mutual interdependence emphasized. Moltmann's approach celebrates the interrelationality of all creation, from the lowest microorganism to humanity as the image of God: "Thus, one cannot regard humankind as an almighty king of the earth or as a lone gardener in contrast to all other creatures. Humanity is first of all a creature in a grand community of God's creation."[51] Therefore, Moltmann's theocentric proposal provides a viable—and sympathetic—alternative to complement Ivone Gebara's ecofeminist challenge:

---

47 Jürgen Moltmann, "'The Fear of the Lord Is the Beginning of Wisdom': Science and Wisdom," in *Experiences in Theology: Ways and Forms of Christian Theology*, trans. Margaret Kohl (Minneapolis: Fortress Press, 2000), 339.
48 Moltmann, "Ecology," 1.
49 Moltmann, "Ecology," 1.
50 Moltmann, "The Fear of the Lord is the Beginning of Wisdom," 339.
51 Moltmann, "Ecology," 3.

> A shared planetary dimension must permeate all our actions, even the simplest of our daily tasks and include all people in the responsibility for their lives and for the common life. It should also touch theologies as means of explaining what we believe. For this to be the case, the most diverse educational processes must be woven by a broad and inclusive idea of interdependence and the common good in order to favor the necessary dialogue between different groups.[52]

Ultimately, a praxis of cooperation and mutual interdependence is best advanced by the radically inclusive ethos of the preferential option for the poor.

Conclusion

Despite our close genetic proximity to other animal life, we are—for the moment—the only species that continues to refine its natural ability to shape habitats for maximal survival to such a degree that we are affecting evolutionary processes themselves, as evidenced by humanity causing global climate change.[53] A theological defense of human uniqueness acknowledges and embraces the human capacity to transform nature on a broad scale in order to find positive solutions for adverse and destructive climate change by encouraging more meaningful dialogue and cooperation between religious beliefs and the natural sciences.

Is Charles Darwin's theory of evolution fundamentally incompatible with the Christian belief in a divine Creator? Darwin could be described as a deist insofar as he rejected divine revelation and supranatural agency in everyday life but maintained a very high regard for the beauty and magnificence of nature in all its complexity, remaining open to the possibility of a Creator who authored the underlying laws of nature. Without compromising his belief that science seeks natural explanations for the workings of

---

52 Ruether, "Ecofeminism," 13-4.
53 Ecosystem engineers, like beavers, can shape the environment for maximal survival, but nowhere near the extent humanity has been able to impact climate change on a global scale.

creation, Darwin seems to suggest such complexity is not accidental: "The whole history of the world, as at present known, although of a length quite incomprehensible by us, will hereafter be recognized as a mere fragment of time, compared with the ages which have elapsed since the first creature, the progenitor of innumerable extinct and living descendants, was created."[54] Some of Darwin's language even echoes the Genesis creation story (Gen. 2:7) as he acknowledges someone or something breathed life into the first simple organism: "Therefore I should infer from this analogy that probably all organic beings which have ever lived on this earth have descended from some primordial form, into which life was first breathed."[55]

Arguably, Darwin's worldview leaves room for a Creator who ordered the universe according to eternal and unchanging laws and established the processes of natural selection and evolution by which the natural order continues to create itself free from divine interference. Without espousing Christian dogma about the nature and character of God, Darwin affirms belief in an originating act by a divine hand. He then concludes *On the Origin of Species* by acknowledging that, from this first act of breathing life into the simplest organism, the divinely ordered laws of nature give rise to higher orders of animals—even human life—via a natural process that might appear random and blind to the suffering it causes but is in fact awe-inspiring in scope:

> Thus, from the war of nature, from famine and death, the most exalted object which we are capable of conceiving, namely, the production of the higher animals, directly follows. There is grandeur in this view of life, with its several powers, having been originally breathed into a few forms or into one; and that, whilst this planet has gone cycling on according to the fixed law of gravity, from so simple a beginning endless forms most beautiful and most wonderful have been, and are being evolved.[56]

---

54 Charles Darwin, *On the Origin of Species* (1859), in *From So Simple a Beginning: The Four Great Books of Charles Darwin*, ed. Edward O. Wilson (New York: W. W. Norton, 2006), 759.
55 Darwin, *On the Origin of Species*, 756.
56 Darwin, *On the Origin of Species*, 760.

Despite popular mythmaking by Richard Dawkins and other figures associated with the "new atheism" that Darwin not only abandoned the Christian faith but became an atheist,[57] evidence suggests that while he no longer believed in the God of the Bible and Christian tradition, Darwin remained receptive to some of the arguments of natural theology. Until the end of his life, Charles Darwin insisted one could be both "an ardent theist and an evolutionist."[58] In the same letter, Darwin goes on to say, "I have never been an atheist in the sense of denying the existence of a God—I think that generally (and more and more so as I grow older) but not always, that an agnostic would be the most correct description of my state of mind."[59]

While there is much ambiguity concerning Darwin's religious beliefs, his father's death caused him to sever his commitment to Christianity, and the death of his youngest daughter at the age of ten from tuberculosis undermined his belief in a benevolent and loving God in a more fundamental way, even if he still left the door open to a theoretical belief in a Creator who established the laws of nature. Though he did not write extensively about this loss, it is evident from his correspondence that her death greatly affected his physical and mental health, and the memorial he wrote for her hints at the depth of his suffering: "We have lost the joy of the Household, and the solace of our old age— she must have known how we loved her; oh that she could now know how deeply, how tenderly we do still and shall ever love her dear joyous face. Blessings on her."[60] While there

---

57 See Richard Dawkins, *The God Delusion* (Boston: Houghton Mifflin Harcourt, 2006) and *The Blind Watchmaker: Why the Evidence of Evolution Reveals a Universe without Design*, reprint (W. W. Norton, 1996); Sam Harris, *The End of Faith: Religion, Terror, and the Future of Reason* (New York: W. W. Norton, 2005); Daniel C. Dennett, *Breaking the Spell: Religion as a Natural Phenomenon* (New York: Penguin, 2006).

58 Charles Darwin to John Fordyce, May 7, 1879, Darwin Correspondence Project, "Letter no. 12041," https://www.darwinproject.ac.uk/letter/?docId=letters/DCP-LETT-12041.xml.

59 Darwin, "Letter no. 12041."

60 Charles Darwin, "Charles Darwin's Memorial of Anne Elizabeth Darwin," Darwin Correspondence Project, April 30, 1851, https://www.darwinproject.ac.uk/people/about-darwin/family-life/death-anne-elizabeth-darwin.

is much ambiguity concerning Darwin's religious beliefs, it becomes clear that he wanted nothing to do with a God who would allow the death of an innocent child or condemn a good man like his father to eternal suffering. Yet, there is nothing in Darwin's understanding of natural selection and evolution that necessarily contradicts belief in God—or that requires abandoning belief in the goodness of God.

John Polkinghorne (1930–2021), a theoretical physicist, Anglican priest, and theologian, confronted the argument that the "wastefulness" of natural selection undermines belief in a good and loving God with the counterargument that the long and slow process of evolution, which admittedly entails much death and suffering, can actually be interpreted as a compassionate act of God's design, whose established laws help species better adapt to their environment, such that "from so simple a beginning endless forms most beautiful and most wonderful have been, and are being, evolved."[61] Polkinghorne devoted a lifetime to making belief in God both reasonable and compatible with science by articulating a natural theology far removed from Paley's "divine watchmaker" argument that nevertheless encourages human consciousness to reflect on the Creator. Unlike Paley, who found direct evidence of divine agency in the world, Polkinghorne acknowledged that in the modern era we must be contented with "general hints of the divine presence."[62] Modern science, however, has identified two areas where such hints are most evident:

> One is the vast cosmos itself, with its fifteen-billion-year history of evolving development following the big bang. The other is the "thinking reed" of humanity, so insignificant in physical scale but, as Pascal said, superior to all the stars because it alone knows them and itself. The universe and the means by which that universe has become marvellously self-aware—these are the centres of our enquiry.[63]

---

61 Darwin, *On the Origin of Species*, 760.
62 John Polkinghorne, *Belief in God in an Age of Science* (New Haven, CT: Yale University Press, 1998), 1.
63 Polkinghorne, 1–2.

Akin to Adam Frank's cosmological argumentation, Polkinghorne looks at both the vastness and complexity of the cosmos, alongside the reality that humanity is (for the moment) the only life-form we know capable of complex, self-reflective thought, and concludes that an anthropocentric perspective is too narrow and limiting, while also affirming that humanity has a unique role in planetary evolution.

Polkinghorne responds to Darwin's assertion that the sheer volume of suffering and death that accompanies natural selection contradicts belief in a benevolent God by arguing that an undirected and natural process entails genetic mutation (chance) as "the engine driving biological evolution."[64] Consequently, "the agonizing fact of cancer is not gratuitous, something that a Creator who was a bit more competent, or a bit less callous, could easily have avoided. It is the necessary cost of a world in which creatures make themselves."[65] Recalling Blaise Pascal's assessment of humanity's place in the universe, he states, "A human being is only a reed, the weakest in nature, but he is a thinking reed."[66] Polkinghorne affirms human uniqueness without contradicting natural selection, confident that "only a universe to whose physical fabric the free-process defense applied could give rise to beings to whom the free-will defense applies."[67]

In the end, the hopeful vision offered by ecofeminist theology—echoed in the theocentric proposal articulated by Moltmann—can only move forward to overcome cultural and societal resistance to environmental sustainability by cooperating with the scientific worldview. This entails a critical engagement of the natural sciences that addresses the objections of secularism while also offering alternative theological frameworks from which to counter destructive patriarchal theologies of domination. This perspective assumes that the natural sciences and theology are both human pursuits in search of answers to discrete questions about the universe that, over the centuries, have intersected and interacted. While many assume that the age of science has superseded the age of faith,

---

64 John Polkinghorne, *Theology in the Context of Science* (New Haven, CT: Yale University Press, 2009), 111.
65 Polkinghorne, 111.
66 Blaise Pascal, *Pensées and Other Writings*, trans. Honor Levi (Oxford: Oxford University Press, 1999), 72 (¶231).
67 Polkinghorne, *Theology in the Context of Science*, 113.

and mistakenly accept conflict as the only accurate way of describing the relationship between Christian belief and the natural sciences, the brief discussion above on the compatibility of theism with evolutionary theory demonstrates how conflict need not be the inevitable conclusion to the narrative relating theology to science.

Ivone Gebara's plea for a return to theological thinking *with* scientific reasoning, as opposed to a conflictual struggle against, yields a hopeful vision for a future in which humanity stands within nature in a divinely ordered communion rather than dominating and subduing nature:

> Our science and technology cannot eliminate the bitter taste of our finitude. As limited, contingent, and therefore imperfect beings, we would like to anchor ourselves in something that does not perish and be immortal. That is why I dare to say that we have to return to God, perhaps, no longer as the almighty Father, but as a consoling force of reciprocity, as a mystery that guides us or as a protection for our steps guaranteed by our neighbors, those and those who are our image and likeness.[68]

Like Moltmann's theocentric proposal, Gebara's God overcomes humanity's resistance to environmental sustainability by locating humanity properly within the creation as interdependent and interrelated to all other life. Rather than contradicting a scientific worldview, this conceptualization of God as inseparable from the cosmos restores the sense of awe and wonder that motivates both religious mythopoesis and scientific inquiry. Heidegger warned that we are chained to technology. Only a radical shift away from the Enlightenment's emphasis on instrumental reason can free humanity from the self-destructive bonds of unchecked technocratic capitalism.

The image of God immanent in every facet of creation—the God who makes a preferential option for the poor and disenfranchised—keeps hope alive because hope arises where God wills and not where we expect or desire it. A scientific understanding of human finiteness is not cause for despair but helps us realize our role in the bigger picture: "There will

---

68 Gebara, "Interdependence, Christianity, and Environmental Crisis," p. xx in this volume.

always be a tomorrow, even though I myself personally might not be here, although I never had children nor even planted a tree. 'God is my hope' means there is a place for my personal responsibility within the historical process. But this process is much grander and more complex than my simple analysis: it involves a thousand and one actors, and I cannot maintain the pretense that my analysis is the only one, or even the best one."[69] In cooperation with scientific learning, a theological framework can transform human attitudes—not all, but perhaps a critical mass—to create and foster a spirit of planetary solidarity.

---

69 Gebara, *Intuiciones ecofeministas*, 147–48.

CHAPTER 9

WORLD CHRISTIANITY AND ECOLOGY: ECOWOMANISM

Melanie L. Harris

Introduction: Ecowomanism

Ecowomanism is an approach to environmental justice that centers the voices and perspectives of women of color and specifically women of African descent. Like womanist theory and praxis, it insists on an ethical principle of justice. Therefore, ecowomanism is deconstructive and uses intersectional analysis to point out the correlation between environmental injustice and the maintenance of unjust systems that devalue the worth of all earthlings or, in the words of Delores S. Williams, "defile"[1] the sanctity of earth, beingness, and the innate dignity and worth of earthlings, including black women. Ecowomanism critically examines the logics of domination used to silence the earth and devalue—even destroy—the voices of women of African descent. Noting the similarities between the logic of domination that has historically silenced black women and the logic of domination that has limited the flourishing of earth, ecowomanist analysis points out the harm that takes place with the use of dualistic frameworks that have been foundational for the environmental movement, while often excluding the epistemologies of Indigenous people and communities of color. Calling for ecological reparations, ecowomanism offers a constructive approach and a more inclusive lens to environmental movement work. It does so by highlighting the voices, perspectives,

---

1   Delores S. Williams, "Sin, Nature and Black Women's Bodies," in *Ecofeminism and the Sacred*, ed. Carol Adams, (New York: Continuum, 1993), 24–29.

theologizing, and ethical meaning-making processes conceptualized by women of color and especially women of African descent engaged in earth justice.

In this sense, ecowomanism is not only deconstructive in its analytical approach. It is also constructive. It honors, uncovers, and validates the sources of Indigenous communities, Indigenous women, communities of color, and women of color, particularly women of African descent whose epistemologies, religious beliefs, spiritual activism, and values are devoted to the wholeness and thriving of earth and all earthlings. Finally, ecowomanism focuses on developing ethical frameworks by highlighting the moral arches in the earth-her-stories of women of African descent who are in communion with the earth and studies how this connection with the earth promotes the work of earth justice and social justice—since for ecowomanism, the two forms of justice are the same.

Ecowomanism as a Decolonizing Ecotheology

Ecowomanism can be described as a "decolonizing ecotheology" in that it promotes the use of intersectional analysis, including sociopolitical and spiritual-cultural critical lenses, to interrogate religious language and worldviews that are steeped in colonial frames and hierarchies. S. Lily Mendonza and George Zachariah's definition of decolonizing ecotheology is helpful here. The scholars define decolonizing ecotheology as "a spiritual and political vocation for all those who are committed to restoring Earth's—and earthlings'—flourishing."[2] Ecotheologies are "attempts to transform religions into public-oriented religions" or empower what Layli Maparyan terms "spiritual activism."[3] The work of decolonizing ecologies helps to reset theological foundations for "engaging creation-care and initiating programs for the restoration of creation," in part by pointing out some critical mis-alignments in ecotheologies that separate earth justice from social justice and use colonial frameworks to allow anthropocentric hierarchies to exist.

---

2   S. Lily Mendonza and George Zachariah, eds., *Decolonizing Ecotheology* (Eugene, OR: Pickwick Publications, 2022).

3   Layli Maparyan, *The Womanist Idea* (New York: Routledge, 2011), 114–144.

One of the great problems of ecotheologies that are void of a political frame and attention to justice is that they ignore the "least of these" being impacted most by climate change. It has often been said that those who contribute the least to the climate crisis are the ones who are paying the most. Across the entire globe, it is mostly Indigenous and communities of color who are bearing the brunt of the weight of climate change, facing remarkable disaster and displacement as a result of rising waters, soil pollution, deforestation, and so much more. Taking a decolonizing turn, ecowomanism points out these realities and highlights these particular voices. It does so in part by moving beyond the modes of conservation and preservation that have cemented whiteness and elevated maleness as core frames for the environmental movement. By recentering the voices of the Indigenous and communities of color, and by adapting environmental justice frameworks created by Robert Bullard, Dorceta Taylor, Chris Carter, Monica White, Sofia Betancourt, and so many other African American environmental justice keepers in the sciences, ecowomanism helps us to think differently about the norms of environmental work. It helps us to recenter the ecological worldviews of Native American Indigenous peoples, highlight the history of African American environmentalism, and intentionally include voices across communities of color in the United States and globally.

Ecowomanist Spirituality

Ecowomanist spirituality is a form of African and African American religion that centers planetary care and connection to the environment and raises awareness about the realities of climate change as central tenets for theological exploration. It can be understood as a form of spiritual activism that offers a response to the pain and suffering caused by climate change while lifting up hope for communities engaged in climate justice work, creating "ways out of no way" with the power of spiritual practices and rituals and a true devotion to earth justice. As such, ecowomanism highlights the research, religious orientations, spiritual activism, and religious practices of African and African American women environmentalists, climate scientists, religious leaders, policymakers, and researchers—such as Wangari Maathai and Alice Walker. The life work and incredible writings and scholarship of these women radically alter traditional norms in ecotheological discourse because they inherently resist colonial frames that dominate the shaping or normative categories in the field. As thinkers whose environmental justice strategies, writings, and spiritual practices guide the work of ecowomanism, they open the discourse of ecowomanism to insist on interfaith and interreligious approaches that can reshape ecological visions of justice.

Especially pertaining to the study and practice of religion, ecowomanism suggests that the way we connect with the earth opens alternative visons of how to live in more environmentally just ways of being. That is, when we consider an African cosmological vision that honors the interconnection between the divine, natural, and human realms, for example, we are presented with a moral prescription and theological base from which to explore questions about humanity's responsibility to care for and be with the earth in just and ethical ways that honor all of earth's being. As an approach that invites interreligious and constructive theological framings, ecowomanism ascribes to an African cosmology wherein the earth (nature), humans, and the divine/ancestors are all interconnected and function best in harmony with one another. That is, as we see modeled in the work of Wangari Maathai, the Kenyan mother of the Green Belt Movement, an ethical imperative for earth justice doesn't just refer to human-to-human encounters. Rather, true wholeness, true justice for the planet, exists in the beauty of all beings thriving and being fully in love together.

For some additional study, one might consider the following questions that inform the theological exploration into ecowomanist spirituality: What religion and what kinds of spiritual practices helped the descendants of enslaved Africans who were escaping the brutality and generational trauma of chattel slavery and later Jim and Jane Crow through the Great Migration? What earth wisdom did these grandparents and forebearers of ecowomanist spirituality have to assist families dealing with the agony of being separated from the soil of their birth? What spiritual practices empowered their courage to withstand and resist racial attacks and white supremacy even as they tried to build a new life of freedom? And what are the theological truths and underpinnings that shaped their relationship to the earth and honored the agricultural epistemology that they brought as remnants from Mother Africa?

ECOWOMANIST COURAGE, FACING TRUTH, AND THE CALL FOR ECOLOGICAL REPARATIONS

The eerie sounds of Billie Holiday's crackling, jazzy voice as she sings "Strange Fruit" hang in the air as we focus on the truth of where we are and what we need now—ecological reparations. Ecological reparations can be defined as the work and movement to shape environmental policy and theology that is reparative, restorative, and inclusive of the earth's voice and that shows compassion for all beings. Ecological reparations demand justice first. Similar to a womanist ethical approach that insists that justice is a primary tenant, a reparations framework acknowledges protection and sustainability as important values but privileges justice above all.[4] Beyond ecowomanism, this privilege of justice is noted by the great black theologian James H. Cone. In his book *The Cross the Lynching Tree*, Cone brilliantly draws out the connections between the most referenced symbol of Christianity, the cross, and the legacy of white supremacist theology and action practiced with an almost religious devotion through the act of lynching Black people. Finding strength in the Black faith that inspired, enabled, and emboldened Black people to live despite the threat of death and racial violence on every side, he writes about the necessity to look at both these symbols together:

> The cross can heal and hurt; it can be empowering and liberating but also enslaving and oppressive. There is no one way in which the cross can be interpreted. I offer my reflections because I believe that the cross placed alongside the lynching tree can help us to see Jesus in America in a new light, and thereby empower people who claim to follow him to take a stand against white supremacy and every kind of injustice.

An ecowomanist look at ecological reparations is also an offering to help us see America and even religion, religious practice, and racial healing in a new light.[5]

---

4   Robin Morris Collin and Robert Collin, "Environmental Reparations," in *The Quest for Environmental Justice: Human Rights and the Politics of Pollution*, ed. Robert D. Bullard (San Francisco: Sierra Club Books) 209–221.

5   It is important to note that while ecowomanist approaches recognize the complex racial landscape and the impact of white supremacy on day-to-day

Ecowomanist Method and Praxis

Ecowomanist method details seven steps that point toward the direction of ecological reparations and earth justice. The steps include:

1. honoring experience
2. reflecting on experience
   - connection with the earth
   - earth as sacred
   - shared experiences of beauty and suffering
   - parallel oppressions between Black women and the earth
3. conducting womanist social analysis
4. critically exploring tradition
5. engaging transformation
6. sharing dialogue
7. taking action for justice and sharing in justice work as a protest to the logic of domination, racial ignorance, and white supremacy

---

life in the US, especially for peoples of color, ecowomanism is not limited to a US-only lens. It also doesn't focus only on African American life or religion. Many African scholars, especially African women scholars such as Mercy Amba Oduyoye and Rose-Mary Amenga-Etego, have shaped African women's theology in ways that are epistemically linked to an ecowomanist vision that prioritizes attention to gender, theology, and ethics. For example, in my book *Ecowomanism: African American Women and Earth Honoring Faiths*, Mercy Amba Oduyoye's voice is referenced as central to ecowomanist discourse in that it reflects ecowomanism's inclusion of spiritual practices across the African diaspora that honor the earth as sacred. For more see Mercy Amba Oduyoye, "Earth Hope: A Letter," in *Ecowomanism, Religion and Ecology* (Boston: Brill, 2017), 81–86 and Rose-Mary Amenda-Etego, "Nankani Women's Spirituality and Ecology" in *Ecowomanism, Religion and Ecology* (Boston: Brill, 2017), 13–26.

While an ecowomanist method can be applied linearly, like most feminist liberative theological methods, the method works like a spiral, each step weaving in and out, being applied at different points of analysis. The method is especially helpful in charting a path toward ecological reparation because it honors a bridge to sustainability and equity that has both spiritual and ecological dimensions. That is, ecological reparations address more than repairing the earth. They also entail reshaping the moral imagination that has resulted in the Anthropocene, racial violence, ecological devastation, and continued assault on those striving to raise consciousness about climate change. Ecological reparations involve correcting ethical systems built into religions, cultural codes, and values and constructing new ethical frameworks and approaches that take into account the layers of environmental injustice and racial and climate violence that impact deeply vulnerable communities, including women and communities of color globally.

ECOWOMANIST MOTHERS: FANNIE LOU HAMER

Significantly, ecological reparations also demand a shift in the environmental and historical framework that has been used to study African Americans' relationship to the earth. That is, as religious and ecological scholars Monica M. White and Christopher Carter suggest in their works "A Pig in a Garden" and "The Spirit of Soul Food,"[6] respectively, a new approach in environmental studies is emerging. It shifts the focus from a non-liberative framework that "emphasizes the conditions of exploitation [of African Americans] that primarily structured the relationship to the land—from slavery through sharecropping and Jim Crow era discrimination against black farmers"[7] to a liberative framework that highlights African Americans' knowledge and use of agriculture "as a basis for

---

6   Christopher Carter, *The Spirit of Soul Food: Race, Faith and Food Justice* (Champaign, IL: University of Illinois Press, 2021).

7   Monica M. White, "'A Pig and a Garden': Fannie Lou Hamer and the Freedom Farm Cooperative," in *Food and Foodways* 2017, 25, no. 1, 20-39, http://dx.doi.org/10.1080/07409710.2017.1270647/.

resistance."[8] Engaging a liberative analysis of Fannie Lou Hamer's Freedom Farm Cooperative, White explains:

> Contrary to perspectives that emphasize the legacies of oppression of black farmers and farmworkers in agricultural communities, and the long history of disenfranchisement/enslavement tied to agriculture, Hamer made food and its production an act of resistance and a strategy to build a sustainable community. Freedom Farm represented her vision of the centrality of food and agriculture in building self-reliant communities as a base for political activism.[9]

A careful look at White's analysis of Hamer's life and the Freedom Farm Cooperative reveals values maintained and modeled by Hamer and those who worked alongside her in order to create self-reliant communities. Having all but given up on the American promise and having toiled endlessly as a leader in the Civil Rights Movement to bring about change, fight for the African American right to vote, and create a living and true democracy, Hamer toward the end of her life used her platform and international acclaim to build up her community in a fashion that interrupted white supremacy and poverty at the same time. Creating a model of resistance based on the right and value of quality of life, Hamer sought to "develop a cooperative intentional community, with housing, employment, educational opportunities, health care and access to healthy food, [reflective] of a self-determined, politically engaged, liberated community."[10]

As a proto-ecowomanist, Fannie Lou Hamer stands a pioneering figure in the tradition. Not only is she a model of one who aligned the political, socialpolitical, religious-ethical, and racial justice agenda with an earth justice agenda, but she did so by using her organic intellectualism, spirituality, and strategies in grassroots movement building and organizing. The combination of sources from which Hamer found courage and fortitude to do her work presents a wholistic model not only of an authentic life and noble character but also of what it means to be a woman,

---

8   White, "'A Pig and a Garden,'" 22.
9   White, "'A Pig and a Garden,'" 33.
10 White, "'A Pig and a Garden,'" 33.

womanist, spiritual being, leader, farmer, mother, partner, politician, and activist. These identities are ones that are embodied by many womanist scholars, thinkers, and activists today. Thus, seeing Hamer from this new perspective is helpful.

ECOWOMANIST MOTHERS: CHARTING AN ECOWOMANIST ETHIC OF SUFFICIENCY

Often in womanist religious scholarship, there is a role model of womanist ethical living. Alice Walker (who coined the term "womanist") attests in her writings about uncovering the work of Zora Neale Hurston that the present generation has only to dig deep, doing the work of uncovering the Black women's literary tradition, to discover a path, however partial or fragmented, that Black women made before.[11] When searching for a model of Black womanhood, strength, and strategies of survival, examining historical Black women and how they blazed a trail in their lives and liberative work often reveals roots and grounding that provide a scaffold for a new beginning. In this case, an ecological reparative ethic, the ethic of sufficiency.[12]

In order to do this work of uncovering a model for an ecological reparative ethic, or an ethic of sufficiency, I return to the methodological steps of a womanist virtue ethic. As I explicate in my book *Gifts of Virtue, Alice Walker, and Womanist Ethics*,[13] this method foregrounds three steps used to mine values for the shaping of a life map, ethical path of living, or path for when facing a crisis. Informed by the model and Black womanist ethic of Katie G. Cannon, the womanist virtue ethic method

---

11 Alice Walker, "Looking for Zora," in *In Search of Our Mothers' Gardens* (New York: Harcourt Brace Jovanovich, 1983), 93–116.

12 Having experienced a real sense of "lostness" and disconnection as a result of loss and isolation due to the COVID-19 pandemic, many Black women have a strong desire to seek a path of community. That is, as countries, communities, and individuals navigate global realities of health care disparities, racial injustice, and climate change, many Black women (and others) are looking for answers, ways to become stable, and new alternatives of viewing and understanding life that highlight the value of connection with other beings.

13 Melanie L. Harris, *Gifts of Virtue, Alice Walker and Womanist Ethics* (New York: Palgrave Macmillan, 2010).

helps to glean womanist values helpful in shaping the moral lives and enhancing the quality of life of Black women and the earth community. Recognizing virtues for an ethic of sufficiency begins with highlighting experiential themes recorded in an analysis of Fannie Lou Hamer's life and the Freedom Farm Cooperative. For the purpose of this chapter, Monica M. White's work serves as a primary source for this investigation. Though not an exhaustive source, White's positive and liberative frame used to examine Hamer's life and work is helpful in showcasing the full vision and success of the Freedom Farm Cooperative. The second step in the method is to glean ethical implications and sift values from these themes. The third step is naming and explicating each of the virtues gleaned and framing a list of values. For the purpose of this work, these values serve as the skeleton for a fuller explication of a womanist ethic of sufficiency, a constructive echo of the method applied in this paper, and a move toward hope as evidence of God's love in (and as) the cosmos. These values are:

- liberation
- resistance
- self-reliance
- self-determination
- food
- quality of life
- political activism
- connection with the earth
- community
- solidarity

Uncovering the ethical building blocks or set of values that guided Fannie Lou Hamer provides a base for an ecowomanist theological ethic of sufficiency, thus creating a middle path between an ethic of scarcity and an ethic of abundance, often referenced in creation care discourse.

The new ethic raises the question of what is enough while simultaneously critiquing a culture of overconsumption. Rather than lifting values of greed, an ethic of sufficiency highlights the values of sharing, feeling fulfilled, being satisfied, and living in community with all beings in the earth community. During the last years of Fannie Lou Hamer's life, she worked as a self-sustaining farmer and believed fiercely in Black people's right to farm, harvest, and grow for themselves—apart from the white supremacist template of sharecropping (a form of slavery). Taking lessons from this, an ecowomanist ethic of sufficiency also provides theological reflection on earth-honoring faith strategies for the care of the self, planet, and community. Some of the earth stories and wisdom emerging from the life and work of Black women such as Fannie Lou Hamer and abolitionist Harriet Tubman provide sources from which to garner values and contemplate new insights about facing climate change when we understand the earth as partner, protector, healer, and liberator.

To begin the dialogue about an ecowomanist theological ethic of sufficiency, it is first helpful to set the stage by revealing the extreme alternative theological ethics that function normatively in many theologies adopted by creation care churches and ministries. The first is an ethic based on what Walter Brueggemann calls "the myth of scarcity."[14] This ethic suggests to Christian communities (and all communities) that they exist solely in a culture of scarcity and therefore must always measure their ability to give, conserve, and even create with a sharp blade of theological subtraction. One of the outcomes of the myth of scarcity is a practice of consumerism out of fear of lack. It aligns with a theological assumption that the total sum provided by God (creation) can never be replenished or re-imagined. This form of theology understands God to be challenged in giving, a scrooge, penny-pincher, or absent following the placement of the original gift. No generosity here! Rather, a calculating God, who accounts for every cent, carbon footprint, and non-recycled bulletin that a church puts out, is presented before us.

A theology of abundance counters this first model and suggests that God gives generously and wants us, as human members of the earth

---

14   Walter Brueggemann, "The Liturgy of Abundance, the Myth of Scarcity," in *The Christian Century*, 116, no. 10 (March 24, 1999): 342–347.

community, to do the same. A branch of this theology that acknowledges the reality of multilayered oppressions comes from the rich southern black women's culture of womanism. Articulated best by womanist historian Rachel Harding in the volume *Remnants: A Memoir of Spirit, Activism, and Mothering,* honoring the work and scholarly writings of her mother, Rosemarie Harding, Harding writes:

> *There is no scarcity. There is no shortage. No lack of love, of compassion, of joy in the world. There is enough.*
> *There is more than enough.*
> *Only fear and greed make us think otherwise.*
> *No one need starve. There is enough land and enough food.*
> *No one need die of thirst. There is enough water. No one need live without mercy. There is no end to grace. And we are all instruments of grace. The more we give it, the more we share it, the more we use it, the more God makes. There is no scarcity of love. There is plenty. And always more. This is the universe my mother lived in. Her words. Her ways. This is the universe she was raised in, by parents from rural Georgia who came up in a generation after slavery. People who lived with many terrors but who knew terror was not God's final say. This is the universe she taught me. Whatever I call religion is this inclusive, Christian, indigenous, Black, southern cosmology of compassion and connectedness. It is the poetry of my mother's life.*[15]

Rosemarie Freeney Harding believed in a world of abundance, where there was enough for all to eat, to live, to breathe, to be. Battling against the structural racism that was a deep part of the lives of African Americans in the US at the time of Rosemarie Harding's life, Harding still held a deep belief in an ethic of sufficiency: that God was an abundantly loving God and saw deep worth in every being, every Black life, and every Black soul regardless of the daily evidence of white supremacy. Allowing for the

---

15   Rosemarie Freeney Harding with Rachel Elizabeth Harding, *Remnants: A Memoir of Spirit, Activism, and Mothering* (Durham, NC: Duke University Press, 2015), ix.

acknowledgment of both evil (white supremacy) and a theology of resistance and divine love, this theology of abundance was much more than food or money—it was the wealth of being and was filled with the inner knowing of one's worth and value as a child, a cherished creation of God.

How race is constructed, how racism is woven into the theology of scarcity, and how it manifests in this later form of the theology of abundance is significant for us in the work and development of new ecotheologies. We see the differences in these theologies when we compare the womanist theology of abundance to the theology of scarcity, which emerged out of a classical form of theological understanding and is practiced in mainly white, Protestant churches.

A final example and powerful living model of a womanist leader living out what I would call an "ecowomanist ethic of sufficiency" is Dr. Iva C. Carruthers, professor emeritus and former chairperson of the sociology department at Northeastern Illinois University. Her nuanced work and scholarship on the development of a theology of sufficiency and her special noticing of the presence of lament even within a theology is key to ecowomanism. That is, Carruthers explains that while the language of scarcity is common in social, political, and theological discourse, the language of abundance has also been unhelpful. Prosperity gospel movements have often been associated with detrimental values of abundance, including extravagance, divine favor, and exclusion.[16] When the abundance of material things (proof of the love of God) is placed on one side and scarcity marked by the abandonment of God (the scale of God's love) is on the other, presence and giving become weighted by obedience to the proclaimers of such prosperity gospel. The theology does not take into account structure, evil, or sin. It is considered ahistorical, ignoring for example the history of slave codes, legalized segregation, and separate but unequal access to education. According to Carruthers, these forms of abundance theology (prosperity gospel) give "false hope by ignoring the structural issues that keep many from real opportunities for education, good health, and a good job." The scarcity-abundance binary does not leave room for the living out of Christian community in ways that build

---

16   David P. King, "Beyond Abundance: Is Stewardship Ethical?" *Word & World*, 38, no. 3 (2018): 301–308.

up community and negate individualism. In order to offer a constructive theological correction, Carruthers reclaims a fuller theology of abundance where the church is encouraged to embrace the celebration of plenty but also the reality of lament. As a form of earth stewardship, an ecowomanist ethic of sufficiency raises the importance of including lament into our ecotheology. One framing of this might be lamenting that the world is not as we would hope it might be; asking for forgiveness for our own sins, what we have done and left undone; working to make sure all of God's children (all of creation) have what they need; and sitting in lament before we act or move to challenge the church. Another framing of this lament in ecotheology would be to actively include practices of lament into our new ecotheologies and earth-honoring faiths; not only for the species that have been lost and the ecosystems that no longer exist but also for every innocent Black man or woman who was ever been shot down unjustly and murdered by the police.

Adding this form of lament into our ecotheologies brings us on our way to what Cone called for when he said, "We need theologians and ethicists who are interested in mutual dialogue, honest conversation about justice for the earth and all of its inhabitants. . . . Dialogue requires respect and knowledge of the other—their (environmental) history, culture and religion. No one racial or national group has all the answers, but all groups have something to contribute to the earth's healing."[17] We honor the work of the ecowomanist mothers before us and engage the challenge of James Cone and others, who saw a deep connection between earth justice and social justice; we are the scholars, activists, theologians, ethicists, and environmental justice keepers called to speak up with the earth in this time. We do so honoring the earth and making room for the fullness of earth stories long silenced. Coming to voice earth stories long silenced will help us break forth into ecowomanist hope even in such a time as this.

---

17   King, "Beyond Abundance," 301.

CHAPTER 10

EMBRACING LIFE AND CULTIVATING HOPE: THE ECOLOGICAL DIMENSION OF LIBERATION THEOLOGY[1]

Luis Martínez Andrade

INTRODUCTION

Since the seventies, different reports by the Club of Rome have alerted us to the limits of growth. The reports have analyzed five significant trends: accelerated industrialization, rapid population growth, widening undernutrition, the decay of non-renewable resources, and the degradation of the environment. The 1972 report warned of the terrible consequences of the continuation of this model of development.[2] In terms of the position of the church, Olivier Landron considers that contemporary historians of Catholicism have not studied in depth the relationship between the church and nature for two main reasons: because the relationship between God and humanity has been seen as privileged and because of suspicion toward pantheism.[3] From the debates at the First Vatican Council (1869–1870) and the Second Vatican Council (1962–1965), we see a recomposition of theology concerned with the creation and its different manifestations. In France, the theology of creation was deeply marked by Thomism, which had little interest in the relationship between the Creator and the universe. On the other hand, the work of the Jesuit Paul Beauchamp highlights the renewal of Christian thinking regarding nature and the human sciences.

---

[1] Translated from Spanish by Stephen Di Trolio Coakley.
[2] René Dumont, *L'utopie ou la mort!* (Paris: Seuil, 1974), 19.
[3] Olivier Landron, *Le Catholicisme Vert: Histoire des relations entre l'église et la nature au XXe siècle*, Histoire (Paris: Cerf, 2008), 7.

Since the eighties, a number of theologians emerged in the francophone sphere who privileged their reflections around the subject matter of nature. In the Protestant world, it was the world of the Lutheran theologian from Strasburg, Gérard Siegwalt, and the reformed theologian from Lausanne, Pierre Gisel, who roused interest in a theology of creation. In the Catholic ambit, it was the work of Pierre Ganne, René Coste, Jean-Michel Maldamé, François Euvé, Jacques Arnould, and Adolphe Gesché. Additionally, in 1988 the French publication of *Gott in der Schöpfung: Ökologische Schöpfungslehre* by German theologian Jürgen Moltmann marked a point of inflection in taking account of the ecological crisis through theological means. On the other hand, the figure of Pierre Teilhard de Chardin occupies an important place in contemporary thought around these matters, through theology (Christogenesis), philosophy (holism), and science (paleontology). Finally, we should point out that the Brazilian theologian Leonardo Boff integrates the *noosphere* concept in his anti-hegemonic critique just as in his questioning of the capitalist system that destroys nature.[4]

LIBERATION CHRISTIANITY AND ECOLOGY OF THE POOR

Undoubtedly, liberation theology represented a vital inflection point in the intellectual history of Latin American critical thinking. Since the beginning of the 1970s, there began to circulate the first written documents of those who would later be its leading proponents: Gustavo Gutiérrez, Leonardo and Clodovis Boff, Enrique Dussel, Hugo Assmann, Jon Sobrino, Frei Betto, Pablo Richard, Rubén Dri, Jorge Pixley, and Juan Luis Segundo. In addition, the sociologist Michael Löwy uses the Weberian concept of *elective affinities* to not only understand the relationship between Christianity and socialism but to explain the new religious cultures that produced the emergence of liberation theology.[5] For Michael Löwy, two foundational events between 1958 and 1959 would later lead to the

---

4 Luis Martínez Andrade, *Ecología y teología de la liberación. critica de la modernidad/colonialidad* (Barcelona: Herder, 2019).

5 Michael Löwy, *La lutte des dieux : christianisme de la libération et politique en Amérique latine : avant-propos de Leonardo Boff* (Paris: Van Dieren Éditeur, 2019).

development of a liberationist Christianity. On the one hand is the election of Pope John XXIII, who was responsible for the organization of the Second Vatican Council. On the other hand is the Cuban Revolution, which with its anti-imperialist, anti-capitalist program laid the groundwork for what would later be known as *guevarismo*. Löwy additionally points out the specific impact of French anti-capitalist progressive Christianity (predominantly Catholic but also ecumenical), which would influence the emergence of liberationist Christianity in Brazil. In the 1970s, in Brazil, a *progressive Christianity*, known as the *Esquerda católica*, began to arise, which in later years would grow throughout Latin America. This is the case because the French Catholic Church has had a privileged relationship with the Brazilian Catholic Church; a clear example of this is the Catholic student union known as *Juventude Universitária Católica* (JUC).

Michael Löwy highlights a few key moments that would be instrumental in developing a new religious culture during the first two years of the 1970s and would antecede the emergence of liberation theology. First, the document presented by the JUC in 1960 was called "Algumas diretrizes para um ideal histórico para o povo brasileiro" and outlined the nefarious mechanisms of capitalism. Second, the article entitled "Juventude cristã hoje," published in 1962 by Herbert José de Souza "Betinho" (who was a representative for JUC), embodied the anti-capitalist Catholic *ethos*. The third event was a conference of progressive Protestants, which was called "Cristo e o processo revolucionário brasileiro" and took place in 1962 in the city of Recife. The fourth was the creation of the movement *Ação Popular* (Popular Action) in the city of Belo Horizonte in 1962, which unified the JUC members with the *Educação Popular* movement (in the line of Paulo Freire) with the expressed purpose of fighting for socialism and using the Marxist method. In 1964, *Ação Popular* distanced itself from the church to join the ranks of the *Partido Comunista de Brasil* (PCdoB). These events indicate the burgeoning "new religious culture," configured in an even more radical iteration of the "spirit of Vatican II." In this sense, Löwy proposes that we should understand *liberation Christianity* as a social movement whose spiritual and intellectual expression was liberation theology. In this regard, the *elective affinities* between Christianity and socialism as identified by Löwy are: (1) a profound critique of individualist visions of the world (liberal-rationalist, empiricist, hedonist) toward a faith with *trans-individualist* values; (2) both visions hold the poor as the victims of injustice; (3) both share *universalism* as internationalism and Catholicism (in its etymological meaning), that is, they conceive of humanity as a totality whose substantial union is beyond race, ethnicity, or nations; (4) the value of community and communitarian life; (5) the critique of capitalism and the doctrines of liberalism; (6) both share a hope for a future kingdom of justice and liberty, peace, and fraternity among all of humanity.

The massive occupation of the Amazon began with the military government in Brazil expressing the objective of pillaging its natural resources. Without accounting for the detriment to Indigenous populations, the bishops of the northeast of Brazil published on May 6, 1973 a document entitled "Eu ouvi os clamores do meu povo," a prophetic text that echoes Exodus 3:7 by denouncing poverty, hunger, and oppression—an oppression that the government carefully hid under the veneer of development (in the sense of dependency theory). This commitment to the oppressed led to the assassination in 1976 of two priests, Rodolfo Lunkenbein and João Bosco Burnier. Nevertheless, this document, written over thirty years ago, continues to be relevant because it lays out the horrible conditions of life of the *campesinos*, who are trapped between the interests of the ruling classes, national and international. Among the bishops who participated in the writing of the document were Hélder Câmara, José Lamartine Soares, and José Maria Pires.

Founded in 1975, the Comisión Pastoral de la Tierra de Brasil (CPT) focused on the problem of the redistribution of lands. From its beginning, this commission embraced the cause of the rural workers, which denounced the murders and oppression of the rural activists in the world while asking for agrarian reform. In terms of liberationist Christianity, Tomás Balduino and Pedro Casaldáliga became emblematic figures of the fight for agrarian reform. In 1971, Pedro Casaldáliga published a pastoral letter entitled "A Church in the Amazons in Conflict with Large Estate Holders (Latifundio) and Social Marginalization," where he dealt with the question of the destructive logic of capitalism.

Fighting against deforestation in the Amazons, the CPT joined the spirit of the eco-economist Joan Martinez-Alier, who has been called the "environmentalism of the poor."[6] Against the military dictatorship and even during the democratically elected governments, the CPT mobilized to defend the oppressed, denouncing the alliance between the government and large agribusiness. Therefore, it is fortuitous that one of the members of the CPT, the Benedictine monk Marcelo Barros, developed a theology of the land, where the land is considered the place of life, an anthropological, sociopolitical, and religious totality. In this perspective, the cosmogonies of Indigenous communities and the sensibilities of the *campesinos* are rehabilitated since each, in their manner, respects the natural cycles of the land.[7]

Marcelo Barros also affirms that capitalism does not hold a respectful relationship with nature.[8] The inherent dynamic to the movement of valorization of capital transforms land into a commodity, that is, an object that can be bought and sold. Revalorizing the agrarian style and the festiveness of the liturgy, the CPT works as a catalyst for the feelings of the rural population. The liberation of the oppressed rural peoples of the world and the liberation of the land go hand in hand. The CPT is occupied with the fight against deforestation, precarious and inhumane work conditions, the expulsion of farmers, the taking of land parcels, and the destruction of the land. Though the CPT does not openly discuss the ecological dimension, this does not mean that this aspect of their work is not present. In their work, we can see the convergence between the environmentalism of the poor and liberation Christianity.

In Latin America, the spirituality of liberation Christianity, rural communities, and Indigenous peoples have significantly contributed to the fight for socio-environmentalism.[9] Without a doubt, the community

---

6   Juan Martinez-Alier, *The Environmentalism of the Poor: A Study of Ecological Conflicts and Valuation* (Cheltenham, UK: Edward Elgar, 2002).

7   Luis Martínez Andrade, "Elective Affinities between Liberation Theology and Ecology in Latin America," in *Religion in Rebellions, Revolutions, and Social Movements*, ed. Warren S. Goldstein and Jean-Pierre Reed, Routledge Studies in Religion and Politics (London: Routledge, 2022), 219–30.

8   Marcelo Barros, *Para Onde Vai Nuestra América. Espiritualidade Socialista Para o Século XXI* (São Paulo: Nhanduti Editora, 2011), 40.

9   Luis Martínez Andrade, "Biocolonialité Du Pouvoir et Mouvements Sociaux Dans l'Amérique Latine," *Écologie & Politique* 55 (2017): 153–64.

that stands out among those fighting for liberation in our continent is the Indigenous peoples of the southeast of Mexico organized around the Ejército Zapatista de liberación Nacional (EZLN). Inside the traditions that form the Zapatista movement, we must mention: a considerable Indigenous (Maya) resistance, the experience of the guerrilla, and the work done around the ecclesial base communities (CEBs)[10] inspired by liberation theology. On this last point, Samuel Ruiz García was fundamental to developing an incarnated liberation theology or Indigenous theology. Named bishop of San Cristóbal de las Casas in 1959, Ruiz was influenced by the fresh winds of the Second Vatican Council and, of course, by the Indigenous meetings in Melgar (1968) and Xicotepec de Juárez (1970). Over time Samuel Ruiz gradually moved from a conservative position to one increasingly linked to liberation theology. In 1974, Ruiz organized El Congreso Indígena, a pivotal event that raised consciousness around the issues of the Indigenous communities. Some members of his catechist network would later join the ranks of the EZLN.[11] Though it may be correct, as held by Graham McGeoch,[12] that the neo-Zapatista movement did not have the same impact as the Cuban Revolution on the sociopolitical imagination of liberation Christianity, its influence was fundamental in the new configuration of social movements.[13]

Another struggle, equally as important, was that of Chico Mendes, who pointed out three important aspects of the sociopolitical imagination of the region: (1) the ecological struggle of the poor, where the defense of nature is an issue of life or death; (2) a liberation Christianity represented by the work of the CEBs; and (3) the inheritance of the heterodox Marxist tradition. (Regarding the third aspect, the influence that Euclides Fernandes Távora, who had been the lieutenant of Luis Carlos Prestes, had

---

10 Comunidades Ecclesiales de Base.
11 Samuel Ruiz García, *Cómo me convirtieron los indígenas*, Colección servidores y testigos (Santander, Spain: Sal Terrae, 2003).
12 Graham McGeoch, "Liberation Theology: Problematizing the Historical Projects of Democracy and Human Rights," *Revista Sociedade e Cultura* 23 (2020).
13 Raúl Zibechi, *Los arroyos cuando bajan. Los desafíos del zapatismo* (Málaga, Spain: Zambra/Baladre, 2019), https://traficantes.net/libros/los-arroyos-cuando-bajan.

on Chico Mendes cannot be sidestepped.) The fight that Mendes represented was a pivotal moment in the eco-socialist struggle in Latin America. Up until then, the problem of the environment had not been linked to social justice issues. Following this, we can hold that *ecological sensibility* does not exclusively belong to developed nations; instead, it is a vital issue for societies at the periphery. Countries have been looted for over five hundred years by the deadly dynamics of modernity and coloniality. In fact, in 1975, the same year that Chico Mendes and Wilson Pinheiro started the union of Brazilian rural workers, the Brazilian CPT was started. The role of the CPT was fundamental in developing environmental battles against large-scale agribusiness in Brazil with the support of *campesino* movements such as the Movimento dos Trabalhadores Rurais Sem Terra (MST). Through the CEBs, the CPT launched formidable work to raise awareness in rural areas, resulting in the emergence of new syndicalism, which only strengthened the link between traditional leftist notions and liberation theology. Through periodic meetings, reflecting, systematizing the needs of farmers, these rural populations underwent a process of constituting new forms of self-identity directly linked to their liberatory reading of the Bible, where the theme of land acquired a new meaning. Thus, the fight for access to land now found a religious justification. It should not be foreign to us that the work of the CPT should have had such a profound impact on the formation of the Movimento dos Trabalhadores Rurais Sem Terra (MST). The CPT contributed to the MST, strengthening the socioreligious dimension of its cause, where the importance of the *mística* should not be overlooked.[14] In the words of João Pedro Stedile (the founder and national

---

14 The term *mística* has generated much confusion not only because of its difficulty of translation but also because of what it implies in a theological context. Following the approaches of some liberation theologians (Juan Luis Segundo, Leonardo Boff or Marcelo Barros), theologian Graham McGeoch argues that *mística*, specifically that of the MST, is not ideological or alienating because it is rooted in the experiences of struggle, resistance, and redistribution of the earth. In this sense McGeoch recognizes that although liberation theology does not have a systematic reflection on the *mística* of the MST, it does offer general reflections on it. See Graham McGeoch, "Marxismo, mística e o MST: qual é o segredo do MST na luta pela reforma agraria no Brasil?", *Debates do NER*, Porto Alegre, 33 (2018), 174–196.

representative), the mystical nature inside the MST is not a metaphysical or idealist distraction but a source of unity in the daily life of its members, where there is no contradiction between faith and struggle.[15] The MST is the protagonist of an anti-state, anti-imperialist, and anti-capitalist struggle. We can see the mystical expressed through symbols (flags, slogans, hymns, songs, and many others) that nourish and allow for the affirmation of the movement's identity. The symbolic-religious aspect becomes a source of inspiration (of the struggle, utopia, and rebellion). Far from alienating the movement, memory, identity, or myths of the MST, it gives it a radical strength to its sociopolitical horizon.

The MST became the subject of its own liberation by practicing an offensive strategy of agrarian political reforms that created *assentamentos*, parcels of lands on which the landless *campesinos* settled. In 2009, there were about eight thousands of these *assentamentos* across Brazil. However, the struggle of the MST is not limited to merely the possession of land but also sheds light on a new society in which *campesino* agriculture is in harmony with nature and opposed to large agribusiness.[16] The MST has expressed solidarity with Indigenous groups not only in the access to land but in their struggle with agribusiness and monocultures. However, holding tight to its convictions, the MST opposes the pharaonic projects of building hydroelectric dams in the Amazon. These projects tend to benefit the country's elites and large transnational corporations, who are responsible for terrible detriment to the environment.

We must comment on the "pharaonic project" of moving the Rio de San Francisco which, undoubtedly, found resistance among the river-dwelling communities as well as among members of the Catholic Church, such as the bishop of the Diocese of Barra, Luís Flávio Cappio. In 2005 and 2007, Cappio underwent two hunger strikes (in line with a nonviolent position) to oppose the work on the river since it was considered a direct attack on the people and communities that depended on the river as their life source. Additionally, this project had the objective of satiating the large industrial corporations that are the most responsible for contamination

---

15   João Pedro Stedile and Bernardo Mançano, *Brava Gente: A trajetória do MST e a luta pela terra no Brasil* (São Paulo: Fundação Perseu Abramo, 2005).

16   Michael Löwy, *Écosocialisme: l'alternative radicale à la catastrophe écologique capitaliste*, Les petits Libres, n° 77 (Paris: Éd. Mille et une nuits, 2011).

and pollution. Therefore, Cappio found resonance among popular ecological movements, including the MST. In the same way, for João Alfredo Telles Melo, the project of this river did not resolve issues of drought when unaccompanied by an agrarian and water reform. The conflict around the river was political, economic, cultural, and environmental. These questions needed to be thought out from criteria that aimed to conserve the means of sustenance and life of the communities. Rather than merely solving immediate political issues or those based on the instrumental rationality of modernity and coloniality, the fight against the redirection of the river, according to Telles Melo, "not only had an anti-imperialist character but fundamentally, an anti-capitalist one which was expressed in the direct opposition to treating water as merchandise."[17] From this vantage point, this struggle becomes a prophetic act against the forces of death in capitalism. If, as highlighted by Martínez Alier, ecological politics is concerned with distributive environmental conflicts, then following this, we would not be remiss in naming this struggle of redirecting the Rio de San Francisco as a succinct case of the *environmentalism of the poor* or popular environmentalism.

THE DEFENSE OF HUMAN AND NONHUMAN LIFE

Liberation theology is a theology of life.[18] For the feminist theologian Maria Clara Lucchetti Bingemer, "those who fight for life find God in history and before God in history."[19] Allan Coelho holds that the distinction between the gods of life and those of fetishes is fundamental to understanding the critique of liberation theology.[20] In effect, as pointed out by Graham McGeoch, we cannot get around the fact that liberation theology always

---

17 João Alfredo Telles Melo, *Direito Ambiental, Luta Social e Ecossocialismo* (Fortaleza, Brazil: Demócrito Rocha, 2010), 287.

18 Marcelo Barros and Frei Betto, *O amor fecunda o Universo: ecologia e espiritualidade* (Rio de Janeiro: Agir, 2009).

19 Maria Clara Lucchetti Bingemer, "Direitos humanos, direitos divinos," in *Fé cristã e direitos humanos*, ed. Daniel Ribeiro de Almeida Chacon and Frederico Soares de Almeida, 1st ed. (São Paulo: Edições Loyola, 2021), 45.

20 Allan da Silva Coelho, "Fé capitalista e a devoção dos cristãos: o sacrifício dos direitos dos pobres," in *Fé cristã e direitos humanos*, ed. Daniel Ribeiro de

underlines the themes of *liberation* and, in this sense, goes far beyond a mere reflection on democracy and human rights. Therefore, following the tenets of the German theologian Jürgen Moltmann (cosmic love, ecological spirituality) and Brazilian theologian Ivone Gebara (interdependence, interrelationality, environmental crisis), we will explore some aspects of the evident ecological connection to liberation theology.

The "theology of the hoe," as proposed by the Belgian theologian José Comblin, is another way of thinking about liberation theology that begins in the rural world. Having proposed in the 1970s a theology of revolution, Eduardo Hoornaert states that José Comblin breaks away from the pedagogical traditions of over sixteen centuries and rehabilitates a Christian pedagogy existent prior to the fifth century.[21] More pedagogy than theology, the theology of the hoe revives catechism and oral education from the place of popular religiosity. Inspired by the ideas of Joseph Cardijn and by Paulo Freire, Comblin developed a project in which pedagogical reciprocity is an antecedent to religious experience, evangelization, and interpersonal relationships found in the heart of the Church. The theology of the hoe is a metaphor that remits us of the worldview of the farmers of the northeast of Brazil, those who do not use a plow but rather work the earth by opening it with a hoe and later sow and plant. The theology of the hoe has an ecological dimension, though it may not be fully evident, in that it tries to establish a harmonious relationship with nature. A vision of the world in which the *campesinos* live, where a sense of community is fundamental, is positioned against the formation of social hegemony, the modernity and coloniality that genuinely exists.[22]

In the 1970s, theologians such as Rosemary Radford Ruether articulated the fight against sexism as an issue of environmentalism. She denounced the androcentric categories of theological discourse at the heart of the power structures of the church that maintain women in

---

Almeida Chacon and Frederico Soares de Almeida, 1st ed. (São Paulo: Edições Loyola, 2021), 281–92.

21   Eduardo Hoornaert, "L'audace d'un Théologien," in *Joseph Comblin, Prophète et Ami Des Pauvres*, ed. Philippe Dupriez (Brussels: Lessius, 2014), 95–102.
22   Martínez Andrade, *Ecología y teología de la liberación. crítica de la modernidad/ colonialidad*.

positions of marginality and, at the same time, consolidate the patriarchy.[23] Even though feminist theologians share some commonly held points (the critique of patriarchal structures, androcentrism, and the domination of women's bodies), it is worth noting that they are far from being a homogeneous discourse.[24]

Influenced by the work of Rosemary Radford Ruether and Dorothee Sölle, the Brazilian theologian Ivone Gebara has been working since the 1980s on feminist theology in the key of liberation.[25] Through her mediation through gender, Gebara tries to overcome the epistemological dualism of hegemonic theology that, with its dominating anthropological vision, has legitimized the submission of women. Gebara considers it necessary to overcome hierarchical, unjust, and discriminatory relationships in society and the church.[26] In the 1990s, she cultivated an ecofeminist theology in which the poor and nature are designated as victims of the current hegemonic system. In her book, *Intuiciones ecofeministas*, Ivone Gebara explains from a holistic perspective how women and nature are exploited and dominated, through patriarchal discourses, by the modern logic of capitalism. Consequently, for Gebara ecofeminism is a way of thinking and a social movement that challenges the systems of hierarchy and patriarchy since these systems exploit women and nature. She writes:

---

23   Rosemary Radford Ruether, "Ecofeminism and Healing Ourselves, Healing the Earth," *Feminist Theology 9*, 1995.

24   Articulating together queer theory and liberation theology, Marcella Althaus-Reid sought to fill the void between the asexual discourse of the poor and of new sexual identities to subvert the heterosexual models used by so many theologians, including liberation theologians. See Marcella Althaus-Reid, *La Teología indecente: perversiones teológicas en sexo, género y política*, Serie general universitaria (Barcelona: Bellaterra, 2005).

25   Ivone Gebara, *Intuiciones ecofeministas: ensayos para repensar el conocimiento y la religión* (Madrid: Trotta, 2000).

26   Ivone Gebara speaks of the "zôè-diversity" of God to qualify the diversity of discourses about God. In this regard, respect for ecosystems becomes an ethical imperative. See Ivone Gebara, *Le mal au féminin: Réflexions théologiques à partir du féminisme*, Collection Religion et Sciences Humaines (Paris: L'Harmattan, 1999).

> Ecofeminism as a way of thinking and social movement refers to the ideological connection between the exploitation of nature and the exploitation of women within the system of hierarchy-patriarchy. From this philosophical and theological point of view, ecofeminism can be considered as a type of wisdom which tries to recover ecosystems and women ... As Carolyn Merchant well reminds us, modernity—though historians do not speak of this—begins with the torture of witches and the establishment of a new scientific method ... Modernity begins, thus, with the redefinition of the roles of women as homemakers, subordinated by marital and familial relationships. At the same time, nature, now freed from the power of spirits, gradually dispelled of its secrets, is gradually dominated by the masculine scientific spirit.[27]

The theological project of Ivone Gebara clearly shows the convergence between feminist liberation theology and concern for the environment from a perspective that places the defense of human and nonhuman life at the center of its focus.

The analysis of Iñaki Ceberio de León of the work of theologian and revolutionary Sandinista Ernesto Cardenal's *Cántico cósmico* shows the ecological themes as opposed to the capitalist subject.[28] Published in 1989, *Cántico cósmico* denounces both the destructive logic of capitalism and the instrumental rationality of hegemonic modernity. In this way, Ernesto Cardenal weaves a link between the environment, politics, and religion.

The social poetry of Ernesto Cardenal represents yet another expression of *liberation Christianity*.[29] A fierce opponent of the Somoza regime, Cardenal participated in the formation of Bible studies and ecclesial base communities, which would later become protagonists of the Nicaraguan Revolution. After the fall of the dictatorship, Ernesto Cardenal was named

---

27 Gebara, *Intuiciones ecofeministas: ensayos para repensar el conocimiento y la religión*, 18.
28 Iñaki Cebeiro de León, "El Sujeto Ecológico En La Poesía de Ernesto Cardenal," *Ontology Studies* 11 (2011): 345–54.
29 Jean-Pierre Reed, *Sandinista Narratives: Religion, Sandinista, and Emotions in the Making of the Nicaraguan Insurrection and Revolution* (Lanham: Lexington Books, 2020).

minister of culture of Nicaragua. However, Cardenal would be reprimanded by John Paul II during his trip to Nicaragua in 1983 and would later fall victim to the cold ecclesial winter by being punished *a divinis* by the Vatican.[30]

This is a committed poetry; the poetry of liberation and life are some of the traits of the work of Ernesto Cardenal. Revolution and spirituality, ecology and politics, mystery and praxis, are crisscrossed to form his aesthetics. In the poem *Nueva Ecología* from the 1980s, Cardenal creates a beautiful quartet:

> *We are going to decontaminate Lake Managua.*
> *Liberation was not only yearned for by humans.*
> *All of creation was groaning. The Revolution*
> *is also of the lakes, rivers, trees, animals.*[31]

The social poetry of Ernesto Cardenal prefigures a utopia where the idea of "the true insertion of humanity in nature" is made concrete.[32] To this topic, we read the poem "Gaia":

> *The largest living creature on Earth*
> *is Earth.*
> *We have seen her in photographs:*
> *that blue sapphire amid white fleece*
> *with shining white caps at its poles.*
> *The new notion of Gaia—a living Earth.*
> *The planet Earth one whole living self-creature.*
> *It was this long before there was "life" on its surface.*
> *There is nowhere else to live but in the sky,*
> *this way,*

---

30 Ernesto Cardenal, *La Revolución Perdida: Memorias*, vol. 3 (Managua: Anama, 2003), https://www.iberlibro.com/REVOLUCION-PERDIDA-Memorias-Tomo-III-Cardenal/3119881644/bd.

31 Ernesto Cardenal, *Vuelos de victoria* (Madrid: Visor, 2012). Translation my own.

32 Ernst Bloch, *El principio esperanza*, vol. 2, Colección Estructuras y Procesos—Serie Filosofía (Madrid: Trotta, 2007), 282.

leaving its equatorial region, the sun
made herself a sphere to revolve around her.
A living being which did not need arms nor mouth nor anus
instead in its roundness, spins and spins around the sun.
It spun fast (days of 5 hours and nights of 5 hours),
the moon creating the tides from that moment on.
It created for itself the conditions to hold organisms
and later organisms with consciousness, persons; and later
an organism that is at the same time community and persons.
Burning and arid, humid; dripping lava, melting glass,
the Earth seemed to not have a future.
Who would have thought that from that flaming lava
forests would emerge and cities and songs and nostalgias.[33]

Without a doubt, it is in the work of the Brazilian theologian Leonardo Boff that the ecological dimension of liberation theology is found succinctly.[34] During the 1990s, liberation theology began to cultivate previously unexplored terrains. In this sense, this theological current was enriched by positions that began to open themselves on questions of gender, race, and of course socio-environmental concerns. The *poor* ceased to be merely an abstract category. Although liberation theology was criticized for abandoning its primary interest—the poor—those critiques seem unconvincing.

Leonardo Boff officially abandoned the structure of the Catholic Church in 1992. He continued to wor on concerns he had on issues of the environment. In his works *Nova Era*, *Principio-Terra*, and *Ecologia*, these issues are placed at the center of his theological, social, and political reflections.[35] The clamor of the *victim* (the poor and the earth) is taken as the departure point for a *new ecotheological paradigm* since, for Boff, liberation

---

33 Ernesto Cardenal, "GAIA," July 24, 2012, http://polis.revues.org/4278.
34 Martínez Andrade, *Ecología y teología de la liberación: Crítica de la modernidad/colonialidad*.
35 See Leonardo Boff, *Nova era: a civilização planetária : desafios à sociedade e ao cristianismo*, Série Religião e cidadania (São Paulo: Editora Atica, 1994); Leonardo Boff, *Ecologia: grito da terra, grito dos pobres* (Rio de Janeiro: Sextante, 2004).

theology and ecological discourse share the same wounded victims.[36] On the other hand, the painful situation of misery afflicts a large part of humanity, alongside the suffering of the earth, a planet that has been pillaged for centuries by an economic system that only has the production of *surplus value on its horizon*.[37]

We can criticize the bio-centric concept proposed by Leonardo Boff to overcome the pseudo-concrete notion of anthropocentrism of modern thinking. However, Boff established a critical dialogue with *deep ecology* to show the limits and contradiction of modernity expressed in the idea of *dominium terrae*. Supporting the complexities of science, Boff starts with a holistic vision (a Greek term referring to "totality") to understand the interrelationship between the whole and its parts.[38]

After the "Cumbre de la Tierra" (*Eco-92*), which took place in Rio de Janeiro, where the participation of Leonardo Boff had been crucial in the event's organization, he began to think into a new ecotheological paradigm. Among the elements of this new way of thinking are the following: (1) a critique of the classic concept of development, (2) a self-critique of the responsibility of Christianity for the ecological crisis, (3) the acknowledgment of the intimate relationship between ecological and social justice, 4) the denouncement of *anthropocentrism* and a reevaluation of the seeming bias of technology. Later, through his work *Ecologia: grito da terra, grito dos pobres*, Boff would successfully articulate a prophetic denunciation of liberation theology with an environmental critique. In this way, Boff calls for the possibility of entering a paradigmatic change process, where the origin myths (*Pacha Mama*) or the *Gaia* hypothesis form an organic union: Earth-humanity.

The theologians Afonso Murad and Marco Túlio Procópio are convinced that the eco-centrism proposed by Leonardo Boff articulates the singularity of humanity on Earth extraordinarily.[39] Following this,

---

36 See Paulo Agostinho Nogueira Baptista, Libertação e ecologia: a teologia teo-antropocósmica, ed. Leonardo Boff, 1st ed., Coleção Interfaces (São Paulo: Paulinas, 2011), http://catdir.loc.gov/catdir/toc/fy13pdf04/2013336872.html.

37 Leonardo Boff, *Ecologia: grito da terra, grito dos pobres* (Rio de Janeiro: Sextante, 2004).

38 Boff, *Ecologia*.

39 Marco Túlio Murad, Afonso and Procópio, "Dignidade dos animais e direitos humanos: uma leitura teológica inclusiva," in *Fé cristã e direitos humanos*, ed.

the Earth and humanity share the same identity. Therefore, the *ecological conversion* proposed by Boff finds agreement with the proposals of the German theologian Jürgen Moltmann.

Now, after enumerating some of the cardinal points in Boff's ecotheological perspective, we think of the profound crisis we are facing today, not only evident in economic terms but at the environmental level, calling us toward alternative strategies to avert the catastrophe that is coming. Today—more than ever—we need theoretical and political proposals that go against capitalism's destructive logic, which drives us toward the total destruction of human and nonhuman life.

Conclusion

In Rome on March 13, 2013, Jorge Mario Bergoglio, then the cardinal of Buenos Aires, was elected Pope Francis. The election of this pope from the Global South aroused great enthusiasm in the Catholic world, especially among liberation theologians. Greeted by Leonardo Boff as the bearer of hope for the Church and the world, Pope Francis seems to break with the party line of his predecessors. His sober treatment of protocols, his critique of the financial world, his concern for the poor, and his call for the protection of nature make this pope someone who can restore the Church.[40]

Leonardo Boff affirmed that Pope Francis had requested some texts related to environmental questions since he was writing an encyclical on ecology,[41] which would be presented on May 25, 2015 would be entitled *Laudato Si': On Care for Our Common Home*. In terms of what is at stake in this encyclical, it is no less than the *essence of humanity* that ecological concerns cannot be spoken of without a holistic understanding. Moreover, since aspects of the environment, economics, social, and human issues are intimately interconnected, without putting in relation the *wounds* of the "natural environment" and those of the "social environment," the

---

Daniel Ribeiro de Almeida Chacon and Frederico Soares de Almeida, 1st ed. (São Paulo: Edições Loyola, 2021), 253.

40 Leonardo Boff, Teodoro Nieto, and Maria Jose Gabito, *Francisco de Roma y Francisco de Asís: ¿una nueva primavera en la Iglesia?*, 1st ed., Colección Estructuras y procesos (Madrid: Editorial Trotta, 2013).

41 Personal conversation with author.

cause of the ills cannot be elucidated.[42] So, it becomes about associating justice issues with the "perspective of the rights of peoples and cultures," the ecology of everyday life, and how to live alongside the poorest.[43] Intending to reach all human beings, since we are all inhabitants of our common home, the encyclical exhorts each one of us as citizens of the world. We are to commit to a more responsible way of living for the earth and choose a lifestyle that considers the cultural, ethical, and spiritual dimensions of things from an individual to a communitarian and collective level. The recipient of *Laudato Si'* remains the believer—precisely, the Catholic faithful—as a few of the proposals call for the moral considerations of holistic environmentalism, such as the defense of all life, which includes condemning abortion and stigmatizing gender theory. However, we must recognize that the encyclical seeks to "listen to the clamor of the earth as well as the clamor of the poor," question the commercialization of nature, and emphasize the social consequences of inequality on a planetary scale, the deterioration of nature, and the myth of infinite growth.[44] On our behalf, one cannot reject that it does not openly denounce the basic foundations of the capitalist system: the logic of value that is valued, the centrality of exchange values, et cetera.

In recent years, the term *Anthropocene* has gained a lot of weight both in the theological arena and in some social movements, but it is more of an ideological move (as it holds all human beings responsible for environmental collapse) than a relevant notion for questioning the destructive dynamics of capitalist modernity.[45] In this sense, the relevance of liberation theology is fundamental to denounce the structures of exploitation and domination that destroy both human beings and nature.

---

42 Pope Francis, *Encyclical Letter Laudato Si' of the Holy Father Francis on Care for Our Common Home*, 2015, 6.
43 Pope Francis, *Laudato Si'*, 144.
44 Pope Francis, *Laudato Si'*, 49. Number 120 and 136; number 155.
45 Joerg Rieger, *Theology in the Capitalocene: Ecology, Identity, Class, and Solidarity* (Minneapolis, Fortress Press, 2022.

CHAPTER 11

HEARING THE WORDS OF CREATURES: CONTEMPLATIVE KNOWLEDGE IN THE ORTHODOX TRADITION

Elizabeth Theokritoff

It is a premise of the present volume that there are voices in Christian ecological thinking that are not being heard, or perhaps are partially heard and then rapidly subsumed into the dominant narrative. It is ironic, however, that those eager to dethrone the claims of colonial Christianity to speak for newer Christian communities in the Global South often fail to question a position no less blinkered—the assumption that historical Christianity can be equated with the Roman Catholic and Protestant tradition of western Europe. For too many Christians of Western tradition, whichever part of the world they hail from, the entire Eastern Christian tradition is simply written out of the picture. So is it not entirely surprising that today some church historians even use the language of "proto-colonialism" in speaking of the historical relationship of the West to the Eastern Churches and the resultant difficulty for Orthodox theology to escape over centuries from defining itself in Western terms.[1]

The reason for pointing this out is not at all to stake yet another claim to grievance or to foster hostility and suspicion. Rather, it is to suggest how it could have happened that so much Christian ecological thinking was able to swallow, largely without question, an idea of the default "Christian

---

[1] See, for instance, George Demacopoulos, "'Traditional Orthodoxy' as a Post-colonial Movement," *The Journal of Religion* 97, 4 (2017): 475–7 and notes.

attitude to nature" that is so woefully unrepresentative of Christian tradition as a whole.[2] Ivone Gebara's essay in this volume seems a variant on this depiction of Christianity, barely recognizable to the Orthodox Christian (or, I suspect, to most Western Christians). Yet even a brief outline of the Eastern Christian tradition will indicate, I hope, that the "ontological friendship of all that exists" that she had discovered in the writer calling himself Dionysius the Areopagite, along with the "interdependence" she urges, is not an isolated if promising "ancient statement" but a defining and continuing feature of Christian cosmology.

THEOLOGY OF CREATION IN THREE WAVES

To understand Orthodox ecological theology, it is helpful to bear in mind that this represents the third major wave of theological preoccupation with creation as a whole and its relationship to God. The first belongs to the early Christian centuries, when Christian theology was being articulated against the challenge of opposing cosmologies: Greco-Roman paganism in its many forms and various Gnostic sects that denied the goodness of the material world. The responses to these challenges have been definitive for theological cosmology ever since. Popular paganism, which divinized idols, animals, and Roman emperors, was seen as insulting their true creaturely nature and alienating them from their Creator. The world is full, not of gods, but of God's creatures, which image, reveal, and speak of their Creator. So the world is not primarily something that we use, although of course we do that, too. It is offered to us for contemplation, so that through understanding and using it, we "read" about its Creator. "Contemplation," *theoria,* is the Greek term for the spiritual meaning of Scripture; the possibility of "natural contemplation" implies that the "book of nature," like the book of Scripture, is to be read on multiple levels. "Wherever you turn

---

2   For a devastating critique of this blind spot, see J. J. Heckscher, "A 'Tradition' That Never Existed: Orthodox Christianity and the Failure of Environmental History," in *Towards an Ecology of Transfiguration: Orthodox Christian Perspectives on Environment, Nature and Creation,* ed. John Chryssavgis and Bruce V. Foltz (New York: Fordham University Press, 2013), 136–51.

your eyes, there is God's symbol," Saint Ephrem the Syrian wrote in the fourth century.[3] But we must not superimpose on this an impoverished modern notion of "symbol": the sense in which a creature images God is as much, if not more, a part of its inner truth as its physical constitution and function. So the human's creation "according to God's image" has a context—a world in which imaging God is what creatures do, each in its own distinct way.

Gnostic contempt for the material creation was countered by the enormously influential second-century bishop Irenaeus of Lyon. He firmly established the Eucharist as key to the continuity between God's work of creation and salvation worked by Christ: if Christ can declare bread and wine his own body and blood, which give immortal life, that is because he is the Son of the Creator who gives wheat and grapes to sustain our physical life. The burial and resurgence of wheat, the "eucharisted" bread that becomes the food of immortality and the transformation of our own bodies at the resurrection, represent the same recurring pattern of divine activity.[4]

Compared to Gnostic dualism, the pantheism of the Stoic was considerably easier to "baptize." The idea of a world held in balance by the *Logos* ("word, rationality, inner principle") that pervades it, of the seminal words in all things, provided images for the Christian intuition about the world which we might today label with abstractions such as "panentheism," "interdependence" or "cosmic Christ." So Origen, for instance, talks about the world in all its variety as a harmony, or more particularly something analogous to a *body*: an immense animate creature, held together by the power and *Logos* of God as by a soul.[5] Rather more carefully phrased, the imagery of the world as a body becomes commonplace in the writings of church fathers. "Our need for everything binds us with a love for

---

3 Hymns on Virginity 20:12; Sebastian Brock, *The Luminous Eye: The Spiritual World Vision of Saint Ephrem the Syrian* (Kalamazoo, MI: Cistercian Publications, 1992), 42.
4 For example, *Against Heresies* IV.18.5.
5 Origen, *On First Principles*, trans. G. W. Butterworth (Gloucester: Peter Smith, 1973), 76–80.

everything," as Saint Ephrem says, clearly echoing Saint Paul's image of the church as a body.⁶

These ways of thinking about creation as a whole did not disappear when creation ceased to be a matter of theological controversy; they remained deeply entrenched and were developed with more precision by church fathers in the ascetic and contemplative tradition. This indicates that they accord with the reality of the world as perceived through prayer and worship. One of these contemplative teachers is Pseudo-Dionysius the Areopagite, with his strong sense of the unity of all things by virtue of their common source. That is why he coined the term hierarchy, meaning not a pyramidal power structure but a community and ordering. In this sense, Pseudo-Dionyisius's hierarchy is more akin to a living organism than to the common association of hierarchy with pyramidal power. It is a way of envisaging how enormously disparate creatures can function together as one whole ordered toward God.⁷ Hierarchy is about participation in God, which means very different things for different creatures, but is nevertheless essentially communal; it involves dependence on other creatures and responsibility to them.

The great cosmic theologian Maximus the Confessor elaborates Dionysius's insights about the unity of creation, especially in his commentary on the Divine Liturgy: God "holds all things together round Himself, since He is their cause and beginning and end, causing them to incline toward each other . . . by force of the relationship with Himself as their origin."⁸ Maximus speaks at length about how the cosmos, the Church, and the human being image each other as a unity of different things and different levels, each demonstrating how the spiritual and the physical coexist and reveal each other.

It is Maximus who develops most fully the Christian notion of *logoi*, integral to the way he understands the interconnectedness of all things. The Logos of a creature—its "word," rationale, essential principle—expresses

---

6   Letter to Hypatius, in Brock, *Luminous Eye*, 167.
7   See Eric Perl, "Hierarchy and Love in St. Dionysius the Areopagite," in Chryssavgis and Foltz, *Towards an Ecology*, 29.
8   *Mystagogy*, 1; *Maximus Confessor: Selected Writings* (Mahwah, NJ: Paulist Press, 1985), 186.

the creative will of God—God's presence within that thing but also its own inner essence. The word of God is uncreated yet at the same time wholly present in the infinite variety of creatures, inscribed upon them as if by letters, just as God will be embodied in Scripture, and finally and most perfectly in the incarnation. The inscription of the word of God on all things is also what enables us to read something of the Creator in his creation. Again, this in no way conflicts with valuing things for themselves—since one and the same *Logos* "makes [each thing] to be distinctly itself and at the same time draws it toward God."[9]

The second wave of thinking about creation comes from Russian religious philosophy of the nineteenth century. The catalyst in this case was not a theological challenge but a general cultural unease with an increasingly fragmented way of seeing the world, including a growing gulf between humans and nature. This places it within a very broad quest across European culture for a reintegrated vision of creaturely reality and of creaturehood with the divine. It is no accident that Vladimir Soloviev (1853–1900) was writing of his visions of personified divine wisdom ("God's body, the matter of divinity")[10] within a decade of Ernst Haeckel's coining the term "ecology" to describe the material world as unity, organic, and inorganic natures interacting in a system of active forces. But whereas Haeckel himself developed his insight philosophically into a pantheistic monism,[11] Soloviev and Sergei Bulgakov (1871–1944) can be seen as proposing an alternative and broader ecology, embracing the interactions of creatures (humans included) on a spiritual as well as a physical level. With an eschatological perspective, these thinkers gave great prominence to the idea of the ultimate deification of all things with and through the human. Their immediate inspiration came from the philosophy of Schelling, but

---

9   Metropolitan Kallistos (Ware) of Diokleia, "Through the Creation to the Creator," in *Towards an Ecology*, 91.

10 Oliver L. Smith, "Vladimir Soloviev (1853–1900)—The Ultimate Spiritualisation of All Created Matter," *Creation and Salvation Volume 2: A Companion on Recent Theological Movements*, ed. Ernst M. Conradie (Zurich: Lit Verlag, 2012), 13–19.

11 Andrea Wulf, *The Invention of Nature: The Adventures of Alexander von Humboldt, the Lost Hero of Science* (London: John Murray, 2015), 307, 313.

Bulgakov in particular progressively shifted his attention to patristic and liturgical sources in his quest for the cosmological aspect of Christianity.

Soloviev sees human activity and the world—like humanity and its natural environment—as part of a "mutually conditioning relationship," such that each realizes itself in the other—a relationship that humanity distorts at its peril.[12] Bulgakov, the economist and former Marxist, speaks of economic activity and consumption—within which he encompasses all human activity in the world—as a "natural communion" with the material world, the way we become inextricably interconnected with the whole world so that it joins us in union with God.[13]

Another watchword in Russian religious philosophy of the time, especially among Slavophils and Bulgakov, is "sobornost," denoting unity without uniformity and the essential contribution of every member to the whole. Sobornost arises out of a vision of the church: the Slavonic translation of *katholike* in the Nicene Creed, *sobornaya*, carries the sense of gathering all together. Think of Maximus's image of the church and the universe mirroring each other as the place where all things are brought into unity and of course behind that is Saint Paul's image of members of one body. We will see clear echoes of this way of thinking in how more recent Orthodox writers speak of the place of humanity in creation and their insistence that a sense of solidarity with all creatures is an extension of human communion, never a substitute for it—"a cosmology of communion has its place within a sociology of communion."[14]

The thinkers of the nineteenth to early twentieth century reflect a time of great optimism about human work and the shaping of the world despite the beginnings of unease about the potential dark side of human activity and, especially, technology. While emphasizing that humans take the whole world with us in our spiritual journey, the philosophers saw

---

12   Oliver L. Smith, "Is Humanity King of Creation? The Thought of Vladimir Solov'ev in the Light of Ecological Crisis," *Journal for the Study of Religion, Nature & Culture* 2/4 (2008): 463- 482 (469, 478).

13   Sergei Bulgakov, *Philosophy of Economy: The World as Household* (New Haven, CT: Yale University Press, 2008).

14   Olivier Clément, "Le sens de la terre (Notes de cosmologies orthodoxe)," *Contacts* 59-60 (1967/3-4): 297.

the relationship as largely one-way, giving scant attention to the contribution of nonhuman creatures. The potential is all there, however, for an understanding of divine wisdom in all creation that gives full measure to the interdependence of all creatures, such as we can find in more recent writing.[15]

Ecological theology, then, is for Orthodoxy a third wave of intense cosmological thinking. The Orthodox encounter with specifically environmental issues initially came largely through the World Council of Churches, and this had a long-lasting influence on the way the discussion was framed. The predominantly Protestant ecological thinking of the 1970s and 1980s not only grappled with human responsibility for damage to the earth on an alarming scale but also responded to a pointedly anti-Christian strain in nascent environmentalism. Often it even internalized the notion that Christian teaching itself bears responsibility for the ecological crisis and requires radical revision. Its response was thus preoccupied with the meaning of human dominion over earth and full of anxiety that traditional Christianity had been anthropocentric in a way that devalued the claims of other creatures. Orthodox writings and statements of this period tend to accept that starting point, initially adopting the language of stewardship, albeit in combination with other images of the human's role. One of these terms, "priest of creation," was developed especially by Metropolitan John Zizioulas, who in the 1990s proposed it as an alternative to "steward."[16] Certainly, priestly imagery has positive implications for the manner in which we use the world. It means recognizing that nothing in creation is ours: all is "God's own," in the words of the Divine Liturgy, so that any use and shaping must be a fitting thank offering to God. But the crucial point, almost never made explicit, is that "priest" cannot be seen simply as an alternative job description for the human in the world. It is an image on quite a different level, pointing to the liturgical and eucharistic character of the world we live in—a world that worships God and is created for transfiguration to reflect God's glory. Humanity's (mis)treatment of its natural

---

15 George Theokritoff, "The Cosmology of the Eucharist," in *Towards an Ecology*, 131–135.

16 Metropolitan John (Zizioulas) of Pergamon, "Proprietors or Priests of Creation?" in *Towards an Ecology*, 163–71.

environment is the pressing and practical point; but the abiding conviction for Orthodoxy is that the problem cannot be addressed apart from the total context within which dominion—however we paraphrase it—is exercised. Focusing on the narrow question of man's relationship to his natural environment creates a frame of reference that is itself inevitably anthropocentric, whatever answers one may come up with. Furthermore, the preoccupation with interpreting Genesis 1 deflects attention from all the other aspects of Christian tradition, not least other parts of Scripture, that help provide the necessary context. Even the more recent language of caring for creation, despite its apparent practical value, can obscure the bigger picture in which caring for creation is not a human task—it is a divine task carried out *through the way that all creatures serve each other.*

Nevertheless, the anthropocentric questions of ecological theology cast a long shadow. And this is true even though some of the fundamental problems with them, from an Orthodox point of view, were identified clearly and trenchantly in the mid-1970s by Metropolitan Paulos Mar Gregorios, the most prominent Orthodox voice on environment at the time.[17] Mar Gregorios makes quite clear that the concept of nature as nonhuman material creation is not native to the Christian tradition and needs to be replaced with the traditional and inclusive Christian language of creation (as a whole) in contradistinction to God, so that the modern juxtaposition of man and nature becomes irrelevant. The human has a unique role, but one *within,* not vis-á-vis, creation. Mar Gregorios is among the first to use the image of priest for man's role in creation, and he favors it precisely because "the priest has to be an integral part of the people he represents"[18]—a point that Zizioulas will echo. This implies that the rest of creation is not only the matter that is offered but also the community that offers.[19] For Mar Gregorios, human affairs, including "science-technology,

---

17 See Metropolitan Paulos mar Gregorios, *The Human Presence* (Chennai, India: The Christian literature Society, 1980).

18 Gregorios, *Human Presence,* 85.

19 On "priest of creation" language and its implications, see Elizabeth Theokritoff, "Priest of Creation or Cosmic Liturgy?" in *Rightly Dividing the Word of Truth: Studies in Honour of Metropolitan Kallistos of Diokleia*, ed. Andreas Andreopoulos and Graham Speake (Oxford: Peter Lang, 2016), 189–211.

political economy and value choices," are part of creation's *self*-offering to the Creator.[20]

Mar Gregorios responds robustly to the suggestion that Christianity is inherently dualistic, dividing matter from spirit. As a representative of the Indigenous Church of India, he was well placed to point out that Christianity too is an Eastern religion with potential for overcoming "pernicious dichotomies," including the duality between vertical and horizontal—the assumption of "one realm (nature) where man is master and another (grace-supernatural) as coming from God."[21] Writing more than forty years ago, Mar Gregorios evinces an optimism about technological "mastery" of the world for the benefit of all humankind that may today seem naive, but he is adamant that any such "mastery of nature must be held *within* the mystery of worship."[22]

The approach that Mar Gregorios outlines avoids at least three pitfalls common in modern ecological theology: the separation of environmental and social concerns; the narrow focus on human use of the world without reference to the wider relationship of Creator and creation; and the consequent temptation to bracket human use and manipulation of the world as, at best, a necessary evil, rather than another aspect of creaturely activity. As a guide to the mystery that provides context for human mastery, Mar Gregorios is able to draw on not only the cosmic theology of church fathers such as Gregory of Nyssa and Maximus the Confessor but also modern writers whose work was eclipsed in the scramble of early ecotheology. Already in 1958, Olivier Clément was writing on "the human in the world."[23] But he began not with instructions to Adam in paradise but with Saint Maximus's vision of the human calling to bridge the divisions in creation and ultimately unite creation with the Creator. This was a task in which Adam failed, but which was accomplished in potential by the second Adam, Christ. The task of the Christian is therefore to actualize the potential by building up the body

---

20   Paulos Gregorios, *Science for Sane Societies* (New York: Paragon House, 1987), 230–1, 97.
21   Gregorios, *Science for Sane Societies,* 104–6.
22   Gregorios, *Human Presence,* 89. Italics added.
23   Olivier Clément, "L'homme dans le monde," *Verbum Caro* XII:45: 4–22.

of Christ through communion with others and sanctification of things. The spiritual destiny of the human being is inseparable from that of humankind as a whole and from the material world whose substance we share. It is through us that the material world, our extended body, can attain eternity, says Clément, and this gives us a responsibility for the world "down to the last blade of grass."[24]

Not that the working of divine grace in the world is mediated solely through the human. The world has its own connection to God; it is bathed in his omnipresent glory. Clément too invokes here the "divine idea," the Logos in each thing, which is also a word addressed to us. All things pray in us, but they in turn assist our prayer. It is the ascetic effort of purification that enables us to hear the "music" of other creatures and receive their words; this is the same ascetic path that culminates in tenderness, infinite vulnerability, and infinite prayer for all the sorrow of the world.[25]

Clément speaks for Orthodox tradition as a whole in insisting that cosmology cannot be understood as static: it belongs in a historical and eschatological context that demands our ceaseless effort to sanctify and transfigure.[26] This is to recognize that neither we humans nor anything else in the world has attained its final state and that the journey is a collaborative effort. As is so often the case in Orthodox writings, the Eucharist is the prime example, the "centre and meaning of cosmic life." Natural processes and human labor and understanding come together "so that bread and wine become *fully themselves* [my italics], the glorified body of the Lord. And *the effect is also the cause*, as the fire spreads to the rocks and stars whose substance is present in the holy gifts."[27] This vision of the world is lyrically expressed, but the reality of it is hard to deny if we take seriously both the incarnation and the nature of matter.

Some thirty years before Western theologians starting talking about "deep incarnation," the significance of the incarnation for creation as a whole is set out incisively by Paul Evdokimov: "Christ walked this

---

24 Olivier Clément, "Le sens de la terre (Notes de cosmologie orthodoxe)," *Contacts* 59–60 (1967/3–4): 252–323.
25 Clément, "Le sens de la terre," 252.
26 Clément, "Le sens de la terre," 255.
27 Olivier Clément, "L'homme," 13. Italics added.

earth ... there is nothing in this world which has remained a stranger to His humanity"; "the matter of the cosmos... becomes the conductor of grace." "Nature" cannot be thought of apart from "the mystery of the Church and its sanctifying action"; the sacraments in which we see the physical world and our interaction with it restored to their true meaning and destiny; the symbolic quality of the material world, offering "a reading of 'God's poetry' written in its flesh"; or the eschatological destiny of matter, "the flesh of the resurrection" glimpsed in the lives and experience of people of holiness.[28]

These writings from the dawn of the modern environmental movement, or before, are the foundation for a remarkable triad of sermons given in 1989 by the late Patriarch of Antioch Ignatius IV.[29] These address the preoccupation of the time with "the responsibility of Christians," but the practical action comes out of the vision of a world destined to "become eucharist," a world whose very existence is "ontological praise."[30] This approach looks not simply to the protection of creation but to its ultimate transfiguration.

None of these writings set out to be a new theological construct: they are a guide to reading the tradition of the church. They express a tacit recognition that contemporary questions such as environmental issues cannot be addressed simply on the basis of biblical exegesis or theological discourse, ancient or modern. Rather than combing Scripture and the church fathers for references to the human place in the natural world and then making our own extrapolations, we begin from the way Scripture and patristic theology have been lived—in worship, prayer, lives of faith, and holiness. This is why even that most systematic of Orthodox ecological theologians, Metropolitan John Zizioulas, repeatedly insists

---

28 Paul Evdokimov, "Nature," *Scottish Journal of Theology* 18 (March 1965): 1–22.

29 Ignatius IV, Patriarch of Antioch, "Three Sermons: A Theology of Creation; A Spirituality of the Creation; The Responsibility of Christians," http://www.orth-transfiguration.org/wp-content/uploads/2016/05/Lecture_HB-Ignatius-1989-Lecture-Nr-1.pdf, http://www.orth-transfiguration.org/wp-content/uploads/2016/05/Lecture_HB-Ignatius-1989-Lecture-Nr-2.pdf, http://www.orth-transfiguration.org/wp-content/uploads/2016/05/Lecture_HB-Ignatius-1989-Lecture-Nr-3.pdf.

30 Ignatius IV, "Three Sermons."

on the priority of ethos over ethics: good ecological practice should be shaped by our experience of worship. The role of ecological theology is not to rewrite Christian doctrine but to reveal the theological valence of the ways we interact with and experience the material world in our life of faith and then translate this into the very different languages of environmental questions and ecological science.

Sources of Contemplative Knowledge: Incarnation and Sacrament

This understanding of creation and our place in it is theological to its core, grounded in the very heart of Christian faith: God manifested in the flesh. Every source in the church for understanding the nature of the world in which we live depends either on the incarnation itself (sacramental life, icons, holy relics and places), the process of growing into Christ (holiness), or the way that creation is structured in view of the incarnation (praise and service of God from all creatures, which are mirrors and symbols of the word of God).

The great mystery of the incarnation is extended into the mysteries of the church. In the sacramental use of things like bread, wine, and oil, we rediscover a world in which the same natural elements, the same physical actions and natural processes, the same technologies that enable our physical life and flourishing, also convey God's blessings for eternal life. The matter used sacramentally is for the most part shaped by humans. This is not a blanket blessing on human use and shaping of the world but demonstrates how this characteristically human activity can equally serve the manifestation of God's glory and must be judged by that yardstick. The spectacular exception to this rule is water: Christian life begins at baptism, with God working through an element essential for physical life, untouched by human activity. The message is clear: the elements, and all things, serve and glorify their Lord and Creator alone. If they also serve humans, physically or spiritually, that is entirely at his behest. The sharp distinction between natural process and human activity is broken down; both are characteristic creaturely activities appointed by God, working together to serve him through each other.

The incarnation and the mysteries of the church reveal matter as permeable to the divine. This appears first of all in the human body—that of Christ, visibly suffused with glory in the transfiguration, and then of his saints. That is why Orthodoxy venerates the relics of saints—in recognition that the Holy Spirit who filled them in life "does not depart from their souls *or their bodies in the tombs*," as Saint John of Damascus wrote in the seventh century.[31] Indeed, unless one believes that salvation and deification are a matter for disembodied spirits only, it could hardly be otherwise. But what is of particular significance for our ecological understanding is that this grace does not stop at the human body; it extends to the natural and manmade environment of the saint, their clothing and possessions, and the place where they lived and died. This continues to be the Orthodox experience today. A pilgrim to the monastic republic of Mount Athos speaks of discovering the mountain as a whole as "a sacrament of the divine presence. The monks, the monasteries and the icons are enfolded . . . within an all-embracing context of sacred space. . . . The very rocks and earth of the Mountain, with all its flowers, shrubs and trees, possess an intrinsic sacredness."[32] It is a vivid reminder that our responsibility toward our natural environment starts from our entanglement with it. It is not primarily a matter of management but of awareness that both stand or fall together.

The capacity of the material world to connect us to God stands at the heart of the Orthodox experience in the form of the icon. The very fact that we can now make an image of God the word is a constant reminder of the meaning of the incarnation: we honor the matter that wrought our salvation.[33] Equally, the way that the world is depicted in the icon strives to convey matter fulfilling its calling to be the abode of God. As Metropolitan Anthony writes of the icon *The Transfiguration* by Theophanes the Greek, "One has the impression that these rays of divine light touch things and

---

31 Saint John of Damascus, *On the Divine Images: Three Apologies against Those Who Attack the Divine Images*, trans. David Anderson (Crestwood: St. Vladimir's Seminary Press, 1980), 27.
32 Bishop Kallistos of Diokleia, "Gerald Palmer, the Philokalia and the Holy Mountain," *Friends of Mount Athos Annual Report* 1994: 26–7.
33 John of Damascus, *On Divine Images* 1.16; *Three Apologies*, 23.

sink into them, so that from the core of . . . all things created, the same light reflects and shines back as though the divine life quickens the . . . potentialities of all things and makes all reach out toward Itself."[34]

In the making of an icon, all elements of the material world are brought together to depict the face of Christ: animal, vegetable, and mineral products, plus human skill. If all this can be formed into an icon of God incarnate, it is because the created world is already an icon. The veneration of icons—honoring God through his visible and material image—reminds us of the primary service that other creatures offer to us: they speak to us of our common Creator. From the transfigured world of the icon, we turn back to see the ordinary world with new eyes. Its potential and its calling give us the criterion for all our dealings with other creatures.

HEARING THE WORDS OF CREATURES: PRAYER AND WORSHIP

Visitors to Orthodox worship sometimes describe it as "otherworldly." There is some truth here, but it is also misleading. Orthodox worship is replete with materiality—not only the icons but the incense and candles, bread, wine, water, oil, et cetera, as well as our own bodies and all our senses with which we interact with these things. Worship brings us into the presence of an unseen world, but one inextricable from this world *perceived otherwise*—in its inner being, its relationship to its Creator. In the words of one of the great spiritual fathers of our day, "Everything undergoes a wonderful transformation. Time, space and matter, all the 'flesh' of this world which was assumed by the Word of God, become as limpid as crystal in His eucharistic body, which is here present among us."[35]

The use of the material world in worship is not a matter of co-opting things into a purely human activity. Rather it reveals on a human scale what creaturely activity essentially is: we are all part of a worshipping cosmos. All those psalms that speak of the earth and its creatures praising

---

34 Metropolitan Anthony of Sourozh, "Body and Matter in Spiritual Life," in *Sacrament and Image,* ed. A.M. Allchin (London: Fellowship of St Alban and St Sergius, second edition 1987), 45.

35 Archimandrite Aimilianos, "The Experience of the Transfiguration in the Life of the Athonite Monk," *The Living Witness of the Holy Mountain* (South Canaan: St Tikhon's Press, 1996), 200.

and rejoicing in the Lord—including many creatures inconvenient to humankind—are not simply poetic expressions of human joy, but intuitions of a relationship between God and all his creatures that are largely hidden from us.[36]

Awareness of cosmic worship is also strongly associated with private prayer, especially the Jesus Prayer ("Lord Jesus Christ, Son of God, have mercy on me" is one of its most common forms). The nineteenth-century Russian classic *The Way of a Pilgrim* describes how the pilgrim acquires through the Prayer the "knowledge of the speech of all creatures," the ability to hear them glorifying God. We hear their doxology and offer it back; the Russian émigré scholar Nadejda Gorodetzky speaks of the name of Jesus as a mystical key to the world through which we offer up "people, books, flowers, to all things we meet, see or think."[37] It is hardly surprising that the name of the incarnate word should tune us to the frequency of the words of creatures. "All creation mysteriously utters the Name," writes Father Lev Gillet. And so, by pronouncing it over the things of this world, we "speak aloud [their] secret" and "bring them to their fulfillment."[38]

COME AND SEE: SAINTS AND ASCETICS

The most compelling ecological examples come from the lives of saints ancient and modern, both in their sensitivity to the wonder and beauty of all creation and in their restored relationships with their natural and human environment. This transformation in relationships, including all creatures, has been highly typical of holy ascetics, Eastern and (especially earlier) Western, down the centuries. This must be underlined not least because of the widespread misunderstanding of asceticism in some ecotheologies, which assume it to be a dualistic contempt for the material world. But rather than jumping to conclusions about the meaning of such unfamiliar phrases as "despising the flesh," "cutting off the will" or

---

36 See Theokritoff, "Liturgy, Cosmic Worship," 295–306.
37 Nadejda Gorodetzky, "The Prayer of Jesus," *Blackfriars* xxiii (1942): 74–78 (76).
38 Lev Gillet, *On the Invocation of the Name of Jesus* (London: Fellowship of St Alban and St Sergius, 1949), 15–16.

"resisting the passions," it is more instructive to "come and see" the lives of those shaped by the ascetic tradition.[39] Monastics are the masters of the tradition and provide most of the best examples, but asceticism does not mean monasticism. The most obvious and universal form of asceticism is fasting (abstinence from animal products), practiced by most observant Orthodox Christians for approximately half the days of the year. Asceticism in whatever form is the way we learn freedom: we cease to be slaves of our desire to possess and consume, and this opens our eyes to other created things—people included—in their full reality and dignity in relation to their Creator.

When thinking of those who might be described as "ecological saints," two things must be kept in mind. First, that to pigeonhole them in this way is actually rather misleading because they illustrate so clearly the Anthonite saying that "anyone who loves God loves not only his fellow man but the entire creation as well: the tree, the grass, the flowers. He loves everything with the same love."[40] And, second, that the holy people who would most obviously attract that label include some of the most deeply loved, influential, and authoritative figures of contemporary Orthodox Christianity.

We may think of Saint Herman (1837), a hamble monk and missionary to Alaska who served, protected, and ministered to the local people as well as the local wildlife. Or the Elder Amphilochios of Patmos, equally beloved locally, known for speaking of an unwritten commandment to "love the trees!"[41] His teaching and influence are evident alike in the charitable works that he initiated and in the impressive greening of the once-bare hillsides in his part of the island. The more recent Anthonite Elders Paisios and Porfyrios, both now recognized as saints, continue to be revered as towering spiritual figures and tireless intercessors for everyone who visited

---

39　John Chryssavgis, *Cosmic Grace, Humble Prayer: The Ecological Vision of the Green Patriarch Bartholomew I* (Grand Rapids, MI: Eerdmans, 2003).

40　Archimandrite Ioannikios, *An Athonite Gerontikon: Sayings of the Holy Fathers of Mount Athos,* trans. Maria Derpapa Mayson and Sister Theodora (Zion) (Kouphalia—Thessaloniki, 1997), 31.

41　Kallistos Ware, *Towards an Ecology of Transfiguration: Orthodox Christian Perspectives on Environment, Nature and Creation*, ed. John Chryssavgis and Bruce V. Foltz (New York: Fordham University Press, 2013), 86–105.

or wrote to them. Elder Paisios had an acute sense of the presence of God in all his creation; he could speak of the grass and stones as icons filled with God's grace or pluck a leaf and give it to a visitor as a blessing.[42]

Elder Porfyrios, who spent much of his life as chaplain at a clinic in central Athens, was known for his childlike delight in nature, a "poetic" sensibility that he encouraged his spiritual children to cultivate: all the plants, animals, flowers, and the elements are "little loves through which we attain to the great Love that is Christ."[43] And when the late Abbess of Chrysopigi in Crete sought his advice about construction of the new monastic buildings up the mountainside, he urged her to keep the perimeter walls low enough that the Sisters could look out and be inspired by the beauty of the forest and the sea beyond. It is hardly coincidental that Chrysopigi is one of the monasteries most active in conservation, sustainable living, and environmental education.[44] Another such monastery is that of Saint John the Baptist in central Greece,[45] whose involvement in the growing and exchange of heritage vegetable seeds began with an observation from Elder Porfyrios to some of the Sisters that "the world will die of hunger, because we don't take care of seeds." It is a saying of characteristic simplicity, which captures exquisitely the nexus of interdependence, including the least of creatures, in and for which we are created.

CONTEMPLATIVE KNOWLEDGE EMBODIED IN CULTURE

It is not only great saints who have an inner vision of a communion of creatures, of all things serving and glorifying God. Pointers to it are embedded

---

[42] Alexander Belopopsky and Dimitri Oikonomou, eds., *Orthodoxy and Ecology Resource Book* (Bialystok, Poland: Syndesmos, 1996), 55.

[43] Elder Porphyrios, *Wounded by Love: The Life and Wisdom of Elder Porphyrios*, ed. Sisters of the Holy Convent of Chrysopigi (Limni, Greece: Denise Harvey, 2005), 218.

[44] See "The Protection of the Environment as Applied to the Environmental Education Programme of the Holy Monastery of Chrysopigi, Crete," *The Free Library*, December 1, 201,8, https://www.thefreelibrary.com/The+Protection+of+the+Environment+as+Applied+to+the+Environmental...-a0577908351.

[45] Saint John's Monastery, http://www.saintjohns-monastery.gr/?lang=en.

also in the culture of Orthodox peoples. Often a pre-Christian intuition of the spiritual in nature has been "baptized," replacing nature-worship with a culture "captivated by the vision of the transfigured cosmos."[46] There may be an element of nostalgic romanticism in Nicolas Zernov's depiction of Slavic Orthodoxy, yet it captures well the spirit that we find, for instance, in the remarkable twentieth-century Russian Akathist hymn "Glory to God for all things," composed by a priest imprisoned in a Soviet camp:

> Glory to Thee, showing me the beauty of the universe/ Glory to Thee, spreading out before me heaven and earth/ Like the pages in a book of eternal wisdom . . . O Lord, how lovely it is to be Thy guest . . . All nature murmurs mysteriously, breathing the depth of tenderness. Birds and beasts of the forest bear the imprint of Thy love. Blessed art thou, mother earth, in thy fleeting loveliness[47]

A similar intense feeling for nature is found in writings of the acclaimed Serbian theologian Bishop Nikolai Velimirovich, whose *Prayers by the Lake* echo the Psalms in their vision of a world that serves the Lord and where "all creation is merely a story about Him."[48] His profound sense of the universe as symbolic enhances rather than diminishes; it is an awe-filled delight in creatures in themselves. Striking also is the way he reverses the clerical tendency that can attend priest of creation language: "I feel mute and inarticulate, my luxurious Lord . . . Therefore, I beseech the entire universe to kneel down with me and speak in my stead, since I am incapable, and inarticulate . . . truly, I am not worshipping stone, but rather I, together with the stone, am worshipping the living Lord.'" (xxviii)

The "baptism" of pre-Christian cultures continues, as we see in many features of Indigenous Orthodox Christianity in Alaska, traditional ways of seeing the world in which the nineteenth-century Russian missionaries

---

46 Nicolas Zernov, *The Russians and Their Church*, 3rd ed. (Crestwood, NY: St Vladimir's Seminary Press, 1994), 180.

47 See "The Akathist Hymn: 'Glory to God for All Things,'" http://www.saintjonah.org/services/thanksgiving.htm.

48 Nikolai Velimirovich, *Prayers by the Lake*, A Treasury of Serbian Orthodox Spirituality, vol. 5 (Grayslake, IL: Serbian Orthodox Metropolitanate of New Gracanica, 1999).

could discern resonances with Orthodox cosmology.[49] The life-force in every creature, indicated in traditional masks by depicting one eye as a human face, was seen as an intimation of the *Logos* of each creature, its echo of the divine word in whose image humans likewise are created. This fellow-feeling is reflected in a profound respect and gratitude to the animals who are seen as giving their lives so that humans can survive. That understanding speaks strikingly of a world in which self-giving even unto death is the deep order of the universe and is practically manifested in an insistence that no part of the animal is allowed to go to waste. Faithfulness to customs and practices intended to mirror in daily life the pattern of the universe clearly accords with the vision of a symbolic cosmos in which the spiritual world is not separable from the material but reveals its meaning, its *Logos*.

Conclusion

It is examples such as these, familiar to most Orthodox as a living tradition, that make it hard to join in the self-flagellation of many Western ecotheologians concerning the ecological credentials of traditional Christianity. Orthodox statements and homilies on ecology often speak instead of our own need for repentance, *metanoia*—a change of heart, which involves learning to live consistently with the faith we profess. And this starts with listening for the words that the Creator has placed in all his creations.

Hearing the words of things does not exclude use of the world or indeed the development of technologies for that purpose. What it does preclude is the Baconian idea that discovering the physical secrets of nature and putting them to practical use for human benefit restores the dominion appointed in paradise. There is no secular shortcut to reappropriating that authority in creation, which is restored only in Christ.

As the Patriarch of Antioch taught more than thirty years ago,[50] the human is able to apprehend the world at various levels—contemplative,

---

49   See Michael Oleksa, "The Yua as Logoi," in *Re-Imagining Nature: Environmental Humanities and Ecosemiotics*, ed. Alfred Kentigern Siewers (Lewisburg, PA: Bucknell University Press, 2013), 147–241.

50   Ignatius, "Three Sermons."

artistic, and scientific. But there has to be a synergy of these different levels of knowing, in contrast to the modern disjunction between a rationality that deals in quantifiable abstractions and a spiritual knowledge of the world that perceives the great divine *Logos* suffusing all things—a split that he sees as lying at the root of environmental destruction. "Reason as instrument has disenchanted the world . . . reason as contemplation has now to teach us to admire and respect it."[51]

Reason as contemplation also points us to where human responsibility lies: not in saving the earth by our own skill and ingenuity, but in learning from all creation how to cooperate in the divine work of saving the world.

---

51 Ignatius, "Three Sermons."

PART 4

EARTH-KEEPING APPROACHES FROM THE GLOBAL SOUTH

CHAPTER 12

NATIVE RELIGIONS AND HIDDEN MOANA ECOLOGIES

Jione Havea

Maui Kisikisi was the son of a woman from Koloa to Maui 'Atalanga, whose father Maui Motu'a lived in Pulotu (underworld). Maui Motu'a was blind, but he enjoyed roasted yams—for there was fire in Pulotu. At that time, there was no fire in Tonga.

One day, Maui Kisikisi sneaked behind his father when he went to visit Maui Motu'a and to work at the garden at Pulotu. The father and grandfather did not know that Maui Kisikisi also came (his first visit to Pulotu).

Maui 'Atalanga went to the garden, and Maui Kisikisi crept up to his grandfather and tasted the peels from his roasted yams. Yum. So, he took one of the two yams and climbed up a *nonu* tree. When Maui Motu'a reached out for the yams, one was missing. Maui Kisikisi had eaten it, then he took a bite of a nonu fruit and threw it down at his grandfather. Maui Motu'a felt the bite mark and cried, "The teeth of Maui Kisikisi."

Maui 'Atalanga heard the name of his son. He saw Maui Kisikisi on the tree and to cut a long story short, he chased Maui Kisikisi back to Koloa. Maui Kisikisi scooped up live coals with his body wrap, and upon reaching Koloa he told the fire to hide in the trees. When Tongans rub two sticks, fire would come out so they could eat cooked food.

One of the Tongan sacred stories on the genesis of fire[1]

---

[1] Translated by the author.

Native people have religions. Native religions enlighten people with senses of belonging, ways to make sense of their world(view)s, skills to survive with one another, and passions to communicate religious learnings to future generations. These assertions are true of the native people of Pasifika (for the Pacific islands, Oceania)[2] as well. Put differently, no people are without a religion that enriches them with sacred texts (in oral, visual, and performative forms), qualified teachers, certified healers, and contextually conscious rituals.

In Pasifika, prior to Western colonization (misrepresented in some accounts as "arrival" or "contact"), each island group had native religious wisdoms and practices that were shaped by our oceanic world. Those religious wisdoms and practices in turn shaped our worldviews. When Western colonization came uninvited with the established religion of Christianity, native religious wisdoms and practices were demonized and banned. But some were hidden (went underground) in the genres of legends and myths, customs and traditions, and those were then shifted to the disciplines of anthropology, ethnography, and subdisciplines of cultural studies instead of religious studies—where they rightly belong.

The key objective of this chapter is to offer a Moana reading of one of the Tongan sacred texts, about the genesis of fire, that has been made a legend, with special attention paid to its hidden ecological teachings. To set this up, i[3] also revisit another sacred text, one of the Tongan creation stories, which has been formative in my work in framing Moana hermeneutics and Moana theologies.

The hopes in this chapter are twofold: to celebrate native religious wisdom and to offer alternative responses from Pasifika to the crises of

---

2   Pasifika one of the native renderings of the label "Pacific" that Europeans gave to our waters and islands. I use the term as a reminder of our colonial history, a history that has not ended.

3   I use the lowercase "i" (except at the beginning of a sentence) because i also use the lowercase with you, we, she, he, they, it, and other. This is a sign of my affirmation that i (as an individual) do not exist without relating to others and to the surroundings, a sign of my resistance against the privileging of the so-called independent modern self, and a sign of my rebellion against the colonial English language.

climate change, responses that are free of the traps of victimhood into which Western ecological conversations have lured us.[4]

Hidden

Pasifika islands are drifting in the vast open sea, and *being hidden* is part of our oceanic condition. Geographically, we are hidden in the open, deep sea. Politically, we are hidden under the interests of colonial powers.

Hidden World/views

Pasifika is hidden in more ways than one. Not only is our island world (space) hidden from the eyes and experiences of people who are outside of our waters, but so are our worldviews (wisdom).

First, Pasifika is the part of the so-called Asia-Pacific region that people fly over. From the West Coast of the Americas, businessfolk, politicians, and tourists fly over to Asian nations in and across the arch stretching from Australia to Japan, with no need to stop at the Pasifika islands. Our beaches and cultures may be exotic, but airfare and lodging are too expensive in comparison to tourist hot spots in Asia. And in the other direction, Asians take the twelve-or-more-hour journey across to the American "promise land" with no need to touch and be touched by Pasifika.

Second, the population and economy of Pasifika nations are too small to be of interest to the operators of the machineries of global capitalism. Pasifika does not have excess workers to be able to push the cost of production down or enough resources and consumers with excess wealth to push the profit margins up. Pasifika is on the radar of some donors as an altar where they might seek expiation for their exploits, but many more opt to stay away (in case, we think, they are moved to give some assistance). There is not much in Pasifika to capitalize on, so it is better to fly over and away from our island(er)s.

Third, when academic institutions and scholars organize programs and projects to showcase the Asia–Pacific region, it is a rare occasion when

---

4   See Jione Havea, "The Politics of Climate Change, a Talanoa from Oceania," *International Journal of Public Theology* 4 (2010): 345–355.

10 percent of the contributors are of Pasifika heritage.[5] To be fair, the population and land space of Asia are larger than ours and there are only a handful of Pasifika scholars. Among that handful, token Pasifika scholars cannot speak on behalf of our rich diversities. Put another way, even the Pasifika tokens (myself included) fly over other parts of Pasifika.

Many outside people romanticize our island world. They fly over to Asia, where they buy Pasifika souvenirs that were made in Taiwan and China and island handicrafts and fabrics that were made in Indonesia and Thailand, and then they return to their isolation—in body, mind, and soul—away from Pasifika. Hence the Pasifika world is basically hidden. Isolation is the existential condition of Pasifika island(er)s and the political choice of outsiders.

However, there are some benefits to being hidden. For instance, we are less susceptible to exploitation. But there is a toll as well. We can be caricatured, according to someone else's fantasy, illusion, and project.

Hidden No Longer

In the early days of contact between colonial and missionary Europeans and Americans and Pasifika islanders, Western anthropologists and historians furnished "the authorized version" on the Pasifika world and worldviews. They paid the fee and owned the copyright to native Pasifika matters.

The name "Moana" (see next section) is a recent case in point. When the 2016 Disney animation *Moana* was dubbed into the European languages, it was discovered that some non-native person had registered the name in Europe. To avoid trademark issues, Disney changed the title of the movie and the name of the leading character to "Vaiana"—claiming that the new name means "water [*vai*] cave [*ana*]"—in the German, French, Spanish, and Italian versions. This change proceeded without consultation with the natives of Pasifika, whose cultures Disney claims to present in the movie.

---

5   It is different when a Pasifika native is involved in organizing the project. See, for example, Jione Havea and Peter Lau, eds., *Reading Ecclesiastes from Asia and Pasifika* (Atlanta, GA: Society Biblical Literature, 2020).

While it is true that *vai* and *wai* translate to "water" in several of the native Pasifika languages, Disney did not take into consideration the fact that these terms refer to freshwater, not saltwater. Saltwater is the world of Moana, and Disney avoided the copyright police and again misrepresented the native Pasifika world and worldviews.

Even when European and American scholars buy into "the white man's burden" by consulting and promoting native voices, the natives tend to support their white sponsors and celebrate their becoming "noble savages." We are therefore hidden because someone else speaks for us and because token natives promote the cause of the white masters. To put it sharply, we are damned when we don't and damned when we do—uncritically and naively, instead of natively.

In the disciplines of theology and hermeneutics, we have begun to set up platforms in the space of the white masters where native Pasifika scholars speak for our worldviews and interests.[6] This chapter comes in the ripples of those voices, pushing our native agenda into the shadows of religious studies.

Moana

In the beginning, there was only Moana (sea) and Pulotu (underworld). At the southern edge of Moana, a reef rose up to become the island of 'Ata. One day, a plover (*kiu*, named Tangaloa 'Atulongolongo) from the sky visited 'Ata. It dropped a seed onto the island. The next time Tangaloa 'Atulongolongo visited, it found a creeper that had grown from the seed. It pecked at the root of this creeper until it split in two.

A few days later, Tangaloa 'Atulongolongo returned to find that the root had rotted and a fat, juicy maggot (*'uanga*) was curled up in it. It pecked the maggot in two. The top section turned into a

---

6   See for example two of the projects that i edited: *Sea of Readings: The Bible in the South Pacific* (Atlanta, GA: Society of Biblical Literature, 2018) and *Theologies from the Pacific* (New York: Palgrave, 2021). The contributions for both collections were hatched at conferences organized by two local associations: Talanoa Oceania (which meets in Australia and Aotearoa New Zealand) and Oceania Biblical Studies Association (which meets in the Pasifika islands).

person named Kohai [who was female]. The bottom section turned into another person named Koau [who was male]. Then Tangaloa 'Atulongolongo felt a crumb (*momo*) on its beak; it shook the crumb off and it turned into a third person named Momo [whose gender is forgotten, maybe because they were queer]. Kohai, Koau, and Momo were the first humans on 'Ata.

Maui brought partners for them from Pulotu and they became the ancestors of the native peoples of Tonga.

One of the creation stories from Tonga

I have recently offered two readings of this native sacred text,[7] and i add a third one here. It is appropriate that i read and reread native sacred texts, as i do with other sacred texts. No one reading or reader can say everything about a sacred text, and each reading has agendas, concerns, and directions. In other words, no reading or reader is innocent. And this applies to those of us who read natively. We too are not naive or unbiased.

The intentional multiplying of readings and the bluntness concerning the limits of readers and readings are features of my version of "Moana reading." In the fluid Moana world/views, finality and fixity are illusions.

Reading

The name "Moana" is used across Pasifika to refer to *the deep ocean* that links our "sea of islands."[8] In the Tongan story of creation above, "Moana" refers to this deep sea.

But Moana is not limited to space (of the sea plus the (is)lands). With respect to Moana reading, i use the term "Moana" to refer to the

---

7   In "Homing Woman-Eve in Native World(view)s: A Moana Reading" in *The Routledge Companion to Eve*, ed. Caroline Blyth and Emily Colgan (New York: Routledge, 2024); and "Theologizing Moana and Pasifika World(view)s" in *Political Theology in the Asia Pacific*, ed. Kwok Pui-lan (Waco, TX: Baylor University Press, forthcoming).

8   Epeli Hau'ofa, "Our Sea of Islands," *The Contemporary Pacific* 6/1 (1994): 148–61.

modes, frames, opinions, and positions of interpretations that have been conditioned by the Moana world/views. In this connection, to avoid confusion, in this chapter i use "Pasifika" in reference to the sea and our sea of islands (as space or context) and "Moana" in reference to mindset and wisdom.

In my work, there are two key characteristics of Moana reading. First, a Moana reader looks for the four bodies in Moana world/views—sea, land, sky, and underworld—in texts. These four bodies are named in the Tongan story of creation above: through the *sea*, a reef came up from the *underground* (Pulotu) to form an is*land* ('Ata), and a plover bird (*kiu*, named Tangaloa 'Atulongolongo) came from the *sky* to begin the process that led to the hatching of native Tongans. In Moana worldviews, what takes place with one body affects or is affected by what happens with the other bodies. A Moana reader looks for these four bodies in texts.

To illustrate, i appeal to Genesis 1:1-2 (drawing on my own translation): "When 'elohim began to construct *the skies* and *the earth*—the earth was chaotic, and darkness covered the face of *the deep*—a wind from 'elohim swept across the face of *the waters*." The *sky* and the *land* (earth) are named in the first verse. My translation presents a Moana reading according to which "the deep" represents the *underworld*, a body whose face was covered (blindfolded) by darkness. And as the biblical story unfolds, the waters were divided into two bodies (waters above and waters below, the dome), with the waters below turning into the *sea*. The four Moana bodies are present or made present by this Moana reading of a biblical sacred text.

The second characteristic of Moana reading is that the Moana reader also looks for points where the Moana bodies meet (interweave, overflow). In the biblical creation story, three entities play linking functions: First, the waters link both the *sky* to the *sea* (verse 7) as well as the *sea* to the *land* (verse 9). Second, the wind (from 'elohim) links the *sky* to the waters from which the *sea* came. And third, darkness (which was over the deep, the *underground*) is the hidden linking agent that transitioned the creation processes into the day-to-day; there was evening (darkness) and there was morning, as the creation ticks on—across the four Moana bodies.

In this reading, the four Moana bodies are present and interlink in Genesis 1:1-2. Moana reading works on this biblical sacred text, and it can also work on native sacred texts.

Creation

A reef came up from Pulotu (underground), through the sea, to form an island. A bird came from the sky to plant a seed, which grew into a creeper, out of whose dismemberment a maggot was formed; the bird returned to sever the maggot into two big pieces, plus a crumble, from which the native Tongans emerged. With human eyes, one could confidently argue that this sacred story is about the creation of an island to be the home of the first Tongan humans—female, male, and queer—sealed by Maui bringing partners for them from Pulotu. However, two ecological details are overlooked by—or hidden under—such an anthropocentric reading.

First, the Moana bodies—sea, underground, sky, (is)land—are ecological bodies. The underground (Pulotu) was responsible for the creation of the island, and i imagine something similar to what we see today when volcanic eruptions form islands in the middle of the sea. The island in the Tongan sacred story is named 'Ata, which is an uninhabited island at the southern end of the Tonga group of islands. The magic of this native creation story is in the formation of the island, which comes up through the sea, rather than in the possibility that it could happen as in the logocentric biblical creation story.

On 'Ata, a bird came from the sky to plant a seed that led to the first Tongan natives—who emerged as gendered adults. And as the (is)land came up from Pulotu, so were partners brought up from Pulotu to generate the ancestors for native Tongans. Maui, a demigod in native sacred stories, brought the partners, but he did not create the humans.

So, who created the native Tongans? While Pulotu did the heavy lifting, it is fair to say that the creation was a collaboration between the four Moana bodies. Tongans were not created by divine power or magical words but by a collaboration between ecological bodies whose images we are—we are images of sea, land, sky, and underworld. This is the first ecological detail that anthropocentric readers overlook. As natives, we are (composed of) sea, land, sky, and underworld. And so are other humans.

Second, i call attention to two ecological creatures that cross between the four Moana bodies. First, the *kiu* (plover) crossed from the sky to the island. Second, Maui crossed from Pulotu through the sea to the island. Both creatures carried "seeds," with Maui bringing—to borrow categories from the second biblical creation story (see Gen. 2:18)— "partners" to be "helpers" for Kohai, Koau, and Momo. In other Tongan sacred stories, Maui fished up islands from the deep sea, but he did not play such a significant role in this story.

When my late grandmother told me this story, she wanted me to learn that Tongans came from a fat, juicy maggot and that a bird was responsible. The *kiu* was significant in her world/view because it lived in two spaces—in the sea and on the (is)land (compared to the stork in European baby delivery stories). But i found the maggot more interesting because, at the end of our lives, our bodies will return to fat, juicy maggots, who will convert our remains into the food chain. The human destiny, dust to dust and ashes to ashes, is possible thanks to fat, juicy maggots.

Anthropocentric readers would find the famous Maui more interesting than Tangaloa 'Atulongolongo the *kiu* because Maui brought partners for the purpose of procreation, and he thereby fit the bill of patriarchy. But my grandmother's Moana worldviews had a more ecological twist: native Tongans are sons and daughters of a fat, juicy maggot that spawned at the root of a fallen creeper.

Later in life, i wondered how Tangaloa 'Atulongolongo the *kiu* dropped the seed onto the island. Did the seed drop from its beak or through its cloaca? The beak plays dismembering roles in the chopping of the creeper and the butchering of the maggot, but the cloaca would fit better with my grandmother's ecological leanings. A seed that came through the cloaca would have a better chance of taking root and sprouting on a new (is)land.

Theocentric readers would also be drawn to Maui, as a demigod, but overlook that he was a trickster. We find this aptitude in another Tongan sacred text (a translation of my grandmother's version is presented at the top of this chapter), to which i turn next.

Food

Three generations of Maui are in the Tongan sacred story presented at the top of this chapter—grandfather (Maui Motu'a), father (Maui 'Atalanga), and son (Maui Kisikisi). I assume that the Maui in the creation story (who brought partners from Pulotu) was Maui Kisikisi, but that Maui could also have been the father or even the blind grandfather. All three Mauis were sons of legends, three demigods with special powers who, in sacred stories, crossed between the four Moana bodies.

In traditional readings, which are drawn and disseminated through retellings, there are two key functions of this sacred story: to explain that fire was brought up from Pulotu (etiological purpose) and to teach Tongans that rubbing sticks will produce fire (practical purpose). This is one of the Tongan versions of the genesis of the civilization of fire, and we share the main gist of this sacred story with other native Pasifika islanders (but mindful that the proverbial devil is in the details).

Tonga is at the southwest end of the so-called Pacific Ring of Fire, so the premise of this sacred story—fire is underneath the sea and the islands—is easy to accept. That was true in the days of the Mauis and is also true today. In Tonga, on January 15, 2022, the sea of fire flowing in the underworld erupted through a submarine volcano between Hunga Tonga and Hunga Haʻapai, spewing water particles up to a hundred kilometers into space.[9] This was a very powerful eruption, considering that commercial airplanes fly from 10 to twelve kilometers above sea level. The eruption generated tsunami waves that ran freely through nearby islands, and the explosion was so powerful that it was heard all the way from Alaska.

There are fires under us and in the trees. Both assertions are not unique to the Tongan worldview. The Tahitian and Hawaiʻian sacred stories are more powerful, involving Pele, creator of the islands and the goddess of volcanoes and fire. Both assertions can pass the tests of experience.

But the Tongan sacred story fails the womanist test. The native woman from Koloa, who mothered Maui Kisikisi, is not named. She is hidden in the story and in readings that do not consider her as a possible influencer for Maui Kisikisi's courage and prudence. With respect to this

---

9   Jane J. Lee and Andrew Wang, "Tonga Eruption Blasted Unprecedented Amount of Water Intro Stratosphere," *NASA Jet Propulsion Laboratory*, August 2, 2022, https://www.jpl.nasa.gov/news/tonga-eruption-blasted-unprecedented-amount-of-water-into-stratosphere; Jonathan Amos, "Tonga Volcano Eruption Continues to Astonish," *BBC News*, December 13, 2022, https://www.bbc.com/news/science-environment-63953531.

unnamed native mother, even though she is more legendary than historical, i call attention to two ecological details that are hidden from readings that limit this sacred story to the etiology of fire.

First, the Tongan sacred story is also about a son crossing into Pulotu to visit his blind father. But Maui 'Atalanga was not crossing over for a family reunion or a holiday, with the chance to rest and relax (from the duties at home). His visits involved working in the garden. At this point in her retellings, my grandmother would raise a grand/motherly kind of question: For whom was the garden? This is not a question of ownership, but of beneficence—who benefits from the garden.

Since there were other dwellers in Pulotu—in other sacred stories, the most famous are Hikuleʻo (goddess) and Felehuhuni (female trickster)—then the garden would have also been for them. They too would have worked in and eaten from this garden. This reading subverts the privileging of the Mauis: the garden could have been a community garden for other dwellers at Pulotu, whose children and grandchildren, from Koloa and other Moana islands, would have come to visit (which involved working in the garden). Maui 'Atalanga would not have had to work alone but would have been among others for whom the garden was the basis for their relationships.

Better yet, the garden could have also been for the people of Koloa and other Moana islands. In this regard, not only did Maui 'Atalanga come to work at the garden on behalf of his blind father (in Pulotu), but also to take food for his unnamed wife and for their neighbors (outside Pulotu). Community gardening was and still is common in Tongan villages. This reading opens the "gates" of Pulotu so that natives on (is)lands (in the world of the living) may also benefit from the resources of Pulotu (in the world of the spirits).

Second, the purpose and value of fire in the Tongan sacred story had to do with food—with fire, Tongans could eat cooked food. In this sacred story, a blind man was cooking yams.[10] But in Tongan villages, women also cook. And as Tongan society has become more patriarchal, women do more cooking than men.

---

10   Yams are at the top of the Tongan noble foods. See Mikaele N. Paunga, SM, "*Ko e Mana Fakahā 'Otua 'o e Fakatupu*: Creation as Sacrament," in *Theologies from the Pacific*, ed. Jione Havea (New York: Palgrave, 2021), 31–46.

Since Maui 'Atalanga had been going back and forth between Koloa and Pulotu, he would have enjoyed cooked food. In the story, i assume that one of the two yams that Maui Motu'a roasted was for Maui 'Atalanga. So why didn't Maui 'Atalanga consider bringing fire to Koloa? He brought food from Pulotu but not fire. Was he a *kaipō* (someone who does not share their food) kind of husband?

Maui Kisikisi's feat has traditionally been read as that of a trickster. He tricked his grandfather, the keeper of fire at Pulotu, and brought fire to Koloa and Tonga. What this etiological reading overlooks is that Maui Kisikisi enjoyed his grandfather's roasted yam, and so i suggest that his delight with the cooked yam was the motivation for him to bring fire to Koloa. He saw that fire was good for cooking, and he experienced the cooked yam as a delight in his mouth compared to the bitter raw *nonu* fruit that he threw at his grandfather, so he scooped up coals in order to take fire back to his people so that they, too—to echo Genesis 3:6—would experience his delight. This is a story not just about the daring of a trickster but also about the fondness of a discoverer who chose to share (as other discoverers, local and foreign, tend to do) his discovery with his people.

Both roles—trickster, discoverer—could have been the influences of his unnamed native mother. She would have enjoyed cooked food thanks to her son, much better than the raw food that her *kaipō* husband had been feeding her. She would have also been proud of her son, even with his recklessness—especially with hiding fire in trees, which is dangerous for flora and fauna, in the context of modern bushfires. Maui's feat thus fails the ecological test.

This Moana reading brings a Tongan sacred story into the kitchen (which, in Tonga, could be an open space). In the orbit of food, the destructive forces of fire could be harnessed. Food is a favorite subject for Pasifika natives. Our world and views circle around food. But these affirmations do not deny that food is an anthropocentric concern and the cause for a lot of ecological turmoil.

Religion

When native peoples are identified as "Indigenous" because they are said to hold primeval spiritualities and cultures, we are put on a platform where we are *not* considered to be, as natives, religious beings. The platform of religion is, on the other hand, reserved for the spiritualities and cultures that have been institutionalized, which the Europeans and Americans brought to Pasifika. Natives can become religious by adopting Jewish, Christian, and Muslim principles and practices—which are foreign to our Moana world/views—but not by observing native ways and wisdoms. In this connection, saying that we are "Indigenous" is a polite way of saying that our ways and customs have expired.

Against such demeaning whitewashings, in the spirit of what may be called the "politics of indigeneity," i read two Tongan sacred texts above as evidence that our people had a native religion—insofar as one of the marks of a religion is having sacred texts that address matters related to living—prior to invasion by foreign religions. I read two Tongan sacred texts, but there is a sea of sacred texts across Pasifika that have been shaped by Moana world/views. As a collective, native Moana religions and sacred texts were and are oral in form and energies.

Caveat: Mainline theologies have labels—pantheism, panentheism, deism, animism, totemism, shamanism, paganism—that discredit native religions. Shedding such demeaning theological positions is required for the affirmation of native religions to bear fruits. The required shedding task is for the gatekeepers of mainline theologies, and directions have been given by Pasifika people inviting them onto the paths of decolonization.[11] To put it bluntly, the ball is in the courts of white *and* native masters who benefit from mainline theologies.

Ecologies

Native Pasifika religions are this-worldly, and Pulotu is included in this world. In the Tongan sacred stories read above, Pulotu is not removed from the (is)lands of the living. Pulotu is located in the underworld, but the underworld interlinks with (is)land, sea, and sky. Sea and sky are present *in*

---

11   See Konai Helu Thaman, "Decolonizing Pacific Studies: Indigenous Perspectives, Knowledge, and Wisdom in Higher Education," *The Contemporary Pacific* 15.1 (2003): 1–17; Linda Tuhiwai Smith, *Decolonizing Methodologies: Research and Indigenous Peoples* (Dunedin, FL: University of Otago Press, 1999).

front of people, but their depths are beyond the human ability to fathom. So is Pulotu, the entry point to which, according to my grandmother, is the place where the sea meets the sky. Pulotu is on the horizon, *in front of* people. People could (close their eyes and) choose to see it.

Being this-worldly, native Pasifika religions are alert to ecological energies and embodiments, both the healthy and the sickening ones. Considering the Moana reading above, i close this reflection with four invitations as contributions from Pasifika to the conversations on the climate crisis.

First, native Pasifika religions invite and encourage reconsideration of worldviews toward the (is)land, sea, sky, and underworld. The Tongan sacred stories invite us to think of the sky not as the home of gods but of birds that can spark life on (is)lands, and Pulotu as a place overflowing with fire that forms islands. The (is)lands did not drop from the sky but came up from the deep, and the sea links islands and provides resources for islanders (qua those who live on islands, which include pests, animals, and plants). According to the Moana worldview, if humans are not responsible, then our (is)lands will disappear back to the deep. The lower (is)lands will go first and the higher ones will come later—depending on the movements of the sea, sky, and underworld. They interlink, and to harm one will result in harming the others. Similarly, to restore one will result in restoring the others.

Of course, changing worldviews is vanity without changing worlds. And changing world/views require changing behaviors. Here, it would help if humans would stop behaviors that destroy the Moana bodies and the lives and livelihoods that depend on them. Modern humans are driven by progress and success, to the sickness and death of (is)land, sea, sky, underworld—and their inhabitants.

Second, native Pasifika religions invite and encourage deep respect for and working toward restoring the interlinks of sea, (is)land, sky, and underworld. Climate crises multiply because of opinions and actions that disconnect these four Moana bodies, as though the harm to one body does not hurt the other three.

The nuclear tests that the British, US, and French governments conducted up to 1996 on reefs and islands across Pasifika also harmed the sea, sky, and underworld—and their inhabitants. The threats of nuclear disaster have not passed. Even in 2023, North Korea still tests atomic weapons (to deter South Korea and Japan, allies of the US) and threatens to turn Pasifika into a "firing range,"[12] and Japan has dumped nuclear contaminated water into the sea.[13] Both nations do not seriously consider that harming the sea will also harm the (is)land, sky, and underworld—and their inhabitants. However, both nations know that the half-lives of radioactive isotopes (from the production and testing of nuclear weapons) can be thousands of years. In other words, there are two disconnections in the worldviews of these powerful nations: disconnection of the four Moana bodies in their worldviews and disconnection between their knowledge and their actions. Pasifika is still hidden by and under these disconnections.

For the climate crisis to slow down and level out, humans who live on (is)lands need to also respect and restore the health of sea, sky, and underworld, who are critical for the survival of (is)lands and their inhabitants—plants, animals, humans, and other kinds. It is therefore not only what humans can do that will make a difference but also what humans can stop doing. For the sake of the living and the dying, a healthier call to action is to *just stop it*.

Third, native Pasifika religions invite and encourage the sharing of resources and knowledge. In the Moana reading above, Pulotu is filled with fire, but it is also a place where a garden produces sweet yams for the inhabitants of the world of the living. Resources and knowledge from Pulotu provided Tongans with (is)land, partners, food, and fire for cooking. In the eyes of native religions, Pulotu is the birthplace, as well as the inspiration for the sharing of innovations and civilizations.

---

12 Reuters, "North Korea Fires Ballistic Missiles, Warns of Turning Pacific into 'Firing Range,'" *RNZ*, February 20, 2023, https://www.rnz.co.nz/news/world/484523/north-korea-fires-ballistic-missiles-warns-of-turning-pacific-into-firing-range; Kelly Ng and Jean Mackenzie, "North Korea Parades Largest Long-Range Missile Array," *BBC News*, February 10, 2023, https://www.bbc.com/news/world-asia-64577925.

13 Sakura Murakami, "Fukushima Wastewater Released into the Ocean, China Bans All Japanese Seafood," August 24, 2023, https://www.reuters.com/world/asia-pacific/japan-set-release-fukushima-water-amid-criticism-seafood-import-bans-2023-08-23/.

Resources and ways of knowing are not products to sell and buy. On the other hand, resources and knowledge are shared for the sake of delight and survival. Sharing is about exchanging, and doing so builds relationships. Relationality and reciprocity are transactional, and they embody native economic systems that seek to grow communities more than to increase profits (as in the capitalist economic system).[14]

Fourth, native Pasifika religions invite and encourage simplicity, practicality, and humility. Humans are sons and daughters of (is)land, sea, sky, and underworld—and their inhabitants. Humans are images of this world, which we exhaust and burn because we hunger for more than food. The hunger of the images is eating up the model, and it does not help that the otherworldly inclinations of some religions and theologies distract us from the well-being of this world. In these regards, the ball is in our courts, in front of us.

---

14 Presenting native Pasifika economic systems is the task for another reflection: Brian F. Kolia and Michael Mawson, eds., "Moana Economies: A Theological Invitation" in *Unsettling Theologies: Memory, Identity, and Place* (New York: Palgrave, forthcorming).

CHAPTER 13

TWO MILLION TREES PLANTED: THE GREEN REFORMATION AND GHANA'S CHURCH OF PENTECOST

David Douglas Daniels III

As one of Ghana's major Protestant (specifically Pentecostal) denominations, the Church of Pentecost planted nearly two million trees between 2021 and 2023 as a part of its creation care initiative. Their Pentecostal green theology emerged out of the denomination's widening of its civic vision to include the care of the creation as it seeks to address climate change. In addition to planting trees, the Church of Pentecost has implemented initiatives to counter "unhealthy practices that contribute to environmental degradation" and programs to promote constructive practices that advance the sustainability of the earth.[1]

As a conservative Protestant denomination, Scripture is key to this church's ecological vision. If its Pentecostal theological perspective would engage contemporary conversations about ecological spirituality, the greening of the church, and eco-justice, it would do so by drawing upon the Bible and its own theological resources as a Ghanaian Pentecostal church. The Church of Pentecost understands itself as being an ecclesial citizen of Ghanaian society as well as citizens of heaven. While having congregations in over a hundred countries, the headquarters and largest constituency of the denomination are in Ghana.

The denomination balances its commitment to the common good through, on one hand, its efforts to advance education, healthcare, public

---

[1] Church of Pentecost News, "Environmental Care Campaign," November 22, 2018, https://thecophq.org/news/environmental-care-campaign-launched/.

safety, job creation, and the environment and, on the other hand, its commitment to evangelism, discipleship, and spiritual renewal. It follows this path rather than juxtaposing evangelism and social ministry; rather than being either-or, it is both-and. Evangelism and social ministry are for them complementary instead of contradictory. The church's theological orientation is Trinitarian, squarely theocentric, Christocentric, and pneuma-centric with a plain reading of the Bible and conservative views of the Christian lifestyle, while at the same time recognizing creation care as part of the Christian witness and a prominent focus of the church.[2]

THE GREEN REFORMATION

Jürgen Moltmann, in his essay "Ecology as the Capacity for Love," calls for a "Green Reformation." According to Moltmann, a Green Reformation, as a successor to the sixteenth-century Reformation, should produce a new theology, spirituality, view of nature, understanding of humanity, reading of Scripture, and experience of God. A paradigm shift from an anthropocentric to biocentric framework is sought. Moltmann explains that "ecological questions are no longer merely ethical questions but call for an ecological shift to the entire theological enterprise." He writes:

> As a reformed theologian, I have chosen the expression "Green Reformation" because every reformation in the church and in theology looks back to defining biblical texts from the Christian tradition in order to discover something new and grasp God's future. Biblical hermeneutics is the key to Christian theology. In this chapter, I will develop a doctrine of creation, which reads Genesis 1 no longer anthropocentrically, but ecologically. . . . I will seek a theology of the earth, and a corporal and sensual spirituality, which sanctifies earthly life.[3]

---

2   See David D. Daniels, "Progressive Pentecostalism, Pentecostal Philanthropy: The Church of Pentecost," in *African Pentecostal Missions Maturing: Essays in Honor of Apostle Opoku Onyinah*, ed. Lord Elorm Donkor and Clifton R. Clarke (Eugene, OR: Wipf and Stock, 2018).

3   Jurgen Moltmann, "Ecology as the Capacity for Love," p. xx in this volume.

Moltmann suggests that the Green Reformation also calls for "changes [of] the inner attitude of humanity." It is "a fundamental shift from the view of humanity to the earth, to the view of the earth to the human race." The change in the human attitude about nature and relations to nature has been called "planetary solidarity," according to some scholars Moltmann notes.[4]

THE GREEN REFORMATION: AN EMBEDDED GREEN THEOLOGY OF THE CHURCH OF PENTECOST

In the presentation "Direction on Environmental Care Campaign," part of a Bible study series, the Church of Pentecost proposes something akin to Moltmann's Green Reformation. Within a section entitled "Greening Our Communities," the denomination explores what could have been called "Greening the Church" as well as "Re-Greening the Earth." The study recognizes that theological beliefs "inform how people consider the environment and the care that must be given to it," and they assign "responsibility as to how one cares for God's creation."[5]

The Church of Pentecost utilizes various phrases to express its theological commitment to creation: creation care, environmental care, "safeguarding the environment," sustainable use of the earth, greening, "caring for God's creation," and "caretakers of our Father's property." Each phrase reflects an embedded theology. Creation care is the one that best registers the theological perspective gesturing toward a Green Reformation.

The denomination reads the creation account in Genesis as about all creation rather than just humanity being the zenith of this divine initiative. As will be discussed, the first two chapters of Genesis are interpreted by the church's embedded green theology through the hermeneutic of interdependence, specifically the interdependence of humanity and nature. This interdependence is cast within the wider Creator-creation relationship. As Moltmann comments, the Green Reformation includes yet exceeds ethics; a rethinking of theology is required.[6]

---

4 Moltmann, "Ecology," p. xx in this volume.
5 "Direction on Environmental Care Campaign" [PowerPoint], slides 1, 24, 39. PowerPoint presentation in the author's possession.
6 Moltmann, "Ecology," p. xx in this volume.

The denomination's embedded green theology is theocentric. In an address, the current chair and chief ecclesial officer Apostle Eric Nyamekye acknowledges God as "the creator and sustainer of the worlds." The Creator-creation relation is key for this theology; a relationship with the Creator involves more than human beings; the Creator created all creation and relates to all creation graciously. How God treats the creation mirrors how humanity should treat nature; by acting accordingly, humans honor God. The "Greening the Communities" bible study says it this way: "Since God created the world, respect for the environment means respect for God."[7]

Nyamekye recognizes the vital role of the church in the world as also being part of the Creator-creation relation. The church is the gift of the Creator to creation or the world. In the chair's words, "the dual identity of the Church [is] that the church is called out of the world to belong to God and sent back into the world to witness and to serve." The church can serve the world, according to "Green the Communities," by recognizing that "God [has] assigned the responsibility for the care of the land into our care (Genesis 2:15)." The coordinator of the denomination's environmental care campaign, Samuel Gakpetor, called the church "God's agent of change on earth." He believes the church "must act proactively to proffer solutions and actually get involved in handling the [ecological] crisis."[8]

Interdependence is a vital component to the embedded green theology of the Church of Pentecost. Their understanding of interdependence parallels Ivone Gabara. She describes interdependence with these words:

> In this sense, interdependence is not only an external physical relation between different elements but a process of perceiving the world through varied attitudes, forms, and valuations that also emerge from ourselves. We are intrinsically implicated in our perceptions and discoveries. For this reason, interdependence refers not only to physical phenomena, but also to our own subjectivity and, therefore, to the ethical relations that we establish in our world.[9]

---

7   Nyamekye, 1; "Directions," slide 24.
8   "Directions," slide 24; Samuel Gakpetor, "The Sustained Intervention of the Church Safeguarding the Environment—The Church of Pentecost Story," 1.
9   Ivone Gabara, "Interdependence, Christianity, and Environmental Crisis," p. xx in this volume.

Gebara's description of interdependence resonates with the embedded green theology of the Church of Pentecost. Each recognizes the connectedness of the "physical phenomena" and human subjectivity. Attitudes and practices are held together. In the Environmental Care Campaign of the denomination, education is prioritized in order to focus on "attitudinal change" regarding positive ways of viewing and engaging with the environment; it calls for "conscious and sustained" ecological engagement. Gebara and the Church of Pentecost join together attitudes and practices in order to advance the sustainability of the earth and human flourishing.[10]

For the Church of Pentecost, the Creator-creation relation embedded in its green theology expresses the interdependence of humans and nature. While using traditional language for God as Father and the earth as God's property, the embedded green theology affirms the "interdependence of plants and animals" with humankind. Their green theology draws upon Genesis 1 and 2 and Proverbs 27:18. Humans "depend on the environment to survive," and we are called to "maintain the different kinds of plants" and "to repress luxuriance." In other words, we are to resist overharvesting the earth. Human beings, especially Christians, must introduce careful ways of relating to nature; at times nature should be allowed to grow "spontaneously... [as it] certainly did at the creation." At other times, careful practices of farming, gardening, and harvesting should be implemented because humans are called by God to cultivate the land and replant "where feasible." "As caretakers of our Father's property," humans, especially Christians, are called to care for the earth and "desist from destroying" it. The mistreatment of the earth "will cause humanity to suffer, which may lead to [the] loss of lives." The careful treatment of the earth, or "to engage in greening," lets humankind express the reality that they are created "in the image and likeness of God."[11]

This church's green theology, reflected in the Creator-creation relation, explores eight aspects of the interdependence of humanity and nature. After creation, according to this theology, humanity was commanded to:

---

10   Gakpetor, 4.
11   "Directions," slides 40–43.

1. live in interdependence with nature;
2. relate constructively with "nonhuman creatures";
3. find sustenance from the earth;
4. be prudent in building living, working, cultural, recreational, and religious facilities that take away land for natural usage;
5. implement and "ensure sustainable use of plant resources";
6. implement and ensure sustainable "use of the earth's resources";
7. appreciate "the need to green the environment";
8. And calculate and mitigate against the "consequences of excessive harvest[ing] of plants without replanting."[12]

These eight aspects of the interdependence of humanity and nature parallel the paradigm shift proposed by Moltmann from an anthropocentric to a biocentric framework; yet the Church of Pentecost's paradigm shift goes from anthropocentric to Creation-centric. The interdependence it advances might include elements that could be included in the "planetary solidarity" to which Moltmann gestures.[13]

A Green Reformation: The Environmental Care Campaign of the Church of Pentecost

The Environmental Care Campaign of the Church of Pentecost could be seen as including what Gebara calls a "planetary agenda."[14] Sallie McFague describes the planetary agenda, as discussed in chapter 2, as involving "all things and each person. It involves everything because we know that all things and all beings and processes on the planet are interrelated."[15]

---

12 "Directions," slides 40–42.
13 Moltmann, "Ecology," p. xx in this volume.
14 Gebara, "Interdependence, Christianity, and Environmental Crisis," p. xx in this volume.
15 Sallie McFague. *The Body of God. An Ecological Theology* (Minneapolis, Fortress Press, 1993), 8.

Related to a planetary agenda is "the path of simplicity in the midst of the complexity of relations." Gebara states: "By simplicity, I understand many things, but above all a movement to return to everyday life, to facts, to people's little anecdotes, listening to stories and learning to tell them, preparing and sharing food together."[16]

The planetary agenda of the Church of Pentecost, with its focus on big and small projects as well as the earth-sustaining household practices, is lodged in the Environment Care Campaign that was launched by Nyamekye on November 22, 2018 in Accra, Ghana. The motto of the campaign is Environmental Care, My Responsibility. While the campaign is a denomination project, it solicits a wide range of individuals to participate, from ecclesiastical leaders to laypeople, while also promoting denominational partnerships with government departments and commercial entities.[17]

The campaign consists of five major components: ecology education, tree planting, recycling plastic waste, lobbying for the governmental enforcement of ecology-focused laws, and cleanup projects. Over a hundred thousand leaders in the Church of Pentecost have been educated on biblical perspectives and Christian practices related to creation care.[18]

THE GREEN REFORMATION: CREATION CARE AND THE CIVIC VISION OF THE CHURCH OF PENTECOST

Creation care is part of the civic vision of the Church of Pentecost. While the Church of Pentecost casts its civic vision in terms of promoting the "spiritual, social, and political well-being" of society, its creation care vision advances the sustainability of the earth along with human flourishing. According to the denomination, in addition to caring for creation, Christians are called to serve the "least of these," as demanded in Matthew 25—the poor, prisoners, the shelter-less, and those with health challenges.

---

16   Gebara, "Interdependence," p. xx in this volume.
17   Gakpetor, 2.
18   Gakpetor, 5.

(One's shelter and health might be negatively impacted by climate change.)¹⁹ The civic responsibility of the Church of Pentecost has been framed in terms of "partnership[s] with governments, communities, and other like-minded organizations." The set goal is to empower poor communities to reach economic sustainability through an array of initiatives, including the Environmental Care Campaign. As a denomination, the Church of Pentecost takes seriously its role as vital sector within civil society.²⁰

The civic vision of the denomination preceded the creation care focus. Daniel Walker identified the Church of Pentecost's turn to political engagement with the nomination in 1992 of the chairman of the Church of Pentecost, Prophet Martinson Yeboah, by the newly elected president Jerry Rawlings to the twenty-five-member Council of State, an advisory body to the president of Ghana. By 1998, male and female leaders in the denomination, including elders and deaconesses, ran for office, and some won their elections as members of Parliament. According to Church of Pentecost's Apostle Daniel Okyere Walker, by 2009 "there were fifteen elders and officers of the CoP [Church of Pentecost] serving as parliamentarians in various constituencies and political parties in Ghana." A tradition has emerged wherein the chair of the denomination addresses political and social issues at the general council meetings, an event that includes government officials. The denomination has encouraged its members to be political officials to advance the common good, which includes creation care.²¹

During the 2010s, the former chair Apostle Dr. Opoku Onyinah convened a meeting of the members of parliament who belonged to the Church of Pentecost. In 2016, he extended the invitation "to all members actively involved in politics." In his address, Onyinah stated, "We have met here as Christians to fellowship and dialogue on the way forward for the development of the country. We therefore take this opportunity to appeal

---

19   Daniel Okyere Walker, "The Pentecost Fire Is Burning: Models of Mission Activities in the Church of Pentecost" (PhD diss., University of Birmingham, 2010), 116; Ghanaweb, "Widows and Orphans Receive 400 Million-cedi Fund," April 24, 2006, https://etheses.bham.ac.uk/id/eprint/1177/1/Walker10PhD_A1a.pdf; Walker, 25.
20   Walker, "The Pentecost Fire Is Burning," 24.
21   Walker, 143.

to other God-fearing politicians to conduct themselves in the fear of the Lord."[22]

The Church of Pentecost also engages in leveraging the public policy of the government toward expanding public services, especially to the poor, and confronts corruption in electoral politics. The Church of Pentecost encourages its members who feel the call to political engagement to run for elected office. If they win, they should participate in efforts to craft government programs and partnerships that advance the political well-being of the poor, the common good of society, and the sustainability of the earth.[23]

In its publication *Vision 2023*, the Church of Pentecost includes creation care in its ecclesial responsibility to contribute to the national development of Ghana. The denomination works to equip "the Church to transform every sphere of society." Its vision is "to contribute" to Ghana being:

> a God-fearing society with hardworking and committed citizens; a society where there is the display of Christ-like behavior and the demonstration of a high level of integrity; a society with a considerable reduction in social injustice, corruption, crime rate and other social vices; a society whose members are law-abiding citizens and where there is a reasonable reduction in wayward or deviant characters; a transformed society that is very concerned about the environment, keeping it clean and prompting others within the society to do the same and a society where citizens in deprived communities have improved access to basic amenities.[24]

As this vision indicates, the focus goes beyond evangelism and charity. Yet in one sense the vision is limited to the nation-state. There exists a tension

---

22 Church of Pentecost, "Chairman Interacts with Christian Politicians," June 15, 2016, http://thecophq.org/expo_churchnews.php?id=2042#sthash.mIrYEwev.dpuf.
23 Church of Pentecost.
24 The Church of Pentecost, *Vision 2023: Five-Year Document for the Church of Pentecost Covering the Period 2018–2023*, 9.

between the nation-state focus in *Vision 2023* and the planetary focus of the embedded green theology explored above. The Church of Pentecost offers specific features of the society that it seeks to address. In the report, the denomination identifies twelve indexes that it seeks to reduce: corruption; gender-based, sexual, and domestic violence; teenage pregnancy; and property crime. It seeks to increase the percentage of citizens who feel "'very safe' in their daily lives," the number of rural households with portable water, the use of "public dump site[s]," the percentage of adults who feel the government takes their views seriously, the graduateation rate across all levels of education, and the "level of access to health facilities" for citizens.[25]

The focus of these efforts is on local communities, demonstrating the ways a Pentecostal denomination serves communities through social ministries. Especially in at-risk urban and rural communities absent of key functioning institutions, social actions directed by the Church of Pentecost provide vital services, illustrating its civil engagement.

In the Environmental Care Campaign, the denomination identifies additional indexes: reforestation, decreased environmental degradation, increased sanitation, reduction in the use of plastics, multiple uses of those plastic-constituted items remaining, recycling of all plastics no longer usable, and a clearer, more sustainable environment.

Creation care is a recent focus for the Church of Pentecost, yet this focus builds on the civic engagement of the denomination. It is a new frontier for the role of the church, expanding from the narrow lens of society to include broader nature and from the nation-state to include the planet.

THE GREEN REFORMATION: THE CHURCH OF PENTECOST AND OTHER PENTECOSTALS

Other Pentecostal denominations have been participating, one could argue, in the Green Reformation. Pentecostals in Ecuador and Chile have been addressing ecological issues since the late twentieth century. In South Korea, ecology is a theme in the theology of the late David Yonggi Cho. A ministry that Cho founded developed a model environmental garden

---

25   The Church of Pentecost, 10.

and taught environmental issues. Some Pentecostal denominations in Burundi, Tanzania, and Kenya have engaged in tree planting and environmental education.

According to a report of the Swedish Pentecostal Churches' aid organization Pingstmissionens Utvecklingssamarbete (PMU) on "Pentecostalism and Ecological Sustainable Development":

> Spiritually motivated Pentecostals have "begun to articulate a distinctive Pentecostal ecology" with concern for the "ecological and eschatological well-being of creation." The ecological and climate crisis calls "for deep moral, psychological, political and spiritual changes," [and] while Pentecostals need to step up in theology and commitment, they also carry great potential and a substantial hope to make vital difference to the issues of environment and climate change.[26]

The Church of God in Christ is a Black-majority Pentecostal denomination headquartered in the United States and has congregations in over a hundred countries. In 2013, it approved a climate change resolution in its general assembly. The resolution frames creation care in terms of exercising "good stewardship over the earth and its creatures." While it acknowledges the negative "impact of climate change" on many communities, it makes special mention of the suffering of "the poorest among them." Although more anthropocentric than the embedded green theology of the Church of Pentecost, this resolution called for "measure stewardship actions that will reduce energy consumption, use sustainable practices in our houses, buildings and houses of worship, and seek good counsel in peer-reviewed climate scientists that will increase our knowledge and actions to confront change." The resolution also "recognize[d] the facts about climate change from the United Nations Intergovernmental Panel on Climate Change" as "important foundations for an informed approach to the challenge

---

26 Pingstmissionens Utvecklingssamarbete, "Pentecostals, Transformation, and Social Engagement-A Research Overview," 2022, 22, https://pmu.se/wp-content/uploads/2022/09/Pentecostals-transformation-and-socia_2022_webb.pdf.

of climate change." Among some leaders of the denomination, environmental racism and eco-justice need to be added as topics of a Pentecostal ecotheology and ecological concern.[27]

The Church of God in Christ found similar biblical texts as the Church of Pentecost to make its theological claims: the first two chapters of Genesis, Psalms 24, Proverbs 12:15, and Proverbs 15:22. The creation account is prominent as a biblical and theological foundation.[28]

Having a dialogue among Pentecostals and other Christians across various continents could strengthen the embedded green theologies of denominations like the Church of Pentecost.

Conclusion

The embedded green theology of the Church of Pentecost emerges out of praxis of planting nearly two million trees in two years while reading the Bible from a creation care perspective. As a conservative Protestant denomination, it balances intelligently its commitment to evangelism and social ministry. It remains faithful to its plain reading of the Bible and conservative views of the Christian lifestyle while at the same time recognizing creation care as part of the Christian witness and a prominent focus of the church. Its green Pentecostal theological perspective is shaped by efforts to foster an ecological spirituality, the greening of the church, the sustainability of the earth, and human flourishing.

Moltmann's concept of the Green Reformation provides an insightful way to frame the Environmental Care Campaign of the Church of Pentecost and its embedded green theology. A theology of interdependence appears to anchor the perspectives of Moltmann, Gebara, and the Church of Pentecost while the Creator-creation relationship provides a theological framework that the Church of Pentecost can embrace for its green theology. Categorizing the five major components to the Environmental Care Campaign with the concept of planetary agenda offers great potential. Environmental care fits well in the expanded civic vision of the Church

---

27 Church of God in Christ, General Assembly (April Call Meeting 2013), Resolution #042013-7, "Climate Change."
28 Church of God in Christ, General Assembly.

of Pentecost and enables the church to shift from an anthropocentric focus to a creation one.

The Green Reformation includes Pentecostal denominations in addition to the Church of Pentecost. Having a dialogue among Pentecostals and other Christians across various continents could strengthen the embedded green theologies of the Church of Pentecost as it explores ways to advance the sustainability of the earth, human flourishing, and the renewal of the Christian witness. Pentecostal denominations like the Church of Pentecost contribute their tree planting efforts and other environment enhancement projects to the earth's sustainability and their embedded green theology for Pentecostal, ecumenical, and interreligious dialogue.

CHAPTER 14

AN ASIAN ECO-SPIRITUALITY

Kwangsun Choi

The ecological crisis has become the main theme for Christian faith and practice in the contemporary world. As one of the first attempts of the World Council of Churches (WCC) to tackle this theme head-on, the World Convocation on Justice, Peace and Integrity of Creation (JPIC) convened in Seoul, Korea, in 1990. This convocation in turn became the core theme for a series of case studies in Asia. Gradually, the due care for creation and justice took the center stage of the WCC work on climate change. In 2013, the tenth Assembly of the World Council of Churches made a new statement on mission entitled *Together Towards Life: Mission and Evangelism in Changing Landscape*.[1] The aim of the new ecumenical discernment was to "seek vision, concepts, and directions for a renewed understanding and practice of mission and evangelism in changing landscape."[2] Likewise, the Lausanne movement, representing evangelical Protestants, addressed climate change during its meeting in Cape Town in 2010. The third Lausanne Congress collaborated to produce the *Cape Town Commitment*, which declares the importance of the care for God's creation. It notes:

> Probably the most serious and urgent challenge faced by the physical world now is the threat of climate change. This will disproportionately affect those in poorer countries, for it is there that

---

[1] World Council of Churches, *Together towards Life: Mission and Evangelism in Changing Landscapes*, e. Jooseop Keum (2013 WCC Publications: 2013).
[2] World Council of Churches, 3.

climate extremes would be manifested most severe and where there is little socio-politico-economic capability to adapt to them. World poverty and climate change need to be addressed together and with equal urgency.[3]

Both *Together Towards Life* and the *Cape Town Commitment* underscore the common theme of creation and life as a theological imperative and emphasize justice for the poor. Within Catholicism, Pope Francis has also called on Christians and all people of good will to work together to care for the earth, our common home.[4]

The purpose of this study is to explore an ecological Christianity in order to overcome the current ecological crisis besetting us. The present context of the ecological crisis and the bio-geological change demands an urgent, comprehensive response in order to restore the integral functioning of the earth's processes. What is needed for the feasible journey of the earth community is not merely a replacement of the existing theologies that have contributed to the crisis; rather we need a recontextualization of theology. To envision a mutually enhancing human-earth relationship, I will pay particular attention to the ecological wisdom found in East and South Asia.

Review on Asian Context

Here I review the Asian context highlighting three distinctive features—religious diversity, economic poverty of the people, and ecological destruction. This analysis will lead us to delve not only into the ecological wisdom of Asia but also into the ecological vision of the basic earth communities that I propose later in this paper. Asia is the home of the so-called great religions—Hinduism, Buddhism, Islam, Judaism, and Christianity—as well as Confucianism, Taoism, Shintoism, and other religions with fewer adherents. With few exceptions, Christians comprise a small minority

---

3   Lausanne Movement, "Cape Town Commitment: A Confession of Faith and a Call to Action," http://www.lausanne.org/content/ctc/ctcommitment

4   Pope Francis, *Encyclical Letter Laudato Si' of the Holy Father Francis on Care for Our Common Home*, 2015.

in Asian countries. Rooted in such a diverse religious worldview, various cultures flourish in Asia.

Aloysius Pieris, Sri Lankan liberation theologian, is inspirational.[5] He asks, How do Asian Christians become the agents of liberation from the poverty of the poor and the conflict among religions? The overwhelming poverty that exists in Asia, with the exceptions of some developed countries, should be taken into serious consideration. This poverty is intensified by colonial and neocolonial exploitation. Military dictatorships and widespread corruption also contribute to the increase of poverty. Many Asians realize that nation-building and economic growth are not sufficient to end colonialism. New forms of colonialism continue to form at the expense of the poor and the rest of creation. It is worthwhile to mention the ecological crisis, which is not only the result of certain economic, political, and social factors but is also deeply related to moral and spiritual crises. The current ecological crisis reveals how certain problematic aspects of these have contributed to the crisis itself. That is, the ecological crisis results in part from a failure of theology to integrate humans into a flourishing human-earth relationship. Accordingly, we must come to understand the answer to the question, What makes humans the most destructive species in the earth community? Why are many religiously devout people silent about the ecological crisis? Why is the Church's response to the fate of the earth, devastated by a plundering commercial-industrial system, inadequate? What gives meaning and value to life, as well as the spiritual-psychic energy to overcome the present crisis? It is difficult to escape criticisms leveled at a Christian faith that has brought the merciless exploitation of

---

5   Aloysius Pieris holds five reasons why he regards liberation theology as the correct method of doing theology in Asia. First, the features of the methodology are contained in Jon Sobrino's lucid comparison of European and Latin American theologies. Second, there is the primacy of praxis over theory. Third, this way is the way of the cross, the basis of all knowledge. Fourth, it is a liberational theology demanding an asceticism of renunciation and a voluntary poverty that rejects acquisitiveness. Finally, the encounter of God with humanity is seen as the obligation to use all human potentialities to anticipate the kingdom. See Aloysius Pieris, *An Asian Theology of Liberation* (Maryknoll, NY: Orbis, 1988), 82–83.

the poor and the rest of creation, which becomes the source of the misery of millions of Asians.

While these three features are inseparable, how are we going to face this accusation to a Christianity seriously concerned with the well-being of all creation and with the protection of the poor? Using socioeconomic, and religio-cultural analysis, it is clear that salient theological movements have emerged in Asia, including minjung theology in Korea, pain of God theology in Japan, water buffalo theology in Thailand, third-eye theology among the Chinese, yin and yang theology among Chinese and Korean Christians, theology of change in Taiwan, and Indian and Sri Lankan theology.

Nonetheless, no established voice for Asian ecotheology and eco-spirituality has been heard yet. The emerging ecological awareness alongside religious conflict and social justice suggests the need for further theological reflection in an integral manner. To dissolve the criticisms of merciless exploitation, Christianity in Asia should develop a new perspective embracing not only humanity but also the earth community. In this chapter, I contend that Asian ecotheology has two kinds of important references: liberation theology in Latin America and ecological wisdom in Asian religions. Many Asian theologians accept the contributions made by liberation theology concerning the preferential option for the poor as the subject of theology. They also employ the method of social analysis to read the signs of the times. They further regard contemplative commitments as the act of doing theology. Although liberation theology has laid much of the theological basis for Asian theologians, they recognize that this theology must be supplemented with ecological insights and practices derived from Asian religious resources and perspectives. This is what I attempt to do in this paper. To overcome the ecological crisis and suggest an alternative future for Christianity, I suggest a turn to basic earth communities that integrate liberative Christian praxis and the ecological worldview of Asian people.

A Cosmological and Ecological Worldview

It is today's critical task to recover a cosmological dimension for ecotheology and eco-spirituality. It is often said that there are three metaphysical factors for doing theology—God, humanity, and the rest of creation. Since the sixteenth century, theology has mainly focused on God and humanity, and spirituality has focused on the God-human relationship as a redemptive-centered spirituality. Thus the rest of creation has become marginalized in Christian thought. Combined with the mechanistic worldview of modern times, such an anthropocentric theology has contributed to the development of the current ecological crisis. When we reflect on the creation account of Genesis, as the prologue of the Gospel of John shows, the most profound context for doing theology is actually cosmological. Indeed, the ecological crisis necessitates a turn to the cosmological context.

The current ecological crisis is due primarily to a dysfunctional cosmology whose foundations are rooted in anthropocentrism and a dualistic mindset. Here cosmology is not understood as a static conceptual system. When a given cosmology becomes too problematic and/or dysfunctional to deal with contemporary pressing challenges, a new cosmology eventually emerges. As the foundation for reflection on meaning and value amid crises, an emerging cosmology offers new answers to the questions of who we are, where we are going, and what our relationship is to God, the rest of creation, and other people. In fact, any religious interpretation of an object or event relies on cosmology because it provides the ground for reflecting on human meaning and purpose in the world.

From this point of view, Elizabeth A. Johnson calls for the need of a new understanding of the cosmological context. For her, the ecological crisis not only requires that "we just think through a new theology of creation, but that cosmology be a framework within which all theological topics be rethought and [become] a substantive partner in theological interpretation."[6] Denis Edwards, John Haught, and Sallie McFague echo Johnson's proposal that we need to not only turn to cosmology but make cosmology the heart of the theological enterprise.[7] For the development of

---

6   Elizabeth Johnson, "Turn to the Heavens and the Earth: Retrieval of the Cosmos in Theology," *CTSA Proceedings* 51(1996), 14.

7   Julia Brumbaugh and Natalia Imperatori-Lee, eds., *Turning to the Heavens and the Earth: Theological Reflections on a Cosmological Conversion: Essays in Honor of Elizabeth A. Johnson* (Collegeville, MN: Liturgical Press, 2016).

an eco-spirituality, Charles Cummings also insists that there should be a new focus for the theological enterprise:

> The three major areas of theology are God, Humans and Nature. The early ages of theological studies laid heavy premium on the understanding of God; the next period placed much emphasis on the study of the Human; it is true that our attention should now turn to Nature, a much neglected discipline in the curriculum of the theological enterprise.[8]

Cosmology becomes an important subject for exploring contemporary spirituality. When old cosmologies become dysfunctional, a new worldview eventually emerges. Just as cosmology is not fixed, spirituality is evolving to deal with contemporary pressing challenges such as the ecological crisis.

How Much Would One Grain of Rice Weigh?

While I admit limitations of Asian traditions to respond to the ecological crisis, I explore their ecologically friendly cosmologies for the healing of the earth community. Asian religions contain the radical experiences of intimate relationships between humans and the rest of creation. Here I introduce a Korean song as an example that reveals a non-dual, organic, and interrelated worldview.

Reflect on a grain of rice, not a kernel of wheat, since rice is the main crop and staple of Asian people. Imagine that you put it on the palm of your hand. Have you ever looked carefully at one grain of rice? Have you thoughtfully considered the meaning and value of a grain of rice? Please do not limit yourself to seeing the rice only in a materialistic dimension. Expand your imagination to the end of the universe and to the unseen dimension of reality. The following lyrics might help you in this expansion. Consider the lyrics of the Korean song "How Much Would One Grain of Rice Weigh":

---

8   Charles Cummings, *Eco-Spirituality: Towards a Reverent Life* (Mahwah: Paulist Press, 1991), vi.

> *How much would one grain of rice weigh?*
> *I put it on the palm of my hand to feel the weight*
> *Winds, thunders, rain, and sunshine*
> *And the lonely starlight, they all have brushed by*
> *Including the farmer's dawn*
> *One grain of rice embraces the whole universe*
> *I try to weigh one grain of rice*
> *The one lonely grain deserted, the weight of the universe*
> *It sings the song of this world*
> *One grain of rice is as heavy as life*
> *One grain of rice is as heavy as peace*
> *One grain of rice is as heavy as the farmer*
> *One grain of rice is as heavy as time*
> *One grain of rice is as heavy as the universe*

When reading the song's lyrics, you may be able to sense the worldview of the Asian people. They are people who see a grain of rice as representative of the interrelatedness and interconnectedness of all beings that exist in the universe. Asian religion and culture have sprouted from this worldview, which places high value on diversity and communion without neglecting the value and subjectivity of each grain of rice.

In India, the cosmos is perceived as an interconnected whole described in Buddhism as Indra's net. The Buddhist point of view encourages people to embrace rather than conquer or control the environment. All beings are linked to each other, and all life-forms are also interlinked. Such a view voices more clearly the relationship between humanity and nature. Thich Nhat Hanh upholds the strong interconnectedness of all creation, which echoes with the following:

> Although we human beings are animals, a part of nature, we single ourselves out from nature, thinking of other animals and living beings as "nature" and acting as if we are not a part of it. Then we ask ourselves, "How should we deal with nature?"[9]

---

9 Thich Nhat Hanh, "Interbeing," 1992, https://www.parallax.org/mindfulnessbell/article/environmental-interbeing.

The answer is simple. We should deal with nature the way we should deal with ourselves! We should not harm ourselves; we should not harm nature. Harming nature is harming ourselves, and vice versa. If we knew how to deal with our self and our fellow human beings, we would know how to deal with nature. Human beings are inseparable. Therefore, by not caring properly for any one of these, we harm them all.[10]

In Confucianism, the human is understood as a microcosm against the macrocosm of the universe. Chang Tsai, a neo-Confucian scholar, explains:

> Heaven is my father and earth is my mother, and even such a small creature as I find an intimate place in their midst. Therefore that which extends throughout the universe I regard as my body and that which directs the universe I consider as my nature. All people are my brothers and sisters, and all things are my companions.[11]

Asian religious worldviews are often associated with cosmological interrelatedness and interconnectedness with each other. That is why one grain of rice is as heavy as life, peace, the farmer, time, and the universe.

Cosmological Principles for Asian Eco-Spirituality

Let us go back to the lyrics of the rice song. If you try to understand the reality of a grain of rice, you need to see it in a triadic communion among heaven, earth, and humanity. Without seeing reality in a cosmological dimension, one cannot understand the reality of rice as it is. What is needed is to see reality not only in a human (e.g., farmer or peace) and nature dimension (e.g., winds, thunders, rain, and sunshine) but also in a cosmological dimension (e.g., starlight or the universe). For this reason, I draw a more integral and cosmological perspective to propose three cosmological principles for Asian ecotheology based on Berry's three cosmological

---

10 Thich Nhat Hanh, "Interbeing," 1992, https://www.parallax.org/mindfulnessbell/article/environmental-interbeing.
11 Zhang Zai, *Western Inscription*, quoted in Thomas Berry, *The Dream of the Earth* (San Francisco: Sierra Club Books, 1988), 15.

principles of the universe: communion (intimacy, interrelatedness), differentiation (diversity), and subjectivity (interiority, self-organization).[12]

According to Berry, differentiation is the first principle of the universe, which is somewhat like the Creator God who creates an amazing world with the power to develop greater complexity through the unfolding process of the universe. Diversity means that everything is coded to be distinctly different from everything else. Nothing is identical to anything else in the divine mystery of the awesome web of life. Understanding and accepting diversity is crucial for Asian mission. If you do not appreciate diversity in Asia, you simply slip into exclusivism, which leads to discrimination toward Asian culture and religion as well as Asian people.

Thomas Aquinas describes the whole universe as participating in divine goodness:

> For he brought things into being in order that His goodness might be communicated to creatures, and be represented by them; and because His goodness could not be adequately represented by one creature alone, He produced many and diverse creatures, that what was wanting to one in the representation of the divine goodness might be supplied by another. For goodness, which in God is simple and uniform, in creatures is manifold and divided and hence the whole universe together participates in the divine goodness more perfectly, and represents it better than any single creature whatsoever.[13]

For Aquinas, all that exists is to participate in the perfection of God's goodness in the universe, representing itself more fully as a whole rather than as any single creature. For Aquinas, diversity is the way of showing reality in the universe. We need to recognize that in the midst of a magnificent

---

12   Thomas Berry, *The Great Work: Our Way into the Future* (New York: Bell Tower, 1999), 162–3; Brian Swimme and Thomas Berry, *The Universe Story: From the Primordial Flaring Forth to the Ecozoic Era—A Celebration of the Unfolding of the Cosmos* (San Francisco: HarperOne, 1994), 71–78.

13   Thomas Aquinas, *Summa Theologia: A Concise Translation,* 1. a.47, a.1, ed. Timothy McDermott (Westminster: Christian Classics, 1989), 89.

diversity of cultures, peoples, and religions in the world, we are God's one family and live in God's one house, the earth community.

Second, each differentiated object in the universe has its own subjectivity because from the beginning everything has both a material-physical dimension and a psychic-spiritual dimension. Each being in the universe contributes to the unfolding story of the universe in its own unique way according to its nature and context. Subjectivity describes the innate potential and right of every single organism to grow, develop, and blossom into its full potential. Every being has inner beauty and value. Asia is a land of religion and a land of diverse cultural roots. In Asia, many countries also have colonial experience at the imperial hands of the West. Some Asian theologians have attempted to transplant Western theology into Asia, lacking understanding of the subjectivity of the Asian heritages. The task of Asian ecotheology is to respect the subjectivity of Asian culture and religion.

The third principle is the communion of each reality of the universe with every other reality in the universe. Just as the grain of rice shows its interrelatedness with all that exists in the universe, we humans live in an awesome interconnected and interdependent web of life. To be at all is to be in relationship. During a visit to Indonesia, I had a chance to participate in an angklung performance in Bandung. Angklung is a musical instrument made of bamboo that plays when shaken. Each instrument plays one tone. While participating in the angklung performance, I was able to better understand the meaning of communion. Each one makes a different sound, but finally every participant harmonizes beyond their perceptions, thoughts, or religions. I realized I had experienced the communion of the Holy Spirit through participating in the performance.

The three cosmological principles for Asian ecotheology do not arise from a thematic approach but from a more radical understanding of the Asian context. For instance, there are increasing religious conflicts between Christianity and other Asian religions. I might apply the principle of diversity to the base of interfaith dialogue among religions and to solving tensions among countries related to migration. Subjectivity can relate to such topics as human trafficking, human rights, women's rights, domestic violence, and discrimination. It also provides a sense of the ongoing ecocide, mass extinction of life, and geocide—the killing of the earth community. Finally, communion provides a mutually enhancing manner to develop an ecological community beyond the human community, including the rest of creation as subjects for doing theology.

Toward the Basic Earth Communities

On the basis of Asian cosmology which can be explained with three cosmological principles, I propose the Basic Earth Communities (BECs) drawing on the vision of Berry for the future of Asian ecotheology. The primary concern of the BECs is the survival of the earth community, which is integral with Basic Christian Communities of Latin America (BCCs) and the Basic Human Communities (BHCs) of Asia. The BCCs, also called "basic ecclesial communities," are Christian movements originating from and inspired by liberation theology in Latin America. When liberation theology came to Asia, Asian theologians further expanded the BCCs, turning them into BHCs. In fact, Asian theologians attempted to integrate the insightful fruits from liberation theology into the Asian context, the reality of Asia inseparable from social injustice and religious diversity.

For instance, Aloysius Pieris notes, "a Christian participation in and a christic explication of all that happens at the deepest zone of concrete ethos where religiousness and poverty, each in its liberative dimension, coalesce to forge a common front against mammon."[14] In this regard, Pieris proposed the BHCs, where members of Christian and non-Christian groups—Buddhists, Hindus, and Marxists—would strive together for the liberation of life. The BHCs are not a group that has come together for interreligious dialogue. The culmination of the activities of a BHCs is ideally the total liberation from the oppression of human society. It is within the process of this ongoing liberative praxis that each member of the BHCs discovers the uniqueness of their own faith.

While the BCCs are relevant to the poor in the context of Latin America, and the BHCs are relevant to the poverty and religious diversity in Asia, the BECs are relevant to the poor and the earth community integral to ecological discipleship of Jesus Christ. For the future of humanity

---

14   Aloysius Pieris, *An Asian Theology of Liberation* (Maryknoll, NY: Orbis, 1988), 88.

and the rest of creation, it is time to further develop the BECs. A BCC is a place where Christians in Latin America come together to read the Bible, reflect on what it means in relation to their own life experiences, and find meaning of life. A BHC is a community of people who transcend religions pursue common human values and meanings while resisting unjust dictatorships in Asia.

Here I take the term "earth" from both the Bible and the "Earth Charter" to describe the importance of life community. In the Old Testament, the book of Proverbs, Chapter 8 notes that the entire earth is the dwelling place of wisdom. The earth as the dwelling place is wisdom's womb. The "Earth Charter" describes the earth as the key world. The document contains four overarching principles: first, respect and care for the community of life; second, ecological integrity; third, social and economic justice; and fourth, democracy, nonviolence, and peace.[15] BECs is a community that values these four principles, is spiritually awakened to the sacred aspects of our global community, is committed to ecological justice for ecological refugees and the poor, and plays a leading role in the ecological civilization transition for a promising future. In BECs, the earth is not only the sacred dwelling place of wisdom but also the responsibility of humanity.

There are a few distinctive emphases that characterize the BECs. First, the BECs provide a critical understanding of eco-justice that integrates social justice and ecological justice. By recognizing that the well-being of people is inseparable from the well-being of the earth, eco-justice provides a dynamic framework for thought and action that fosters socioeconomic justice and ecological integrity. James Profit, who drew on the work of Leonardo Boff, writes:

> The cry of the poor is indeed the voice of Earth who is suffering from death and destruction wrought by humans. The cry of the Earth is also the cry of Jesus. Jesus is suffering the erratic weather systems caused by the heating of Earth's atmosphere. Jesus is suffering in the crisis caused by the near extinction of the cod, not

---

15   Earth Charter International, "The Earth Charter," https://earthcharter.org/read-the-earth-charter/.

only because of the suffering of the fishers, but because one more revelation of God's presence is being put to death. The passion of Earth, including the passion of suffering people, is the passion of Jesus. The cry of the poor is the cry of the Earth is the cry of Jesus.[16]

When we hear the passion of the poor and the earth, we become aware of the deeply intertwined link between economic, social, and ecological justice. This awareness of Jesus's presence amid the suffering of people and of the rest of the earth community can foster an appropriate response to the ecological crisis through an integral understanding of ecological justice and economic justice.

Second, a BEC is a living and contemplative community that reveals the discipleship of Jesus Christ. Ecological crisis is not only the result of certain economic, political, and social factors. It is also deeply related to failure of discipleship of Jesus. For Asian theologians, discipleship is not a natural consequence of doing theology. Rather for them the discipleship is more important than theology in Western rational categories. I name this discipleship "contemplative commitment." Drawing from Tissa Balasuriya, commitment is a response to God and a source of empathetic understanding responding to the exigencies of reality; and contemplation is a union with God that leads to and is nurtured by commitment. This is an approach toward a spirituality of action that is holistic, unitive, and mystical."[17] Therefore, the BECs start with the realization of reality in contemplative ways and respond to God's call through a praxis of liberation of humanity and the rest of creation.

Third, the BECs attempt to read the Christian Bible with a lens of ecological hermeneutics. It is an example of the ecological readings

---

16   James Profit, "Connecting with the Earth: Experiencing the Sacred," in *Sacred Earth, Sacred Community: Jubilee, Ecology and Aboriginal Peoples* (Toronto: Canadian Ecumenical Jubilee Initiative, 2000), 201. See Leonard Boff, *Cry of the Earth, Cry of the Poor* (Maryknoll, NY: Orbis, 1997).

17   Tissa Balasuriya, "Divergences: An Asian Perspective," in *Third World Theologies: Commonalities and Divergences*, ed. K.C Abraham (Maryknoll, NY: Orbis, 2004), 114.

developing now among Australian scholars. Norman C. Habel and Peter Trudinger, for instance, set the aims of the Earth Bible Project:

> As Western interpreters we are heirs of a long anthropocentric, patriarchal, and androcentric approach to reading the text that has devalued the Earth and that continues to influence the way we read the text; that we are members of the endangered Earth community in dialogue with ancient texts; to recognize Earth as a subject in the text with which we seek to relate empathetically rather than as a topic to be analyzed rationally; to take up the cause of justice for Earth and to ascertain whether Earth and Earth community are oppressed, silenced, or liberated in the text; and to develop techniques of reading the text to discern and retrieve alternative traditions where the voice of Earth and Earth community has been suppressed.[18]

This statement is innovative, timely, and urgently required if we are to read the Bible with ecological sensitivity. These theologians provide valuable critiques of biblical readings that have contributed to the ecological crisis and most importantly critiques of anthropocentrism as a mode of separation from the earth. Moreover, they offer a valuable set of eco-justice principles: intrinsic worth, interconnectedness, voice, purpose, mutual custodianship, and resistance.

Finally, remember the song "How Much Would One Grain of Rice Weigh" again. Asians are seeking the unity of knowledge and action, theory and practice within the cosmological context. In the BECs, the practice of ecological cultivation is grounded in the origin, structure, and functioning of the universe, and ecological virtues might enable us to live in accordance with the functional processes of earth's history. In this view, the BECs provide not only dispositions for the moral potential of humanity but also a type of discipline that cultivates the ecological practices of the Christian faith.

---

18 Norman C. Habel, "Introduction," *Exploring Ecological Hermeneutics*, ed. Norman C. Habel and Peter Trudinger (Atlanta, GA: Society of Biblical Literature, 2008), 4.

As a conclusion, I note that Asian churches are the agent for Basic Earth Communities. The survival of humanity is threatened, and the Christian faith cannot be separated from the current ecological crisis. At this juncture in time, the Asian churches can contribute to world Christianity through the development of a mutually enhancing relationship between the Christian faith, the well-being of humanity, and the rest of creation.

CHAPTER 15

CHRISTIANITY IN ABYA YALA: MOTHERLAND, SUSTAINABILITY, AND ECOCIDE

Yenny Delgado-Qullaw

INTRODUCTION

To understand the arrival of Christianity on the continent currently known as North America, it is necessary to first reframe our understanding of the land and its people by grounding the discussion in the land's name and location. *Abya Yala* comes from the Guna language and means "land in full maturity and land of vital blood." The Guna people inhabit the meeting points of the North and South Americas, and their language symbolically represents the connectivity of the lands. The name Abya Yala comes from the Guna language and means "land in full maturity and land of vital blood." This name focuses on reflections on the land and its native people rather than colonization and invasion. In the 1970s, native activists, historians, politicians, and theologians adopted Abya Yala as the unified name instead of North America (English and French speakers) and Latin America (Spanish and Portuguese speakers), which perpetuated colonial divisions.[1]

Christianity arrived in Abya Yala over five centuries ago; European soldiers, settlers, and Christian missionaries brought the cross and sword to rule our land. The implications of colonization on the native population led to a sizable reduction of people, forcing assimilation into normative European practices that led to a loss of ancestral and

---

[1] Yenny Delgado and Claudio Ramírez, "Abya Yala Theology," https://publicatheology.org/2022/04/06/abya-yala-theology/.

spiritual practices where only Christians are saved and native practices are seen as pagan. The vision of the Gospel that the newcomers brought assumed that only things coming from Europe were Christian, whether it was faith or death. This reductionist understanding of the Gospel, where Christian Europeans were considered superior and blessed by the Divine, led to the enslavement, abuse, and death of native populations for centuries. This removed any aspects of liberation inherent in the message of Christ, which reflects a new life into fullness missing from the first arrival of Christian kingdoms in Abya Yala. This historical and theological past is the starting point for our reflection on how Christianity arrived to Abya Yala and its lingering effects on native populations and the motherland.

In this chapter, I present as a native descendant theologian a theological reflection focusing on three aspects of Christianity's arrival in Abya Yala: the motherland, sustainability, and the ecocide imposed on the land. This chapter also presents a liberating message of Christianity in Abya Yala that can lead to a renewed theological understanding that provides a return path to greater harmony and sustainability, promoting a better future for the next generations.

Christianity in Abya Yala

Over 530 years ago, native people in Abya Yala lived well and prospered in practice, providing unity between a naturalistic cosmology and a spiritual practice that is a sample of what they managed to do in their constructions of temples and altars that even now show us their greatness. The practice of Good Living, or Sumaq Kawsay in Quechua, emphasizes a community well-being, and a holistic approach to life where we can live in harmony with nature.[2] A fundamental principles of Good Living is harmony with nature; our ancestors sought to live in balance, protect ecosystems, and use resources sustainably.

Three practices were interwoven in the practice of Good Living:

---

2 Sofía Chipana Quispe, "El restablecimiento del equilibrio y armonía desde la cosmovisión Andina," https://publicatheology.org/2022/05/23/el-restablecimiento-del-equilibrio-y-armonia-desde-la-cosmovision-andina/.

Community and Solidarity: Good Living emphasizes the importance of community and collective decision-making. Native peoples have strong social bonds and communal traditions that support all members' well-being. As Patricio Guerrero writes, "the good life . . . will not be possible . . . if we do not create 'a good feeling, a good thought, a good saying and a good doing,' which implies that for the fulfillment of these principles Cosmic ethics demand having 'a clean heart, clean head, clean speech, and clean hands.'"[3]

Sustainable Agriculture: Traditional subsistence agriculture practices led to self-sufficiency and maintained independence and resilience. Traditional farming techniques, such as crop diversity and terracing, are often used to ensure food security and protect the land from degradation.

Spiritual Connection: Spiritual beliefs and practices are integral to Good Living. Native communities often have deep spiritual connections to the land and natural forces that guide their way of life. Communities additionally often have traditional conflict resolution and justice methods that prioritize reconciliation and healing.

In this context, native populations were surprised by the arrival of Europeans in 1492. The story of colonization was precipitated by actions in the Mediterranean world—the Byzantine Empire's fall. Indeed, the Ottoman conquest of Constantinople sparked the search for an alternative route to the East due to a desire not to go through primarily Muslim trading routes and high fees. Europeans arrived in Abya Yala via a geographic mistake. Their encounter with an unknown reality was then seen as a new possibility to take control of a "new land" that had spices, fruit, vegetables, gold, minerals, and extended virgin land. At the same time, they could spread Christianity, evangelizing the native population.

In order for Abya Yala to be Christianized, Europeans played the roles of missionaries and colonizers at the same time. The Bible on one

---

3   Patricio Guerrero Arias, *La Chakana del corazonar. Desde las espiritualidades y las sabidurias insurgents en Abya Yala.*, (Quito, Ecuador: Universidad Politécnica Salesiana, 2018), 32. Author's translation.

hand and the sword on the other; a dual approach to evangelization and colonization. The missionaries enslaved native people and pillaged their extensive lands, which were rich in minerals, gold, silver, and abundant fruit trees, and plants. The missions reported to their church and the conquistadores to their monarchs. Religion and politics were interwoven in a show of power. They saw this "new world" as the new heaven, the promised land, a new start that was an opportunity to transform impoverished, uneducated, and struggling Europeans into positions of wealth and power based on the colonization and oppression of native peoples and the brutal extractive actions taken against nature and the motherland. Myrna Santiago writes in "Extracting Histories: Mining, Workers and Environment," "Gold and Silver, what sixteenth-century Europeans considered 'species,' are the precursors of contemporary Latin American mining. For three hundred years, mining fueled colonialism, nourishing Europe's rise to global prominence."[4]

The invasion of Abya Yala by Europeans was disguised as massive migration. Not only missionaries, prisoners, merchants, and militaries but also rich and impoverished Europeans migrated to Abya Yala and performed acts of violence on the native populations that practiced different forms of spirituality. Such an ideology allowed them to claim the right and legitimacy to "civilize," "Christianize," and "rule" this territory. To make this possible, a papal bull granted permission for the colonization process. In return, they would receive compensation from God for extending the Gospel. They received the land, control of native peoples, and resources.

THE DOCTRINE OF DISCOVERY

The doctrine of discovery developed through a number of papal bulls during the fifteenth century and made it permissible for non-Christian people to be captured, enslaved, murdered, vanquished, and have their

---

4   Myrna Santiago, "Extracting Histories: Mining, Workers, and Environment," in *New Environmental Histories of Latin America and the Caribbean* (7/2013), 81, RCC Perspectives, ed. Claudia Leal, José Augusto Pádua, and John Soluri, https://www.environmentandsociety.org/sites/default/files/2013_i7_englisch.pdf.

possessions and land seized by the Christian monarchs of Spain and Portugal.[5] It provided a papal blessing for Christian Europeans to colonize and take the land from native populations.

At the end of the fifteenth century, Spanish and Portuguese monarchs divided Abya Yala and took possession of it in accord with the Treaty of Tordesillas (1494), which amended Pope Alexander VI's bull *Inter Caetera* of 1493 and was sanctioned by Pope Julius II in 1506. Under this collusion between church and empire, native peoples received "civilization" and were forced to convert to Christianity. As Walter Brueggemann put it, "The Doctrine of Discovery served to dispossess native people of their lands and resources and was especially important in the colonial practices . . . [T]he doctrine illuminates our theme of superiority and supremacy."[6] Later, the English and the French joined in the land grabbing and colonized the northeast of Abya Yala. This colonization process affected the lives of the native population and their descendants; the land became private property that colonizers could sell and buy, violating it through extractive agricultural and mining practices.

Since the land was considered unproductive and empty, the narrative of striving Europeans seeking freedom becomes a much simpler story. History books until today described them as "pioneers," daring "explorers," and "missionaries." In the book *Harvest of Souls*, Carole Blackburn writes:

> Colonial documents, whether the product of missionaries, such as the Jesuits, or of explorers, officials, or administrators, were instrumental in producing a body of knowledge about the colonized and colonizers that both came from and shaped the ideologies informing colonialism. This knowledge was linked to the technology of colonial rule. Indeed, administrators often systematically acquired this knowledge in order to make rule more effective.[7]

---

5   The Bull Romanus Pontifex, The Doctrine of Discovery, https://doctrineofdiscovery.org/the-bull-romanus-pontifex-nicholas-v/.
6   Walter Brueggemann, *Tenacious Solidarity Biblical Provocations on Race, Religion, Climate, and the Economy* (Minneapolis: Fortress Press, 2018), 114.
7   Carole Blackburn, *Harvest of Souls: The Jesuit Missions and Colonialism in North America, 1632–1650* (Montreal: McGill-Queen's University Press, 2000), 10.

In such accounts, one can see that the Christianity that arrived in Abya Yala by the hands of European invaders was critical to shaping up the colonization of the land.

In the sixteenth century, British colonists, inspired by their reading of the Hebrew Bible stories, envisaged "America" as a new promised land. In his book *Manifest Destiny*, Anders Stephanson writes, "Puritans were unsure initially about the intended extent of the New Canaan and were inclined anyway to see the land beyond as a hideous and desolate wilderness, full of wild beasts and wild men."[8] The imaginary recasting of Abya Yala colonization as a God-ordained process to take control of a promised piece of land came from individuals who were no longer under a Hebrew Bible covenant but who instead professed Christianity and a risen Christ—not Judaism.

Not only did Europeans begin to view themselves as God's chosen people, but they placed themselves on top of a God-ordained pyramid of humanity. They then asserted that native populations were pagans because they did not worship the Christian God. In the words of Wilder Kent, quoted by Jeannine Fletcher, "It was the will of God that 'the red men of the forest' have been supplanted by a much nobler race of beings of European blood. . . . It would have been a sin and perversion of the duties and design of the human race to permit roving savages of the forest to maintain these lands as a savage and frightful desert."[9]

This orchestration of ideologies to maintain the new system of law and order in Abya Yala was created and sustained by both business ventures and European Christian churches for centuries. Historian Roxanne Dunbar-Ortiz succinctly points to a reality that was far from the whitewashed history created by Europeans to control the land:

> It was not a virgin wilderness but a network of indigenous nations, peoples of the corn. These were civilizations based on advanced agriculture. It is essential to understand the migration and

---

8   Anders Stephanson, *Manifest Destiny: American Expansion and the Empire of Right* (New York: Hill and Wang, 1995), 25.
9   Jeannine Hill Fletcher, *The Sin of White Supremacy: Christianity, Racism, and Religious Diversity in America*, (Maryknoll, NY: Orbis, 2017), 20.

indigenous people's relationship before the European invasion—North and South, and how colonialism cut them off. The targeted and deliberate decision to reduce the indigenous people who lived here for thousands of years was not by accident and not because of God's providence but just a cruel act of power.[10]

Abya Yala, Our Motherland

Inextricably linked with colonial and settler thinking is the vision of land and nature as a resource that exists only for extractive purposes. On the other hand, understanding Abya Yala as a motherland means reimagining the harmonious relationship between the land, its children, and all creation, a new way of sustainability where everyone has a place to live, food, and a "good living practice."

Abya Yala refers to the land as alive and filled with vital blood and maturity. This name implies mainly two things: First, it references the "maturity of our motherland that grows and produces food for their children; at the same time, native peoples maintain the ways of understanding the world in holistic ways." On the other hand, this is "the land of vital blood," meaning that there "is a connection between the native peoples." Furthermore, it implies the continuous existence of peoples who have suffered the impact of colonization and who struggle to assimilate into the "European culture" established with the ultimate goal of erasing "all ways to connect with [their] ancestors."[11]

The theological implications of this conception of Abya Yala as a motherland leads us to reflect on the deep connections we have with the place where we live. In this way, Abya Yala is understood as a motherland that has been the victim of a hegemonic, patriarchal, and colonialist historical process that violated and divided it into pieces, separating its children, giving it to strangers, and breaking the relationship between the land and communities that previously lived there.

---

10   Roxanne Dunbar-Ortiz, *An Indigenous Peoples History of the United States* (Boston: Beacon Press, 2014), 30.
11   Delgado Yenny and Ramírez Claudio, "Abya Yala Theology," April 6, 2022, https://publicatheology.org/2022/04/06/abya-yala-theology/.

For this reason, the forceful denial of our ancestry as the children of Abya Yala that resulted from colonization and the equally forceful assimilation into European Christianity became a source of continuous pain and confusion for the surviving native communities and their descendants.

The reimagination of Christianity in Abya Yala from the perspective of native peoples is a possibility to bring liberation for the peoples who live on the continent. One on the first steps for that to happen is the recognition that Indigenous spiritual practices are sacred for the native population and are compatible with Christianity. That realization can be an eye-opening experience for many who have been raised to think that their traditions are in conflict with the Christian faith. However, the practice of an inclusive understanding of how humans can worship and have a relationship with God and believe in Christ can significantly renew faith on the land. This will require taking seriously the liberating message that Jesus shared with us to take care of each other and live in community. It will also require believing that the Christian message is relevant for the native population too, instead of it being a hegemonic religious system under the control of European Christians.

We can also proclaim a God that heals all wounds, restores those who have been broken, and who, above all, after the pain of the crucifixion, resurrects—provides hope. The native people and their descendants who have been crucified for centuries under colonizing powers, experiencing oppression and genocide, rise today as believers of this message, witnessing firsthand the resurrection of the motherland and all their children.[12]

SUSTAINABILITY: A WAY TO LIVE IN HARMONY WITH MOTHER NATURE

Abya Yala is known for its rich biodiversity, vast rainforests, diverse plant life, and abundant water resources. However, degradation risks the lives of the new generations and their good living practices. Rapid urbanization

---

12 Delgado Yenny and Ramírez Claudio, "Abya Yala Theology," April 6, 2022, https://publicatheology.org/2022/04/06/abya-yala-theology/.

in many places has converted natural areas into concrete jungles, further contributing to the loss of green spaces and biodiversity.

Sustainability and the need to care about nature can sound modern and is, above all, a Western proposal. However, the native peoples of Abya Yala have been doing sustainable work for centuries. Sustainability in such a context refers to not believing that nature resources are unlimited; it means living in harmony with nature, including practices that range from caring for and protecting other animals to respectfully using land resources with permission from the motherland that the Quechua call "*Pachamama*."[13]

The extractive process of colonization carried out by the Europeans followed by processes of industrialization in the fledgling republics produced a barbarity without remorse toward nature to satisfice a hunger for gold, minerals, and goods needed in Europe. By contrast, the harmonious living the native population has practiced in Abya Yala shows profound respect and care for the motherland. In addition to that, they advanced ways to improve sustentative agronomic practices to produce a variety of seeds that meet the nutritional needs of the people, who then give back to the land in a cycle of mutual coexistence.

According to our ancestral knowledge, we are people of the land, we are people of the mountains, people of the forest, people of the water. We do not see nature only as limitless resources to use; native peoples lived harmoniously with the land for millennia. As Aymara theologian Sofia Chipana states:

> When we approach the contexts and realities of Abya Yala, our lands and territories have suffered the systematic subjugation and extermination of our peoples for more than five hundred years, since extractives policies see the ancestral plural worlds that resist

---

13 *Pachamama* is the Quechua word in the Andean highlands for "Mother Earth"; it implies a profound and mystical connection between nature and religion. Michael Pye, "Pachamama" in *Macmillan Dictionary of Religion*, Dictionary Series (London: Palgrave Macmillan, 1994), https://doi.org/10.1057/9780230379411_16. See also David Mesquiati de Oliveira, "Pachamama, Paqarina e Pachakamaq: uma perspectiva religiosa quéchua sobre natureza e religião," *Estudos de Religião* 31/1 (2017): 61–76.

as a threat, to die and fight to continue being and being in connection with the *Pacha* (earth).[14]

The experience of colonization brought to the land a new way of relating to nature. Europeans saw nature as private property, which gave them permission to use it as they saw fit. The colonialist dynamic in Abya Yala is complex. The land began to suffer extraction in a way that has never been seen before; vast areas of land were looted and biodiversity was destroyed. Everything was exploited. Massive resources were concentrated in the hands of a few, generating in Europe enormous capital for future expansions without care for the natural resources being exploited to produce that wealth. The original population was forced to work night and day to feed the hungry. Such exploitative conditions contributed to the colossal genocide of native people, leading to the enslavement of Africans to work in the plantation systems.

The discourse of the hegemonic religious system got under European Christian's skin. Guillermo Bonfil in his book *Utopia and Revolution* writes, "The very essence of evangelizing work, whatever the church that carries it out, has always been ethnocidal: a permanent attack, subtle or violent, against the worldview, beliefs, social habits, and forms of organization of peoples, 'pagans' or 'gentiles.'"[15] The work of evangelism was at the end of the day a work against shared practices of the native cultures that also impacted the care of the land, being common to both Catholic and Protestant expansion in Abya Yala. The role of the Protestant churches, especially at the turn of the twenty-first century, is incredibly telling. Author Khyati Joshi writes, "Christian privilege and Christian normativity are part of the larger construct of white Christian supremacy. In the US, as in Europe before it, religion has been central to the construction of race."[16]

---

14   Sofia Chipana, *Cosmovivencias, Saberes y Sabidurías Andinas*, March 10, 2022, https://publicatheology.org/2022/03/10/cosmovivencias-saberes-y-sabidurias-andinas/.

15   Guillermo Bonfil Batalla, *Utopia and Revolution: The Contemporary Political Thought of the Indians in Latin America* (Monterey, CA: Monterey Institute of International Studies, 1984), 15.

16   Khyati Y. Joshi, *White Christian Privilege: The Illusion of Religious Equality in America* (New York: New York University Press, 2020), 63.

It is clear that when missionaries traveled to convert people to Christianity, these encounters were followed by private corporations and foreign government troops soon after. Christianity's first idea for the native population was to reduce and simplify their cultures so they would adopt normative values and be assimilated into the worldview associated with white Christianity. "While whiteness does not align with collective suffering, the suffering Christ continues to be imaged as white. The image of Christ as white was part of the cultural production of a white Christian nation."[17] This reductionist view of Christianity removed any aspects of the liberating message inherent in the Gospel, according to which all humans are the creation of God, regardless of sex, gender, economic background, race, ethnicity, or nationality, because we are all one in Jesus Christ.

Ecocide: Reaches Their Ultimate Consequences

Trees that are over a thousand years old have witnessed centuries of secret wisdom where the cosmos unites with Mother Earth to give growth to the beauties of nature. In that regard, the Amazon rainforest is one of the most important places on earth. However, it is also one of the most threatened. The green lungs of Abya Yala have not only been attacked in recent years, but there are increasingly concerns about the destructive impact of state policies affecting it.[18] Abya Yala has a diverse natural biodiversity of threes, plants, minerals, animals but, if not deterred, privatization of the lands, intentional fire, and the destruction of trees will have ultimate consequences . As Sam Ordoñez points out, "It is particularly important to understand that the burning of the Amazon is the continuation of colonialism, a centuries-long process of genocide, land seizure, environmental degradation and exploitation."[19]

The destruction of our motherland through the continuous deforestation of ancient trees; monocultural agricultural practices; the

---

17 Joshi, *White Christian Privilege*, 150.
18 Nguyen Tien Hoang, Keiichiro Kanemoto. "Mapping the Deforestation Footprint of Nations Reveals Growing Threat to Tropical Forests," *Nat Ecol Evol* 5 (2021): 845–853, https://doi.org/10.1038/s41559-021-01417-z.
19 Sam Ordóñez, "Amazon Deforestation, the Result of Colonialism, U.S. Imperialism," *Workers World* https://www.workers.org/2019/08/43486/.

contamination of water through the extraction of minerals, gas, and the use of fertilizers; and the genocide of the native population are the root causes of an ecocide of immense consequences. A reflection on this historical situation shows the oppressive, destructive, uninterrupted nature of the colonizing process that affects not only *Pachamama* but all those who live in it. In the words of theologian Ivone Gebara:

> Marginalized people are growing. The destruction of different species of plants and animals are growing too. The richness of the world is becoming more and more in the hands of a small elite. We are killing and we are cloning ourselves. Our body becomes merchandise without limits, without knowing who we are and where we are going. We are destroying ourselves as an interconnected body.[20]

After centuries of colonization and destruction, "our motherland is no longer the place of the spirits, the jungle of the gods, and the mountain of prayers."[21] Abya Yala became the land of private properties, imaginary borders, and a generator of wealth and "progress" for the colonizers. Entire communities were pushed to the periphery of those borders, which have become increasingly contaminated territories where suffering, lack of water to cultivate, and a shortage of resources make the lives of the native people extreme and brutal.

The many recent cases of murders of native activists are a frightening example of the persistence of such nrutality. The victims include the environmental activist Berta Caceres from Honduras, who was murdered in 2016; Indigenous chief Emyra Waiapi, who was murdered in Brazil in 2019; and also the mistreatment and threats received by Maxima Acuña in Peru because of her struggle against the pollution of water by large mining companies. These are just a few examples of how native peoples continue to be denied the right to live well and in peace. As journalist

---

20   Ivone Gebara, "**Ecofeminism: A Latin American Perspective,**" *All Creation*, http://www.allcreation.org/home/ecofeminism-lap.
21   Delgado Yenny and Ramírez Claudio, *Abya Yala Theology*, https://publicatheology.org/2022/04/06/abya-yala-theology/.

Teresa Tomassoni states, the "Amazon region has become a 'war zone' in which peoples are on the front lines protecting the world's largest rainforest, which produces 20 percent of the planet's oxygen. 'They're paying with their lives.'"[22]

Such an extensive land exploitation and contamination puts at risk the life of native populations. How can we approach the text in Genesis 2:7 (ESV), which states, "Then the Lord God formed the man of dust from the ground and breathed into his nostrils the breath of life, and the man became a living creature"? In this creation story, God takes dust from the ground to create us. How can we engage with our motherland as part of the creation? If we are from the dust, why contaminate and destroy it?

God formed us from the dust and gave us the breath of life. At the same time, we have in our ancestral memory the understanding that when we die, we are going to return to it, as stated in Genesis 3:19. A focus on the intimate connection with the land in the creation of humanity, therefore, is crucial for our existence.

This is why native people understand life and creation as a cycle. From the perspective of the native peoples of Abya Yala, one can also see the creation of our body from the land in different narratives. The motherland gives us life; the people are the children of the motherland, children of the corn. Native people lived well and prospered holding a cosmovision that provided unity between a naturalistic cosmology and an integral spirituality. The land, its resources, and the whole of nature are part of God's creation, part of God. However, when we separate ourselves from creation, we fail to protect all of our environment, the earth where we live.

Abya Yala, a land of many creation stories, still protects our ancestral memories that connect us with *Pachamama*. By contrast, Europeans based their theological and political ideology of superiority on the control of the creation narrative.[23] Five centuries later, the struggle resulting from colonization persists. Native people are still being disposed of every day in their

---

22 Teresa Tomassoni, "We Are in Great Danger": In Amazon, Indigenous Waiapi Chief Is Killed by Illegal Miners," *NBC*, https://www.nbcnews.com/news/latino/we-are-great-danger-amazon-Indigenous-waiapi-chief-killed-illegal-n1035806?ex=digest.

23 Willie James Jennings, *The Christian Imagination: Theology and the Origins of Race* (New Haven, CT: Yale University Press, 2010).

motherland. Paradoxically, native people and their descendants struggle as a people without a land.

A decolonizing understanding of creation is needed to reframe that narrative and our relationship with the land. God created Abya Yala and acknowledged the wisdom and ancestral memories that affirm that the motherland, nature, and all creation live in a harmony through which God speaks to all people.

Conclusions

As Christian Europeans arrived to Abya Yala and colonization abruptly became a reality, the oppression that emerged from that collision caused a number of negative consequences for the people and the land—destruction, contamination, and genocide all part of efforts for increased control and power.

Native peoples and their descendants continue working on many levels to maintain the environment throughout Abya Yala, including by protesting oil pipelines to prevent the further destruction of the Amazon. A theological perspective from Abya Yala demands a new understanding of God, placing the divine as speaking from and to all the people of Abya Yala. The Christian message should not be one of oppression but one of liberation of the people and the land. We must teach that Jesus died to liberate all oppressed beings, not for their forced enslavement or to justify the taking of limited resources from the land and nature. No, his sacrifice and message are about caring for one another and the environment, promoting ways for everyone to live well in a loving community marked by deep solidarity.

As we move forward with fostering a decolonial theology, which is more urgent today than ever, Abya Yala has a particular contribution to offer, reclaiming ways of practicing Christianity that are in line with the wisdom that native peoples have practiced for centuries to protect their motherland and all creation. The practice of Good Living and respect for human rights is sustainable and promotes coexistence, pointing to ways we all can live well and in harmony.

BIBLIOGRAPHY

Ackerman, Thomas. "A Scientist's Perspective." In *Loving the Least of These: Addressing a Changing Environment.* Edited by Dorothy Boorse. Washington, DC: National Association of Evangelicals, 2011.

Aimilianos, Archimandrite. "The Experience of the Transfiguration in the Life of the Athonite Monk." In *The Living Witness of the Holy Mountain*, edited by Alexander Golitzin. (South Canaan: St. Tikhon's Press, 1996).

Althaus-Reid, Marcella. *La Teología indecente: perversiones teológicas en sexo, género y política.* Serie general universitaria. Barcelona: Bellaterra, 2005.

Alves, Rubem. "Towards a Theology of Liberation: An Exploration of the Encounter between the Languages of Humanistic Messianism and Messianic Humanism." PhD diss., Princeton Theological Seminary, 1968.

Amenga-Etego, Rose Mary. "Nankani Women's Spirituality and Ecology." In *Ecowomanism, Religion and Ecology*. Boston: Brill, 2017.

Anderson, Leith. Preface to *Loving the Least of These: Addressing a Changing Environment*, ed. Dorothy Boorse. Washington, DC: National Association of Evangelicals, 2011.

Anthony, Metropolitan of Sourozh. "Body and Matter in Spiritual Life." In *Sacrament and Image: Essays in the Christian Understanding of Man.* Edited by A.M. Allchin. 2nd ed. Oxford: Fellowship of St. Alban and St. Sergius, 1967.

Aquinas, Thomas. *Summa Theologica: A Concise Translation.* Edited by Timothy McDermott. Westminster, MD: Christian Classics, 1989.

Arendt, Hannah. *The Human Condition.* Chicago: The University of Chicago Press, 1958.

Asproulis, Nikolaos. "Un messaggio congiunto per la tutela del creato. Una riflessione ortodossa orientale," *Concilium* 58/3 (2022): 151–155.

———. "Metropolitan Kallistos Ware of Diokleia, between the Neo-patristic Synthesis and the Russian Religious Renaissance: An Example of the Reception of the Patristic Tradition," *International Journal for the Study of the Christian Church* 19/4 (2019): 212–229.

Ayre, Clive W. and Ernst M. Conradie, eds. *The Church in God's Household: Protestant Perspectives on Ecclesiology and Ecology.* Pietermaritzburg, South Africa: Cluster Publications, 2016.

Balasuriya, Tissa. "Divergences: An Asian Perspective." In *Third World Theologies: Commonalities and Divergences*, edited by K.C Abraham. Maryknoll, NY: Orbis Books, 2004.

Baptista, Paulo Agostinho Nogueira. *Libertação e ecologia: a teologia teoantropocósmica de Leonardo Boff*. 1st ed. Coleção Interfaces. São Paulo, SP, Brasil: Paulinas, 2011. http://catdir.loc.gov/catdir/toc/fy13pdf04/2013336872.html.

Barreto, Raimundo C. "A Response from a Latinx/Latin American Perspective." In *T and T Clark Handbook of Christian Theology and Climate Change*, edited by Hilda Koster and Ernst Conradie, 174–177. London: T and T Clark, 2020.

Barros, Marcelo. *Para onde vai nuestra América: Espiritualidade socialista para o século XXI*. São Paulo: Nhanduti Editora, 2011.

Barros, Marcelo and Frei Betto. *O amor fecunda o Universo: ecologia e espiritualidade*. Rio de Janeiro: Agir, 2009.

Bauckham, Richard. *The Bible and Ecology: Rediscovering the Community of Creation*. London: Darton, Longman and Todd, 2010.

Bedford-Strohm, Megan. "Your House Is Left to You Desolate: On Christian Grief and Faith for Africa and Earth in Climate Crisis." In *Mother Earth, Mother Africa: World Religions and Environmental Imagination*, edited by Sophia Chirongoma and Ven. Scholar Wayua Kiilu, 15–36. Stellenboach, South Africa: African SUN PReSS, 2022.

Belopopsky, Alexander and Dimitri Oikonomou, eds. *Orthodoxy and Ecology Resource Book*. Bialystok, Poland: Syndesmos, 1996.

Beros, Daniel, Eale Bosela, Lesmore Ezekiel, Kambale Kahongya, Ruomin Liu, Grace Moon, Marisa Strizzi, Dietrich Werner, eds. *International Handbook on Creation Care and Eco-Diakonia*. Geneva: WCC, 2022.

Berry, Thomas. *The Great Work: Our Way into the Future*. New York: Bell Tower, 1999.

Biehl, Michael, Berndt Kappes, and Bärbel Wartenberg-Potter, eds. *Grüne Reformation*. Hamburg: Missionshilfe Verlag, 2017.

Bingemer, Maria Clara Lucchetti. "Direitos humanos, direitos divinos." In *Fé cristã e direitos humanos*, edited by Daniel Ribeiro de Almeida Chacon and Frederico Soares de Almeida. 1st edition. São Paulo: Edições Loyola, 2021, 43–59.

Blackburn, Carole. *Harvest of Souls: The Jesuit Missions and Colonialism in North America, 1632–1650*. Montreal: McGill–Queen's University Press, 2000.

Blasu, Ebenezer. *African Theocology—Studies in African Religious Creation Care*. Eugene, OR: Wipf and Stock, 2020.

Bloch, Ernst. *Das Prinzip Hoffnung*. Frankfurt: Suhrkamp, 1959.

———. *El principio esperanza*. Colección Estructuras y Procesos—Serie Filosofía. Madrid: Trotta, 2007.

Blumhardt, Christoph. *Ansprachen, Predigten, Reden, Briefe: 1865–1917*. Edited by Johannes Harder. Neukirchen-Vluyn, Germany: Neukirchener Verlag, 1978.

Boff, Leonardo. *Cry of the Earth, Cry of the Poor.* Maryknoll, NY: Orbis, 1997.
———. *Ecologia: Grito da terra, grito dos pobres.* Rio de Janeiro: Sextante, 2004.
———. *Ecologia, mundialização, espiritualidade.* São Paulo: Editora Record, 2008.
———. *Nova era: A civilização planetária: desafios à sociedade e ao cristianismo.* Série Religião e cidadania. São Paulo: Editora Atica, 1994.
Boff, Leonardo, Teodoro Nieto, and Maria Jose Gabito. *Francisco de Roma y Francisco de Asís: ¿Una nueva primavera en la Iglesia?* 1st ed. Colección Estructuras y procesos. Madrid: Editorial Trotta, 2013.
Bolaane, Maitseo and Gwen Lesetedi. "Women Shaping the Narrative within the Fire Churches Environment in Gabarone, Botswana." In *Mother Earth, Mother Africa and Mission*, edited by Seblewengel Daniel, Mmapula Diana Kebaneilwe, and Angeline Savala, 159-184.. Stellenbosch, South Africa: African SUN PReSS, 2021.
Bonfil Batalla, Guillermo. *Utopia and Revolution: The Contemporary Political Thought of the Indians in Latin America.* Mexico City: New Image, 1988.
Bonhoeffer, Dietrich and Maria von Wedemeyer. *Love Letters from Cell 92: The Correspondence Between Dietrich Bonhoeffer and Maria von Wedemeyer, 1943-45*, edited by Ruth Alice von Bismarck and Ulrich Kabitz. Nashville, TN: Abingdon Press, 1995.
Bosch, Rozelle Robson. "Mother Earth in a Theological Perspective: A Sacramental Unveiling." In *Mother Earth, Mother Africa and Theology*, edited by Sinenhlanhla S. Chisale and Rozelle Robson Bosch, 19-29. Cape Town: AOSIS Publishing, 2021.
Brock, Sebastian. *The Luminous Eye: The Spiritual World Vision of Saint Ephrem the Syrian.* Kalamazoo, MI: Cistercian Publications, 1992.
Brown, Alease. "The Discourse of Drought: Ongoing Gendered Inequality of Water Access in Cape Town, and the Implications for Public Theology." In *Mother Earth, Postcolonial and Liberation Theologies*, edited by Sophia Chirongoma and Esther Mombo, 117-137. New York: Lexington Books, 2021.
Brueggemann, Walter. "The Liturgy of Abundance, the Myth of Scarcity" in *The Christian Century*, Volume 116, Issue #10, March 24, 1999.
———. *Tenacious Solidarity Biblical Provocations on Race, Religion, Climate, and the Economy.* Minneapolis: Fortress Press, 2018.
Brumbaugh, Julia and Natalia Imperatori-Lee, eds. *Turning to the Heavens and the Earth: Theological Reflections on a Cosmological Conversion: Essays in Honor of Elizabeth A. Johnson.* Collegeville, MN: Liturgical Press, 2016.
Bujo, Benezet. *The Ethical Dimension of Community: The African Model and the Dialogue between North and South.* Nairobi: Paulines Publications, 1998.
Bulgakov, *Philosophy of Economy: The World as Household.* New Haven, CT: Yale University Press, 2008.

Burkett, Maxine. "Climate Reparations." *Melbourne Journal of International Law* 10 (2009): 2.
Butler, Judith. *The Psychic Life of Power.* Redwood City, CA: Stanford University Press, 1997.
Buxhoeveden, D., and Gayle Woloschak, eds. *Science and Eastern Orthodox Church.* Farnham, UK: Ashgate Publishing, 2011.
Cardenal, Ernesto. *Amour, secret du monde.* Paris: Éditions du Cerf, 1972.
———. *La revolución perdida.* Managua, Nicaragua: Anama, 2003.
———. *Vuelos de victoria.* Madrid: Visor, 2012.
Carson, D.A. "Love." In *New Dictionary of Biblical Theology*, edited by T. Desmond Alexander and Brian S. Rosner, 646–650. Downers Grove, IL: InterVarsity Press, 2000.
Carter, Christopher. *The Spirit of Soul Food: Race, Faith, and Food Justice.* Champaign, IL: University of Illinois Press, 2021.
Catling, David C. *Astrobiology: A Very Short Introduction.* Oxford: Oxford University Press, 2013.
Ceberio de León, Iñaki. "El sujeto ecológico en la poesía de ernesto cardenal." *Ontology Studies* 11 (2011): 345–54.
Chireshe, Excellent. "Access to Land Ownership and Gender in the Light of African Indigenous Religion in Zimbabwe among the Shona in Chiredzi District, Masvingo Province, Zimbabwe." In *Mother Earth, Mother Africa and African Indigenous Religions*, edited by Nobuntu Penxa Matholeni, Georgina Mwanima Boateng, and Molly Mangonganise, 155–167. Stellenbosch, South Africa: SUN PReSS, 2020.
Chirongoma, Sophia, and Silindiwe Zvingowanisei. "Karanga Women's Utilisation of Indigenous Knowledge Systems on Climate Change Adaptation and Mitigation in Zimbabwe." In *Mother Earth, Mother Africa: World Religions and Environmental Imagination*, edited by Sophia Chirongoma and Wayua Kiilu, 127–151. Stellenbosch, South Africa: SUN PReSS, 2022.
Chisale, Sinenhlanhla. "When Women and Earth Connect: African Ecofeminist or Ecowomanist Theology?" In *Mother Earth, Mother Africa and Theology,* edited by Sinenhlanhla S. Chisale and Rozelle Robson Bosch, 9–17. Cape Town: AOSIS Publishing, 2021.
Choi, Kwang Sun. *Ecozoic Spirituality: The Symphony of God, Humanity, and the Universe.* New York: Peterlang, 2015.
Chryssavgis, John. *Creation as Sacrament: Reflections on Ecology and Spirituality.* London: T and T Clark, 2019.
———. *Cosmic Grace, Humble Prayer: The Ecological Vision of the Green Patriarch Bartholomew I.* Grand Rapids, MI: Eerdmans, 2003.
Chryssavgis, John, ed. *In the World, Yet Not of the World: Social and Global Initiatives of Ecumenical Patriarch Bartholomew.* New York: Fordham University Press, 2010.

Chryssavgis, John, and Nikolaos Asproulis, eds. *Priests of Creation: John Zizioulas on Discerning an Ecological Ethos*. London: T and T Clark, 2021.

Clément, Olivier. "Le sens de la terre (Notes de cosmologies orthodoxe)." *Contacts* 59–60 (1967/3–4).

———. "L'homme dans le monde." *Verbum Caro* XII:45: 4–22.

Cummings, Charles. *Eco-Spirituality: Toward a Reverent Life*. Mahwah, NJ: Paulist Press, 1991. Olivier Clément, "L'homme dans le monde". *Verbum Caro* XII:45: 4–22.

Coelho, Allan da Silva. "Fé capitalista e a devoção dos cristãos: o sacrifício dos direitos dos pobres." In *Fé cristã e direitos humanos*, edited by Daniel Ribeiro de Almeida Chacon and Frederico Soares de Almeida, 281–92. 1st ed. São Paulo: Edições Loyola, 2021.

Collin, Robin Morris, and Robert Collin. "Environmental Reparations." In *The Quest for Environmental Justice: Human Rights and the Politics of Pollution*, edited by Robert D. Bullard. San Francisco: Sierra Club Books, 2005.

Cone, James. "Whose Earth Is it Anyway?" In *Earth Habitat: Eco-injustices and the Church's Response*, edited by Dieter T. Hessel and Larry Rasmussen, 32–32. Minneapolis: Fortress Press, 2001.

Conradie, Ernst M. "Doing Ecotheology in the South African Context." *Journal of Systematic Theology* 1:5 (2022), 1–35.

———. *Saving the Earth? The Legacy of Reformed Views on "Re-creation."* Berlin: LIT Verlag, 2013.

———. "Why Can't the Term Development Just be Dropped Altogether? Some Reflections on the Concept of Maturation as Alternative to Development Discourse." *HTS Theological Studies* 72:4 (2016), 1–11.

———. "The Salvation of the Earth from Anthropogenic Destruction: In Search of Appropriate Soteriological Concepts in an Age of Ecological Destruction." *Worldviews: Global Religions, Culture, Ecology* 14:2–3 (2010), 111–140.

Conradie, Ernst M., Sigurd Bergmann, Celia Deane-Drummond, and Denis Edwards, eds. *Christian Faith and the Earth: Current Paths and Emerging Horizons*. London: T and T Clark, 2014.

Conradie, Ernst M., and Andrew E. Warmback. "Theology and the Environment: A Select Bibliography of Contributions from Africa." *Bulletin for Contextual Theology in Africa* 8/2&3 (2002): 121–134.

Conradie, Ernst M., and Lai Pan-chiu. eds. *Taking a Deep Breath for the Story to Begin*. Eugene, OR: Wipf and Stock, 2021.

Conradie, Ernst M. and Hilda Koster eds. *The T and T Clark Handbook on Christian Theology and Climate Change*. London: T and T Clark, 2020.

Cox, Stan. *The Green New Deal and Beyond*. San Francisco: City Lights Books, 2020.

Daly, Mary. *Beyond God the Father: Toward a Philosophy of Women's Liberation*. Boston: Beacon Press, 1993.

Daneel, Marthinus. *African Earthkeepers: Environmental Mission and Liberation in Christian Perspective*. Pretoria: Unisa, 1999.

Daniel, Seblewengel. "Fertility of Women and Mother Earth: An Ethiopian Theological Perspective." In *Mother Earth, Mother Africa and Theology*, edited by Sinenhlanhla S. Chisale and Rozelle Robson Bosch, 129-143. Cape Town: AOSIS Publishing, 2021.

Daniels, David. D. "Progressive Pentecostalism, Pentecostal Philanthropy: The Church of Pentecost." In *African Pentecostal Missions Maturing: Essays in Honor of Apostle Opoku Onyinah*, edited by Lord Elorm Donkor and Clifton R. Clarke. Eugene, OR: Wipf and Stock, 2018.

Darwin, Charles. *On the Origin of Species (1859)*. In *From So Simple a Beginning: The Four Great Books of Charles Darwin*. Edited by Edward O. Wilson. New York: W. W. Norton, 2006.

Dawkins, Richard. *The God Delusion*. Boston: Houghton Mifflin Company, 2006.

———. *The Blind Watchmaker: Why the Evidence of Evolution Reveals a Universe without Design*. W. W. Norton, 1996.

De Gruchy, Steven M. *Keeping Body and Soul Together: Reflections by Steve de Gruchy on Theology and Development*. Pietermaritzburg, South Africa: Cluster Publications, 2015.

De León, Iñaki Cebeiro. "El Sujeto Ecológico En La Poesía de Ernesto Cardenal." *Ontology Studies* 11 (2011): 345-54.

Demacopoulos, George. "'Traditional Orthodoxy' as a Post-colonial Movement." *The Journal of Religion* 97/4 (2017): 475-7.

Dennett, Daniel C. *Breaking the Spell: Religion as a Natural Phenomenon*. New York: Penguin, 2006.

Dotson, Kristie. "Tracking Epistemic Violence, Tracking Practices of Silencing." *Hypatia* 26/2 (2011): 236-257.

Dostoyevsky, Fyodor. *The Brothers Karamazov*. Translated by Constance Garnett. Dar Es Salaam, Tanzania: Global Publishers, 2023. Kindle.

Dube, Musa W. "Fifty Years of Bleeding: A Storytelling Reading of Mark 5:24-43." *The Ecumenical Review* 51/1 (1999): 11-17.

———. "Mother Earth, Gender and Biblical Imagination." In *Mother Earth, Mother Africa and Biblical Studies: Interpretations in the Context of Climate Change*, edited by Sidney K. Berman, Paul L. Leshota, Ericka S. Dunbar, Musa W. Dube, and Malebogo Kgalemang, 237-250. Bamberg, Germany: University of Bamberg Press, 2021.

Dumont, René. *L'utopie ou la mort!* Paris: Seuil, 1974.

Dunbar-Ortiz, Roxanne. *An Indigenous Peoples History of the United States*. Boston: Beacon Press, 2014.

Dutta, Soumya, Soumitra Ghosh, Shankar Gopalakrishnan, C. R. Bijoy, and Hadida Yasmin. *Climate Change and India*. New Delhi: Daanish Books, 2013.

Evdokimov, Paul. "Nature." *Scottish Journal of Theology* 18 (March 1965): 1–22.
Edwards, Denis. *Deep Incarnation: God's Redemptive Suffering with Creatures*. Maryknoll, NY: Orbis, 2019.
Elkington, Bianca, Moana Jackson, Rebecca Kiddle, Ocean Ripeka Mercier, Mike Ross, Jennie Smeaton, and Amand Thomas. *Imagining Decolonization*. Wellington, New Zealand: Bridget Williams Books, 2020.
Field, David F. "Love." In *New Dictionary of Christian Ethics and Pastoral Theology*, edited by David J. Atkinson, David F. Field, Arthur F. Holmes, and Oliver O'Donovan, 9–14. Downers Grove, IL: InterVarsity Press, 1995.
Frank, Adam. *Light of the Stars: Alien Worlds and the Fate of the Earth*. New York: W. W. Norton, 2018.
Fiorenza, Elisabeth Schüssler. *In Memory of Her: A Feminist Theological Reconstruction of Christian Origins*. New York: Crossroad, 1994.
Fletcher, Jeannine Hill. *The Sin of White Supremacy: Christianity, Racism, and Religious Diversity in America*. Maryknoll, NY: Orbis Books, 2017.
Freire, Paulo. *Pedagogy of the Oppressed*. New York: Continuum, 1986.
Gebara, Ivone. *Intuiciones ecofeministas: Ensayo para repensar el conocimiento y la religión*. Translated by Graciela Pujol. Madrid: Editorial Tratto, 2000.
———. *Le mal au féminin: Réflexions théologiques à partir du féminisme*. Paris: L'Harmattan, 1999.
Gerick, Nicole. *Recht, mensch und tier, nomos*. Baden-Baden, Germany: Nomos Verlag, 2005.
Gichaara, Jonathan, "Issues in African Theology." *Black Theology* 3/1 (2005): 75–85.
Gillet, Lev. *On the Invocation of the Name of Jesus*. Oxford: Fellowship of St. Alban and St. Sergius, 1949.
Global Buddhist Climate Change Collective. "Buddhist Climate Change Statement to World Leaders." Published October 29, 2015. https://plumvillage.org/articles/buddhist-climate-change-statement-to-world-leaders-2015/
Golo, Ben-Willie Kwaku. "In Search of a Sustainable Society in Africa: Christianity, Justice and Sustainable Peace in a Changing Climate." In *Philosophia Reformata: An International Philosophical Journal of Christianity, Science and Society*, 83, no 1 (2018): 68–89.
———. "Redeemed from the Earth? Environmental Change and Salvation Theology in African Christianity." *Scriptura: International Journal of Bible, Religion and Theology in Southern Africa* III (2012): 348–361.
———. "The Groaning Earth and the Greening of Neo-Pentecostalism in Twenty-first Century Ghana." *PentecoStudies: An Interdisciplinary Journal for Research on the Pentecostal and Charismatic Movements* 13, no. 2 (2014): 197–216.
Golo, Ben-Willie Kwaku, Majeed Mohammed Hasskei, and Nancy O. Mills. "Akan Religious Ontology and Environmental Sustainability in Ghana." *Worldviews* 27 (2003): 86–114.

Gomez-Barris, Macarena. *The Extractive Zone: Social Ecologies and Decolonial Perspectives*. Durham, NC: Duke University Press, 2017.

Gorodetzky, Nadejda. "The Prayer of Jesus," *Blackfriars* xxiii (1942): 74–78.

Gregersen, Niels Henrik. "Deep Incarnation: From Deep History to Post-axial Religion." *HTS Teologiese Studies/Theological Studies* 72/4 (2006): 1–12.

Gregorios, Paulos Mar. *The Human Presence*. Madras: The Christian Literature Society, 1980.

———. *Science for Sane Societies*. New York: Paragon House, 1987.

Habel, Norman C., and Peter Trudinger, eds. *Exploring Ecological Hermeneutics*. Atlanta, GA: Society of Biblical Literature, 2008.

Hadebe, Nontando, "The Cry of the Earth is the Cry of Women: Ecofeminisms in Critical Dialogue with *Laudato Si'*." in *Mother Earth, Postcolonial, and Liberation Theologies*, edited by Sophia Chirongoma and Esther Mombo, 83–98. New York: Lexington Books, 2021.

Hallman, David G. "Climate Change and Poverty–Science, Theology and Ethics: A Discussion Paper for the National Religious Partnership on the Environment." Unpublished paper, September, 2005.

Hallman, David G., ed. *Ecotheology: Voices from South and North*. Geneva: WCC, 1994.

Hau'ofa, Epeli. "Our Sea of Islands." *The Contemporary Pacific* 6.1 (1994): 148–61.

Harris, Melanie L. *Ecowomanism: African American Women and Earth-Honoring Faiths*. Maryknoll, NY: Orbis Books, 2017.

———. *Gifts of Virtue, Alice Walker, and Womanist Ethics*. New York: Palgrave Macmillan, 2010.

Harding, Rosemarie Freeney, and Rachel Elizabeth Harding. *Remnants: A Memoir of Spirit, Activism, and Mothering*. Durham, NC: Duke University Press, 2015.

Harris, Sam. *The End of Faith: Religion, Terror, and the Future of Reason*. New York: W. W. Norton, 2005.

Havea, Jione. "The Politics of Climate Change: A Talanoa from Oceania." *International Journal of Public Theology* 4 (2010): 345–355.

———. "Homing Woman-Eve in Native World(view)s: A Moana Reading." In *The Routledge Companion to Eve*, edited by Caroline Blyth and Emily Colgan, 382–390. New York: Routledge, 2024.

———. "Theologizing Moana and Pasifika World(view)s." *Political Theology in the Asia Pacific*. Edited by Kwok Pui-lan. Waco, TX: Baylor University Press, forthcoming.

———. ed. *Sea of Readings: The Bible in the South Pacific*. Atlanta, GA: Society of Biblical Literature, 2018.

———. ed. *Theologies from the Pacific*. New York: Palgrave, 2021.

Havea, Jione, and Peter Lau, eds. *Reading Ecclesiastes from Asia and Pasifika*. Atlanta, GA: Society of Biblical Literature, 2020.

Heckscher, J. J. "A 'Tradition' That Never Existed: Orthodox Christianity and the Failure of Environmental History," in *Toward an Ecology of Transfiguration: Orthodox Christian Perspectives on Environment, Nature, and Creation,* edited by John Chryssavgis and Bruce V. Foltz, 136–51. New York: Fordham University Press, 2013.

Heidegger, Martin. "The Question Concerning Technology." In *Martin Heidegger: Basic Writings,* edited and translated by David Farrell Krell, 295–96. New York: Harper and Row, 1977.

Heschel, Abraham J. *The Sabbath: Its Meaning for Modern Man.* Boston: Shambhala, 2003.

Hessel, Dieter T., and Rosemary Radford Ruether. *Christianity and Ecology.* Cambridge, MA: Harvard University Center for the Study of World Religion, 2000.

Hoang, Nguyen Tien, and Kanemoto, Keiichiro. "Mapping the Deforestation Footprint of Nations Reveals Growing Threat to Tropical Forests," *Nat Ecol Evol* 5 (2021): 845–853. https://doi.org/10.1038/s41559-021-01417-z.

Hoornaert, Eduardo. "L'audace d'un théologien." In *Joseph Comblin, prophète et ami des pauvres,* edited by Philippe Dupriez, 95–102. Brussels: Lessius, 2014.

Huechante, Luis Cárcamo. "Mapuche Historians Write and Talk Back: Background and Role of ¡. . .Escucha, winka. . .! Cuatro ensayos sobre Historia Nacional Mapuche y un epílogo sobre el futuro." *Decolonial Gesture* 11/1 (2014): 4.

Ikuenobe, Polycarp A. "Traditional African Environmental Ethics and Colonial Legacy." *International Journal of Philosophy and Theology*, 2, no. 4 (2014): 1–21.

Ioannikios, Archimandrite. *An Athonite Gerontikon: Sayings of the Holy Fathers of Mount Athos.* Translated by Maria Derpapa Mayson and Sister Theodora (Zion). Kouphalia—Thessaloniki: The Holy Monastery of St. Gregory Palamas, 1997.

Jennings, Willie James. *After Whiteness: An Education in Belonging.* Grand Rapids, MI: Eerdmans, 2020.

———. *The Christian Imagination: Theology and the Origins of Race.* New Haven, CT: Yale University Press, 2010.

John of Damascus, Saint. *On the Divine Images: Three Apologies Against Those Who Attack the Divine Images.* Translated by David Anderson. Crestwood, NY: St. Vladimir's Seminary Press, 1980.

Jones, James. "The Son of Man Came Eating and Drinking." In *Consumption, Christianity, and Creation.* Unpublished paper from an academic seminar held on July 5, 2002 at the Centre for Sustainable Consumption. Sheffield, England: Sheffield Hallam University, 2002.

Johnson, Elizabeth. "Turn to the Heavens and the Earth: Retrieval of the Cosmos in Theology." CTSA PROCEDDINGS 51(1996).

Johnson, Tore. *Sami Nature-Centered Christianity in the European Arctic: Indigenous Theology beyond Hierarchical Worldmaking*. Lanham, MD: Lexington Books, 2022.
Joshi, Khyati Y. *White Christian Privilege: The Illusion of Religious Equality in America*. New York: New York University Press, 2020.
Julian of Norwich. *Showings*. Translated by Edmund Colledge and James W. Walsh. New York: Paulist Press, 1978.
Kanyoro, Musimbi R., and Nyambura J. Njoroge, eds. *Groaning in Faith: African Women in the Household of God*. Nairobi: Acton Publishers, 1996.
Kaoma, Kapya. *God's Family, God's Earth: Christian Ecological Ethics of Ubuntu*. Zomba, Malawi: Kachere Series, 2013.
Katongole, Emmanuel. *Born from Lament: The Theology and Politics of Hope in Africa*. Grand Rapids, MI: Eerdmans, 2017.
Kauffman, Stuart. *At Home in the Universe*. Oxford: Oxford University Press, 1995.
Kebaneilwe, Mmapula Diana, and Kgomotso Scotch. "Reimagining Mission through Inculturation: Pentecostalism and Sustainable Environment." In *Mother Earth, Mother Africa, and Mission*, edited by Seblewengel Daniel, Mmapula Diana Kebaneilwe, and Angeline Savala, 13–32. Stellenbosch, South Africa: African SUN PReSS, 2021.
Keller, Catherine. *On the Mystery. Discerning God in Process*. Minneapolis: Fortress Press, 2008.
———. *Political Theology of the Earth: Our Planetary Emergency and the Struggle for a New Public*. New York: Columbia University Press, 2018.
Kim, Grace Ji-Sun. *Making Peace with the Earth: Action and Advocacy for Climate Justice*. Geneva: WCC, 2016.
Kim, Grace Ji-Sun, and Hilda P. Koster, eds., *Planetary Solidarity. Global Women's Voice on Christian Doctrine and Climate Justice*. Minneapolis: Fortress Press, Minneapolis, 2017.
King, David P. "Beyond Abundance is Stewardship Ethical?" *Word and World* 38, no. 3 (Summer 2018).
Krueger, Frederick W. *Transfiguring the World: Orthodox Patriarchs and Bishops Articulate a Theology of Creation*. Independently-published, 2022.
Landron, Olivier. *Le Catholicisme vert: Histoire des relations entre l'église et la nature au XXe siècle*. Paris: Cerf, 2008.
Lenkabula, Puleng. "Economic Globalisation, Ecumenical Theologies and Ethics of Justice in the Twenty-first Century." *Missionalia* 38:1 (2010), 99–120.
Lorz, Albert. *Tierschutzgesetz. Kommentar*. Munich: C.H. Beck, 1987.
Lovelock, James. *Gaia: A New Look at Life on Earth*. Oxford: Oxford University Press, 2016.
Löwy, Michael. *Écosocialisme: l'alternative radicale à la catastrophe écologique capitaliste*. Les petits Libres, n° 77. Paris: Éd. Mille et une nuits, 2011.

———. *La lutte des dieux : christianisme de la libération et politique en Amérique latine : avant-propos de Leonardo Boff.* Paris: Van Dieren Éditeur, 2019.

Mackay, John Alexander. *Ecumenics: The Science of the Church Universal.* Englewood Cliffs, NJ: Prentice Hall, 1964.

Madigele Tshenolo J. M., Patricia K. Mogomotsi, and Goemeone E. J.Mogomotsi. "Water Deficiency, Poverty, Ecology and Botho Theology in Botswana." In *Mother Earth, Mother Africa and Theology*, edited by Sinenhlanhla S. Chisale and Rozelle Robson Bosch, 87–95. Cape Town: AOSIS Publishing, 2021.

Makgoba, Thabo. "Hope and the Environment: A Perspective from the Majority World." *Anvil* 29:1 (2013), 55–70.

———. "Water Is Life, Sanitation Is Dignity." *Anglican Theological Review* 100:1 (2018), 113–118.

Maluleke, Tinyiko. "Black and African Theologies in Search of Comprehensive Environmental Justice." *Journal of Theology for Southern Africa* 167 (2020), 5–19.

———. "A Response to Willis Jenkins." In *T and T Clark Handbook of Christian Theology and Climate Change*, edited by Hilda Koster and Ernst M. Conradie, 83–89. New York: T and T Clark, 2020.

Mangonganise, Molly and Godfrey Museka. "The Sedated Sacred: A Socio-Religious Analysis of Zimbabwe's Land Reform Programme and Environmental Degradation." In *Mother Earth, Mother Africa, and African Indigenous Religions*, edited by Nobuntu Penxa Matholeni, Georgina Mwanima Boateng, and Molly Mangonganise, 67–84. Stellenbosch, South Africa: Sun PReSS, 2020.

Maparyan, Layli. *The Womanist Idea.* New York: Routledge, 2011.

Mariman, Pablo, Sergio Caniuqueo, Rodrigo Levil, and José Millalen. *¡. . .Escucha, winka. . .! Cuatro ensayos de Historia Nacional Mapuche y un epílogo sobre el future.* Santiago, Chile: LOM Ediciones, 2006.

Martínez Andrade, Luis. "Biocolonialité Du Pouvoir et Mouvements Sociaux Dans l'Amérique Latine." *Écologie & Politique* 55 (2017): 153–64.

———. *Ecología y teología de la liberación: critica de la modernidad/colonialidad.* Barcelona: Herder, 2019.

———. "Elective Affinities between Liberation Theology and Ecology in Latin America." In *Religion in Rebellions, Revolutions, and Social Movements*, edited by Warren S. Goldstein and Jean-Pierre Reed, 219–30. Routledge Studies in Religion and Politics. London: Routledge, 2022.

Martinez-Alier, Juan. *The Environmentalism of the Poor: A Study of Ecological Conflicts and Valuation.* Cheltenham, UK: Edward Elgar, 2002.

Masenya, Madipoane. "All from the Same Source? Deconstructing a (Male) Anthropocentric Reading of Job (3) through an Eco-bosadi Lens." *Journal of Theology for Southern Africa* 137 (2010), 46–60.

———. "Ecological Hermeneutics and Postcolonialism." In *The Oxford Handbook of the Bible and Ecology*, edited by Hilary Marlow, and Mark Harris, 49–62. Oxford: OUP, 2022.

Maturana, Humberto and Francisco Varela. *A árvore do conhecimento. As bases biológicas da Compreensão humana.* São Paulo: Palas Athena, 2001.

Mbiti, John S. *African Religions and Philosophy.* London: Heinneman, 1969.

McFague, Sallie. *The Body of God: An Ecological Theology.* Minneapolis: Fortress Press,1993.

McGeoch, Graham. "Marxismo, mística e o MST: qual é o segredo do MST na luta pela reforma agraria no Brasil?" *Debates do NER*, Porto Alegre, 33 (2018), 174–196.

———. "Liberation Theology: Problematizing the Historical Projects of Democracy and Human Rights." *Revista sociedade e cultura* 23 (2020).

Mendoza, Lily, and George Zachariah, eds. *Decolonizing Ecotheology: Indigenous and Subaltern Challenges.* Eugene, OR: Pickwick Publications, 2022.

Merchant, Carolyn. *The Death of Nature: Women, Ecology, and Scientific Revolution.* New York, Harper and Row, 1983.

Moe-Lobeda, Cynthia. "Climate Change as Race Debt, Class Debt, Climate Colonialism: Moral Conundrums, Vision, and Agency." In *Ecological Solidarities: Mobilizing Faith and Justice for an Entangled World*, edited by Krista Hughes, Dhawn Martin, and Elaine Padilla, 61–80. State College: Pennsylvania State University Press, 2019.

Moltmann, Jürgen. *Gott in der Schöpfung. Ökologische Schöpfungslehre.* Munich: Chr. Kaiser, 1985; "Ökologie," in *Theologische Realenzyklopädie* (TRE), edited by Gerhard Müller, vol. XXV, Berlin, 1995, 36–46.

———. "Der Gott der Auferstehung. Christi Auferstehung—Auferstehung des Fleisches—Auferstehung der Natur." *"Sein Name ist Gerechtigkeit." Neue Beiträge zur christlichen Gotteslehre.* Gütersloh, Germany: Gütersloher Verlagshaus, 2008, 45–82.

———. "A Common Earth Religion: World Religions from an Ecological Perspective." *The Ecumenical Review*, 03/63 (2011): 16–25.

———. *Hope in These Troubled Times.* Geneva: WCC Publications, 2010.

———. "'The Fear of the Lord Is the Beginning of Wisdom': Science and Wisdom." In *Experiences in Theology: Ways and Forms of Christian Theology.* Translated by Margaret Kohl. Minneapolis: Fortress Press, 2000.

Moltmann-Wendel, Elisabeth. *Wer die Erde nicht berührt, kann den Himmel nicht erreichen. Autobiographie.* Zurich: Benziger Verlag, 1997.

Mombo, Esther. "The Missionary Initiative of Vegetable Gardens: Benefits and Shortcomings from an Eco-centric Perspective." In *Mother Earth, Mother Africa, and Mission*, edited by Seblewengel Daniel, Mmapula Diana Kebaneilwe, and Angeline Savala, 68–84. Stellenbosch, South Africa: African SUN PReSS, 2021.

Moore, Stephen, ed. *Divinanimality: Animal Theory, Creaturely Theology*. New York: Fordham University Press, 2014.

Morrison, Toni. *The Origin of Others*. Cambridge, MA: Harvard University Press, 2017.

Mpofu, Sifiso. "A Theology of the Land and Its Covenant Responsibility." In *People and Land: Decolonizing Theologies*, edited by Jione Havea, 77–90. London: Rowman and Littlefield, 2020.

Munteanu, Daniel. "Cosmic Liturgy: The Theological Dignity of Creation as a Basis of an Orthodox Ecotheology," *International Journal of Public Theology* 4/3 (2010): 332–344.

Murad, Afonso, and Procópio, Marco Túlio. "Dignidade dos animais e direitos humanos: uma leitura teológica inclusiva." In *Fé cristã e direitos humanos*, edited by Daniel Ribeiro de Almeida Chacon and Frederico Soares de Almeida, 245-62. 1st edition. São Paulo: Edições Loyola, 2021.

Murphy, Ngahuis. "Menstruation, Whakapapa and the Revival of Matrilineal Maori Ceremony," in *Decolonization in Aotearoa: Education, Research, and Practice*, edited by Jessica Hutchings, and Jenny Lee-Morgan. Wellington, NZ: NZCER Press, 2016.

Mwale, Nelly Mwale. "The Mother Earth Centre: A Narrative of the Comboni Missionary Sisters' Contributions to Environmental Sustainability" in *Mother Earth, Mother Africa: World Religions and Environmental Imagination*, edited by Sophia Chirongoma, and Wayua Kiilu. Stellenbosch, South Africa: SUN PReSS, 2021, 95–110.

———. "Women and Sustainable Agriculture in the Context of the Kasisi Agricultural Training Centre: A Catholic Initiative in Zambia" in *Mother Earth, Mother Africa, and Mission*, edited by Seblewengel Daniel, Mmapula Diana Kebaneilwe, and Angeline Savala, 141-158. Stellenbosch, South Africa: SUN PReSS, 2021.

Naicker, Linda. "Sisters in Solidarity: Resistance and Agency Through Urban Community Food Gardens." *African Journal of Gender and Religion* 27/1(2021): 24–41.

Nantsou, Theodota, and Nikolaos Asproulis, eds. *The Orthodox Church Address the Climate Crisis*. Volos, Greece: Volos Academy Publications, 2021.

Nesteruck, Al. *Light from the East: Theology, Science, and the Eastern Orthodox Tradition*. Minneapolis: Fortress Press, 2003.

Nicolaidis, Eftymios. *Science and Eastern Orthodoxy: From the Greek Fathers to the Age of Globalization*. Baltimore: Johns Hopkins University Press, 2011.

Nieuwerth, Kees, Peter Pavlovic, and Adrian Shaw, eds. *Every Part of Creation Matters*. CEC Series No. 8. Geneva: Globethics Publications, 2022.

Nixon, Rob. *The Slow Violence and the Environmentalism of the Poor*. Cambridge, MA: Harvard University Press, 2011.

Njagi, Catherine. "African Cosmological View: The Role of African Indigenous Knowledge Systems in the Preservation of Mount Kenya Forest." In *Mother Earth, Mother Africa: World Religions and Environmental Imagination*, edited by Sophia Chirongoma and Wayua Kiilu, 111–125. Stellenbosch, South Africa: SUN PReSS, 2022.

Nürnberger, Klaus. *Prosperity, Poverty and Pollution: Managing the Approaching Crisis*. Pietermaritzburg, South Africa: Cluster Publications, 1999.

Oduyoye, Mercy A. *Beads and Strand: Reflections of an African Woman on Christianity in Africa*. Maryknoll, NY: Orbis, 2004.

———. *Regaining Sanity for the Earth*. Pietermaritzburg, South Africa: Cluster Publications, 2011.

———. "Earth Hope: A Letter" in *Ecowomanism, Religion, and Ecology*. Boston: Brill, 2017.

Ofori, Samuel Appiah, Samuel Jerry Cobbina, and Samuel Obiri. "Climate Change, Land, Water, and Food Security: Perspectives from Sub-Saharan Africa." *Frontiers in Sustainable Food Systems* 5: 680924 (2021) doi: 10.3389/fsufs.2021.680924.

Oleksa, Michael. "The Yua as Logoi." In *Reimagining Nature: Environmental Humanities and Ecosemiotics*, edited by Alfred Kentigern Siewers, 147–241. Lewisburg, PA: Bucknell University Press, 2013.

Oliveira, David Mesquiati de. "Pachamama, Paqarina e Pachakamaq: uma perspectiva religiosa quéchua sobre natureza e religião," *Estudos de Religião* 31/1 (2017): 61–76.

Origen. *On First Principles*. Translated by G. W. Butterworth. Gloucester: Peter Smith, 1973.

Owusu-Ansah, Sylvia, and Beatrice-Joy Owusu-Ansah. "Women, Religion and Sustainable Development: Redeeming the Environment for Human Survival." In *Mother Earth, Mother Africa and Theology*, edited by Sinenhlanhla S. Chisale and Rozelle Robson Bosch, 45–62. Cape Town: AOSIS Publishing, 2021.

Pascal, Blaise. *Pensées*. New York: Penguin Books, 1995.

———. *Pensées and Other Writings*. Translated by Honor Levi. Oxford: Oxford University Press, 1999.

Paunga, Mikaele N. "*Ko e Mana Fakahā 'Otua 'o e Fakatupu*: Creation as Sacrament." In *Theologies from the Pacific*, edited by Jione Havea, 31–46. New York: Palgrave, 2021.

Pelser, André J., and Rujeko Samanthia Chimukuche. "Climate Change, Rural Livelihoods, and Human Well-Being: Experiences from Kenya." *IntechOpen*. http://dx.doi.org/10.5772/intechopen.104965.

Phillips, Mary, and Nick Rumens. "Introducing Contemporary Ecofeminism." In *Contemporary Perspectives on Ecofeminism*, edited by Mary Phillips and Nick Rubens, 1–16. London: Routledge 2015.

Pico della Mirandola, Giovanni. *Über die Würde des Menschen*. Zurich: Manesse, 1989.
Pieris, Aloysius. *Asian Theology of Liberation*. London: T and T Clark, 1988.
Polkinghorne, John. *Belief in God in an Age of Science*. New Haven, CT: Yale University Press, 1998.
Porphyrios, Elder. *Wounded by Love: The Life and Wisdom of Elder Porphyrios*, edited by Sisters of the Holy Convent of Chrysopigi. Limni, Greece: Denise Harvey, 2005.
———. *Theology in the Context of Science*. New Haven, CT: Yale University Press, 2009.
Profit, James. "Connecting with the Earth: Experiencing the Sacred." In *Sacred Earth, Sacred Community: Jubilee, Ecology and Aboriginal Peoples*. Toronto: Canadian Ecumenical Jubilee Initiative, 2000.
Puleo, H. Alicia. *Ecofeminismo para outro mundo posible*. Madrid: Ediciones Cátedra, 2011.
Pye, Michael. "Pachamama" in *Macmillan Dictionary of Religion*. London: Palgrave Macmillan, 1994. https://doi.org/10.1057/9780230379411_16.
Rabie-Boshoff, A.C. "Imago mundi: Justice of peace." *HTS Teologiese Studies/ Theological Studies* 78/2 (2022): 1–7.
Radford Ruether, Rosemary. "Ecofeminism and Healing Ourselves, Healing the Earth." *Feminist Theology* 9 (1995).
———. *Women Healing Earth: Third World Women on Ecology, Feminism, and Religion*. Maryknoll, NY: Orbis, 1997.
———. "Ecofeminism—The Challenge to Theology." *Deportate, esuli, profughe: Rivista telematica di studi sulla memoria femminile*, No. 20 (2012): 27.
Rakoczy, Susan. *In Her Name: Women Doing Theology*. Pietermaritzburg, South Africa: Cluster, 2004.
Reed, Jean-Pierre. *Sandinista Narratives: Religion, Sandinismo, and Emotions in the Making of the Nicaraguan Insurrection and Revolution*. Lanham, MD: Lexington Books, 2020.
Reijnen, Anne-Marie. "Is Green the Colour of Our Redemption?" In *Returning to Tillich. Theology and Legacy in Transition*, edited by Russell Re Manning and Samuel Andrew Shearn, 87–96. Berlin: De Gruyter, 2018.
Resane, Kelebogile T. "Earth-Centred Trinitarian Models: The Trinitarian Synergy and Symbiosis in the Creation Narrative." In *Mother Earth, Mother Africa, and Theology*, edited by Sinenhlanhla S. Chisale and Rozelle Robson Bosch, 31–42. Cape Town: AOSIS Publishing, 2021.
———. "The Theological Responses to the Socio-economic Activities that Undermine Water as a Resource," *HTS Theological Studies* 66 (2010): 1–7.
Ress, Mary Judith. *Ecofeminism in Latin America*. Maryknoll, NY: Orbis, 2006.
Rieger, Joerg. *Theology in the Capitalocene: Ecology, Identity, Class, and Solidarity*. Minneapolis: Fortress Press, 2022.

Ripple, William J., Christopher Wolf, Thomas M. Newsome, Phoebe Barnard, and William R. Moomaw. "World Scientists' Warning of a Climate Emergency," *BioScience* 70/1 (2020), 8–12.
Roper, Garnett. "Empire 2.0: Land Matters in Jamaica and the Caribbean." In *People and Land: Decolonizing Theologies*, edited by Jione Havea, 101-112. London: Rowman and Littlefield, 2020.
Ruiz García, Samuel. *Cómo me convirtieron los indígenas*. Colección servidores y testigos. Santander, Spain: Sal Terrae, 2003.
Russell, Cathriona. "Burden-sharing in a Changing Climate: Which Principles and Practices Can Theologians Endorse?" *Studies in Christian Ethics* 24, no.1 (2011): 67–76.
Salazar, Marilú Rojas. "Decolonizing Theology: Panentheist Spiritualities and Proposals from the Ecofeminist Epistemologies of the South." *Journal of Feminist Studies in Religion* 34/2 (2018): 92–98.
Santmire, Paul H. "Healing the Protestant Mind: Beyond the Theology of Human Dominion." In *After Nature's Revolt: Eco-Justice and Theology*, edited by Dieter Hessel, 57–58. Minneapolis: Fortress Press, 1992.
Scheler, Max. *Die Stellung des Menschen im Kosmos*. Munich: Nymphenburger Verlagshandlung, 1947.
Serres, Michel. *Polegarzinha*. Rio de Janeiro: Bertrand Brasil, 2013.
Setiloane, Gabriel M. "Toward a Biocentric Theology and Ethic—via Africa." *Journal of Black Theology* 9:1 (1995): 52–66.
———. *African Theology. An Introduction*. Johannesburg: Skotaville Publishers, 1986.
Shore, Christopher. "A Development Worker's Perspective." In *Loving the Least of These: Addressing a Changing Environment*, edited by Dorothy Boorse, 29–36. Washington, DC: National Association of Evangelicals, 2011.
Sjöö, Monica, and Barbara Mor. *The Great Cosmic Mother: Rediscovering the Religion of the Earth*. New York: Harper and Row, 1987.
Smith, Linda Tuhiwai. *Decolonizing Methodologies: Research and Indigenous Peoples*. Dunedin, FL: University of Otago Press, 1999.
Smith, Oliver. "Vladimir Soloviev (1853-1900)—The Ultimate Spiritualisation of All Created Matter," *Creation and Salvation: A Companion on Recent Theological Movements*, edited by Ernst M. Conradie, 13–19. Zurich: Lit Verlag, 2012.
———. "Is Humanity King of Creation? The Thought of Vladimir Solov'ev in the Light of Ecological Crisis." *Journal for the Study of Religion, Nature & Culture* 2/4 (2008): 463- 482.
Spivak, Gayatri. "Can the Subaltern Speak?" In *Marxism, and the Interpretation of Culture*, edited by Cary Nelson and Lawrence Grossberg, 271-313. New York: Macmillan, 1988.

Stassen, Glen H. and David P. Gushee. *Kingdom Ethics: Following Jesus in Contemporary Context*. Downers Grove, IL: InterVarsity Press, 2003.

Stedile, João Pedro, and Bernardo Mançano. *Brava gente: A trajetória do MST e a luta pela terra no Brasil*. São Paulo: Fundação Perseu Abramo, 2005.

Stephanson, Anders. *Manifest Destiny: American Expansion and the Empire of Right*. New York: Macmillan, 1995.

Swatuk, Larry, Gregg Brill, Charon Büchner-Marais, Kirsty Carden, Ernst Conradie, Jenny Day, Joanna Fatch, Jessica Fell, Mafaniso Hara, and Bongani Ncube. *Toward the Blue-Green City—Building Urban Water Resilience*. Pretoria: Water Research Commission, 2021.

Swimme, Brian, and Thomas Berry. *The Universe Story: From the Primordial Flaring Forth to the Ecozoic Era—A Celebration of the Unfolding of the Cosmos*. San Francisco: HarperOne, 1994.

Tabe, Jennet. "Gendered Bodies and the Forgotten Mothers of Nature: An African Woman's Rethinking of the Ngbokondems and Forest Preservation among the Ejagham of Cameroon." In *Mother Earth, Mother Africa, and Mission*, edited by Seblewengel Daniel, Mmapula Diana Kebaneilwe, and Angeline Savala, 123–140. Stellenbosch, South Africa: African SUN PReSS, 2021.

Talia, Maina. "The *Fakalofa* Lies before You," in *An Earthed Faith, Vol. 2: How Would We Know What God is Up To?*, edited by Cynthia Moe-Lobeda and Ernst Conradie, 177–190. Eugene, OR: Wipf and Stock, 2023.

Telles Melo, João Alfredo. *Direito ambiental, luta social e ecossocialismo*. Fortaleza, Brazil: Demócrito Rocha, 2010.

Thaman, Konai Helu. "Decolonizing Pacific Studies: Indigenous Perspectives, Knowledge, and Wisdom in Higher Education." *The Contemporary Pacific* 15.1 (2003): 1–17.

Theokritoff, Elizabeth. "Priest of Creation or Cosmic Liturgy?" In *Rightly Dividing the Word of Truth: Studies in Honour of Metropolitan Kallistos of Diokleia*, edited by Andreas Andreopoulos and Graham Speake, 189–211. Oxford: Peter Lang, 2016.

Tinker, Tink. "Walking in the Shadow of Greatness: Vine Deloria Jr in Retrospect." *Wicazo Sa Review* 21/2 (2006): 167–177.

Tollefsen, Torstein Theodor. *The Christocentric Cosmology of St Maximus the Confessor*. Oxford: Oxford University Press, 2008.

Townes, Emile. *Breaking the Fine Rain of Death*. Eugene, OR: Wipf and Stock, 2006.

Tutu, Desmond M. *No Future without Forgiveness*. London: Rider, 1999.

Velimirovich, Nikolai. *Prayers by the Lake*. A Treasury of Serbian Orthodox Spirituality, volume 5. Grayslake, IL: Serbian Orthodox Metropolitanate of New Gracanica, 1999.

Walker, Alice. "Looking for Zora" in *In Search of Our Mothers' Gardens*. New York: Harcourt Brace Jovanovich, 1983.

Walker, Daniel Okyere. "The Pentecost Fire Is Burning: Models of Mission Activities in the Church of Pentecost." PhD diss., University of Birmingham, 2010.

Ware, Kallistos. In *Towards an Ecology of Transfiguration: Orthodox Christian Perspectives on Environment, Nature and Creation*. Edited by John Chryssavgis and Bruce V. Foltz. New York: Fordham University Press, 2013.

———. "Gerald Palmer, the Philokalia and the Holy Mountain." *Friends of Mount Athos Annual Report* 1994: 26–7.

Weinberg, Steven. *Dreams of a Final Theory: The Search for the Fundamental Laws of Nature*. London: Hutchinson Radius, 1993.

White, Monica M. "'A Pig and a Garden:' Fannie Lou Hamer and the Freedom Farm Cooperative." In *Food and Foodways* 25 no. 1 (2017): 20–39 (Routledge),. http://dx.doi.org/10.1080/07409710.2017.1270647/.

White, Jr., Lynn Townsend. "The Historical Roots of Our Ecologic Crisis." *Science* 155, no. 3767 (March 10, 1967): 1203–7.

Wilfred, Felix. "Christianity between Decline and Resurgence." In *Christianity in Crisis?*, edited by Jon Sobrino and Felix Wilfred. Concilium, vol. 3. London: SCM Press, 2005.

Williams, Delores S. "Sin, Nature, and Black Women's Bodies." In *Ecofeminism and the Sacred*, edited by Carol Adams. New York: Continuum, 1993.

Wilson, Ken. "A Biblical Basis for Christian Engagement: A Pastor's Perspective." In *Loving the Least of These: Addressing a Changing Environment*, edited by Dorothy Boorse, 9–14. Washington, DC: National Association of Evangelicals, 2011.

World Council of Churches. *Together Toward Life: Mission and Evangelism in Changing Landscapes*. Edited by Jooseop Keum. Grand-Saconnex, Switzerland: WCC Publications: 2013.

Wulf, Andrea. *The Invention of Nature: The Adventures of Alexander von Humboldt, the Lost Hero Of Science*. London: John Murray, 2015.

Zachariah, George. "Decolonizing Ecotheology: Subaltern Social Movements as Theological Texts." in *How Would We Know What God Is Up To*, edited by Ernst Conradie and Cynthia Moe-Lobeda. Cape Town: AOSIS Publishing, 2022.

Zernov, Nicolas. *The Russians and Their Church*. 3rd ed. Crestwood, NY: St. Vladimir's Seminary Press, 1994.

Zibechi, Raúl. *Los arroyos cuando bajan: Los desafíos del zapatismo*. Málaga, Spain: Zambra-Baladre, 2019.

Zizioulas, John. *Being as Communion: Studies in Personhood and the Church*. Crestwood, NY: St. Vladimir's Seminary Press, 1985.

———. *Communion and Otherness: Further Studies in Personhood and the Church*. London: T and T Clark, 2006.

———. "Pope Francis's Encyclical Laudato Si'." In *Ecotheology, Climate Justice, and Food Security*, edited by Dietrich Werner-Elizabeth Geglitza, 179–186. Geneva: Globethics Publications, 2016.

———. "The Eucharistic Vision of the World and Modern Man." In *Christianikon Symposium*, edited by Kostas Tsiropoulos, 183–190. Athens: éd. Estia, 1967.

———. "Preserving God's Creation," *The Eucharistic Communion, and the World*, edited by Luke Ben Tallon. London: T and T Clark, 2011.

Zvingowanisei, Silindiwe. "African Islam and Environmental Sustainability: A Case Study of the Varemba Muslm Women in Zimbabwe." In *Mother Earth, Mother Africa: World Religions and Environmental Imagination*, edited by Sophia Chirongoma and Wayua Kiilu, 57–73. Stellenbosch, South Africa: SUN PReSS, 2021.

INTERNET REFERENCES

African Methodist Episcopal Church. "AME Church Climate Change Resolution." July 2016. http://www.ame-church.com/wp-content/uploads/2016/07/AME-Climate-Change-Resolution.pdf.

Anglican Church of Canada, Episcopal Church, Evangelical Lutheran Church in America, and Evangelical Lutheran Church in Canada. "A Pastoral Message on Climate Change." September 19, 2014. https://www.episcopalchurch.org/publicaffairs/a-pastoral-message-on-climate-change/.

Blue Ocean Law and the Pacific Network on Globalization. "Resource Roulette: How Deep-Sea Mining and Inadequate Regulatory Frameworks Imperil the Pacific and Its Peoples." June, 2016. https://www.blueoceanlaw.com/blog/blue-ocean-law-releases-report-on-risks-and-pitfalls-of-deep-sea-mining-for-pacific-peoples-in-light-of-governments-inadequate-regulatory-frameworks.

Buddhist Climate Project. "The Time to Act Is Now: A Buddhist Declaration on Climate Change." May 14, 2015. https://fore.yale.edu/files/buddhist_climate_change_statement_5-14-15.pdf.

Chipana Quispe, Sofía. "El restablecimiento del equilibrio y armonía desde la cosmovisión Andina." https://publicatheology.org/2022/05/23/el-restablecimiento-del-equilibrio-y-armonia-desde-la-cosmovision-andina/.

Darwin, Charles. "Letter no. 12041." Letter to John Fordyce from Charles Darwin dated May 7, 1879. Darwin Correspondence Project. https://www.darwinproject.ac.uk/letter/?docId=letters/DCP-LETT-12041.xml.

———. "Charles Darwin's Memorial of Anne Elizabeth Darwin." Darwin Correspondence Project. April 30, 1851. https://www.darwinproject.ac.uk/people/about-darwin/family-life/death-anne-elizabeth-darwin.

Church of Pentecost News. "Environmental Care Campaign." November 22, 2018. https://thecophq.org/news/environmental-care-campaign-launched/.

Delgado, Yenny, and Claudio Ramírez. "Abya Yala Theology." April 6, 2022. https://publicatheology.org/2022/04/06/abya-yala-theology/.

Ecumenical Patriarch Dimitrios. "Encyclical Letter on the Day of Protection of the Environment." September 1, 1989. https://www.orthtransfiguration.org/wpcontent/uploads/2016/05/Lecture_HAH-1989-Patr.-Dimitrios-on-Day-of-Prayer-for-Envir.pdf.

European Commission. "European Green Deal." November 7, 2022. https://ec.europa.eu/info/strategy/priorities-2019-2024/european-green-deal_en.

Evangelical Environmental Network. "An Evangelical Declaration on the Care of Creation." 1994. https://creationcare.org/what-we-do/an-evangelical-declaration-on-the-care-of-creation.html.

Evolution of Modern Humans. https://www.yourgenome.org/stories/evolution-of-modern-humans/#:~:text=of%20much%20debate.-,Modern%20humans%20originated%20in%20Africa%20within%20the%20past%20200%25.

Gebara, Ivone. "Ecofeminism: A Latin American Perspective." *All Creation*. http://www.allcreation.org/home/ecofeminism-lap.

Ghosh, Amitav. "The Colonial Roots of Present Crises." *Green European Journal*. October 19, 2022. https://www.greeneuropeanjournal.eu/the-colonial-roots-of-present-crises.

Guerrero Arias, E. Patricio. "La Chakana del corazonar. Desde las espiritualidades y las sabidurias insurgents en Abya Yala." Quito- Universidad Politécnica Salesiana. 2018. https://pure.ups.edu.ec/es/publications/the-heart-chakana-from-the-insurgent-spiritualities-and-wisdoms-0.

Ignatius IV. "Three Sermons: A Theology of Creation."

———. "A Spirituality of the Creation." http://www.orth-transfiguration.org/wp-content/uploads/2016/05/Lecture_HB-Ignatius-1989-Lecture-Nr-2.pdf.

———. "The Responsibility of Christians." http://www.orth-transfiguration.org/wp-content/uploads/2016/05/Lecture_HB-Ignatius-1989-Lecture-Nr-3.pdf.

Indigenous Environmental Network. "Talking Points on the Ocasio-Cortez—Markey Green New Deal (GND) Resolution." February 7, 2019. https://www.ienearth.org/green-new-deal/.

———. "Indigenous Resistance against Carbon." https://www.ienearth.org/Indigenous-resistance-against-carbon.

International Islamic Climate Change Symposium. "Islamic Declaration on Global Climate Change." Istanbul, Turkey. August 17–18, 2015. https://www.ifees.org.uk/about/islamic- declaration-on-global-climate-change/.

Jewish Climate Initiative and the Interfaith Center for Sustainable Development. "Statement by Israel Orthodox Rabbis on The Climate Crisis." https://www.jewishecoseminars.com/statement-by-israel-orthodox-rabbis-on-the-climate-crisis/.

"Joint Statement, Pope Francis, Ecumenical Patriarch Bartholomew and Archbishop of Canterbury Urge Care for Future of the Planet." November 1, 2022. https://www.oikoumene.org/resources/documents/joint-statement-pope-francis-ecumenical-patriarch-bartholomew-and-archbishop-of-canterbury-urge-care-for-future-of-the-planet.

Lausanne Movement. "Cape Town Commitment: A Confession of Faith and a Call to Action." October 15, 2010. http://www.lausanne.org/content/ctc/ctcommitment.

Murakami, Sakura. "Fukushima Wastewater Released into the Ocean, China Bans All Japanese Seafood." August 24, 2023. https://www.reuters.com/world/asia-pacific/japan-set-release-fukushima-water-amid-criticism-seafood-import-bans-2023-08-23/.

Ng, Kelly and Jean Mackenzie. "North Korea Parades Largest Long-Range Missile Array." *BBC News*. February 10, 2023. https://www.bbc.com/news/world-asia-64577925.

Ordóñez, Sam. "Amazon Deforestation, the Result of Colonialism, U.S. Imperialism." *Workers World*. August, 2019. https://www.workers.org/2019/08/43486/.

Parliament of the World's Religions. "Hindu Declaration on Climate Change." Melbourne, Australia. December 8, 2009. https://hinduclimatedeclaration2015.org/english.

Pennelys Droz and Julian Brave Noisecat, eds. "Position Paper: Mobilizing an Indigenous Green New Deal." https://ndncollective.org/app/uploads/2019/09/Position-paperR2.pdf.

Perrin, Sam. "Ecofeminism: The Essentialism Issue." https://ecologyforthemasses.com/2019/11/21/ecofeminism-the-essentialism-issue/.

Pingstmissionens Utvecklingssamarbete. "Pentecostals, Transformation, and Social Engagement-A Research Overview." September, 2022. https://pmu.se/wp-content/uploads/2022/09/Pentecostals-transformation-and-socia_2022_webb.pdf.

Pope Francis. "Encyclical Letter *Laudato Si'* of the Holy Father Francis on Care for Our Common Home." May 24, 2015. https://www.vatican.va/content/francesco/en/encyclicals/documents/papa-francesco_20150524_enciclica-laudato-si.html.

Presbyterian Church (USA). "Affirmation of Creation." 222nd General Assembly. June 22, 2016. https://ncse.ngo/presbyterian-church-usa.

Reuters. "North Korea Fires Ballistic Missiles, Warns of Turning Pacific into 'Firing Range.'" *RNZ*. Published February 20, 2023, https://www.rnz.co.nz/news/world/484523/north-korea-fires-ballistic-missiles-warns-of-turning-pacific-into-firing-range.

Sagan, Carl. "An Open Letter to the Religious Community." Presented at the Global Forum of Spiritual and Parliamentary Leaders Conference in Moscow,

Russia. January 1990. http://earthrenewal.org/open_letter_to_the_religious_.htm.

Santiago, Myrna. "Extracting Histories: Mining, Workers, and Environment." *New Environmental Histories of Latin America and the Caribbean*. Edited by Claudia Leal, José Augusto Pádua, and John Soluri. July 2013. https://www.environmentandsociety.org/sites/default/files/2013_i7_englisch.pdf.

Tariq, Farooq. "After the Floods, Pakistan Needs Reparations, Not Charity." *Climate and Capitalism*. October 10, 2022. https://climateandcapitalism.com/2022/10/10/after-the-floods-pakistan-needs-reparations-not-charity/.

The Bull Romanus Pontifex. The Doctrine of Discovery. https://doctrineofdiscovery.org/the-bull-romanus-pontifex-nicholas-v/.

Earth Charter. "The Earth Charter." September 12, 2023. https://earthcharter.org/read-the-earth-charter/.

The Inequality Lab at the Paris School of Economics. *World Inequality Report 2022*. https://wir2022.wid.world/.

The Shalom Center. "'Elijah's Covenant'—New Rabbinic Statement on the Climate Crisis." January 1, 2020. https://theshalomcenter.org/content/elijahs-covenant-new-rabbinic-statement-climate-crisis.

Thich Nhat Hanh. "Interbeing." August 1992. https://www.parallax.org/mindfulnessbell/article/environmental-interbeing/.

Tomassoni, Teresa. "'We Are in Great Danger': In Amazon, Indigenous Waiapi Chief Is Killed by Illegal Miners." https://www.nbcnews.com/news/latino/we-are-great-danger-amazon-Indigenous-waiapi-chief-killed-illegal-n1035806?ex=digest.

United Nations Framework Convention on Climate. "The Paris Agreement." November 5, 2022, https://unfccc.int/sites/default/files/english_paris_agreement.pdf.

United Nations Human Rights Office of the High Commissioner. "Environmental Human Rights Defenders Must Be Heard and Protected." March 9, 2022. https://www.ohchr.org/en/stories/2022/03/environmental-human-rights-defenders-must-be-heard-and-protected.

Wayman, Erin. "How Africa Became the Cradle of Humankind." https://www.smithsonianmag.com/science-nature/how-africa-became-the-cradle-of-humankind-108875040/.

Weldon, S. "Laudato Si': On Care for Our Common Home." September 2015. https://inhabitingtheanthropocene.com/2015/09/21/laudato-si-on-care-for-our-common-home/.

World Council of Churches (WCC). "The Living Planet: Seeking a Just and Sustainable Global Community." October 2022. https://www.oikoumene.org/sites/default/files/2022-10/ADOPTED-PIC01.2rev-The-Living-Planet-Seeking-a-Just-and-Sustainable-Global-Community.pdf.

World Meteorological Organization (MNO). "Africa Suffers Disproportionately from Climate Change." 2013. https://public.wmo.int/en/media/press-release/africa-suffers-disproportionately-from-climate-change.
World Wildlife Fund. "Living Planet Report 2016: Risk and Resilience in a New Era." 2016. https://wwf.panda.org/discover/knowledge_hub/all_publications/living_planet_report_timeline/lpr_2016.

INDEX

Abya Yala, 297–310
Ação Popular, 213
activism, 198, 199, 204, 206
Acuña, Maxima, 308
Adam, 166, 237
Adriatic Sea, 137
African Americans, 74, 199, 203, 204, 208
African cosmologies, 74, 157, 164–65, 200
African Initiated Churches, 91
African Women's Theology (AWT), 85
agape, 160–61
agribusiness, 215, 217, 218
Akan, 165
Alaska, 244, 246, 260
Alliance of Small Island States (AOSIS), 122
Amazon, 119, 137, 214, 218, 307, 309, 310
ancestral knowledge, 116, 117, 305
androcentrism, 180–82, 220–21, 294
animism, 131, 163
anthropocentrism, 4, 9–12, 25, 45, 56, 60, 64, 74, 146, 169, 180–81, 187, 189, 194, 198, 225, 235–36, 258, 259, 262, 268, 272, 277, 279, 285, 294
anthropomorphism, 164
anti-capitalism, 45, 213, 218, 219
Aquinas, Thomas, 182, 289
Arendt, Hannah, 22, 26
assentamentos, 218
astrobiology, 177, 185–86
'Ata, 255–58
Athanasius of Alexandria, 147, 148

atomic weapons, 265
Australia, 63, 66, 253, 294

Bacon, Francis, 9, 130, 131, 247
Balkans, the, 141
Baltic Sea, 137
Bandung, 290
baptism, 240, 246
Barros, Marcelo, 215, 217
Barth, Karl, 15, 19
Belhar Confession, 60
biodiversity, 46, 54, 130, 143, 148, 179, 304–7
Black Sea, 136–37
Bloch, Ernst, 10
bodies, 24, 28, 31, 33, 38, 73, 183, 221, 231, 241, 242, 257–60, 264–65
Boff, Leonardo, 14, 54, 212, 217, 224–26, 292
Bolivia, 121
Bonfil, Guillermo, 306
Bonhoeffer, Dietrich, 15, 16
Botho, 88, 89
Botswana, 87–89, 91
Brazil, 22, 99, 100, 213, 214, 217–19, 220, 308
Brueggemann, Walter, 207, 301
Buddhists, Buddhism, 32, 51, 179, 282, 287, 291
Bulgakov, Sergei, 233–34

Caceres, Berta, 308
Cameroon, 82–83

Index

campesinos, 214, 215, 217, 218, 220
Cape Town, 89, 281
Cape Town Commitment, 281–82
capitalism, 4, 27, 41, 45, 59, 60, 61, 103–4, 110, 111, 184, 187, 195, 212, 213–15, 218, 219, 221, 222, 226, 227, 253, 266
Cappio, Luíz Flávio, 218–19
carbon
    carbon emissions, 45, 99–100, 107, 108, 120, 125, 140, 185, 207
    carbon inequality, 99–100
    carbon markets, 120, 124
    carbon neutral, 120
Cardenal, Ernesto, 11, 222–23
Cardijn, Joseph, 220
Caribbean, 122, 123, 126
Carruthers, Iva C., 209–10
Carter, Christopher, 199, 203
Casaldáliga, Pedro, 214
Catholicism, 4, 63, 91, 92–93, 169, 211, 212, 213–14, 218, 224, 226–27, 229, 282, 306
Chimukuche, Rujeko, 155
Circle of Concerned African Women Theologians, 69–95
Club of Rome, 99, 211
Comblin, José, 220
Comboni, Daniel, 93
Comboni sisters, 93
Comisión Pastoral de la Tierra de Brasil (CPT), 214
Cone, James, 54, 201, 210
Congo, 114, 120
COVID-19 pandemic, 54, 138, 205
creation care, 50, 78, 134–35, 140, 198, 206–7, 267–69, 273–78

Darwin, Charles, 151, 176, 177, 190–94
decolonization, 2, 4, 5, 54, 58, 59, 62, 101, 104–5, 108, 114–18, 127, 198–99, 263, 310

deism, 190, 263
Descartes, René, 9, 130
development, 61–62, 78, 112, 122, 125, 132, 137, 142, 143, 211, 214, 225, 274, 275, 277
Dionysius the Areopagite, 34, 181, 230, 232
Doctrine of Discovery, 300–301
dominium terrae, 9, 12, 180, 225
Dube, Musa, 52, 74, 77

Earth Bible Project, 294
Earth Charter, 14, 292
Eastern Orthodox Christianity, 129–52
ecclesial base communities (CEBs), 216–17, 222
ecofeminism, 52, 69–95, 175–96, 221–22
ecowomanism, 73–74, 197–210
Ecumenical Association of Third World Theologians, 69
Ecumenical Foundation of Southern Africa, 51
Ejagham people, 82–83
El Congreso Indígena, 216
El Salvador, 103
'elohim, 257
Ethiopia, 90, 126
Ewes people, 165

Frank, Adam, 177, 185–87, 194
Freedom Farm Cooperative, 204, 206
Freire, Paulo, 118, 213, 220

Gaia hypothesis, 14, 225
Ghana, 69, 165, 267–79
Good Living (Sumaq Kawsay), 298–99, 303, 304, 310
green and brown agendas, 54–55
Green Reformation, 10, 268–79
greenhouse gas emissions, 99, 100, 106, 120, 174
Guna people, 297

Haeckel, Ernst, 233
Hamer, Fannie Lou, 203–7
Hanh, Thich Nhat, 287–88
Harding, Rosemarie, 208
Hegel, Georg Wilhelm Friedrich, 35
Heidegger, Martin, 187–88, 195
Hindus, 49, 51, 179, 282, 291
HIV/AIDS pandemic, 54

imago Dei, 9, 12, 149–51, 180
imago mundi, 150
India, 63, 66, 98, 99, 100, 106–7, 121, 237, 284, 287
Indigenous Knowledge Systems (IKS), 78
Indigenous NDN Collective, 113
Islam, 48, 49, 51, 91, 94, 179, 263, 282, 299

Japan, 253, 265, 284
Jennings, Willie James, 102, 109, 115
Judaism, 33, 48, 146, 179, 263, 282, 302
Julian of Norwich, 75–76
Juventude Universitária Católica (JUC), 213

Kairos Document, 60
Kant, Immanuel, 130
Katongole, Emmanuel, 113–14
Keller, Catherine, 22, 175–76, 177, 184, 185
Kenya, 78, 277
kiu, 255, 257, 259

Latin America, 22, 63, 66, 113, 119, 212–27, 284, 291–92, 297, 300
Laudato Si', 10, 92, 93, 133, 169, 170, 172, 178, 226–27, 282
Lenkabula, Puleng, 53, 77
liberation theology, 50, 62, 66, 69, 73, 179, 184, 211–27, 283, 284, 291
Löwy, Michael, 212–13
Lutherans, 62, 66, 105, 212

mainline churches, 49, 91, 263
Maximus the Confessor, 145, 147, 149, 232, 234, 237
McFague, Sallie, 32, 272, 285
Mendes, Chico, 216–17
Merchant, Caroline, 22, 222
mística, 217
Moana, 251–66
Mount Kenya Forest, 78–79
Movimento dos Trabalhadores Rurais Sem Terra (MST), 217

native religions, 251–66
neoliberalism, 59, 103–4, 116, 184
net-zero emissions, 120, 124
Ngbokondems, 83–84
Nicene Creed, 10, 18, 33, 64, 234
North America, 55, 66, 100, 297
North Atlantic, 47, 54
North Korea, 265

Oduyoye, Mercy Amba, 69–70, 163, 202
Onyinah, Opoku, 274
Orthodox Christianity, 129–52, 178–79, 229–48

Pakistan, 122, 125–26
Paris Climate Agreement, 124, 132
Partido Comunista de Brasil (PCdoB), 213
Pascal, Blaise, 18, 193, 194
Pasifika, 252–66
Pentecostalists, 267–79
Pieris, Aloysius, 283, 291
Polkinghorne, John, 193–94
pollution, 19, 73, 77, 120, 125, 130, 136, 137, 140, 173, 178, 199, 219, 308
popes
    Pope Alexander VI, 301
    Pope Francis, 10, 92, 133, 138, 164, 169, 170, 178, 226, 282

Index

Pope John Paul II, 17
Pope John XXIII, 213
Pope Julius II, 301
prosperity gospel, 209
Protestants, 64, 209, 212, 213, 229, 235, 267, 278, 281, 306
Protestant Reformation, 33

Quechua, 298, 305

racism, 29, 55, 104, 105, 114, 184, 208, 209, 278
Radford Ruether, Rosemary, 180, 220–21
resurrection, 17–20, 65, 145, 159, 231, 239, 304
Ruiz García, Samuel, 216

Sami people, 105, 120
Shona people, 78–81
Sobrino, Jon, 103, 212, 283
Soloviev, Vladimir, 233–34
South America, 111, 113, 297
South Korea, 265, 276, 281, 284, 286
sub-Saharan Africa, 155–56, 174

Tonga, 251–65
totemism, 79–80, 263

Varemba, 94
Vatican, 223
    First Vatican Council, 211
    Second Vatican Council, 93, 211, 213, 216
Velimirovich, Nikolai, 246

Via Campesina, La, 123–24
Volos Academy for Theological Studies, 141–42

Waiapi, Emyra, 308
Walker, Alice, 199, 205
Walker, Daniel, 274
water, 12, 27, 39, 70, 71, 77, 80, 85, 87–90, 91, 94, 109, 113, 116, 117–19, 136, 156, 163, 184, 208, 219, 240, 242, 254–55, 257, 265, 276, 304, 308
White Jr., Lynn, 77, 130–31
White, Monica M., 199, 203–4, 206
white supremacy, 54, 73, 105, 111, 114–18, 200–202, 204, 207, 208–9
whiteness, 54, 112, 115, 199, 307
womanism, 74, 197, 201, 202, 205–6, 208–9, 260. *See also* ecowomanism
word of God 26, 48, 65, 233, 240, 242
World Council of Churches (WCC), 119, 125, 135, 235, 281
World Summit on Sustainable Development, 51, 61
World Wildlife Foundation, 136, 141

Yeboah, Martinson, 274
ying and yang theology, 284

Zachariah, George, 102, 198
Zambia, 92–93
Zernov, Nicolas, 246
zero-carbon, 120
Zimbabwe, 49, 78, 79, 81, 94
Zizioulas, John, 131, 134, 144–45, 147–48, 235, 236, 239
Zvingowanisei, Silindiwe, 78, 94

www.ingramcontent.com/pod-product-compliance
Ingram Content Group UK Ltd.
Pitfield, Milton Keynes, MK11 3LW, UK
UKHW040245061225
465639UK00002B/42